ANCIENT INDIAN TRADITION & MYTHOLOGY

TRANSLATED BY

A BOARD OF SCHOLARS

AND EDITED BY

Dr. G.P. BHATT

VOLUME 43

ANCIENT INDIAN TRADITION AND MYTHOLOGY SERIES

[PURĀṆAS IN TRANSLATION]

Volumes Released

ŚIVA 1-4
LIṄGA 5-6
BHĀGAVATA 7-11
GARUḌA 12-14
NĀRADA 15-19
KŪRMA 20-21
BRAHMĀṆḌA 22-26
AGNI 27-30
VARĀHA 31-32
BRAHMA 33-36
VĀYU 37-38
PADMA 39-48
SKANDA, PARTS I-XX, 49-68
VĀMANA 72

Volumes Under Preparation

SKANDA, PARTS XXI-XXIII
BHAVIṢYA
BRAHMAVAIVARTA
DEVĪBHĀGAVATA
KĀLIKĀ
MĀRKAṆḌEYA
MATSYA
VIṢṆU
VIṢṆUDHARMOTTARA

THE

PADMA-PURĀṆA

PART V

Translated And Annotated By

DR. N.A. DESHPANDE

MOTILAL BANARSIDASS PUBLISHERS
PRIVATE LIMITED • DELHI

Reprint: Delhi, 2007
First Edition : Delhi, 1990

ISBN: 81-208-0701-4

MOTILAL BANARSIDASS
41 U.A. Bungalow Road, Jawahar Nagar, Delhi 110 007
8 Mahalaxmi Chamber, 22 Bhulabhai Desai Road, Mumbai 400 026
203 Royapettah High Road, Mylapore, Chennai 600 004
236, 9th Main III Block, Jayanagar, Bangalore 560 011
Sanas Plaza, 1302 Baji Rao Road, Pune 411 002
8 Camac Street, Kolkata 700 017
Ashok Rajpath, Patna 800 004
Chowk, Varanasi 221 001

UNESCO COLECTION OF REPRESENTATIVE WORKS— Indian Series
This book has been accepted in the Indian Translation Series of the UNESCO Collection of Representative Works, jointly sponsored by the United Nations Educational Scientific and Cultural Organization (UNESCO) and the Government of India

PRINTED IN INDIA
BY JAINENDRA PRAKASH JAIN AT SHRI JAINENDRA PRESS,
A-45 NARAINA, PHASE-I, NEW DELHI 110 028
AND PUBLISHED BY NARENDRA PRAKASH JAIN FOR
MOTILAL BANARSIDASS PUBLISHERS PRIVATE LIMITED,
BUNGALOW ROAD, DELHI 110 007

PUBLISHER'S NOTE

The purest gems lie hidden in the bottom of the ocean or in the depth of rocks. One has to dive into the ocean or delve into the rocks to find them out. Similarly, truth lies concealed in the language which with the passage of time has become obsolete. Man has to learn that language before he discovers that truth.

But he has neither the means nor the leisure to embark on that course. We have, therefore, planned to help him acquire knowledge by an easier course. We have started the series of Ancient Indian Tradition and Mythology in English Translation. Our goal is to universalize knowledge through the most popular international medium of expression. The publication of the Purāṇas in English Translation is a step towards that goal.

PREFACE

This is Part V of the voluminous *Padma Purāṇa* and Volume 43 in the series of Ancient Indian Tradition and Mythology. It comprises the whole of section IV named *Brahmakhaṇḍa* (chapters 1-26) and part of Section V named *Pātālakhaṇḍa* (chapters 1-67).

Let us here give a brief outline of the contents of this part.

The *Brahmakhaṇḍa* deals mainly with various aspects of *Viṣṇu Bhakti* or devotion to god Viṣṇu. Out of its 26 chapters as many as 19 preach devotion to Viṣṇu directly in most and indirectly in a few, strengthening it with the help of short anecdotes and stories.

Devotion to Viṣṇu is recommended as the quickest and surest way to liberation in this Kali age. No pilgrimage, no bathing in Gaṅgā, in short, nothing else need be done by such a devotee. The characteristics of a devotee of Viṣṇu are described in vv. 21-32 of chapter 1. The story of a thief named Daṇḍaka shows how a solitary and insignificant act performed once destroyed even his gravest sins committed in the past, and the one of a pious brāhmaṇa Vaikuṇṭha and a rat shows how an accidental act of brightening the flame of a lamp burning in a Viṣṇu temple on the part of the rat liberated it.

Observing a fast on a *Jayantī* day is strongly advised. The merits thereof and awful results incurred by its non-observance are described in detail. Six meritorious *Jayantīs* are mentioned, *Kṛṣṇajanmāṣṭamī* and *Rādhāṣṭamī* being the two most prominent ones.

Ekādaśī is said to be Viṣṇu's day and importance of fasting on this day is greatly emphasized. Various means of winning the favour of god Viṣṇu are described in chapter 16.

Worship of Tulasī plant, offering its leaves to the deity, wearing a rosary of Tulasī wood round one's neck and a garland of Tulasī leaves are praised as highly efficacious in destroying one's sins and freeing oneself from the clutches of Yama's messengers. Uttering Viṣṇu's name is regarded highly meritorious and leading to Vaikuṇṭha.

Some minor themes of this Section include deeds responsible for sonlessness, birth of a daughter, of a good son, and for stillbirth; churning of the ocean as initiated by a curse of sage Durvāsa who is reputed to become furious for very flimsy reasons; protection offered to a brāhmaṇa as highly meritorious, illustrated by the story of sage Viśvāmitra and how he averted a tragedy by offering himself as a victim in a *Naramedha* sacrifice in place of a brāhmaṇa boy; purificatory acts recommended for saving oneself from sins incurred by indulging in illicit intercourse and eating feces, drinking urine, sipping wine etc.; and importance of keeping a promise.

The *Pātālakhaṇḍa* devotes its first 68 chapters to the ever well-known *Rāmāyaṇa* story, out of which all but the last are included in this Part. This is a Vaiṣṇava theme par excellence, as Rāma was an incarnation of Viṣṇu born for the divine purpose of eliminating the demons headed by Rāvaṇa.

Most of these chapters from Eight onwards describe Rāma's Horse Sacrifice. Chapters 12-53 narrate a number of interesting episodes associated with the Horse's journey over the whole of the earth, including the various thrilling battles that Śatrughna's army had to fight to free the Horse from the rival kings who for some reason came to challenge the supremacy of Rāma. In chapter 54 the ascetic boy Lava binds the Horse, and chapters 60-66 describe the crushing defeat suffered by Śatrughna's army at the hands of the two ascetic brothers Kuśa and Lava.

Incidentally, chapters 55-59 describe the washerman's scandalous talk about Sītā heard and reported to Rāma by the spies and the consequent banishment of Sītā and birth of Kuśa and Lava in the hermitage of sage Vālmīki under his own loving care, who at an appropriate moment discloses the identity of the two sons of Sītā to Rāma who then owns them as his heirs. Sītā after a lot of persuasion returns to Rāma and the Horse Sacrifice is happily concluded even without the victim who miraculously gives up his equine form at Rāma's touch and assumes a divine form.

Acknowledgements

It is our pleasant duty to put on record our sincere thanks to Dr. R.N. Dandekar and the UNESCO authorities for their kind encouragement and valuable help which render this work more useful than it would otherwise have been. We are extremely grateful to Dr. N.A. Deshpande for translating the text. We are also thankful to all those who have been helpful in our project.

—*Editor*

CONTENTS

SECTION V: PĀTĀLAKHAṆḌA

ABBREVIATIONS

Common and self-evident abbreviations such as Ch(s)—Chapter(s), p—page, pp—pages, V—Verse, VV—Verses, Ftn—footnote, Hist. Ind. Philo.—History of Indian Philosophy are not included in this list.

ABORI	*Annals of the Bhandarkar Oriental Research Institute*, Poona
AGP	S.M. Ali's *The Geography of Purāṇas*, PPH, New Delhi, 1973
AIHT	*Ancient Indian Historical Tradition*, F. E. Pargiter, Motilal Banarsidass (MLBD), Delhi
AITM	*Ancient Indian Tradition and Mythology* Series, MLBD, Delhi
AP	*Agni Purāṇa*, Guru Mandal Edition (GM), Calcutta, 1957
Arch. S.Rep.	Archaeological Survey Report
AV	*Atharva Veda*, Svādhyāya Mandal, Aundh
Bd. P.	*Brahmāṇḍa Purāṇa*, MLBD, Delhi 1973
BG	*Bhagavadgītā*
Bh. P.	*Bhāgavata Purāṇa*, Bhagavat Vidyapeeth, Ahmedabad
Br.	*Brāhmaṇa* (preceded by name such as Śatapatha)
BS. P.	*Bhaviṣya Purāṇa*, Vishnu Shastri Bapat, Wai
BV. P.	*Brahma Vaivarta Purāṇa*, GM, 1955-57
CC	*Caturvarga Cintāmaṇi* by Hemādri
CVS	*Caraṇa Vyūha Sūtra* by Śaunaka, Com. by Mahidāsa
DB	*Devī Bhāgavata*, GM, 1960-61
De or GDAMI	*The Geographical Dictionary of Ancient and Mediaeval India*, N.L. De, Oriental Reprint, Delhi, 1971
Dh. S.	*Dharma Sūtra* (preceded by the author's name such as Gautama)
ERE	*Encyclopaedia of Religion and Ethics* by Hastings
GP	*Garuḍa Purāṇa*, ed. R. S. Bhattacharya, Chowkhamba, Varanasi, 1964

8-13. A devotee of Viṣṇu is delighted on hearing the account of Śrīkṛṣṇa (i.e. Viṣṇu). He who describes it to be false should be known as the greatest (i.e. worst) among the sinners. O brāhmaṇa, the lord of the world does not leave that place where the account of Kṛṣṇa is (being narrated), and does not at any time go (anywhere else). For a man who would create an obstacle in the act of the narration of Viṣṇu's account, there is no escape from hell for a hundred period of Manu. For those who, having heard the account (as narrated) in the Purāṇas, censure or scoff at it, always have the very afflicting hells on their hands (i.e. waiting for them). The sin earned in the previous existences (of him) who desires to listen to the account of Śrīkṛṣṇa, perishes just at that moment only. I do not know what (best) position the man who would devoutly listen to Śrikṛṣṇa's account will have on hearing it.

14-16. All such (blemishes) of the sinner as the sin due to the murder of a brāhmaṇa, untimely death, and also (the sin due to) drinking liquor, perish. The sin of that man who (first) having committed a sin later keeps (himself) away from it, would perish as the heap of cotton perishes (i.e. is burnt) by fire. O brāhmaṇa, Yama's servants do not come near the house of him in whose house there is the book (containing) the account of Śrīkṛṣṇa.

Jaimini said:

17. O preceptor, tell me, whom do they describe as the devotees of Viṣṇu. I have now a desire to know them and also (to know) their excellent greatness.

Vyāsa said:

18-20. O brāhmaṇa, what is the use of bathing at a holy place for that sinful man who devoutly sprinkles upon his head the water (flowing) from the feet of Viṣṇu? O brāhmaṇa, the sins like killing a brāhmaṇa, of him who would have the company of the good for a moment or half a moment, perish. In whichever family (even) one (member) is a devotee of Viṣṇu, the family (even) when full of sins (or sinners), attains salvation.

21-32. Those men (only) who are free from (doing) harm (to others), religious hypocrisy, lust and anger, and also those who are bereft of greed and infatuation, who are devoted to their parents, should be known as the devotees of Viṣṇu, O brāhmaṇa. Those who are devoted to their parents, who are endowed with pity, who are engaged in the well-being of all creatures, who are free from jealousy, and who speak the truth should be known as the followers of Viṣṇu. Also those who are devoted to brāhmaṇas, who are impotent to the wives of others, who are engrossed in the vow of Ekādaśī should be known as the devotees of Viṣṇu. Wearing garlands of Tulasī(-leaves) those who sing the names of Viṣṇu, and who are sprinkled with the water (flowing) from the feet of Viṣṇu should be known as the followers of Viṣṇu. O brāhmaṇa, those also, on whose head or ears an excellent tulasī(-leaf) is usually seen, should be known as the devotees of Viṣṇu. Those who are free from the company of heretics, and free from hating brāhmaṇas, who would sprinkle (water) over the tulasī(-plant) should be known as Viṣṇu's devotees. Those men who worship Viṣṇu, also who worship him with tulasī(-leaves), who are engaged in offering their daughters (to worthy grooms), who honour their guests, who listen to the account of Viṣṇu, should be known as Viṣṇu's devotees, and also the man in whose house the śālagrāma stone would be well-established (is a devotee of Viṣṇu). Those men also, who cleanse the abode (i.e. the temple) of Viṣṇu, who perform rites in honour of the manes, who are full of pity towards the helpless, should be known as the followers of Viṣṇu. Those who look upon the wealth of others and of brāhmaṇas as poison, and those who eat the offering of eatables (after they are) presented to Viṣṇu should be known as the followers of Viṣṇu. And also those men who love Vedas and sacred texts, who protect the tulasī (-plants), who are engaged in practising the vow of Rādhāṣṭamī (or Janmāṣṭamī), and those who devoutly present a lamp before (the image of) Śrīkṛṣṇa, who do not censure others, should be known as the followers of Viṣṇu.

Sūta said:

33. Vyāsa who was asked by Jaimini, told him thus in the (proper) order. (Now) I am telling you what occasionally I heard from my preceptor, O brāhmaṇa.

34. Those best men who listen to the reading (of the account of Viṣṇu), are free from all sins, and go the highest position of Viṣṇu.

CHAPTER TWO

The Importance of Besmearing the Floor of Viṣṇu's Temple

Sūta said:

1. O Śaunaka, listen. I shall tell you (about) the ancient way of life (from) the conversation between Vyāsa and Jaimini, which destroys the sins of the listeners.

Jaimini said:

2. O lord, O preceptor, tell me today by (doing) which acts does a sinful man go to the abode of the lord of the world.

Vyāsa said:

3. That man who besmears (the ground) in the temple of Viṣṇu, is freed from all sins, becomes tranquil and goes to the abode of Hari (i.e. Viṣṇu).

4-5. O Jaimini, listen, I shall tell you in brief about the religious merit of him who smears (i.e. sprinkles) with water (the ground) in the temple of the lord of the world. O best brāhmaṇa, he would live in the abode of Viṣṇu for as many thousands of kalpas as the dust particles are seen there.

6-14. Formerly there was a thief by name Daṇḍaka. He was a terror to the people. He snatched away the wealth of brāhmaṇas; he killed his friends; in the yuga called Dvāpara he told lies; he was cruel; he took delight in going to (i.e. having illicit connection with) others' wives. He ate the flesh of cows; he drank liquor; and kept company of heretics. He cut off (the means of) the livelihood of the brāhmaṇas; he usurped the deposits (kept with him); he killed those who sought his shelter; he ardently longed for the amorous movements of prostitutes. Once that foolish man went to the temple of Viṣṇu belonging to a brāhmaṇa to steal the wealth of Viṣṇu. When he entered (the temple) he put his foot (dirty) with mud at low-levelled ground at the door of the temple. Just by that act the ground was free from slope. With joy he opened the panel of the door with two iron rods. He entered the temple of Viṣṇu adorned with an excellent canopy. It was having a jewelled golden lamp which had dispelled the great (i.e. thick) darkness. It was rich with the fragrance of many flowers; it was full of many vessels. It was filled with the fragrance of fragrant oil. The thief saw (the image of) Viṣṇu clad in a yellow garment sleeping (i.e. lying) with Rādhā on a very lovely bed.

15-22. Having saluted (i.e. when he saluted) the lord of Rādhā he became free from sins. 'Shall I take (away this wealth) or shall I not take away? (In) what (way) would it be (useful) to me? Since I am an all-time thief, I am unable to serve (the lord). The wealth would serve my purpose.' Thinking thus, he made up his mind to take it (away). Dropping on the ground the silken garment of the lord of Lakṣmī and keeping all the things in his hand, he, trembling, tied them (in the garment). O Jaimini, all those things of Viṣṇu, the master of illusory power (Māyā), fell down (on the ground) making a very fearful sound. Abandoning their sound sleep, and running, (saying) 'Oh! what is this?', many people came there. The thief, being frightened, left the things and (other) wealth (there only) and speedily fled somewhere. Being bitten by a black and most piosonous snake, he died and was freed from sins. By Yama's order his messengers with nooses and hammers in their hands and clad in skins and having fangs came (there) to take him (to Yama's abode). They tied him with leather straps and took him along a difficult path. Seeing him, Yama was angry, and asked his counsellor:

Yama said:

23. O wise Citragupta, tell me (about) the entire deed, sinful or virtuous, which he has done.

Citragupta said:

24-25. This fool has committed all the sins that the Creator has created on the earth. I have told the truth; but O lord of the world, listen. He has also (done) some good deed. I think, O brother of Yamunā, that would destroy all his sins.

Dharmarāja (*i.e. Yama*) *said* :

26-27. O minister, tell me what religious merit he has Tell me the real truth. Hearing so, I shall put him where he would be fit.

Hearing the words of Yama, Citragupta, who was afraid, joined the palms of his hands, and spoke to his master, O brāhmaṇa:

Citragupta said :

28-29. This worst sinner among sinners had gone to steal the wealth of Viṣṇu. At the door of (the temple of) Viṣṇu, he threw the mud (clung) to his two feet. That floor was covered (with mud) and free from holes and pits. By the power of the religious merit his great sin has gone out (of him). He is fit for (staying in) Vaikuṇṭha. He is out (of the jurisdiction of) your punishment.

Vyāsa said :

30-31a. Hearing these words he (i.e. Yama) gave him a seat made of gold. He sat there; he was honoured by Yama. With his head (bent down) he saluted him, and politely said to him:

Yama said :

31b-33a. With the dust particles of your feet my abode is purified today. I am blessed, I am lucky, I am lucky; no doubt about it. O good one, now go to Viṣṇu's excellent abode which is full of many enjoyments and which keeps off birth and death.

Vyāsa said :

33b-37. Saying like this, that Dharmarāja (i.e. Yama) placed him whose sins had gone (away), in a divine chariot which was made of gold and to which royal swans were yoked, and sent him to Viṣṇu's place which gives all pleasures. Thus he entered Vaikuṇṭha and lived there for a long time. O best brāhmaṇa, I do not know what will happen to them who do not devoutly besmear the temple of Viṣṇu. The sin of him, earned during crores of existences, who would devoutly listen to this (account) or would attentively recite it, perishes. There is no doubt about it.

CHAPTER THREE

The Importance of Offering a Lamp to Viṣṇu

Śaunaka said:

1. O Sūta, tell me the significance of (the month of) Kārtika. (Tell me) what the fruit of that vow is, and what the blemish of one who does not do it, is.

Sūta said:

2. On a former occasion, O best of sages, Jaimini asked (about) this to Vyāsa, Satyavatī's son. (Then) the sage (Vyāsa) commenced this narration:

Vyāsa said:

3-15. He who would give up sesamum-oil and copulation in the auspicious (month of) Kārtika, becomes free from sins committed during many (previous) existences and goes to Viṣṇu's abode. He, a fool, who does not give up (eating) fish and copulation in Kārtika, would certainly be (born as) a pig in every (subsequent) existence. A man who would worship Viṣṇu with the tulasī-leaves in Kārtikā, obtains the fruit (of the performance) of a horse sacrifice for every leaf (that is offered to Viṣṇu). He who would worship Viṣṇu in Kārtika with the flowers of the muni-tree, obtains through Viṣṇu's grace salvation difficult to be obtained (even) by gods. The best man who eats the muni-vegetable in Kārtika, has all the sin committed during the year destroyed by (just) one vegetable (viz. muni). He who after offering to Viṣṇu eats the fruit of that (tree) in the month of Kārtika dear to Viṣṇu, (has all) his sin (committed) during crores of existences (destroyed). He who gives (an article of food), which is tasty and with ghee, to Viṣṇu, is freed from all sins and would go to Viṣṇu's abode. A man, who offers even one lotus to Viṣṇu in Kārtika, in the end goes, free from all (his) sins, to Viṣṇu's position. He who would (everyday) bathe in the morning in (the month of) Kārtika dear to Viṣṇu, would obtain the fruit which (he would get) on bathing at all the sacred places. That brāhmaṇa, who would offer a lamp into water in Kārtika, is free from sins like the murder of a brāhmaṇa, and would go to the abode of Viṣṇu. O best brāhmaṇa, he who would offer a lamp even for a short time in Kārtika to please Viṣṇu, has Viṣṇu always pleased with him. Everyday the brāhmaṇa who would offer a lamp with ghee to Viṣṇu in his (own) house in Kārtika, obtains the fruit of a horse sacrifice. I (shall) tell you the special significance (of the offering) of a lamp. O best of brāhmaṇas, being attentive, listen to it (as I tell it) with its tradition.

16-26a. Formerly, in Tretāyuga there was a pure brāhmaṇa Vaikuṇṭha by name. A sinner got (himself) liberated by virtue of his company. Once that best brāhmaṇa, having offered a lamp with ghee before Viṣṇu in Kārtika, went home. A rat came there to eat that ghee. When he started eating it from the lamp, the lamp burnt more brightly. The rat too, out of fear of the fire speedidy ran (away); and all the sin of the rat perished due to the grace of Viṣṇu. The rat was bitten by a serpent, and it died. Then, by Yama's order (his) messengers with nooses and hammers in their hands came (there) to take him (to Yama's abode), and tied him with leather-bands. When they made up their mind to take (him to Yama's abode), Viṣṇu's messengers having four hands (each) holding conches, discs and maces and mounted upon Garuḍa came (there). (There was) in the sky an aeroplane also. It was auspicious, and royal swans were yoked to it. It was made of pure gold and through Viṣṇu's grace it moved according to the wish (of the occupant). Having cut off the nooses (with which the rat was tied), the messengers spoke to Yama's servants: "O fools, this is Viṣṇu's devotee. In vain you had tied him. O servants of Yama, go (back) if you desire to live." Having heard (these words) they trembled and asked with politeness: "Please tell us, due to what power of his merit you are taking this great sinner to the city of Viṣṇu".

Viṣṇu's messengers said:

26b-34a. The rat revived the lamp in front of Viṣṇu. Due to that act, O messengers (of Yama), we are taking it to Viṣṇu's abode. He who even without desiring (to do so), revives the lamp of (i.e. offered to) Viṣṇu, abandons his sin earned in crores of (previous) existences, and goes to Viṣṇu's abode. Nobody except Viṣṇu is able to describe the merit of him who would devoutly offer on days of (i.e. auspicious to) Viṣṇu, a lamp (to Viṣṇu). What is the use of performing a thousand horse sacrifices for him who would offer in his house a lamp full of ghee to Viṣṇu? (As he) who performs the horse sacrifice on a day of (i.e. sacred to) Viṣṇu goes to heaven, so also, he who offers a lamp (to Viṣṇu) in Kārtika, would go to Viṣṇu's abode.

Vyāsa said:

Hearing this, (Yama's) messengers went as they had come; (and) Viṣṇu's messengers, having put it in a chariot went to Viṣṇu's abode. He passed a hundred ages of Manu in Viṣṇu's proximity only. Then, through Viṣṇu's grace he was (born) as a princess in the mortal world; and with her sons and grandsons she enjoyed pleasures for a long time. From here (i.e. the mortal world) she again went to the world of cows due to her service to Viṣṇu.

Sūta said:

34b-35. A man who devoutly listens to this excellent importance of the lamp, is freed from all sins and goes to Viṣṇu's abode.

CHAPTER FOUR

The Importance of Fasting on the Jayantī Day

Śaunaka said:

1. O Sūta, tell (me about) the importance of Jayantī (birth day anniversary). When is it celebrated by the people? You are a boat in the ocean of the mundane existence.

Sūta said:

2. O brāhmaṇa, O best sage, listen; since I am asked, I shall tell you. This was formerly asked by Nārada from Brahmā in heaven.

Nārada said:

3. O grandsire, tell me the significance of Jayantī (i.e. birth day anniversary), hearing which I shall go to that highest position of Viṣṇu.

Brahmā said:

4-8. O brāhmaṇa, listen attentively. I shall tell you. He (i.e. a man) goes to Viṣṇu's world by fasting on a Jayantī (day). Jayantī, O sage, burns, through remembering, narrating (the account of Viṣṇu), the sin earned during the (previous) seven existences. The more so in the case of the sin of one who observes a fast (on that day). The Janmāṣṭamī, the auspicious ninth day of the bright half in Caitra, the fourteenth day of the dark half of Māgha, the fourteenth day of the bright half of Caitra, the Durgāṣṭamī in Āśvina, the twelfth day of the bright half of Śrāvaṇa—these six are said to be very meritorious Jayantīs, causing auspiciousness. The Kṛṣṇajanmāṣṭamī (mentioned) first is well-known and destroys sins. It is equal to a crore of sacrifices and to myriads of holy places.

9-18. By fasting on a Jayantī-day, one gets the fruit that is obtained by him who gives a thousand cows everyday. By fasting on a Jayantī-day he obtains the same fruit as by (the gift of) a thousand bhāras of gold at the time of (the auspiciousness) of the planet sun. By fasting on a Jayantī-day he obtains the same fruit as by giving thousands of black antelope-hides and hundreds of sesamum-cows. By fasting on a Jayantī-day a man gets that fruit which he obtains by offering thousands of crores daughters (in marriage). A man gets that fruit by fasting on a Jayantī-day which he obtains by giving this earth with the oceans. By fasting on a Jayantī-day he obtains the fruit which he obtains by constructing a well, a pond etc. in a temple. By fasting on a Jayantī-day a man obtains the same fruit as he, being devoted, does by doing (service) to his mother, father and preceptor. That merit which is obtained by those who, of a truthful vow, have made themselves blessed by resorting to a sacred place for the removal of a calamity, is obtained by fasting on a Jayantī-day. That religious merit which a man obtains by bathing in Gaṅgā or Narmadā, or in the water of Sarasvatī, is obtained by him by fasting on a Jayantī-day. By fasting on a Jayantī-day a man obtains that fruit which the performers of a śrāddha in honour of their dead ancestors on a new moon day, obtain.

Nārada said:

19a. O grandsire, tell me, who formerly observed (a fast on) the Jayantī-day ?

Brahmā said:

19b-26a. (The fast on) the Jayantī-day was formerly observed by Kārtavīrya, Karṇa, the intelligent Kumāra (i.e. Kārtikeya), by Sagara, Dilīpa—the descendant of Kakutstha, by Gautama, Gārgya, the intelligent son of Jamadagni (i.e. Paraśurāma); so also it was formerly observed by Vālmīki, and the good son of Draupadī. (The fast on) the eighth of the bright half of Bhādrapada gives the desired objects. The eighth day is said to be of special importance when in union with the sun. For pleasing the disc-holder (i.e. Viṣṇu), it should be observed every year. The sin earned in crores of existences vanishes in a short time. Having kept awake during the night, a man with his senses controlled, should devoutly worship (Viṣṇu) separately with sandal, flowers and offerings of food. O brāhmaṇa, the sin earned deliberately or without knowledge, of him who observes a fast on a Jayantī-day, perishes in half a watch, by the grace of the son of Devakī (i.e. Kṛṣṇa).

26b-37. There is no doubt that those mean men who eat when the day of Jayantī has arrived (i.e. on a Jayantī-day) suffer the sin produced in the three worlds. All the holy places like the ocean, all the places (which are) the abodes of the liberated, remain in all the parts of the house of him who observes the Jayantī-vow. All the holy places and deities live in the body of that man who devoutly observes (a fast on) the Jayantī-day, dear to Kṛṣṇa. O great sage, I have not seen in the Vedas or the Purāṇas a vow equal or superior to the vow of Kṛṣṇa-Rādhāṣṭamī. The man who does not devoutly observe it, would be (born as) a cruel demon. O brāhmaṇa, that foolish man who eats (food) on a Jayantī-day as on the day (sacred) to Viṣṇu, obtains (i.e. goes to) a great hell. Due to his taking food on a Jayantī-day, one hundred and one preceding and succeeding (members of) his family would fall into a terrible hell. O best sage, what is the use of crores of vows, if a fast is observed when Jayantī would be (i. e. fall) on a Wednesday (when the Moon is) in unison with Rohiṇī ? (A fast on) a Jayantī-day observed according to the proper rule, destroys sin in the Kṛta-age, Tretā-age, Dvāpara-age and Kali-age. The sin earned from birth, of him who, keeping awake, causes to read aloud the Purāṇa of Viṣṇu, burns like a heap of cotton. The sin earned in a crore of existences, of the man who devoutly listens to the Purāṇa on a day (sacred) to Viṣṇu perishes at that moment only. On the day (sacred) to Viṣṇu a man should honour a suppliant, O sage. He liberates a crore (of the members) of his family and is honoured in Viṣṇu's world.

38-50. A man who does not observe a fast on a Jayantī-day and is averse to it, being bereft of all virtue, certainly goes to hell. A man should worship (Viṣṇu) with sandal, flowers, incense, and lamps full of ghee, and should give a present to a brāhmaṇa. O brāhmaṇa, that man who celebrates Jayantī in this manner, would, due to his devotion, liberate twentyone members of (his family). In his house there would be no misfortune, no widowhood, no quarrel, so also no opposition from his children. He never sees (i.e. experiences) loss of wealth. He who observes a fast on a Jayantī-day, obtains all the objects desired by him, and he goes to Viṣṇu's heaven. Those who fix their mind on observing the Jayantī-vow and are very much devoted to Viṣṇu, are blessed, are well-born, are wealthy and wise. Whatever sacred places, vows and restraints are there, they do not deserve (i.e. are not equal to) even the sixteenth part of the Jayantī-day. O child, he who with his wife observes (a fast on) the Rādhā-Kṛṣṇāṣṭamī day in both the fortnights of Bhādrapada, reaches Viṣṇu's proximity. He who always observes the merit-giving vow, who observes a fast on a Jayantī-day, goes to Viṣṇu's Vaikuṇṭha. Jayantī, dear to Viṣṇu, quickly destroys the sin due to want of good conduct, (having) fallen (or been expelled) from the family, (being) deprived of fame, and birth in a bad stock. He who observes a fast on a Jayantī, completely burns all sins comparable to Meru, and those like the murder of a brāhmaṇa. He who desires a son gets a son observing a fast on the Jayantī-day, who desires wealth obtains wealth, who desires salvation obtains salvation. Even Yama is afraid of those who greatly fix their mind on observing (a fast on) the Jayantī-day. They reach the highest position.

Sūta said:

51-53. Having (thus) told Nārada (about Jayantī), he (i.e. Brahmā) went as he had come. O sage, O brāhmaṇa, I have also told you what was asked by you. They too, who devoutly listen to the importance of Jayantī, go to the highest abode (after being) freed from all sins. O brāhmaṇa, similarly sinful men who see the reader of a Purāṇa and him who observes the Jayantī-vow, go to the highest place.

CHAPTER FIVE

The Deeds for Which One Becomes Sonless

Śaunaka said:

1. O you very intelligent one, tell me, due to which act (of a man) he becomes sonless (i.e. does not have a son), and due to (i.e. by doing) which (act) he would have a son.

Sūta said:

2. Formerly this was asked by the magnanimous Nārada from Brahmā. O best sage, listen to what he said (then).

Nārada said:

3-5. O grandsire, O very wise one, O you who have mastered all the truth, O you lotus-born, tell me by (i.e. doing) which deed a mortal would become sonless; due to what sin a woman would be barren. O you who are intent on the well-being of all creatures, tell me, who am listening. Due to which deed a daugther is born, or an important son is born; due to what a child is stillborn. A woman bringing forth a stillborn child is extremely unhappy. O Brahman, tell me due to which religious merit a son would be born.

Brahmā said :

6-7. I shall tell you in brief. Listen to it attentively. You are asking about an amazing account. Listen (to it). It is said that a brāhmaṇa who would snatch away or would cause to snatch away (i.e. who has snatched away or has caused to snatch away) the means of subsistence of a brāhmaṇa, would be sonless.

8-9. That man who in this existence would devoutly listen to a Purāṇa, or would make a present of a land with a crop on it, or who would give a golden cow of many qualities and giving profuse milk along with a present, so also one who would give a golden image (of a deity to a brāhmaṇa), would certainly get a son.

10. That woman who would in her former birth deceitfully kill (i.e. who has deceitfully killed) the child of someone else, would certainly be sonless.

11-12. That woman who, endowed with devotion, would make a present of a golden image (of a deity), and would devoutly drink the water (flowing) from the feet of a brāhmaṇa, would listen to a Purāṇa, or would offer a large present (to a brāhmaṇa), would have many children, and would have her children alive. There is no doubt about this.

13-15. A man or a woman who would not take out a child drowning in water, would certainly be sonless in this world. He who would give a bull, a pumpkin gourd with gold and cloth or would observe the auspicious vow for having a child, or would offer (the image of) a fair virgin, or would listen to a Purāṇa destroying all sins, would have a son.

16-17. That man who in his previous existence would disappoint a guest or would angrily punish him (i.e. who has disappointed or angrily punished a guest), would certainly be sonless. A man should devoutly honour a brāhmaṇa and a guest. He should give food, water, and (should construct) an auspicious temple.

18. That woman or that man who would cause (i.e. who has caused) abortion in her or his previous existence would certainly have a stillborn child.

19. That woman who along with her husband, would observe (a fast on) the day of (i.e. sacred to) Viṣṇu, would have good sons and would be a favourite wife of her husband in every existence.

20-21. A man who would make wealth with cows, or a śūdra who, being infatuated, would kidnap a brāhmaṇa-woman, would be born impotent due to (that) act. O brāhmaṇa, a daughter is born due to (that) act. O brāhmaṇa, a daughter is born by the power of the religious merit (to him) who, having committed this sin, later performs (acts of) religious merit.

22-25. O brāhmaṇa, in Tretāyuga there was a king by name Śrīdhara. He was sonless (but) wealthy. His wife was Hemaprabhāvatī. He asked Vyāsa who knew all sacred texts, who desired the well-being of all people, and who had come to him: "O brāhmaṇa, how (is it that) I am sonless?" (Seated) on a seat made of gold etc. and offered by the king, he, having heard the polite words of the king, answered thus: The king and the queen, being delighted washed his feet, and drank the water (with which) his feet (were washed), and which destroyed all sins.

Vyāsa said:

26-29. O king, hear (about) what you have asked me, (also about) the deed due to which you are sonless. This your queen also is sonless and you observe the vow of having one wife (only). In your former existence, you, the moon, were known by the name Varatanu. Your wife of a fair body was known by the name Śaṅkarī. Once you were going along a path. Though you saw the son of a low (-caste person) drowning in water, you contemptuously went ahead. The son died. By the power of your great religious merit, you became king and queen. (But) as a result of that deed, you would (i.e. did) not have a son.

The king said:

30. O lord, due to which (act of) religious merit, would a son be born (to us)? For, the life of persons having no son is fruitless.

Vyāsa said:

31-32. Give a gift of a pumpkin gourd with gold, cloth and a bull. Observe vow for obtaining a child, give (the image) of a fair virgin, and also listen to a Purāṇa. Then a son, destroying all sins, will be born.

Brahmā said :

33-34. Hearing this, the king gave an excellent gift as told by Vyāsa, and with his sins destroyed listened to a Purāṇa. Then within a year a son honoured by all was born (to them). The king became a sovereign emperor, handsome and the chief of his family.

Sūta said :

35-38. He who having no son, would devoutly listen to this, and make excellent presents, gets a son. I have told (this to you) in brief. O brāhmaṇa, that woman who would devoutly honour a brāhmaṇa according to the rules laid down in the sacred texts, would always have good sons. (So also the man) who would devoutly put on the book (of the Purāṇa) gold, silver, cloth, garland of flowers and sandal—which destroy all sins (would get good sons). A cruel son would be born to the fool who in his former existence has killed a brāhmaṇa or a child, and would be a brāhmaṇa after seven existences.

CHAPTER SIX

Acts Leading to Vaikuṇṭha

Śaunaka said :

1. O Sūta, tell me who am listening, due to which (acts of) religious merit Vaikuṇṭha is obtained (by a man), for you are a boat in the ocean of the worldly existence.

Sūta said :

2-7. O best sage doing auspicious (things) for all, (you have asked) well. I shall tell you in brief (the rite) destroying all sins. Listen, O best brāhmaṇa, hear about the merit of him who would give a house made of clay to a brāhmaṇa devoted to Viṣṇu. That brāhmaṇa, free from all sins, would always live in a palatial building in Viṣṇu's heaven. He is honoured in Viṣṇu's heaven. He who would present a palatial building to a brāhmaṇa devotee of Viṣṇu, would, on reaching Viṣṇu's abode, certainly be a resident of heaven. O brāhmaṇa, he, with a crore of (members of) his family ultimately goes to Viṣṇu's city, and staying in a palatial golden building, he would enjoy pleasures as he pleases. (Even) the Creator, the cause of all, is unable to measure the religious merit that one would get by causing a brāhmaṇa to settle well (in his life), O sage.

8. Dust particles are (i.e. can be) counted; drops of rains are (i.e. can be) counted; (but) the fruit (obtained) by settling well a brāhmaṇa (in his life) cannot be guaged even by the Creator.

9-23. O great sage, listen to what Brahmā, the Creator, the origin of the mundane existence, told Nārada, when he was formerly asked by him. O brāhmaṇa, formerly in Dvāpara age, there was a woman by name Cañcalāpāṅgī; she was very beautiful, her hair was excellent, her eyes were like that of a female deer, her waist was charming, and her smile was lovely. Once she went to another country. Full of all sins, and causing people to fall into hell due to her contact (like that) of liquor, she went to a temple. For a moment she sat there and ate a tāmbūla. Through curiosity she threw the remaining powder on the lowly part of a wall. Then desiring (to secure) a paramour, and to secure wealth (from him) she went to the city. The prostitute rashly made an appointment with some paramour. Being fascinated she went to the appointed place (in) the forest at night. The merchant (her paramour) did not come to the rendezvous. She expected (him) and thought to herself: 'How (is it) that my lover has not come? Has he been eaten up by serpents or tigers? How has he, beside himself due to passion, gone (elsewhere) leaving the place of appointment? Is he hankering after some other unknown woman?' O brāhmaṇa, thinking (like) this in her mind she through the fear of the fort-guard did not arrive into the city as the public road was covered with darkness. O brāhmaṇa, in the meanwhile a hungry tiger that took up any form that he liked, that was sent by the god of death, came there and forcibly ate her up. Then the messengers of Yamunā's brother (i e. Yama), whose forms were fearful, whose bodies resembled mountain-peaks, came there to take her (to Yama's abode) due to her sinful deed. Their feet were crooked, their faces were crooked, their noses were projecting, and they had many jaws. O brāhmaṇa, taking leather straps and hammers the very frantic messengers tied up that licentious harlot with leather straps. The messengers of the magnanimous Viṣṇu who holds a conch, a disc, a mace and a lotus, that were going along the path saw her. They resembled black clouds, their lotus-like faces were throbbing, they formed a group, their noses were charming, and they were adorned with divine ear-rings.

The messengers of Viṣṇu said:

24-27. Who are you of deformed forms, who appear like demons? Where are you going carrying this excellent (lady), the most beloved of Viṣṇu?

Hearing these words of them, they (i.e. Yama's messengers) went (away) quickly. Then those very powerful messengers of Viṣṇu, who were full of anger, struck the messengers of Yama, the lord of the world, with multitudes of weapons like the disc, having the brilliance of that of a crore of suns. All the warriors of Yama ran away, crying; and O brāhmaṇa, they who were frightened, narrated the entire account to Yama. Yama too, having heard that account, said to Citragupta:

Dharma (i.e. Yama) said:

28. O minister, due to which (act of) religious merit has the prostitute gone to (i.e. obtained) salvation? Tell all this according to its merit, to me who am asking (you).

Citragupta said:

29-32. From her birth she had earned very many sins; but, O lord of the world, hear if she might have some merit (to her credit). O lord of Dharma, once (this) prostitute, adorned with all ornaments, seeking wealth and looking for a paramour, went to a certain city. There (i.e. in that city) having remained in the temple, and having eaten a tāmbūla, she threw, out of curiosity, the remaining powder on a wall, By the power of that merit the harlot with her sins gone (away), and free from your punishment, goes to Vaikuṇṭha.

Sūta said:

33-37. Hearing these words the messengers and Yama also set their mind on other work, O brāhmaṇa. That harlot also, mounted in a divine chariot yoked with royal swans and surrounded by Viṣṇu's servants, went to Viṣṇu's world. O brāhmaṇa, she by the order of Viṣṇu stayed along with a crore (members of) her family in a palatial building and enjoyed many pleasures. O best brāhmaṇa, I do not know (i.e. cannot judge) the merit of him who devoutly and carefully puts powder into Viṣṇu's temple (to beautify it). He who would devoutly recite (this) chapter or listen to it with respect, is freed from all sins and goes to Viṣṇu's abode.

CHAPTER SEVEN

The Greatness of Rādhāṣṭamī

Śaunaka said:

1. O very wise one, O you very intelligent one, tell me due to which act a man goes to the world of cows from the ocean of the mundane existence which is difficult to cross and, O Sūta, about Rādhāṣṭamī and its excellent importance.

Sūta said:

2. O brāhmaṇa, O great sage, formerly Nārada had asked this from Brahmā. Listen, in brief, to what he had asked him.

Nārada said:

3-5. O grandsire, O very wise one, O best among those who know all the sacred texts, O dear one, tell me (about) Rādhājanmāṣṭamī. O lord, what is its religious fruit? Who observed it in olden days? O brahman, what would be the sin of those men who do not observe it? In what way is the vow to be observed?

When is it to be observed? Tell me (all) that from the beginning, from whom Rādhā was born.

Brahmā said:

6-12. O child, listen very attentively to (the description of the vow of) Rādhājanmāṣṭamī. I shall tell you in brief the entire (account). O Nārada, except Viṣṇu it is not possible (for anyone) to tell about its meritorious fruit. That sin like the murder of a brāhmaṇa, of them who have earned it through a crore of existences, perishes in a moment, (when) they devoutly observe it (i.e. the vow). The religious merit of Rādhājanmāṣṭamī is hundred times more than the fruit which a man obtains by observing (a fast on) a thousand Ekādaśī (days). The merit due to Rādhāṣṭamī observed (but) once, is hundred times more that the fruit obtained by giving gold equal to the Meru (mountain). People obtain that fruit from the Rādhāṣṭamī, which (merit) they obtain by giving a thousand virgins (in marriage). A man gets that fruit of the Aṣṭamī of the beloved of Kṛṣṇa (i.e. Rādhāṣṭamī), which he would get by bathing in holy places like Gaṅgā. (Even) a sinner who observes this vow casually or devoutly, would along with a crore members of his family go to Viṣṇu's heaven.

13-20. O child, formerly in Kṛtayuga an excellent, very beautiful woman, having a beautiful (i.e. slender) waist, having eyes like those of a female deer, of a beautiful form, having lovely hair, lovely ears, was known by the name Līlāvatī. She had committed very grave sins. Once, she, hankering after wealth, went to another city moving out from her own city. There, in a beautiful temple, she saw many wise people intent on observing the Rādhāṣṭamī vow. They were worshipping devoutly the excellent image of Rādhā with sandal, flowers, incense, lamps, (pieces of) cloth and various kinds of fruits. Some sang, danced, recited the excellent hymn of praise. Some (others) joyfully played upon the lute and beat the drum. Seeing them like that, she, full of curiosity, went near them, and politely asked them: "O you religious-minded ones, what are you, full of joy, doing? O virtuous ones, tell me who am full of politeness (what you are doing)."

21-24. Those devotees, intent upon the observance of the

vow, and interested in obliging and doing good to others, started speaking.

Those who observed the Rādhā (-aṣṭamī) vow said: "Today that eighth day on which—i.e. on the eighth day of the bright fortnight—Rādhā was born, has arrived. We are observing it carefully. This (vow of) the Aṣṭamī which is observed (like this) quickly destroys men's sins like the sin due to the murder of a cow, or arising from stealing, or killing a brāhmaṇa, or which is due to carrying off the wife of another person, or due to (a man's) violating his teacher's bed (i.e. wife)."

25-42. Hearing their words, and repeatedly thinking (to herself), 'I shall observe (this vow) which destroys all sins' she observed that excellent vow there only along with those who were observing it. That pure woman died due to being hurt (i.e. bitten) by a serpent. Then (Yama's) messengers with nooses and hammers in their hands came there by Yama's order, and tied her in a very painful way. When they decided to take her to Yama's abode, messengers of Viṣṇu holding conches and maces came (there). (They had brought with them) an auspicious aeroplane made of gold, to which royal swans were yoked. Having quickly cut off (the nooses) with edges of their discs, they put that woman whose sin had gone (away), into the chariot. They took her to the charming city of Viṣṇu, called Goloka, where she stayed with Kṛṣṇa and Rādhā due to the propitiousness of the vow. O dear one, for him who, a fool, does not observe the vow of Rādhāṣṭamī, there is no acquittance from hell even for hundreds of crores of kalpas. Those women also who do not observe this vow which causes auspiciousness, which delights Rādhā and Viṣṇu, which destroys all sins, go to Yama's city in the end and fall into a hell for a long time. If per chance they get a birth on the earth, they certainly (become) widows. O child, once (this) earth was struck by the groups of the wicked. She, being extremely helpless, became a cow, and approached me. Weeping again and again, she told me (about) her grief. Hearing her words, I went to the proximity of Viṣṇu. I quickly narrated to Kṛṣṇa (i.e. Viṣṇu) the intensity of her grief. He said (to me): "O brahman, with the gods go to the earth. Later I (shall) also go there with my attendants." Hearing that I, along with the gods, came to the earth. Then Kṛṣṇa, calling Rādhā (who was to him) greater than his own life, said (these) words (to her); "O goddess, I am going to the earth to destroy the burden of the earth. You (also) go to the earth." Having heard those (words), Rādhā also then went to the earth. That Rādhikā sprang up by day on the sacrificial ground of Vṛṣabhānu on the day called Aṣṭamī in the bright half of the month of Bhādrapada. When purified for the sacrifice, she, having a divine form, was seen (there). The king, delighted in mind, took her to his house and handed her over to his queen. She, too, nourished her.

43. Thus, O child, the words that I have told you are to be kept secret, to be kept secret, to be kept secret carefully.

Sūta said:

44. He who would devoutly listen to this (account of the vow) giving the fruit of the four goals (of human life), becomes free from all sins and ultimately goes to Viṣṇu's house.

CHAPTER EIGHT

Prelude to the Churning of Ocean

Śaunaka said:

1. O Sūta, O preceptor, why was the ocean churned by the gods in ancient days? Curiosity is produced in my mind to hear it.

Sūta said:

2. O brāhmaṇa, I shall tell you in brief the reason for the churning of the ocean. Listen also to the account of the dialogue between Durvāsas and Indra.

3. Once, the brāhmaṇic sage Durvāsas who had practised great (i.e. severe) penance, who was very lustrous, who was born of a portion of the Lord, went to heaven to see Indra.

4-6a. At that time he saw Śacī's lord (i.e. Indra) mounted on the elephant (called Airāvata). Seeing a garland of Pārijāta (flowers) the great sage gave it to him (i.e. to Indra). O brāhmaṇa, Indra, the lord of gods, taking that garland, and putting it on the head of the elephant went with his army to Nandana (garden). The elephant seizing that garland, cut it off and hurled it on the ground.

6b-7. The great sage, getting very angry, thus spoke to him: "Since, you being endowed with the glory of the three worlds, are thinking lightly (of me), there is no doubt that your glory of the three worlds would perish".

8-12. Then Indra quickly went to his city and then slept. The mother of the worlds saw (this) and disappeared. When she disappeared, the three worlds also disappeared. All (creatures) being hungry and thirsty constantly cried. The clouds did not shower (rain), and reservoirs of water went dry. All the trees were dried up and were bereft of fruits and flowers. All (gods) oppressed by hunger and thirst approached Brahmā. They told the grandsire about their distress and grief. Hearing the words of gods, the Creator, along with hosts of gods and sages like Bhṛgu, went to the milky ocean.

13-16. The Creator, muttering the eight-lettered hymn and meditating (on Viṣṇu), worshipped Viṣṇu, the lord of the world, on the northern shore of the milky ocean. Then Viṣṇu was pleased with all the gods, and the kind lord having mounted upon Garuḍa came there. (Gods) on seeing Viṣṇu who had worn a yellow garment, who had four arms, who had held a conch, a disc and a mace, who was the lord of the worlds, whose eyes resembled lotuses, who was a boat of (i.e. to cross) the ocean of mundane existence, who was adorned with a garland of wood-flowers, who had a curl of hair and the Kaustubha gem on his chest, had their eyes full of tears of joy, and praised with cries of victory and continuously saluted him.

The lord said:

17. O gods, choose a boon. Why have you come to me? I am the giver of boons. So speak (out). I (shall) give you (what you want). (This will not be) otherwise.

Gods said:

18-19a. O kind one, due to the brāhmaṇa's curse, the three worlds are bereft of wealth; O lord, with gods, demons and men they are oppressed by hunger and thirst. Protect all these worlds. We have sought your refuge.

The lord said:

19b-23. O gods, Indirā (i.e. Lakṣmī), due to whose mere glance the world is endowed with glory, has vanished due to the curse of the brāhmaṇa (viz. Durvāsas). Then, O gods, all of you, along with the demons, having uprooted the golden mountain Mandara and making it, with the king of serpents going round it, the churning-rod, churn the milky ocean. O gods, from it Lakṣmī, the mother of the world will spring up. O glorious ones, there is no doubt that because of her you will be delighted. I myself, in the form of a tortoise, shall fully hold the (Mandara) mountain (on my back).

Saying so, that lord Viṣṇu disappeared. O brāhmaṇa, all the gods and demons went for churning the ocean.

CHAPTER NINE

The Churning Starts

Sūta said:

1. Then the hosts of gods with gandharvas and demons uprooted the Mandara mountain and put it into the ocean.

2-7a. Then the glorious, kind, ancient lord of the world supported on his back the bottom of the mountain. (Then the gods) putting Ananta (the lord of serpents) round it churned the milky ocean. When it was being churned on the Ekādaśī day, all of them ran away seeing the Kālakūṭa poison that had come up. Seeing them running away Śaṅkara said these (words): "O hosts of gods, hand over the poison to me. I shall quickly inactivate the great (i.e. severe) poison, viz. Kālakūṭa". Saying so, that lord of Pārvatī, meditating upon Viṣṇu in his heart and uttering the great hymn, took that fearful poison. By the power of the great hymn, that great (deadly) poison was digested.

7b-22. He who, being controlled, would devoutly mutter the three names, viz. Acyuta, Ananta, and Govinda, of Viṣṇu with Praṇava (i.e. Om) at the beginning and Om at the end, has no fear of taking poison, or from fire and also from death. Then gods with their minds delighted, churned the milky ocean. Then Alakṣmī (i.e. Evil Fortune), of a dark face and red eyes, having rough and tawny hair, and having an old body, sprang up. She, the eldest one, said to the gods: "What should I do?" The gods spoke to that goddess, the repository of misery: "O goddess, we are giving you a place in the homes of those men where quarrel takes place. O eldest one, accompanied by evil stay (there). Always remain, causing misery, in the houses of those men who speak cruel and false words and who the mean men, eat at dusk. O eldest one, there is no doubt that your stay will be there where there are skulls, hair, ashes, bones, and chaff fire. Always remain, causing grief and poverty in the houses of those mean men who eat without washing their feet. Stay, always giving grief, and with dissension, in the houses of those who clean their teeth with sand, salt or charcoal. O you eldest one, causing filth, your stay will be in the houses of those mean men who eat mushrooms and a left-over coconut. There is no doubt that you will stay in the houses of those men of sinful thoughts, who eat sesamum-flour, bottle-gourd, garlic, shoots of young plants, a species of kadamba (called kalambaka) and onions. O you inauspicious one, always stay there (i.e. in that house) which is bereft of sacrifices (offered to) preceptors and gods, and bereft of gifts to guests, and where the sound of (the recital of) the Vedas is absent. O you inauspicious one, always stay there, where there takes place quarrel between a husband and his wife, where no worship of the dead ancestors or gods takes place, and where there is (indulgence in) gambling. Causing sins and poverty, always stay in that place where there dwell men who are adulterers, who snatch away the wealth of others, and where brāhmaṇas, good men and old men are not honoured." Having thus directed that eldest of all, who liked (to set up) quarrels, the gods again together churned the ocean.

CHAPTER TEN

The Birth of Lakṣmī

Sūta said:

1-4. Then Airāvata sprang up (from the ocean), so also the horse Uccaiḥśravas. Then (sprang up) Dhanvantari, and the fragrant Pārijāta. So also there was the rise of the celestial nymphs. Then on the twelfth day in the morning, when the sun had risen, the great Lakṣmī, graced with all (auspicious) characteristics, sprang up. All the religious deities saw that great mother of all creatures having her abode in the heart of Viṣṇu, and were delighted. Then, the cool-rayed one (i.e. the Moon), the brother of Lakṣmī, sprang up with nectar. (So also) Tulasī, Viṣṇu's wife, purifying the world, came up.

5-6. Then they, with their desires fulfilled, put the mountain as it was before, and having together praised the mother, muttered the excellent Śrī-sūkta (i.e. hymn in honour of Lakṣmī). Then that goddess, who was pleased, said to all gods: "Well-being to you, O best gods, ask for a boon. I shall grant it."

The gods said:

7-8. O goddess Kamalā, O mother of all, O you who are dear to Viṣṇu, be pleased. Without you the world is a void. Protect our lives.

Thus addressed, that great Lakṣmī, dear to Viṣṇu, said: "Now I shall protect the lives of all creatures."

9-11. Then Viṣṇu, the kind lord of the world, holding a conch, a disc and a mace, suddenly appeared (there). Then the gods saluted the lord of the worlds and praised him. With the palms of their hands joined they spoke with a faltering voice: "O Viṣṇu, accept this Lakṣmī, the mother, your dear queen, who does not go away, for the good of the mundane existence." As long as he did not take the pledge (of marrying her) Lakṣmī said to Viṣṇu:

Lakṣmī said:

12. O Madhusūdana (i.e. Viṣṇu), O lord, how do you

desire to marry me, the younger (sister), without marrying the elder sister, Alakṣmī? Does the younger sister get married when the elder remains unmarried?

Sūta said:

13-18. Having heard this, Viṣṇu, along with the gods, and according to the Vedic text, gave Alakṣmī to Uddālaka. Then the glorious Viṣṇu accepted Lakṣmī. Then all the hosts of gods again and again saluted him. Then they, superior in power, struck all the demons. All of them, crying, went into the ten directions. By the order of Viṣṇu the gods arranged a line in due order to eat (i.e. to drink) the nectar, and said to one another: "You give it, you give it, you give it." Thus they spoke. They said: "I can't, I can't, I can't." Then Viṣṇu stood up, and took up a feminine form and distributed the nectar with a golden vessel.

19-22. When Rāhu ate up (i.e. drank) the nectar, the Moon and the Sun said: "This is a demon, who has come here deceitfully." Then the lord of the world was angry, and struck him with the golden pot. His (i.e. Rāhu's) head dropped on the ground, and came to be known as Ketu. Then, Rāhu and Ketu, afflicted with fear quickly went (away) from there. Now (even) when that day arrives he fights with the Moon and the Sun. The son of Siṁhikā (i.e. Rāhu) would live (in them). That would be a moment difficult to secure. (At that time) all water is like (that of) Gaṅgā, and all brāhmaṇas are like Vyāsa.

23-25. He, who, (at that time) bathes at the Vyāsatīrtha, would obtain the fruit of the bath at Gaṅgā. The gifts given (at that time) would have an inexhaustible merit; and the sin earned (i.e. committed) during crores of existences would completely perish; what then is the use of crores of sacrifices? One who longs for knowledge, gets it. One who desires a son, gets one. One who desires salvation, obtains it. A spell would certainly become effective. Thus, O brāhmaṇa, I have told you (the account of) the churning of the ocean.

CHAPTER ELEVEN

The Importance of Observing a Vow in Honour of Lakṣmī

Śaunaka said:

1-3. Now I desire to hear, O you who were actually instructed by Veda Vyāsa, of the nature of Viṣṇu. O you who have no pride, O you who favour the world, tell me properly as to how (i.e. by doing what) a sinful and very miserable woman would be fortunate. By (doing) what would she be dear to her husband, would she be beautiful, and nectar to (his) eyes? O you, rich in penance, tell me by which (means) wealth is produced.

Sūta said:

4. O brāhmaṇa, if (you think) this is a meritorious account, difficult to be had, (then) listen. I shall tell it to you briefly and properly.

5-13. In the yuga called Dvāpara, there was a king by name Bhadraśravas. He was a resident of the Saurāṣṭra country and had mastered the Vedas and the Vedāṅgas. He had a wife by name Suratacandrikā. From her the king got seven attractive sons. Then a beautiful and truthful daughter, Śyāmābālā by name was born. She delighted her father. Once Śyāmābālā went joyfully with her friends to the ground under a nīpa tree, very difficult to be met with, in the golden sands to play with attractive gems (to be) concealed (and then to be discovered). In the meanwhile, O brāhmaṇa, Lakṣmī, rescuing people from the worldly existence and giving (i.e. teaching) them the right course and having taken the form of an old brāhmaṇa lady, herself came (there); and O brāhmaṇa, thinking in her mind (i.e. to herself), 'Barring the house of the king, the ruler of all the people, to the house of which mean people should I go now ?' she went to the king's abode which had golden walls and which was adorned with banners. Then having crossed the main gate, she said to the door-keeper: "O you of auspicious characteristics who are appointed at the door, leave it (and report to the queen). I am quickly going and seeing queen Suratacandrikā".

14. Hearing those words of her, uttered like the note of a

cuckoo, (the doorkeeper) holding a golden staff in her hand, was extremely delighted.

The doorkeeper said:

15. O old lady, what is your name? Who is your husband? How have you come (here)? What is your business in seeing (i.e. with) the queen? For what reason (do you want to see her)? What (is your intention), O brāhmaṇa lady? I have curiosity to hear it.

The old lady said:

16-18a. Listen, O you (queen's) employee, O you who hold a jewelled staff (i.c. you who are the doorkeeper) of the great king's wife, since you have curiosity for (i.e. to know) the reason for my arrival, I am (that) well-known (goddess) named Kamalā, and the lord of the worlds is known as the lord of my life. (My) city is Dvāravatī by name. O employee, the lord of my life lives in that (city). O you having a jewelled staff in your hand, listen with curiosity. I have come from there. Now, to you, I shall tell the reason for my arrival.

18b-26. Formerly (i.e. in a former existence), your queen, born in a vaiśya family, was unhappy. One day, O employee, that unhappy lady quarrelled with her husband, and then tormented by her husband, she, weeping repeatedly, immediately went out of the house. Hearing her weeping, I approached her. I asked her all (her) account, and was properly told. Then I taught her the excellent vow. On my having taught the vow to her, she gladly practised the vow. O you doorkeeper, due to its propitiousness she became happy. Once she, born in a vaiśya family, died with her husband. Then lord Dharmarāja, who brings about the destruction of all, sent his fearful servants to bring the two (to his abode). The fierce massengers came (there) by Yama's order. They, with iron hammers in their hands exerted to go to Yama's abode.

27-31. In the meanwhile, those messengers of Lakṣmī, who were Viṣṇu's devotees, and who had held conches, discs and maces, came (there) to take them (to her abode). Seeing them like that, Yama's messengers fled (away). (Then) the magnanimous, self-radiant messengers of Lakṣmī cut off the nooses and having put them in a chariot to which royal swans were yoked, they all suddenly went along the aerial path to Lakṣmī's city. For so many thousands of kalpas the two lived in Lakṣmī's city, as many times the excellent vow was practised by the vaiśya lady. To enjoy the remaining religious merit, the two are now born in a royal family. O you doorkeeper, the two, proud of the royal glory, have forgotten the vow. Therefore, to advise her and you also about the vow I have come (here).

The doorkeeper said:

32-33a. O old lady, in what manner is the vow practised? Practised in which month is the vow the best? Which is the deity that is worshipped? O mother, tell properly this to me who am asking you.

Kamalā (*i.e. Lakṣmī*) *said*:

33b-43a. O employee (i.e. O doorkeeper), when the month of Kārtika has passed and the month of Mārgaśīrṣa has arrived, in that month, on a day called Thursday, in the morning, a woman surrounded by those who practise the vow, should worship Lakṣmī along with Nārāyaṇa. O you employee, she should propitiate Lakṣmī with sweets (mixed) with sweetened milk, and (articles of) food mixed with candied sugar, and then should pray like this: "O Kamalā (i.e. Lakṣmī), you who are worshipped by the worlds and you who are dear to Viṣṇu; as you are unshakingly (devoted) to Kṛṣṇa (i.e. Viṣṇu), in the same way remain (firmly) in me. O goddess Lakṣmī, you who rule (everything), O sinless one, give me shelter." Assuring Lakṣmī with many presents, she should please her. She should worship the goddess with great festivity by reciting sacred texts. O employee, then giving the remains of the articles of food to the deity, to the best brāhmaṇa, she should (distribute it among) herself, her husband, sons and other servants. O beautiful lady, listen to the speciality of the second Thursday: She should propitiate Lakṣmī with auspicious fried articles of wheat baked in earthen pots and variegated powders. She should devoutly (worship) Lakṣmī. On the third (Thursday) she should offer present of boiled rice mixed with candied sugar. On the fourth (Thursday) she should carefully and joyfully worship goddess

Lakṣmī with excellent śyāmāka and śāli (rice), O you having a jewelled staff in your hand. Then to please goddess Lakṣmī, she should please brāhmaṇas with (i.e. by giving them) money, cloth, ornaments, various articles of food and fruits.

The doorkeeper said:

43b-47a. O old lady, stay here only; informing the queen (of your arrival) I shall take you (to her). O best one, do not be angry.

Saying so, that beautiful lady went to the queen. O brāhmaṇa, that doorkeeper, having put her joined palms on her head told all that Lakṣmī had said from the beginning to the end to queen Suratacandrikā. Having heard the words of the doorkeeper queen Suratacandrikā went near the brāhmaṇa lady, and the beautiful lady proudly spoke to her.

The queen said:

47b-48a. O old brāhmaṇa lady, to advise what have you come here? Tell it to me quickly, as you please and giving up fear.

The brāhmaṇa lady said:

48b-50a. Seeing your immorality I desire to go quickly. O wicked one, what shall I tell you, since today, on the day of (i.e. sacred to) Lakṣmī, O you cāṇḍālā, you are not observing that vow very difficult to have? I have seen that. Now, O proud one, who will (live) in your house?

50b-52. Hearing these words of the brāhmaṇa lady, she (i.e. the queen) with her eyes red with anger struck the old brāhmaṇa lady. Then that old Kamalā (i.e. Lakṣmī) ran away crying. Then that girl Śyāmā, having penance as her wealth, who was playing, came near that brāhmaṇa lady on hearing her weeping.

Śyāmābālā said:

53-61. O old lady, tell me who caused you pain like this.

O best of brāhmaṇas, having heard her words, Kamalā, with

her voice faltering due to grief, told her the entire account. Śyāmābālā, having heard from her that vow extremely difficult to have, practised it, as told in the sacred texts, with faith and devotion. When the first three days (i.e. Thursdays) were over, and the fourth (Thursday) arrived, her marriage rite was accomplished by the grace of Lakṣmī. The son named Mālādhara, of king Śrīsiddheśvara, having royal lustre, took her and went home. O brāhmaṇa, listen to the wonder (that took place) when she had gone. O brāhmaṇa, it was not known who had taken away the very many rich articles that were there in the house of the queen. She sat without wealth, without ideas and without food and clothes; and to ask (her daughter) for something, she sent her husband with someone to her daughter's house. O brāhmaṇa, after some time he went with difficulty to the village of that Mālādhara, and reached the bank of a lake. Her maids had come there to take water from that (lake). Seeing him who was most unhappy, they, sympathising with him, said (to him).

The maids said:

62. Tell us all that—who you who have lost flesh and blood, whose body and hair are rough, are; wherefrom you have come.

The poor man said:

63-67. I am Śyāmābālā's father. I have come from Saurāṣṭra city. O maids, tell this to Śyāmābālā.

Hearing those words of (i.e. uttered by) him, they who were full of curiosity, laughed after looking at one another's face, and went to their city; and O brāhmaṇa, they told the entire account to Śyāmābālā. Hearing their words, she sent her servants. The beautiful lady gave her father flowers, oil, divine garments, sandal, betel-leaf and a horse. All the servants also went (to him) and having made him well-dressed, took him to Śyāmābālā's house, resembling a palace.

68-71. Then Śyāmābālā also carefully fed her father who was most unhappy, with food of śāli (i.e. boiled rice) with ghee. When four days had passed, she gave him money concealed in a vessel, and sent him (back), O you whose wealth is your penance. Then after entering his house, he found that the money that was there in the vessel (had turned into) a heap of charcoals, and being extremely unhappy he wept. He who had come (back) to his (own) house, went out of it to go to his daughter's house. She also went to the bank of that lake.

72-80. The chaste lady (i.e. Śyāmābālā) honoured her who was dearer to her than her own life, in the same way through affection for her mother. At this time Śyāmābālā thought of making her mother observe (the vow of) the excellent day of Lakṣmī. Her mother, having incurred the wrath of Lakṣmī, experienced poverty, and secretly ate what was left over by young ones of animals. Three days sacred to Lakṣmī passed, and on the fourth one she (i.e. Śyāmābālā) firmly made her observe (that vow). That queen Suratacandrikā came (back) to her city. She saw her house divine like that (i.e. as before) by the grace of Lakṣmī. O best of brāhmaṇas, Śyāmābālā on some occasion again went to the house of her mother with a desire to see her glory. Seeing Śyāmābālā from a distance, she became angry; and saying, "I shall not see her face", she remained hidden. Going into the interior of the house, and taking salt (from there), she (i.e. Śyāmābālā) quietly came to her house resorted to by Lakṣmī. The king, her lord, asked the chaste lady whose husband was her god: "O dear one, tell me what you have brought."

The wife said:

81-84. I have brought the essence of the kingdom; I shall show it to you at (the time of) the meal.

Saying so she cooked food without salt and gave food etc. to king Mālādhara. Then king Mālādhara eating the seasoned article without salt, became sad. Then she gave him (the salt) the essence of the kingdom. O brāhmaṇa, then the king's mind was pleased and he took his meal. And (repeatedly) saying, '(You are) blessed, (you are) blessed,' he praised the woman. One who does not observe this vow with great respect would become poor and luckless in existence after existence.

85-86. He who would listen to this with devotion, or would recite it attentively, would be freed from all sins, and would obtain (i.e. go to) Lakṣmī's world. There is no doubt that for her who observes this vow without listening to its story, the fruit of the vow is lost.

CHAPTER TWELVE

Merit Earned by Protecting a Brāhmaṇa

Śaunaka said :

1. O Sūta, kindly tell (me) due to which other religious merit a man with his sins gone (away) goes to the place of Viṣṇu.

Sūta said :

2-5. That man, O best brāhmaṇa, who protects a brāhmaṇa with his (own) wealth or his (own) life, goes to Viṣṇu's world. Formerly, in the yuga called Dvāpara, there was a king (named) Dīnānātha who was sonless (but who was) a devotee of Viṣṇu and a sacrificer. Once that king politely asked Gālava: "O best sage, O ocean of compassion, tell me due to which religious merit a son is born. I shall practise it by your order. The life of those men who do not have a son is useless."

Gālava said:

6-7. O king, I shall tell you in brief the cause of a son's birth about which you have asked me. Listen attentively. O best king, perform the sacrifice called *Naramedha.* Then you will have progeny endowed with all (good) characteristics.

The king said:

8. O preceptor, O brāhmaṇa, tell me by bringing what kind of man I shall perform the great human sacrifice, the best among sacrifices

Gālava said:

9-22. If a man has a handsome body, a charming face and

is proficient in all sacred texts, then he is fit for sacrifice. He who is crippled, has a black complexion, is a fool, would not be fit (for sacrifice).

O brāhmaṇa, when Gālava spoke like this, that king, the lord of men, sent his messengers, telling them the words of Gālava; and giving much money he selected brāhmaṇas like Gālava who had mastered all Vedic texts. Then by the order of the king the messengers gladly went carefully from country to country, village to village and even to cities, O best brāhmaṇa. Not finding (such a man) anywhere they then went to a country (and the city) called Daśapura which, O brāhmaṇa, was crowded with virtuous brāhmaṇas; where seeing the women having lovely hair and eyes like those of the young ones of deer, men were infatuated, since the women were moon-faced. In that charming city was (i.e. lived) a brāhmaṇa named Kṛṣṇadvija with his three sons and his amiable wife. He was a devotee of Viṣṇu, always spoke agreeably and was engaged in worshipping Viṣṇu. He maintained the (sacred) fire, was devoted to his parents and was a benefactor of the devotees of Viṣṇu. Then the messengers of the king requested the best brāhmaṇa: "O best brāhmaṇa, say, 'give a son, give a son'. O best brāhmaṇa, the king does not have a son who would remove his affliction. For that (son) be initiated into the sacrifice called *Naramedha*. We shall take your son to offer him as a victim in that great sacrifice. O brāhmaṇa, carefully take a lakh of (coins of) gold (in exchange for your son). If, due to your fondness for your son, you would not give your son ungrudgingly, then we shall take him forcibly (because) we carry out the order of the king." Hearing the words of the messengers the brāhmaṇa and his wife were afflicted with grief and with their minds full of fear, they were, as it were dead. "What is the use of wealth, gold, life or house ?" The brāhmaṇa spoke these words to the royal officers.

The brāhmaṇa said:

23-27. O messengers, if you have certainly come to take (away) my son who removes the darkness of grief (in my life), then (please) listen to my words. Who living on the earth desires to disobey the king's order ? But, leaving my son you (please) take me, an old brāhmaṇa (to the king).

Hearing these words of (i.e. uttered by) him, the messengers, full of anger, forcibly left (coins of) gold in his house. When they angrily made up their mind to take away the son, the brāhmaṇa, weeping, and with the palms of his hands joined said: "O men, these words viz. 'leaving the eldest among my sons, take the other excellent one' do not come to my mouth (i.e. my tongue)."

28-30. Hearing the words of the brāhmaṇa, the messengers said to the brāhmaṇa's wife who was weeping: "O best one, give us the younger son." Hearing these words of (i.e. uttered by) them, the brāhmaṇa woman, being extremely grieved, fell on the ground as a plantain-tree falls on the ground due to (strong) wind. Taking up a hammer, she violently struck it on her head: "O messengers, I shall never give you my youngest son."

31-36. O brāhmaṇa, at this time the middle son of the brāhmaṇa, full of modesty and weeping, said to his parents: "Who would be the protector if the mother gives poison (to her son), or the father sells his son, or the king snatches away everything." Saying so, the son, saluting his parents with his head (bowed down), went with the speedy messengers of the king who was initiated. Then the brāhmaṇa and his wife, with their minds afflicted by the separation from their son, wept again and again and became blind. Then they (i.e. the messengers) on their way went to the hermitage of sage Viśvāmitra, which was full of (his) disciples and resorted to by young deer. The sage, seeing the royal officers, respectfully asked them: "O (men), who are you? Where had you gone? What is your profession?"

The king's messengers said:

37-40. O brāhmaṇa, listen attentively. A son is not born to the king. For (i.e. to obtain) that the king is initiated into the sacrifice called *Naramedha*. We are taking this brāhmaṇa-son (to be offered) as a victim in that (sacrifice).

Hearing these words of them, the brāhmaṇa (i.e. Viśvāmitra) became compassionate. 'Let even my life depart; (but) the boy be happy. Those people who in this world cast their life like (a blade of) grass for a child, or a brāhmaṇa, or their master, obtain eternal worlds.'

41-44a. Thus thinking in his mind, the best brāhmaṇa said: "Leaving this brāhmaṇa-son to be offered as a victim in the sacrifice, (please) quickly take me. This is an excellent boy. Having obtained birth in this mundane existence, this child has not got any happiness. How (then) will he die (i.e. Why should he die)? O messengers, when he came from his house, his unlucky parents became unhappy. Indeed he has as it were gone to Yama's house." Having heard these words of him, the messengers said to the brāhmaṇa:

44b-48. "O wise brāhmaṇa, how shall we take an old man like you, without the order of king Dīnānātha?" Speaking thus the messengers then went to the city of the king. The sage also went to the city of the king. The sage also went to the sacrificial chamber with the host of the messengers. The messengers told the king the brāhmaṇa's gesture. He, hearing that, and with his mind full of doubt said to him: "If by performing this sacrifice without a victim I get a son, then you (may) take (back) this son of the brāhmaṇa."

The sage (*Viśvāmitra*) *said*:

49-62a. O king, when the sacrifice is performed, a mighty son will be born. Do not entertain a doubt about this. (Your) seeing (me) will not be fruitless.

Hearing these words of him (i.e. of Viśvāmitra), the king with joy performed the sacrifice with the 'complete oblation' with (the help of) all the sages. Then that best sage took the brāhmaṇa's son (with him) and went to the city named Daśapura; and having gone to his house the sage said (these) words: "O brāhmaṇa, you are staying at home." (The brāhmaṇa said): "O sage, I am staying as if I am dead. The king forcibly took (away) my son. What shall I do? O brāhmaṇa, when our son had gone, our eyes became blind due to weeping." O brāhmaṇa, when the best sage said, "See your son (and) take him (back)", the brāhmaṇa and his wife became glad. For the sake of the son, the two in a moment went out;

and due to perfection of the sage the eyes of the two quickly obtained light (i.e. power of seeing); and then on seeing the son the two drank for a long time the lotus-like face of the son with their bee-like eyes, and repeatedly saluted the sage, and O brāhmaṇa, the two i.e. the brāhmaṇa and his wife, who spoke agreeably, said these words: "O sage, you have indeed made to us a good present of our life." O brāhmaṇa, the sage, the ocean of kindness, having given them blessings, went to his own hermitage. Having the great seat of Viṣṇu at his hand, the magnanimous sage practised a great penance difficult to be obtained (i.e. practised) even by deities. O brāhmaṇa, when some time passed, the king obtained a son. He was handsome, proper for a king, and like the moon in the ocean. O brāhmaṇa, the king too, free from grief and with curiosity arisen in him enjoyed like a god wealth on the earth.

62b-64. He, who protects brāhmaṇas by giving his life and wealth, goes to Viṣṇu's abode, from which a return (to the mortal world) is difficult to have. Those who here (i.e. on the earth) recite or hear devoutly from a brāhmaṇa the story, or the account, or (even) one verse, go to Viṣṇu's abode.

CHAPTER THIRTEEN

The Importance of the Vow of Janmāṣṭamī

Śaunaka said:

1. O Sūta, O you very wise one, tell me (about) Kṛṣṇāṣṭamī, and its excellent importance, (and) emancipate me from the great ocean (of the mundance existene).

Sūta said:

2-8. O brāhmaṇa, he who devoutly observes the (vow) Kṛṣṇāṣṭamī, ultimately goes to Viṣṇu's city along with a crore (members) of his family. O best brāhmaṇa, when Aṣṭamī falls on a Wednesday or Monday in conjunction with Rohiṇī, it gives salvation to a crore (members) of his family. Even if a great sinner observes (this) excellent vow, he is freed from all sins and in the end goes to Viṣṇu's abode. O brāhmaṇa, that mean man who does not observe (the vow of) Kṛṣṇajanmāṣṭamī, meets with misery here (i.e. in this world) and after death he would go to hell. That foolish woman who does not observe the vow of Kṛṣṇajanmāṣṭamī goes to a terrible hell year after year. That foolish man who eats (food) on the day of Janmāṣṭamī, attains to a great hell. I am telling (you) the truth and truth (only). Formerly Dilīpa asked the best sage Vasiṣṭha. Listen to that (conversation), destroying all sins, O you very intelligent one.

Dilīpa said :

9-10. O great sage, tell me, I desire to hear (about) the Aṣṭamī in the dark fortnight of the month of Bhādrapada on which Viṣṇu was born. How was the lord, holding a conch, a disc and a mace, born in (i.e. from) the womb of Devakī, to do what and for what purpose (was he born from her womb)?

Vaiṣṭha said :

11-21. O king, I shall (tell you). I shall tell you for what purpose the lord of the world left the heaven and was born on the earth. Formerly the Earth was oppressed by kings like Kaṁsa. She, struck by Kaṁsa's messenger who was proud of his office, cried again and again, went with her eyes rolling to that place where the chief of gods, the lord of Umā and the bull-bannered god remained to tell him: "O lord, I am struck by Kaṁsa". Tears flowed (down her cheeks); she had become pale and insulted. The great god, seeing her weeping, came, with his lower lip throbbing with anger to the house of the Creator. Having gone to Brahmā he asked him for the destruction of Kaṁsa. (He said to Brahmā :) "O Brahman, along with Viṣṇu, produce (i.e. find out) a means". Having heard those words of the lord (i.e. Śiva), Brahmā went to the milky ocean where Viṣṇu was lying asleep on the serpent. Mounting upon the back of a swan he (i.e. Brahmā) came to Viṣṇu. Having gone there, the Creator, the best among the speakers, joined by gods led by Hara (i.e. Śiva), praised him softly with words: "Salutation to the lotus-eyed one, Viṣṇu, the highest soul, the protector of the world. O you lord of Lakṣmī, salutation to you." Having heard this praise from them, Viṣṇu said to all gods with saddened faces: "How (i.e. for what reason) have you come?"

Brahmā said :

22-26. O god, O lord of the world, listen, I (shall) tell you why we have come, O best of the gods, O cause of the worlds. King Kaṁsa has become arrogant due to the boon given by Śiva. He has become unconquerable. He has struck the Earth; has afflicted her with the blow of his hand. After a boon was granted to him he was deceived by a trick. (He had said:) "O Śiva, I should not meet with death except through my sister's son." Therefore, O god, having gone to Gokula, and obtained birth in (i.e. from) Devakī's womb, go yourself to kill that unconquerable Kaṁsa.

The god, sent forth by Brahmā, said to Śiva: "O lord of gods, hand over Pārvatī. Having remained for a year, she will go."

27-49. With Pārvatī as his protector the god holding a conch, a disc, and a mace, undertook his journey to Mathurā. The mace-holder there (i.e. at Mathurā) obtained birth in (i.e. from) the womb of Devakī. The lotus-eyed Pārvatī resorted to the womb of Yaśodā. Having rested in (Devakī's) womb for nine months and nine days, the lord of the world, the enemy of Kaṁsa and the son of Vasudeva, was born (on) the night when Rohiṇī was in conjunction (with the Moon), when clouds were thundering, of the day called Aṣṭamī, (falling) in the dark fortnight of the month of Bhādrapada. Yaśodā, the daughter of Virāṭa and the wife of Nanda, gave birth to a daughter. Ānakadundubhi (i.e. Vasudeva) seeing his son, having lotus-like navel, and eyes like lotus-petals, began to be joyful, when Devakī, trembling with the fear of the demon, viz. Kaṁsa said (to him): "O lord, go, and hand over the son to Vairāṭī (i.e. Yaśoda). Having given (our) son to Yaśodā, bring (here) her daughter." Hearing her words Vasudeva also was grieved. Placing the son on his side, he went to Yaśodā. On his way Yamunā was full of water, fearful, very long, having deep water and flooded. Seeing this, Vasudeva remained on the bank watching Yamunā and afflicted with grief he cried through anxiety: "What (shall) I do? Where (shall) I go? Even destiny has deceived me. Now, how shall I go to Yaśodā, to Nanda's house?" At that time, Viṣṇu gladly deceived, by means of a trick, his father who watching Yamunā remained on her bank for a moment. He looked (at Yamunā) again. In a moment she became (i.e. her water was) as high as the knee. Happy on seeing her (like that) he rose and started going. The lord of the world resorted to his magical power and fell into the water from his side. Seeing the son fallen (into the water) he wailed loudly and was extremely grieved. That Creator again deceived him by adoptnig a great trick. (He cried): "O lord of the worlds, protect me. O best god, protect my son." Seeing his father crying, (Kṛṣṇa) the enemy of Kaṁsa, sported repeatedly in the water and with compassion again went to (i.e. clasped) the bosom of his father. Then with him the best of the the Yadus went to Nanda's abode. Having given the son to Yaśodā, he brought her daughter. Then having come to his abode, he handed over the daughter (of Yaśodā) to his wife (Devakī). The news that Devakī had delivered was received by the enemy of (Devakī's) son. Then his messengers set out to bring (either) the son (or) the daughter. Those messengers of Kaṁsa, having come (there), proceeded to take the daughter. Having dragged her forcibly from Devakī and Vasudeva, the messengers of Kaṁsa, seized her and gave her to the enemy of gods. That great unconquerable king having held her was frightened. Kaṁsa, the greatest among the demons, seeing her whose complexion was like pure gold, whose face was like the full moon, and whose eyes were like flashes of lightning, and who was smiling, ordered: "Take her and kill her (by dropping) her on a slab of stone." Receiving the order, the demons proceeded to destroy her. Gaurī (i.e. Pārvatī) suddenly went to the sky.

Gaurī (i.e. Pārvatī) said :

50. O king, listen, I shall tell you where your greatest enemy is. O greatest of the demons, your killer is hidden in Nanda's house.

Vasiṣṭha said :

51-57. Having spoken like this, the goddess went to her abode. Having heard the words of the goddess, king Kaṁsa was extremely pained. He said to his sister, Pūtanā: "You go to Nanda's house. Killing the son fraudulently, obtain many things that you desire, which I shall give for killing my enemy. O you auspicious one, go very quickly." That demoness, having received (Kaṁsa's) order, went to Gokula. Taking up an illusory form of a beautiful lady, she entered Gokula. Holding poison in her breasts, she went to kill (Kṛṣṇa). Having entered unnoticed through the door of the cowherds' house, she went inside, took up the child, gave him her breast and obtained beatitude. Then having hurled (the demon) Śakaṭa, and having crushed Tṛṇāvarta and others, and having curbed Kāliya, he went to the city of Madhu (i.e. Mathurā). Having gone there he killed the cruel Kaṁsa and vanquished his wrestlers. O king, I have told you this vow of (i.e. to be observed on) the day of Viṣṇu's birth.

58-62a. On hearing it, the sins (of the person who hears it), perish. (Then) what will happen on observing it? A man or a woman who observes this vow of (i.e. sacred to) Viṣṇu, obtains unequalled wealth as (much as is) desired in this (very) existence. (The vow should) not be observed on the third or the sixth day joined with the previous day. For those who desire religious merit, Aṣṭamī is Ekādaśī; (they should) carefully avoid Aṣṭamī joined with Saptamī. Even without (the rise of) the constellation, Aṣṭamī, joined with Navamī should be observed (as a fast day) if the constellation has risen, and there is partial Aṣṭamī and full Navamī (then the vow should be observed). Aṣṭamī that is united with (i.e. has) Rohiṇī (risen) for a short time, should be (regarded as) complete.

62b-67. O king, what is the use of observing crores of vows if Aṣṭamī with Rohiṇī falls on a Wednesday or with the Moon (i.e. on a Monday). Such Aṣṭamī is obtained or not obtained even after hundreds of years when it falls on a Monday or Wednesday. Without (the rise of) the constellation (Rohiṇī) the vow of Aṣṭamī should not be observed when the Aṣṭamī is joined with Navamī. The vow of Aṣṭamī should be observed even on the seventh day, if it is joined with Rohiṇī. When the eighth day of Kṛṣṇa is (there) even for fortyeight seconds, for kāṣṭhā (i.e. one thirtieth part of a kalā, which is equal to fortyeight seconds) or for a period of fortyeight minutes on the ninth day, the vow of Kṛṣṇāṣṭamī should be observed. That Aṣṭamī is acceptable (i.e. the vow should be observed even) on the ninth day, but not on that eighth day which is united with the seventh day. What (then should be told) about Wednesday and especially about Monday? What (should be told) about Aṣṭamī that is united with Navamī? It gives salvation to crores of the members of the family. If there is the connection with the seventh day, (even) by (the measure of time called) pala, then a man should avoid the vow of Aṣṭamī (on that day) like the pitcher of water full of the water of Gaṅgā coming in contact with a drop of liquor.

Dilīpa said:

68. O great sage, O lord, tell (me), who first observed (this vow). Who brought it to light? What is its religious merit? What is its fruit?

Vasiṣṭha said:

69-77. The great king Citrasena indulged in great sins and in illicit intercourse, and stole the gold of a brāhmaṇa. He was always delighted with (i.e. always drank) liquor and flesh(-eating). Thus he was full of sins, and always took delight in killing animals. He always conversed with cāṇḍālas and the fallen. The king who was like this thought of hunting. Knowing (that there was) a tiger in the forest and carefully surrounding it, he spoke these words to all his soldiers: "I alone shall kill it. If anyone else strikes him, he will be undoubtedly killed." The tiger came along the path of the king. The king, though ashamed, then went after the tiger. With much trouble and difficulty he became intent upon killing the tiger. In the evening he oppressed with hunger and thirst (remained) on the bank of Yamunā. That was the eighth day, united with Rohiṇī—the birth-day (of Kṛṣṇa). O king, cāṇḍāla-girls observed the vow in (i.e. on the bank of) Yamunā with many articles as presents, and very auspicious incense and lamps. Seeing the sandal, the flowers and (other) very charming articles like saffron, and food with many excellences, the kings' mind was perturbed.

The king said:

78a. For want of food my life shall certainly and instantly depart today.

The women said:

78b-85. O sinless king, on the day of Janmāṣṭamī of (i.e.

sacred to) Viṣṇu, you should not eat the hard flesh of a vulture, (of) a crow or of a cow, so also (you should not eat) food. There is no doubt (you have formerly) eaten it. What blemish would not come to the men who in this world eat (on the day of Kṛṣṇāṣṭamī)? For him who, when his vital airs remain in his body (i.e. while alive), has not observed (the vow of) Jayantī, and has not observed a fast (on that day), the punishment is (going to) Yama's abode. His manes do not accept whatever he has offered to them with proper rites. When food is taken on a Jayantī, all the manes are thrown (down).

Hearing this, O king, the king then observed that vow. Being delighted, he brought a few flowers, a little sandal, a small (piece of) cloth, observed the vow, and broke the fast at the end of the (Aṣṭamī) day. By the power of this vow Citrasena along with his dead ancestors got into a divine aeroplane and went to Viṣṇu's abode. Men obtain that fruit from the Aṣṭamī-vow which they get after going to Mathurā and seeing the lotus-like face of Kṛṣṇa. The poor obtain that fruit by observing the Kṛṣṇāṣṭamī-vow which they get by going to Dvārakā and seeing Viṣṇu, the lord of the universe.

CHAPTER FOURTEEN

The Greatness of a Brāhmaṇa

Śaunaka said:

1. O you very wise one, O you ocean of compassion, kindly tell me the importance of a brāhmaṇa, the best of all the castes.

Sūta said:

2-8. O best brāhmaṇa, a brāhmaṇa is the preceptor of all the castes. He should be known to be the resort of all gods, and he is actually Viṣṇu, the lord. O best brāhmaṇa, the wealth etc. of him who devoutly salutes a brāhmaṇa, looking upon him as Viṣṇu, enhances. Viṣṇu would always desire to cut off the head of him who, being proud, does not even casually salute a brāhmaṇa. Those of sinful minds, who hate a brāhmaṇa who has committed an offence, should be known to be hating Viṣṇu. They go to a terrible hell. Yama torments with a heated needle the eyes of him who would look angrily at a brāhmaṇa who has come to make a request. The messengers (i.e. servants) of Yama put (a piece of) heated iron into the mouth of the foolish mean man who threatens a brāhmaṇa. Kṛṣṇa himself along with gods eats in the house of those in whose house a brāhmaṇa with penance as his wealth eats.

9-13a. All the sins, like the murder of a brāhmaṇa, of that man who takes just a drop of water (flowing) from the foot of a brāhmaṇa, perish. I tell you the truth—the man who would devoutly wash the feet of a brāhmaṇa, is freed from all sins. That woman who has no sons or that woman whose child was stillborn, would (respectively) have a son, would have her child alive. Those holy places which exist in the world, those holy places which exist in an ocean, those holy places that exist in a sea, exist in the feet of a brāhmaṇa. He whose head is always sprinkled with the water from the feet of a brāhmaṇa, has (indeed) bathed at all the places (and) is free from all sins.

13b-20. O you Śaunaka, having penance as your wealth, listen, I shall tell you the greatness destroying all sins—the history, of the water (flowing) from the feet of a brāhmaṇa. O best brāhmaṇa, formerly there was a śūdra named Bhīma who was engaged in the occupation of a vaiśya. Even in Dvāpara (yuga), he, a cruel man who killed a thousand brāhmaṇas, was satisfied with a vaiśya wife. That Bhīma had given up the conduct of a śūdra and had illegitimate connection with his preceptor's wife. How can I tell each one (of his sins)? The sins of the śūdra, viz. Bhīma, of a wicked mind, could not be counted. Once he went to a brāhmaṇa's house. He made up his mind to enter the brāhmaṇa's house and to take (away) his money. He remained near the outer gate (of the house) of the brāhmaṇa. He spoke piteous words to the brāhmaṇa, the treasure of penance: "O lord, listen to my words. I think you are kind. I am oppressed with hunger; give me food, (otherwise) my life will soon depart (i.e. I shall die soon)."

The brāhmaṇa said:

21-23. O you who are oppressed with hunger, listen to my words. There is nobody (in my house) to cook food. There is rice. Take it and eat it as (much) as you like. I do not have a father or a mother; I do not have a son or a brother; I do not have a wife or the brother of my mother (i.e. maternal uncle). Leaving me all of them are dead. O guest, being jobless and unlucky I am staying in the house (all) alone. Viṣṇu alone lives in my abode. I do not know anyone else but him.

Bhīma said:

24. O best brāhmaṇa, I too do not have any (relative). I am a śūdra by caste. I shall remain in your house always serving you.

Sūta said:

25-33. Hearing (those) words of (i.e. uttered by) him, the brāhmaṇa who was delighted, quickly cooked food and gave it to him, O ascetic. He too being delighted lived in the brāhmaṇa's house doing to the brāhmaṇa affectionate and good service. 'Today or tomorrow I shall kill him, I shall take away his money and make it mine. Certainly I shall take it (away).' Thinking and deciding like this, he did, by (bowing) his head, whatever work like washing his feet, the brāhmaṇa would tell (him to do); (thus) he was free from sins. The brāhmaṇa having sipped water, everyday put before him under some protext, the water flowing from his feet. Once a thief came there to take away money. At night having drawn out the panels (of the door) he entered the interior of the house. Seeing Bhīma (there), he came with a staff in his hand to strike him. The thief having broken his head, quickly ran away. Then Viṣṇu's soldiers, holding conches, discs, and maces came (there) to take Bhīma whose sins had gone. O brāhmaṇa, a divine chariot to which royal swans were yoked, also came there. Getting into it, he went to Viṣṇu's abode, not easily accessible. I have narrated this greatness of a brāhmaṇa. It destroys the sin of him who listens to it.

CHAPTER FIFTEEN

The Importance of Ekādaśī

Śaunaka said:

1. O illustrious one, tell me the importance of Ekādaśī, and also what its fruit is and the sin (that accrues) to him who does not observe it.

Sūta said:

2-40. Now why should I tell the importance of (the vow of) Ekādaśī? The messengers of Yama, who cause fear to all beings, are frightened on hearing the name of Ekādaśī. There is no doubt about this. A man should observe a fast on the auspicious (day of) Ekādaśī which is the best of all vows, should keep awake and highly decorate Viṣṇu. O brāhmaṇa, the man who worships Viṣṇu with Tulasī-leaves, obtains the fruit of a crore of sacrifices. That sin which is said to be due to illicit intercourse, perishes due to a fast on the (day of) Ekādaśī. O brāhmaṇa, he who would offer a lamp full of ghee (to Viṣṇu) on the Viṣṇu-day (i.e. Ekādaśī), in the end goes to Viṣṇu's place. "Do not bring to me these meritorious beings who observe a fast on (the day of) Viṣṇu's going to bed or his turning aside, and especially on the Prabodhinī (Ekādaśī)." Thus orders Yama to his messengers day and night. Ekādaśī is dear to the lord of the world (i.e. Viṣṇu) and enhances religious merit. Viṣṇu does burn the body (of a man) on (his) eating food on that (day). Fie upon the life, wealth, handsomeness and conduct of those, the most sinful ones, who eat food on (the day of) Ekādaśī! They are the eaters of feces. O best brāhmaṇa, on merely eating food on Ekādaśī(-day), many and various sins attend upon the eater. As a great sin would accrue by having coitus with women on the new moon day, in the same way sin would be there (i.e. would be committed by a man) on eating on an Ekādaśī (-day). Beings (i.e. men) become diseased, crippled, and suffer from cough, and congenital leprosy on eating food on that (day). They become (i.e. are born as) village-pigs and are reduced to poverty. O best brāhmaṇa, people are bound by the king on eating (i.e. if they eat) on that (day), O brāhmaṇa, (all) the sins that are there in the worldly existence resort to food. There would be escape from hell of those who commit all sins (but) drink water (on that day only) through the order (of a superior person etc.). There is no escape (from hell) for those men who eat on Viṣṇu's day. Sin due to crores of brāhmaṇa-murders would accrue to those men for each kind of food that they eat. O men, listen, listen, I tell again, I tell again: On the day of Viṣṇu, (food) should not be eaten, food should not be eaten, food should not be eaten. That fruit is obtained by him who fasts on an (Ekādaśī-) day which is obtained by bathing in Gaṅgā etc. and at holy places or at the (time of) lunar or solar eclipse. He having worshipped (i.e. who worships) with lotus-garlands lord Viṣṇu after having properly broken the fast, does not have a place in mother's womb (i.e. is not reborn). O brāhmaṇa, he who makes a decoration in Viṣṇu's abode (i.e. temple) on an Ekādaśī(-day), gets the highest status and would stay in Viṣṇu's house. Those who having waited for the Ekādaśī-(day) observe a fast on that day, undoubtedly stay in Viṣṇu's city. There is no doubt that those whose minds are clung to the devotion of Viṣṇu, go to the highest place of Viṣṇu. Those too who have no longing for others' wealth and whose minds are contented, certainly have (i.e. go to) Viṣṇu's city. Those best men, who having encountered famine give food to creatures, undoubtedly get (i.e. go to) Viṣṇu's abode. Those, who cast their life for protecting cows, brāhmaṇas, (their) master, and a woman, certainly get (i.e. go to) Viṣṇu's city. Creatures (i.e. men) should never observe a fast on (an Ekādaśī day) joined with Daśamī (i.e. the tenth day). O best brāhmaṇa, it should be avoided like the proximity of a wicked man. Having fasted on that day, if the Ekādaśī-day is joined with Daśamī at the break of day, having fasted on that day, there would be Dvādaśī, and breaking of the fast would be on the thirteenth day. A devotee of Viṣṇu should not observe the Ekādaśī-vow on that day if the day-break is said to be the four ghaṭikās of the morning. This is the time of the bath for the ascetics, and is said to be like the water of Gaṅgā. If at the time of day-break Daśamī is seen (to continue), then on that day Ekādaśī destroying religious merit, worldly prosperity and sensual enjoyments, should not be observed. A wise man should avoid the Ekādaśī joined even a little with Daśamī, as he would abandon a pitcher full of ghee spoiled by the contact of a drop of liquor. When there is the full Ekādaśī (i.e. it falls on the eleventh day) and again continues (in part) on the twelfth day also, then the latter should be observed by ascetics and a householder should observe a fast on the former day. When a part of Ekādaśī does not go beyond Dvādaśī, the merit there is of a hundred sacrifices; and the breaking of the fast (should be done) on the thirteenth day. If the Ekādaśī is omitted and is further united with Dvādaśī, then a man should fast for the entire twelfth day if he desires the highest place. If it is the entire Ekādaśī (day) and if it is there in the morning also, then, if Dvādaśī is after it (commencing on that day) all should observe the (fast of Ekādaśī) on the latter day. Those men whose mind clings to the Ekādaśī-vow, live in heaven and go to Viṣṇu's house. There is no greater means than Ekādaśī for (going to) the next world. He who, full of many sins, observes (a fast on) the day of Viṣṇu, is freed from all sins and goes to Viṣṇu's abode.

41-42. That woman who along with her husband observes (a fast on) the day of Viṣṇu, gets good sons, is fortunate to have a (good) husband, and after death goes to Viṣṇu's abode. O best brāhmaṇa, the religious merit of him, who devoutly offers a lamp before (the image of) Viṣṇu on the day of Viṣṇu (i.e. Ekādaśī), cannot be measured (i.e. is immeasurable).

43-44. O brāhmaṇa, that woman who with her husband keeps awake on the day of Viṣṇu, would stay for a long time with her husband in the abode of Viṣṇu. The religious merit due to an object offered to Viṣṇu on his day is always inexhaustible.

45. Formerly there was (a man) named Vallabha in a city named Kāñcana. The lord of wealth had much wealth.

46-58a. O brāhmaṇa, his very beautiful wife was Hemaprabhā by name. The great characteristic of Kali, viz. being talkative, assaulted (i.e. overpowered) her. O you great ascetic, she would always quarrel with her husband. She would always censure her elders with mean words. She, the impure one, would always secretly eat from the cooking utensils and everyday would offer the remnants of the food to the elders. Her heart was always set on her paramour, (yet) she would say, 'I am a chaste woman.' She always caused anxiety to her husband by her quarrels. Once seeing her who had come (to him), her husband censured her and struck her who was full of all sins. Full of anger, she went to a vacant house, and without anybody's knowledge slept and remained there and did not (drink and) eat water or food. Fortunately for her on that day of Viṣṇu (there was the festival of) Visṇu's turning upon other side[1]—the Ekādaśī-vow, destroying all sins. Then, when it dawned, Dvādaśī with the Śravaṇā (constellation) came. Then that woman with her mind full of anger, observed two fasts, and became pure; and O brāhmaṇa, on the day of the Jayantī, she died at night. By Yama's order, his fearful messengers with nooses and hammers in their hands came there to take her like that (to Yama's abode). When they decided after binding her to take her to Yama's abode, Viṣṇu's messengers holding conches, discs and maces came (there). Having cut off the noose, they put her, free from sins and (therefore) pure, into a divine chariot. Surrounded by them, she then went to Viṣṇu's auspicious house, not easily accessible (even) to gods.

58b-60. O best brāhmaṇa, I have told you the importance of Viṣṇu's day. He who observes this vow even unwillingly goes to Viṣṇu's abode. A man who would go to Viṣṇu's temple on an Ekādaśī-day to offer him a lamp, obtains the fruit of a horse sacrifice at every step. Those who listen to or read the Purāṇas on Viṣṇu's day, obtain, for every letter (listened to or read), the fruit due to the gift of a tawny cow (to a brāhmaṇa).

---

1. **Pārśvaparivartana—Name of a festival on the eleventh day of the first half of Bhādrapada when Viṣṇu is supposed to turn upon the other side in his sleep.**

CHAPTER SIXTEEN

How to Win Favour of Viṣṇu

Śaunaka said:

1. O Sūta, kindly tell (me) that due to which act the sins would perish and grace of Viṣṇu would follow.

Sūta said:

2-4. O Śaunaka, I shall tell you what destroys the sins of the listeners, by which Viṣṇu's grace, destroying sins, would take place. O sage, the sin of him, earned during crores of existences disappears, who, with devotion and in many ways, offers on a full moon day worship to the lord of the world, O sage. Certainly the favour of the lord of Śrī would come to him.

5. The sins of him who would devoutly give food to a brāhmaṇa on Dvādaśī, would perish like darkness at day-break.

6-14. Śrī Viṣṇu instantly loves the man who would bathe (the image of) Viṣṇu with milk, sugar etc. on a Dvādaśī day, O brāhmaṇa. The giver who would offer a stone-like flower to Viṣṇu without any hymn, has a downfall. That man who would give a stone-like gift, a foolish brāhmaṇa, does not have religious merit. The foolish brāhmaṇa who, having no knowledge, accepts a gift like wasted fire at the time of deluge, through delusion, would, due to that, go to hell. O brāhmaṇa, the three, viz. a wooden elephant, or a deer drawn in a picture, or a brāhmaṇa having no knowledge, (simply) bear their names. As the water remaining on a path is purified by means of wind or the sun, in the same way the sin of him who devoutly sees the retinue (of a god), perishes. He who would devoutly offer on the full-moon day of the month of Āśvina parched grain with ghee and cowrie for playing to Viṣṇu goes, free from rebirth, to Viṣṇu's place. A man who through folly would not give to Viṣṇu, Viṣṇu is not pleased with him. He who would offer cowries to Viṣṇu on the full-moon day will certainly live in Hari's abode for as many days as the number of cowries (offered).

15-17. O best of brāhmaṇas, formerly in the city of Karavīra lived a cruel and fearful śūdra whose name was Kāladvija. Engaged in his own duty, he destroyed the business of his master. Once (when) he died, the fearful messengers of Yama came to take him to Yama's abode. Having tied him, they took him (to Yama's abode). Seeing him, Yama asked his minister (Citragupta):

Yama said:

18. O wise minister Citragupta, tell me from the beginning the good or bad deeds of (i.e. done by) him.

Citragupta said:

19-20. This sinner is of a wicked conduct; he has destroyed the business of his master. He does not have religious merit even of the size of an atom. Let him be roasted in hell for a hundred ages of Manu, O king. Then let the cruel one be born in the species of serpents and let him continuously live in a cave.

Sūta said:

21-28. O brāhmaṇa, for that much period he fell into (and lived in) hell, and then, being very unhappy he was born in the species of serpents in a cave. Once, O brāhmaṇa, on the full moon day in the month of Āśvina he threw out from the hole fried grain and cowries. That fell before Viṣṇu. Kind Viṣṇu who removes unhappiness, himself quickly destroyed his sin. When the time for his death arrived, he died. O brāhmaṇa, many messengers of Yama came to take him (to Yama's abode). When after binding him they started taking him to Yama's abode, messengers of Viṣṇu, holding conches, discs and maces came (there). They cut off his nooses and quickly put him whose sins had perished, into a divine chariot. The messengers of Yama ran (away). Surrounded by them the serpent went to Viṣṇu's house. Being free from rebirth he remained before (i.e. near) Viṣṇu. O brāhmaṇa, I certainly do not know what the religious merit of him who devoutly offers fried grain with ghee and cowries to Viṣṇu, would be.

29. O brāhmaṇa, the sins of him who devoutly listens to this chapter destroying sins, perish due to the grace of Viṣṇu.

CHAPTER SEVENTEEN

The Importance of Water Flowing from Viṣṇu's Feet

Śaunaka said :

1. O you ocean of compassion, O you very wise one, tell me from the beginning the greatness of the water (flowing) from Viṣṇu's feet, which destroys sins.

Sūta said :

2-11. The water (flowing) from the feet of Viṣṇu destroys all sins and is auspicious. He who would carry (even) a drop of it, would obtain the fruit of (visiting) all the holy places. O brāhmaṇa, the water (flowing) from Viṣṇu's feet destroys the sin of him who touches it; he does not meet with an untimely death and would obtain the fruit of a bath in Gaṅgā. O brāhmaṇa, there is no doubt that the sin in the body of the sinner who would drink the water (flowing) from the feet of Viṣṇu, would perish. That man who would devoutly carry on his head the water (flowing) from Viṣṇu's feet along with a Tulasī-leaf in the end goes to Viṣṇu's abode. Men obtain that fruit by touching the water (flowing) from Viṣṇu's feet, which is obtained by giving (pieces of) gold resembling Meru. That fruit is surely obtained by offering water to Viṣṇu's feet and touching the water (flowing) from Viṣṇu's feet, which is obtained by (offering) thousands of crores of cows. The fruit that is obtained by touching the water (flowing) from Viṣṇu's feet, is crores of times greater than the fruit which is obtained by performing thousands of crores of sacrifices. O brāhmaṇa, the fruit (obtained) by touching the water (flowing) from Viṣṇu's feet is greater than the fruit got by men by giving a crore of virgins (in marriage to worthy grooms). That fruit which a man obtains by giving a crore of elephants or by giving a crore of horses is obtained by a man by touching the water (flowing) from the feet of Viṣṇu. O brāhmaṇa, a man would get a larger fruit by touching the water (flowing) from Viṣṇu's feet, than that which he would obtain by giving (the earth) with the seven islands along with crops (growing on it).

12. O brāhmaṇa, listen, I shall tell you in brief. (What is the

use of) telling more? By touching the water (flowing) from Viṣṇu's feet, a sinner goes to Viṣṇu's house.

Śaunaka said :

13. O Sūta, kindly tell me which creature formerly reached Viṣṇu's abode by touching and drinking the water flowing from Viṣṇu's feet.

Sūta said :

14-18. Formerly in Tretāyuga there was a sinful brāhmaṇa by name Sudarśana. O best brāhmaṇa, on the day of (i.e. sacred to) Viṣṇu he would always eat (food, i.e. would not observe a fast). He always censured the sacred texts and always condemned the vows. Except his own belly he did not recognise anything else. O brāhmaṇa, when once the time of his death arrived, he died. The messengers of Yama came (to his place), and binding him they took him to Yama's abode. Seeing him, the brother of Yamunā (i.e. Yama) angrily asked his minister: "O minister, tell (me) from the root (i.e. from the beginning) what his merit is and what his sin is. This brāhmaṇa seems to be a great sinner and a man of cruel acts".

Citragupta said :

19-21. Listen to his sins(s). He has no merit even of the size of an atom (to his credit). O lord, even on the day of (i.e. sacred to) Viṣṇu, he always used to eat (food). O king, that mean man who would eat on the day of (i.e. sacred to) the lord of Kamalā (i.e. on the day sacred to viṣṇu), would eat feces and goes to a fearful hell. Give him a place in a hell for a hundred periods of Manu. Then he will be born in the stock of a śūdra.

Sūta said :

22-28. O brāhmaṇa, then, by Yama's order his terrible messengers threw him into feces (where he remained) for more than a hundred ages of Manu. Freed from there he became (i.e. was born as) a village-pig on the earth. For a long time he would remain in hell due to his having eaten food on the day of (i.e. sacred to) Viṣṇu. Then, O brāhmaṇa, the time of his death arrived, and he died. He obtained a birth (i.e. was born) in the stock of crow and always ate feces. O brāhmaṇa, one day this crow of a śabara drank the water, after the śabara's death, (flowing) from Viṣṇu's feet and remaining (i.e. collected) at the door (of the temple) and being killed by a hunter, fell (dead) on the same day. He, the eater of offerings, got into a divine, auspicious chariot to which royal swans were yoked, and went to Viṣṇu's abode. (I have) told you the greatness of the water (flowing) from (Viṣṇu's) feet. The sin of a sinful man who listens to it, perishes.

CHAPTER EIGHTEEN

Purificatory Acts for One Guilty of Illegitimate Intercourse

Śaunaka said :

1. O Sūta, tell me fully, with what can a man who having through delusion had illegitimate intercourse, be purified?

Sūta said :

2-8a. The best brāhmaṇa, who cohabits with a cāṇḍāla woman or an outcaste woman, should observe three fasts, then should observe the Prājāpatya vow, get clean-shaved with (even) the tuft of hair on the crown of his head (removed), and should give a couple of cows (to a brāhmaṇa). The brāhmaṇa becomes purified after giving proper present (to a brāhmaṇa). If a kṣatriya or a vaiśya cohabits with a cāṇḍālī, he should (observe) the Kṛcchra Prājāpatya (vow) and should give two pairs of cows to (a brāhmaṇa). O you ascetic, if a śūdra cohabits with an outcaste woman, he should give four pairs of cows (to a brāhmaṇa) and observe the Prājāpatya vow. If a man being infatuated, cohabits with his mother or sister or daughter, or his daughter-in-law, he should observe three Kṛcchra (-vows). Having observed three Cāndrāyaṇa (-vows), he should give three pairs of cows. Getting clean-shaved with (even) the tuft of hair on the crown of the head (removed), he should drink the mixture of the five products of a cow. O ascetic, in this case he becomes purified even after making offerings into fire.

8b-10. O best brāhmaṇa, if a man through infatuation, cohabits with the wife (other than his mother) of his father, or his mother's sister, or his preceptor's wife, or his maternal uncle's wife, or his brother's wife born in the same family, he should observe a couple of Prājāpatya (-vows). O brāhmaṇa, he should observe three Cāndrāyaṇa-vows, (should give) five pairs of cows to brāhmaṇas and should give them a present. He is (by doing so) purified. There is no doubt about this.

11-14a. That fool who cohabits with a cow, should observe three fasts; there is no doubt that he is purified by giving a cow and food. He who cohabits with a prostitute, a female ass, a female pig or a monkey or a she-buffalow, should remain without eating in mud after having thrown himself there upto his neck. He is purified after three nights. He should observe fast for three nights after having got clean-shaved with the tuft of hair on the crown of his head (removed). Undoubtedly he is purified on remaining in water for a night.

14b-17a. O you ascetic, he who being infatuated by love, would cohabit with a brāhmaṇa-woman should observe three Prājāpatya (-vows) and three Cāndrāyaṇa (-vows). Similarly he should give three cows (to a brāhmaṇa). The brāhmaṇa woman should drink the mixture of the products of a cow for five nights, O brāhmaṇa. There is no doubt that by giving a pair of cows and a present (to a brāhmaṇa) she is purified. When a man cohabits with the wife of someone else he should observe (the vow of) Kṛcchra Sāntapana.

17b-24. A woman is like a bar. Therefore, he should avoid her. If a man (even) once cohabits with a woman out of his caste or a mean one, he should observe Prājāpatya Kṛcchra. There is no doubt that thereby he is purified. A woman is like a burning charcoal. A man is like ghee. Therefore, O brāhmaṇa, he should never remain in her vicinity. O brāhmaṇa, that woman, the destroyer of the family, who conceives (due to cohabitation) with her paramour, should be altogether abandoned. There is no blemish in doing so. That woman who would, leaving her own relatives, go (away) from her house, is spoiled, has fallen from the family. One should have no contact with her again. That woman who, being infatuated, cohabits with another man (who is not her husband), should observe the Prājāpatya Kṛcchra, and then should drink the mixture of the five products of a cow. Then she should give a pair of cows (to a brāhmaṇa). She is (thus) undoubtedly purified. When a childish brāhmaṇa woman, being deluded, cohabits with a stranger, she should be abandoned by (her) men. There is no blemish (in doing so). O brāhmaṇa, that brāhmaṇa who, being deluded by passion of love, would cohabit with a brāhmaṇa-woman, should give a cow and sesamum. Undoubtedly he is (thereby) purified.

CHAPTER NINETEEN

Purificatory Acts for Other Sins

Sūta said:

1. O brāhmaṇa, listen, I shall tell you, how those who, through ignorance, have eaten feces (or drunk) urine or have sipped liquor, are purified.

2-4a. O sage, he should observe two Prājāpatya (-vows); he should go to a holy place. He should give a bull and eleven cows, and then should get himself clean-shaved with the tuft of hair on the crown of the head (removed). Having gone to all crossways he should observe the Prājāpatya (-vow). Then he should give a pair of cows and drink the mixture of the five products of a cow. There is no doubt that he is purified after having fed brāhmaṇas.

4b-8. If a man eats the food of a cāṇḍāla or drinks his water knowingly or while in a difficulty, he should observe Kṛcchra Cāndrāyaṇa; (and) having got himself clean-shaved with the tuft of hair on the crown of the head (removed), he should drink the mixture of the five products of a cow. One or two or three or four cows should be respectively given to brāhmaṇas if he eats the food of a cāṇḍāla or of (i.e. prepared by) a woman recently delivered or food which is not fit to be eaten or water which should not be drunk. If knowingly or while in difficulty he eats the food left over by a śūdra, he should observe two Prājāpatya-vows and three Cāndrāyaṇa-vows. O brāhmaṇa, then he should give a couple of cows and drink the mixture of the five products of a cow. Then, after offering oblations into fire and having fed many brāhmaṇas, he would certainly be purified.

9. There is no doubt that if (a portion of) the food is eaten by rats, mongooses or cats it is purified, when it is sprinkled over with water mixed with sesamum and darbhas, O brāhmaṇa.

10-11. O brāhmaṇa, a man who eats an onion, garlic, a pot-herb, bottle-gourd, a small red variety of garlic and meat, should observe the Cāndrāyaṇa-vow. Due to his doing vile acts a śūdra loves liquor and meat. One should avoid from (i.e. keep at) a distance such a śūdra like a cāṇḍāla.

12. Those who are engaged in serving the twice-born who avoid liquor and meat, who are engaged in giving gifts and in their own duties, should be known to be best vṛṣalas.

13-17a. O brāhmaṇa, if a brāhmaṇa unknowingly eats (food) in a family where impurity is caused by child-birth or by death, he would be purified by reciting the Gāyatrī(-hymn) ten thousand times. O ascetic, a kṣatriya would be purified by reciting it thousands of times, and a cāṇḍāla by (taking) the mixtures of the five products of a cow. A man of a (higher) caste, who, even unknowingly, would drink ghee, or water of curd contained in a vessel of a low-caste man, should observe the Prājāpatya vow. He should give many gifts. By offering oblations into the fire according to the proper rite he is purified. For a śūdra there is no fast. He is purified just by giving gifts. Observing a fast day and night he should get himself clean-shaved with the tuft of hair on the crown of the head (removed).

17b-19a. O brāhmaṇa, a man who is beaten by the low-caste ones with sticks etc. should observe (either) the Prājāpatya-vow or the Cāndrāyaṇa-vow. He should get himself clean-shaved with the tuft of hair on the crown of the head (removed) and should drink the mixture of the five products of a cow. Then he should give a couple of cows and offer oblations of food etc. into fire.

19b-23. O brāhmaṇa, if a man takes liquor knowingly or casually in his house, he should be dropped from (i.e. driven out of) the family. A man who destroys cow's seed or cuts off shoots, or steals gold, should observe Kṛcchra and three Prājāpatya

-vows. Having got himself clean-shaved with the tuft of hair on the crown of his head (removed), he should also drink the mixture of the five products of a cow. In the same way he should thrice offer oblations into fire. O ascetic, food and water from him may be accepted. He should eat in the morning for three days without begging. For three days he should not eat. This is the Prājāpatya -vow.

24-29. O sage, he should drink cow's urine. cow-dung, (cow's) milk, curd, ghee and water mixed with kuśa for two days and should observe fast for a night. This is said to be Kṛcchra Sāntapana which removes all sins. He should eat one morsel for three days in the morning and in the evening without begging and should fast for three days. This vow is (called) Atikṛcchra. O brāhmaṇa, he should drink hot water, milk and ghee for three days. O sage, he should bathe once (a day). This is said to be Tapta-Kṛcchra. Not taking food for twelve days is known as Parāka Kṛcchra, which removes sin and is well-known. He should increase one morsel everyday in the bright half and reduce one morsel everyday during the dark half. He should not eat when the moon has waned (i.e. on the new-moon day). This is known as the Cāndrāyaṇa -vow. A brāhmaṇa should eat four morsels in the morning, four when the sun has set (i.e. in the evening). This is known as Śiśu-Cāndrāyaṇa.

30. A woman who destroys a pumpkin gourd, should drink the mixture of the five products of a cow for three days and should give five pumpkin gourds along with gold and garments (to a brāhmaṇa). (Then) O ascetic, water and food of (i.e. offered by) her may be accepted.

CHAPTER TWENTY

The Greatness of the Worship of Rādhā-Dāmodara

Śaunaka said:

1. O Sūta, (tell me which) you said to be the (deeds of) merit, doing which, the frogs (men) in the blinding well due to darkness, will cross the ocean of mundane existence.

Sūta said:

2-10. That woman who, bathing (every) morning in Kārtika, being dear to Rādhā and Kṛṣṇa, being composed and devoutly worshipping Rādhā and Kṛṣṇa, gives up eating meat etc. and is engaged in serving her husband, goes to Viṣṇu's place called *Goloka* which is very difficult to obtain (i.e. to reach). She who would offer incense and lamp to Rādhā and Dāmodara (i.e. Kṛṣṇa) in Kārtika, goes, with her sin abandoned (i.e. removed), to Viṣṇu's abode. O brāhmaṇa, that woman who would offer a garment to Rādhā and Kṛṣṇa would, for a long time, live in the abode to Śrī Viṣṇu. She who offers to Rādhā and Kṛṣṇa fragrant flowers and garlands in the month of Kārtika, goes to Viṣṇu's abode. Also she who would offer sandal and make an offering like sugar to Rādhā and Kṛṣṇa, would go to Viṣṇu's abode. O brāhmaṇa, the merit of that woman who gives something to a brāhmaṇa in the month of Kārtika to please Rādhā and Kṛṣṇa, becomes inexhaustible. O brāhmaṇa, that woman who devoutly worships Rādhā and Kṛṣṇa in the month of Kārtika goes (to Viṣṇu's abode); she would not live in hell for long, even if she was a widow in a previous existence or was not dear to her husband.

11-18. O brāhmaṇa, in olden days in the Tretāyuga there lived a śūdra named Śaṅkara in the Saurāṣṭra country. His wife was Kalipriyā by name. She always longed for a paramour, and looked upon her husband like (a blade of) grass (i.e. treated him disgracefully). 'This husband is not proper for me, my lord is some other man.' Thinking like this she always gave him food that was left over. The very foolish woman (drank) liquor and ate meat due to the company of mean people. The cruel one always reproached her husband at her will. 'He is a rope (tied to my) feet; why did he not die? When he dies I shall enjoy at will.' O brāhmaṇa, thinking like this to her mind, she made an agreement with a paramour as: "We shall go to another country". O brāhmaṇa, at night she cut off the throat of her husband with a sword for the sake of her paramour, and went to the rendezvous. O brāhmaṇa, the paramour that had come there was eaten up by a tiger. Seeing it she wept and fell down in a swoon. Being composed after a long time the foolish woman wept piteously.

Kalipriyā said:

19. Having killed my own husband, I approached a stranger. Due to my (ill luck) a tiger has eaten up that lord of mine (also). What shall I do? Where shall I go? I am deceived by the Creator.

Sūta said:

20. O brāhmaṇa, then Kalipriyā came to her own house. Putting her mouth into that of her husband she wept.

Kalipriyā said:

21-22. O lord, what a very terrible deed have I done? Which world shall I go to? O lord, speak (at least) a few words. I, who am very much condmened, reproached you at will. O lord, you are not at all speaking. There is not a single sin that I have not committed.

Sūta said:

23-26. She saluted his feet, and went to another city. Having entered it, that woman saw many meritorious people, devotees of Viṣṇu, engaged in bathing in the Narmadā (river) in the morning in the month in Kārtika. Seeing there even women devoutly worshipping Rādhā and Kṛṣṇa with the sounds of conches with great festivity, with sandal and flowers, incense and lamps, pieces of cloth and fruits of various kinds, with perfumes used to scent the breath, asked them modestly: "O ladies, (please) tell me, what is this that you are doing."

The ladies said:

27-33. O mother, in the morning in Kārtika, the best of all months, we offer the auspicious worship to Rādhā and Kṛṣṇa, which removes all sins. (Due to that worship) sin earned in a crore of existences is destroyed, and Viṣṇu's abode is reached.

Giving up (eating) flesh, she performed the worship on the day of (i.e. sacred to) Viṣṇu. O brāhmaṇa, being free from blemish, she died on the full-moon-day. Yama's servants, full of anger, quickly came there to take her to Yama's abode and tied her (body) with leather straps. Then there came in an aeroplane made of gold Viṣṇu's messengers holding conches, discs, maces, lotuses and struck them with the edges of the discs (i.e. with sharp discs); the messengers of Yama ran away. She got into an aeroplane which was made of gold and to which royal swans were yoked. Surrounded by them, she went to Viṣṇu's abode. There she lived for a long time enjoying pleasures as she liked. O brāhmaṇa, she who would worship Rādhā and Kṛṣṇa, goes, due to her sins having perished, to the charming world called *Goloka*.

34. The sin earned during a crore of existences of him who listens to this or the sin earned during a crore of existences of a woman who, being purified, listens to this, perishes.

CHAPTER TWENTYONE

Restrictions While Observing the Kārtika Vow

Śaunaka said:

1. O Sūta, O sage, please tell me properly the rites and restrictions (to be observed) in the best month Kārtika.

Sūta said:

2-7. O best brāhmaṇa, a man, being pure, should (begin to) observe the vow of the Kārtika month on (i.e. from) the full moon of Āśvina (and should continue it) till the Udbodhinī (i.e.

the eleventh day of the bright fortnight of Kārtika). O brāhmaṇa, a man should excrete or pass urine by facing the north during the day time. He should observe silence (while excreting or passing urine); and O you omniscient one, he should excrete or pass urine by facing the south during the night. O brāhmaṇa, he who has undertaken the vow (of Kārtika) should not excrete or pass urine on a path, in water, in a cow-pen, in a crematory or an anthill. He should not excrete or pass urine at excellent places. Taking pure clay he should first wash his left hand with clay and water for cleansing it twenty times. He should apply it (i.e. the clay) once to his generative organ and five times to his anus, ten times to his left hand, and then ten times to both (his hands), and three times to (each of) his feet. Then he should cleanse his face and then resolve to bathe.

8-10a. Meditating on Dāmodara (i.e. Kṛṣṇa) in his mind, he should then recite this hymn: "O Janārdana, in (the month of) Kārtika I shall every morning have a bath that destroys sins, to please Kṛṣṇa with Rādhā. O Śrīkṛṣṇa, my salutation to Paṅkajanābha (i.e. Viṣṇu) lying in water; my salutation to you along with Rādhā. Accept the objects (I am offering and) be pleased with me."

10b-21a. Then he should bathe and put on the mark. If he, being without the Ūrdhvapuṇḍra[1] (i.e. upright lines made on the forehead), does any act, all that (i.e. the entire) act of him becomes fruitless. This is the truth that I am telling. That body of a human being which is without the Ūrdhvapuṇḍra should not be seen. If one sees it, one should look at the sun. Even a cāṇḍāla, on whose forehead white upright lines are made with clay, is of a pure soul. There is no doubt that he is venerable. There is no doubt that on the heads of those mean men who make the Ūrdhvapuṇḍra without a hollow, the foot of a dog is always (placed). O brāhmaṇa, having finished the rite spoken (i.e. laid down) for the morning, he should, according to his capacity,

1. Ūrdhvapuṇḍra—Upright lines made on the forehead with some colouring substance. It is one of the five saṁskāras that a devotee of Vāsudeva was supposed to undergo. The other four are: Tapa (branding on the arm and other limbs), Name (Names of Vāsudeva), Mantra (a hymn), Yāga (worship of the images of Vāsudevao).

worship Tulasī that destroys sins. Then, O brāhmaṇa, having, with his mind concentrated, listened to Viṣṇu's account from a Purāṇa, he who observes the vow, should devoutly and duly worship him. O brāhmaṇa, a man should always avoid (using) the seat of another person, avoid food of others, so also the bed of another person, and another man's wife; (he should) especially (avoid these) in Kārtika. He who observes the vow (of the Kārtika month), should always avoid a jujube, beans, meat and honey, royal beans etc. in Kārtika. O brāhmaṇa, (he should also avoid) the citron fruit, meat, flower and stale food. Masurika (a kind of pulse) is declared among the grains; the milk of cows is said to be vegetarian; O brāhmaṇa, salt is produced from earth; the limb of an animal is meat. O best brāhmaṇa, he should use all fluids bought by a brāhmaṇa, water remaining in a small lake, practice celibacy in the fourth period, and eat food from a dish made of rows of leaves. He should avoid besmearing his body with oil.

21b-35. He who observes the Kārtika-vow, should avoid mushrooms, lotus-stalks, asafoetida, onions, leave of (a kind of herb called) pūtikā, garlic, radish, potherb, so also a gourd, wood-apple, egg-plant, a pumpkin gourd, eating from (a vessel of) bell metal, (food) cooked twice, the food prepared by a lying-in woman, fish, bed and a woman in her period, food prepared by two women and the company of women. O brāhmaṇa, a householder should always avoid the dhātrī-fruit on a Sunday. On (eating) a pumpkin gourd a man would lose his wealth; on (eating) a bṛhatī he would not remember Viṣṇu; on (eating) a cucumber there would be no prosperity; on (eating) a radish there would be a loss of strength. One becomes defamed on (eating) bilva; he is born in the stock of an animal on eating nimba; on eating a palm-fruit there is the loss of the body; there would be folly on (eating) a coconut; a gourd is like the flesh of a cow; on eating kalindaka (the sin) would be (equal to that of) killing a cow. Kidney-beans are said to cause sin. The pūtikā-herb is declared to be causing the murder of a brāhmaṇa. On (eating) the egg-plant one's son would be lost; on (eating) beans one would be ill for a long time. On (eating) meat there would be a great sin (incurred); he should avoid (these) on the first day etc. (of the month). A man should give that food, which he would avoid, to a brāhmaṇa, and have it in his meal at the end of the vow. As elephants flee away on seeing a lion, the messengers of Yama run away on seeing a man who duly observes the Kārtika-vow. O brāhmaṇa, the vow of (in honour of) Viṣṇu is the best; even a hundred sacrifices are not equal to it. By performing a sacrifice he would go to heaven, (while) one who observes the Kārtika-vow would go to Viṣṇu's world. O brāhmaṇa, whatever bad deed a man has done through mind, speech or act, perishes in a moment on seeing him who observes the Kārtika vow. Even the four-faced Brahmā would not be able to narrate the religious merit of him who observes the Kārtika-vow as (already) told, observing which, O brāhmaṇa, all the sin would go (away) through the fear of him who performs the Kārtika-vow (saying to itself): 'Where shall I go? Where shall I stay?' O brāhmaṇa, a man should give according to his capacity food, garments etc. (to brāhmaṇas), and should also feed brāhmaṇas to please Viṣṇu. The observers of the vow should keep awake at night by dancing, singing etc. The sin of him who devoutly listens to this, perishes.

CHAPTER TWENTYTWO

The Greatness of Tulasī

Śaunaka said:

1. O you omniscient one, kindly tell me, for the good of all creatures, the greatness of Tulasī which destroys the sins of those who listen to it.

Sūta said:

2-13. The servants of Yama do not come to his house in the vicinity of which there is a grove of Tulasī, due to the house having the nature of a holy place, O brāhmaṇa. O brāhmaṇa, the Tulasī-grove is auspicious and removes all sins. Those excellent men who plant it do not see the Sun's son (i.e. Yama). O best brāhmaṇa, all the sin of him who plants it, nourishes it, attends upon it, looks at it and touches it, perishes. O brāhmaṇa, those high-souled ones who worship Viṣṇu with tender Tulasī-leaves do not go to Yama's abode. The best rivers like Gaṅgā, the best (gods) Viṣṇu, Brahmā and Śiva, along with deities and holy places like Puṣkara, remain in a Tulasī-leaf. A sinner who, endowed with Tulasī-leaves, casts his life, goes to Viṣṇu's abode. I have told (you) the truth. The man who, besmeared with the clay of Tulasī (i.e. in which Tulasī is growing), casts his life, goes, though full of hundreds of sins, to Viṣṇu's abode. O brāhmaṇa, sin does not touch the body of the man who would wear the sandal-like Tulasī-wood. He goes to the highest position. He, who, though impure and of bad conduct, wears the rosary of (the beads made of) Tulasī-wood round his neck, goes, due to his devotion, to Viṣṇu's house. That man on whose body is seen the rosary made of Dhātrī-fruits or (beads of) Tulasī-wood, is a devotee of Viṣṇu. He again who, putting round his neck the garland (of the leaves) of Tulasī, would worship Viṣṇu, obtains, for each flower, a myriad of cows.

14-19. Those men who, of wicked minds, are sceptics, and who do not wear the (Tulasī)-garland, being burnt by the fire of the wrath of Viṣṇu, do not return from hell. A man should not abandon a garland of Tulasī-(leaves), especially of the fruits of Dhātrī, which destroys great sins and gives religious merit, worldly prosperity and sensual enjoyments. A man lives in Viṣṇu's house for as many thousands of years as the hair (on his body) the Dhātrī-garland would touch. That man who after having offered the rosary of (the beads of) Tulasī-wood to Viṣṇu, devoutly wears it, has no sin at all. On seeing the rosary made of the beads of Tulasī-wood, the messengers of the king of the dead (i.e. king Yama) run away as a leaf shaken up by the wind. O best brāhmaṇa, the dead ancestors of him who offers them piṇḍas in the shadow of Dhātrī in the Tulasī-grove, are emancipated.

20-25. O brāhmaṇa, he who keeps the Dhātrī-fruit in his hand, on his head, round his neck or in his ears should be known as Viṣṇu himself. O brāhmaṇa, the sin earned during crores of existences of him who would worship Viṣṇu with the leaves and fruits of Dhātrī, at once perishes. O brāhmaṇa, sacrifices, gods, sages and holy places always remain by resorting to the Dhātrī-tree in Kārtika. A man who collects a leaf of Dhātrī or a leaf of Tulasī on the twelfth day in Kārtika, would not go to hell full of torment. O brāhmaṇa, the sin, due to the contact of food of the man who eats food under the shadow of Dhātrī in Kārtika perishes for a year. O brāhmaṇa, a man should worship Viṣṇu in a Tulasī-grove and at the root of a Dhātrī in Kārtika; he certainly goes to Viṣṇu's world.

26-27. O best brāhmaṇa, if a sinner devoutly holds on his head the water remaining at the root of Tulasī, he goes to Viṣṇu's abode. He who would hold on his head the water flowing from a Tulasī-leaf, has bathed (i.e. has obtained the fruit of having bathed) at all sacred places, and in the end he goes to Viṣṇu's house.

28-41. O great sage, formerly in the Dvāpara age there was an excellent brāhmaṇa. Once, having bathed and having offered a sacrifice to Tulasī, he went home. He became like the sun in lustre, and like Mārtaṇḍa in religious merit. A glutton, a great sinner, oppressed with thirst, came there, and having drunk the water at the root of Tulasī, had his sins perished. A hunter named Asimardana, came quickly, and said: "The food is eaten." Having eaten it and shattered the food in the cooking vessel has he gone? He killed him. Yama's servants, angry and with nooses and hammers in their hands came by Yama's order to take him to Yama's abode. (When) they thought of binding and taking him, Viṣṇu's servants came (there). Then having cut off the leather-straps, they quickly put him in a charming chariot. They (i.e. Yama's servants) politely asked them: "O good ones, due to which religious merit of him are you taking him (to Viṣṇu's abode?)" They said: "Formerly he was a king. He has done many (acts of) religious merit. He kidnapped some beautiful woman. Due to this sin, the king went to Yama's abode. There you tortured him by Yama's order. Lying there he sported with a woman of a coppery red colour. Due to this sin the king went to Yama's abode. By Yama's order you tortured him there. He remained there. He embraced misery and suffered for a long time. In Yama's abode he was sprinkled with streams of salt water. Then for the remaining part of his stay in hell, he was repeatedly born in sinful stocks, and suffered unhappincss as a result of his own deeds. After drinking the water at the root of Tulasī he goes (i.e. would go) to Viṣṇu's abode." Hearing these words of them the messengers (of Yama) went as they had come. The messengers of Viṣṇu went with him to Viṣṇu's abode. O brāhmaṇa, I have told you Tulasī's abode.

42. O brāhmaṇa, I have told you Tulasī's importance which destroys sins. I do not know what would happen to them who serve (Tulasī) with devotion, O sage.

CHAPTER TWENTYTHREE

The Importance of Viṣṇupañcaka

Śaunaka said:

1. O Sūta, O sage, kindly tell me the importance of the remaining five days of Kārtika, which destroys sins.

Sūta said:

2-16. O Śaunaka, listen. I shall narrate (to you) the importance, which destroys sins, of the remaining five days of Kārtika. O best sage, of the five vows Viṣṇupañcaka (i.e. the vow observed for the remaining five days of Kārtika), is the best. He who, during that (period) worships Śrī Hari (i.e. Kṛṣṇa) with Rādhā, by means of sandal, flowers, incense, clothes and various kinds of fruits, goes, freed from all sins, to Viṣṇu's abode. Without doing the vow of Viṣṇupañcaka, a religious student, (or) a householder, (or) an anchorite, (or) an ascetic does not obtain the highest position. Viṣṇupañcaka removes all sins, is meritorious and well-known. He who would bathe during that (period), would obtain the fruit of (having bathed at) all holy places. He who, to propitiate Viṣṇu, devoutly offers a lamp full of ghee in front of (the image of) Viṣṇu, or near Tulasī, in water, goes to Viṣṇu's abode. A sinner goes to Viṣṇu's abode. I have told the truth. A man should bathe with devotion (the image of) Viṣṇu with honey, milk, ghee etc. What would Viṣṇu being pleased not give to that good man? He should present excellent cooked food to the god of gods. (Even Brahmā) having four faces is not able to measure his religious merit. Being pure, he worships Viṣṇu on Ekādaśī day. Having secured cowdung he duly waits upon (the god) with the sacred hymns. He who observes the vow, should similarly again drink cow urine (reciting) the sacred hymns on the twelfth day. Similarly he should drink milk on the fourteenth day. Having got (these) for the purification of his sins, and having passed the four days, he should, on the fifth day, having bathed and duly worshipped Viṣṇu, devoutly feed brāhmaṇas and should give them presents. Then at night he should eat the mixture of the five products of a cow, which is well consecrated with sacred hymns. He who is unable to do this, should eat fruits, roots and food; O brāhmaṇa, he should offer an oblation according to the rite that is laid down. Lord Viṣṇu who is fit to be known, would himself honour him who would observe (the vow of) Pañcaka with Tulasī-leaves.

17-20. In olden days, in the Tretāyuga, there lived a śūdra, intent on leading the life of a villain, named Daṇḍakara, who always censured religious practices, who told lies, who hurt his friends, who had an ardent longing for anormous gestures of prostitutes, who snatched the wealth of brāhmaṇas, who was cruel, who was interested in another's wife, who killed those who sought his refuge, who kept the company of heretics, who ate cow's flesh, who drank liquor, who always defamed others, who was a traitor, who deprived his kinsmen of their means of livelihood, O brāhmaṇa. Observing him—the cruel one, intent on (committing) sins like that—the kinsmen, being angry, came to his house, O brāhmaṇa.

The kinsmen said:

21-26. O fool, O you of wicked conduct, you are destroying the glory in (i.e. of) our pure family, which was earned by (our) ancestors.

O brāhmaṇa, they who were thus angry, abandoned, out of respect for their family and through fear of bad name, that greatest (i.e. the worst) among sinners. Then, with all his glory lost, he went to a great forest. He would continuously practise the deeds of the villains along with them. O brāhmaṇa, when they were going along the path, they did not get anything to eat through fear. Being oppressed with hunger, they went to another place. Having entered (i.e. gone to) that place, seeing many excellent and meritorious brāhmaṇas who were seated at the root of a Dhātrī (tree) and who were the devotees of Viṣṇu, all the dasyus went (near him). That, Daṇḍakara also went near them, and saluted them.

Daṇḍakara said:

27. O best brāhmaṇas, I am oppressed with hunger. Surely my life will depart (now). Give me something to eat. I have sought your shelter.

28-33. Having heard his words, those (brāhmaṇas), who had a high regard for religious practices said: "How do you have a desire to eat (food) on the day of (i.e. sacred to) Viṣṇu, during the Viṣṇupañcaka, well-known as the remover of sins? Tell (us) your particulars. (Tell us) now what your name is." He joyfully said: "O brāhmaṇas, I am (a śūdra) by name Daṇḍakara. I am full of all sins. How can I be emancipated?" They said (to him): "Observe the best vow (called) Viṣṇupañcaka." O brāhmaṇa, by the order of the brāhmaṇas he observed the (vow of) Viṣṇupañcaka. After death, he got into an excellent chariot, and having reached Viṣṇu's place and his form, he remained (there) free from birth. The sin earned during a crore of existences of him who would devoutly listen to this account destroying sins, perishes at that moment (only).

CHAPTER TWENTYFOUR

In Praise of Giving Gifts

Śaunaka said:

1. O sage, O best among the learned, O you who know the essential nature (of things), tell me in order the importance of vows.

Sūta said:

2-6. O best sage, giving (a piece of) land is regarded as the best gift. He who made that gift (has given) a gift having the fruit of all gifts. O best brāhmaṇa, he who would give a gift of land with a crop (growing in it) to a brāhmaṇa, enjoys happiness in Viṣṇu's heaven as long as (the regimes of) fourteen Indras (last). Then, O king, he, having obtained a birth on the earth, (becomes) a sovereign emperor. Having enjoyed the earth for a long time, he would go to the abode of Viṣṇu. He who gives land of the measure of a cow's hide to a brāhmaṇa, is freed from all sins and goes to Viṣṇu's abode. The sages described that land to be of the measure of a cow's hide (*gocarmamātra*) where a hundred cows and a bull remain uncontrolled.

7-10. He who receives the land and he who gives it, both go to heaven. Wise brāhmaṇas should abandon (i.e. refuse) hundreds of other gifts and accept (the present of) land. That ignorant brāhmaṇa who, being deluded, rejects (the gift) of land, becomes extremely miserable in every existence. To him who, having secured land from some other source, would give it to a brāhmaṇa, the lord of the world gives the highest position. He who destroys the land given to himself or to someone else, goes, along with a crore members of his family to a very fearful hell, O brāhmaṇa.

11-12. O brāhmaṇa, for him who would snatch the land of a deity or a brāhmaṇa, an expiation is not seen for hundreds of crores of kalpas. The religious merit of that king who protects the land given (by him) to someone else would be a crore times greater than that of people.

13-17. A man giving a cow would obtain that merit which is obtained by giving the earth consisting of seven islands, O brāhmaṇa. He, who gives a bull to a member of a poor family, is freed from all sins, and goes to Śiva's world. He who gives gold of the measure of a sesamum to a brāhmaṇa, goes, along with a crore members of his family, to the abode of Viṣṇu. O brāhmaṇa, he who would give silver to a good brāhmaṇa, obtains (i.e. goes to) the world of the Moon and he would always drink nectar there. O best brāhmaṇa, he who gives a coral, a pearl, a diamond or a gem (to a brāhmaṇa) goes to heaven.

18-25. A man would get a crore times more religious merit by giving a śālagrāma stone, than what he obtains by the gift of gold, jewels, or other valuable things equal to his own weight. The giver of a śālagrāma stone gets that religious merit which a man would get by giving the earth consisting of seven islands along with mountains, groves and forests. O brāhmaṇa, he who would give a śālagrāma stone to a brāhmaṇa, has given the fourteen worlds (to a brāhmaṇa). O best brāhmaṇa, he who makes a gift of gold, jewels or other valuable things equal to his own weight (to a brāhmaṇa), is not again born in (i.e. from) the womb of a mother. O best brāhmaṇa, he who gives (in marriage) his daughter that is adorned (with ornaments to a brāhmaṇa), would go to Brahmā's abode. He is not reborn. For a man who sells his daughter, there is no escape from hell; and for one who gives his daughter (in marriage according to the proper rites) there is no coming (back to earth) from heaven. He, who gives sandals or an umbrella to a brāhmaṇa, goes to Indra's city after death, and would live (there) for four kalpas. O best brāhmaṇa, he who gives a divine garment to a good brāhmaṇa, puts on a divine garment and would live in heaven for a long time.

26-27. O brāhmaṇa, he who would give an old cow or an old garment or a young girl in her menses, would go to hell. O brāhmaṇa, a man should not see the face of him who sells his daughter. Having seen (i.e. if he sees) it unknowingly, he should look at the sun.

28-58. O best brāhmaṇa, a man who gives (the gift of) fruits would go to heaven. There he would enjoy for thousands of kalpas the fruit (of his gift) like nectar. O brāhmaṇa, the man who gives vegetables (to a brāhmaṇa) goes to Śiva's abode; and (there) enjoys, with gods, rice boiled in milk for a couple of kalpas. He who gives ghee, he who gives curd, he who gives milk, he who gives butter milk, goes to Viṣṇu's abode (and there) he drinks nectar. The man who gives sandal, who gives flowers goes to the abode of gods. Decorated with sandal and flowers, he would remain (there) for thousands of yugas. He who gives the gift of a bed—the best gift—to a brāhmaṇa, goes to Brahmā's abode, and sleeps (there) on a bed for a long time. The giver of a seat or the giver of a lamp, being free from all sins, would remain, surrounded by a row of burning lamps, on a seat in heaven. A man who would give betel-leaf, happily enjoys the entire earth. He sleeps, being clasped to the bosom by a divine lady, and eats tāmbūla. The best man who makes the gift of knowledge—the best gift—would, after death, live near Viṣṇu for three hundred yugas. O best brāhmaṇa, having obtained there knowledge difficult to be obtained, he, O brāhmaṇa, obtains salvation through Viṣṇu's grace. That best brāhmaṇa who would teach a helpless, miserable brāhmaṇa, goes, free from rebirth, to Śrī Viṣṇu's abode. One who would devoutly and with faith give (the gift of) a book would obtain, for every letter, the merit due to the gift of a crore of tawny cows. One who gives honey, who gives jaggery, goes to the Ikṣu-sāgara. One who gives salt, goes to the world of Varuṇa. O best brāhmaṇa, of all the gifts, the gift of food or water is declared to be the best by all sages knowing the truth. O best brāhmaṇa, he who has given food or water on the earth, has given all (kinds of) gifts, O best among brāhmaṇas. O brāhmaṇa, one who gives food is declared to be the giver (i.e. the saver) of life. Therefore, the giver of food gets the fruit of all (kinds of) gifts. As is food, so is water. The two are said to be equal. O best brāhmaṇa, food would not be prepared without water. O best brāhmaṇa, the two i.e. hunger and thirst are declared to be equal. Therefore, even the wise have declared food and water to be the best. O brāhmaṇa, those best men who make the gift of food on the earth, are freed from all sins, and go to Viṣṇu's abode. O brāhmaṇa ascetic, as many (sins of) brāhmaṇa murders, as the kinds of food a man gives on the earth, perish. O Śaunaka, the sins of those that give food abandon their bodies and go to the bodies of those that receive it. Therefore the wise do not accept the food of the most sinful one. The fools that accept it through delusion, become sinful. O best brāhmaṇa, one should make water remain on the ground (after it flows from the palm of the brāhmaṇa to whom a gift is given). He (who offers a gift) is freed from all sins, and would go to Viṣṇu's abode. O best brāhmaṇa, wealth should be accumulated with effort. A man should spend the accumulated wealth in giving gifts. Those who through miserliness tinkle (i.e. only preserve) their wealth, are extremely unhappy. O sage, in the end, leaving the wealth, they go (i.e. die) wealthless. Those men who by repeatedly giving (gifts) become poor, should not be regarded as poor. They are great lords in the human world. O best brāhmaṇa that which is given to a cruel, relative-less (brāhmaṇa) who does not have proper restraint, does not stand by (the giver) in the other world. One who, when he has wealth, does not (either) enjoy it or give it (to others) should be known as poor, and would leave a sigh (of grief) after death. Those who see the truth have declared that giving gifts is superior even to austerities. Therefore, O best brāhmaṇa, one should give gifts. That giver who gives gifts (to persons of other castes) excluding a brāhmaṇa, goes to a terrible hell, which is fearful to all beings. The giver who does not remember the gift and the recipient who does not ask for it, both remain in hell as long as the moon and the sun last. O best brāhmaṇa, those sins like a brāhmaṇa's murder perish due to giving gifts. Therefore, one should give gifts.

CHAPTER TWENTYFIVE

The Importance of Uttering Viṣṇu's Name

Śaunaka said:

1-4a. That man who devoutly listens to the account of Viṣṇu, which is the abode of glory, which removes all harms, which destroys all sins, which wards off all evil planets, which gives proximity with Viṣṇu, which gives the fruit of the four goals of human life, goes to Viṣṇu's abode in the end. The importance of the utterance of (Viṣṇu's) names is said to be very wonderful; merely by uttering it a man would go to the highest position. Therefore, O Sūta, now tell me the manner of the utterance of (Viṣṇu's) names.

Sūta said:

4b-6. O Śaunaka, listen, I shall tell you the dialogue (between Sanatkumāra and Nārada), which would accomplish salvation. I shall tell you what formerly Nārada asked (Sanat)kumāra. Having heard various kinds of prescribed courses of conduct and their (various) mixtures Nārada, having joined the palms of his hands, once asked Sanatkumāra, of a tranquil mind, who was seated on the bank of the Yamunā:

Śrī Nārada said:

7. O you dear to the lord, tell me how there would be the destruction of the obstacles of dharma about which you had told (me) formerly.

Śrī Sanatkumāra said:

8-13. Listen, O Nārada, dear to Viṣṇu, and knowing the way to reach Govinda (i.e. Viṣṇu). (I shall tell you) that which you asked, viz. the cause of freedom from the world which is beyond the darkness (of ignorance). O brāhmaṇa, even all those mean men who are destitute of (i.e. who do not practise) all (good) ways of behaviour, who are of a wicked mind, who are outcaste, who deceive the world, who are intent upon religious hypocrisy, pride, drinking liquor, and wickedness, who are sinful and cruel, who are interested in another man's wealth, wife or sons, become pure if they resort to the lotus-like feet of Viṣṇu. The name (of Viṣṇu), sure (to succeed) here, protects those sinful men who transgress even him who causes divinity, who, the kind one, the great one, gives salvation to the immobile and the mobile. A man who has done all sins, is freed if he resorts to Viṣṇu. If a contemptible, wicked biped would commit sin against Viṣṇu, and by chance resorts to his name, he is emancipated due to the name. A man falls down due to his sin against (Viṣṇu's) name which is the friend of all.

Śrī Nārada said:

14. O best brāhmaṇa, which are those sins against the

name of the lord, which, when done, impede men's acts and take them to a low status?

Śrī Sanatkumāra said

15-20. The censure of the good causes a great sin against the name (of Viṣṇu). How does (i.e. would) it tolerate the censure of those on account of whom it has become famous? He indeed does ill to the name of Viṣṇu, who, in this world, would regard all (things) about the auspicious Śrī Viṣṇu, as different from his own mind. He who does not disrespect his preceptor, who does not censure sacred texts, who does not look upon Viṣṇu's name as (merely) glorificatory, who does not have a wicked idea about (i.e. to look upon) name (as) sinful, has purification by means of restraints. Indifference to religious vows, sacrifice (for others), offering oblations, all good actions is also a fault. Not having faith, turning away one's face, not listening to advice is also a sin against the auspicious name. He, the mean man, who, even after hearing the greatness of (Viṣṇu's) name, remains without love for it, and is only intent upon 'I', 'mine' etc. (i.e. is selfish), has committed sin against the name (of Viṣṇu). O Nārada, Śiva, with grace, told the sages and me the great name of the lord, bringing happiness. It should always be carefully preserved. They who even knowing (the importance of name), do not suddenly avoid the ten sins against the name, are like children, who being angry, afflict their mother. Being free from sins, always mutter the name (of Viṣṇu). O divine sage, due to name only you will accomplish everything and not by any other means.

Śrī Nārada said:

21. O Sanatkumāra, how is it that those who like rash acts, who are bereft of discrimination and detachment, who are intent upon themselves as they love their own bodies, arise from (amongst) us?

Śrī Sanatkumāra said:

22-29. When somehow a sin or a blemish takes place against the name, the man should always recite the name and seek its refuge only. Names alone remove the sin of those having (i.e. who have committed) the sin against the names (of Viṣṇu), since they alone, employed (i.e. recited) without rest (i.e. continuously) bring wealth. It is the name (alone) which being the characteristic mark, when remembered or heard, either in a pure form or with incorrect syllables, would protect a man, when it is recited without interruption. This alone is the truth. If it is resorted to hypocritically or for greed born of love for body or wealth, it would not quickly produce the fruit here, O brāhmaṇa. O Nārada, this great secret, which removes all inauspiciousness, and keeps off sins, was formerly heard (by me) from Śiva. O Nārada, even those who are intent on committing sins, but who know the names of Viṣṇu, would be liberated merely by reciting them. The entire greatness of the name (of Viṣṇu) is sung (i.e. narrated) in the Purāṇas. Therefore, O you who respect (others), please listen to a Purāṇa. O brother, Śiva, Viṣṇu himself with his followers would be pleased with him who has faith in listening to Purāṇas day after day. The fruit of him who listens with faith is double the fruit that accrues by bathing at the holy place Puṣkara or at Prayāga or at the confluence (of a holy river) with the ocean.

30-37. Those who attentively recite the Purāṇas or listen to them, obtain for every letter the fruit of giving a tawny cow. A man who is sonless obtains a son; he who desires wealth obtains it; he who longs for knowledge gets it; he who desires salvation secures it. Those who listen to the Purāṇas, having destroyed the mass of their sins earned during crores of existences, go to Viṣṇu's abode. O sage, a man should devoutly worship the brāhmaṇa who reads a Purāṇa, with (the gift of) a cow, land, gold, garments, sandal, flowers etc. O ascetic, he should joyfully give (the brāhmaṇa) a pot made of bell-metal, a water-vessel, so also an ear-ring or a ring made of gold, so also a seat, flowers and garlands. He should not do (i.e. show) wickedness in (giving) wealth (to the brāhmaṇa), since, in that case the gift would be without its fruit. O brāhmaṇa, a man should read a Purāṇa for the accomplishment of all objects. He who would devoutly give gold, silver, garments, flowers and garlands, sandal or a book, would go to Viṣṇu's abode. O brāhmaṇa, Citragupta would respectfully write the names of those who would in this manner get the entire book (read).

CHAPTER TWENTYSIX

The Importance of Keeping Promise

Śaunaka said :

1-2. O wise one, I desire to hear, (therefore) tell me fully what the religious merit there is in keeping a promise, and what the sin is in breaking it. O you ocean of compassion, (tell me) what would happen if one takes a false oath or a true one, and by one's offering one's right hand or favouring (someone).

Sūta said :

3-13. O best sage, listen, I am telling it from the beginning. You are the foremost among Viṣṇu's devotees and are engaged in the good of all people. O brāhmaṇa, the merit in (i.e. due to) keeping a promise is a crore times greater than the fruit which a man obtains by giving a hundred cows. There is no doubt that a fool by breaking his promise goes to a terrible hell and is roasted there for a hundred periods of Manu. Then due to his own deeds he obtains birth (i.e. is born) on the earth in the house of a poor person, and bereft of food and garments he is afflicted. One should take an oath truthfully in the vicinity of a deity, fire, or one's preceptor. Till that time the body is burnt; but the family of Viṣṇu is not lost (i.e. continues). O brāhmaṇa, what should I now say about a false oath? O brāhmaṇa, a man (lives) in hell for a hundred periods of Manu due to a false promise. O best sage, he who touches the flowers taken off after Viṣṇu's worship and takes a truthful oath (but does not keep it), is roasted, taking with him seven members (of his family), in hell for a long time. If by chance he gets a birth, then in every existence (he becomes) a leper. This would never happen due to truthful promise. What can be said about (what would happen) due to a false oath? The man who offer his right hand (to give a promise) and keeps it, would obtain Kṛṣṇa. I am telling the truth, (and) the truth (only). The dead ancestors of him who, having offered his hand (to make a promise), does not keep it, are tormented in hell; and undoubtedly the dead one (i.e. he, after death) goes to a terrible hell, and is emancipated by crores of men (of his family, i.e. after a very long time).

Śaunaka said :

14. O sage, tell me, I desire to listen respectfully (to the account of him) who obtained Kṛṣṇa by keeping the promise made by him with his right hand.

Sūta said :

15-18. Formerly in a city lived a śūdra named Vīravikrama. He ate much, was bulky, talked much and was very handsome. He was wealthy, he had sons, was polite, learned, and dear to all people. He always honoured brāhmaṇas and guests. O best brāhmaṇa, he was devoted to his father and always kept his promise. He kept his promise, protected his elders and waited upon Viṣṇu. Once a handsome, young, very intelligent cāṇḍāla, taking up the guise of a brāhmaṇa, came to his house deceptively (i.e. to deceive him).

The brāhmaṇa said :

19-23. O wise one, listen to my words. My auspicious wife is dead. What shall I do? Where shall I go? Kindly tell me today. What is the use of (other) gifts, (visits to) holy places, sacrifices or crores of vows for him who would marry (his daughter) to a brāhmaṇa?

Hearing these words, that Vīravikrama said to that brāhmaṇa: "O brāhmaṇa, listen to my words. I have a virgin daughter. If, O brāhmaṇa, you would desire, I shall give (her to you in marriage) according to the proper rite. Hold my right hand. I shall give her. (This shall) not (be) otherwise." Hearing there words of (i.e. uttered by) him, he held his hand; and the cāṇḍāla being pleased, said these words.

The brāhmaṇa said :

24. Making (i.e. fixing) an auspicious moment, give me your daughter endowed with auspicious (characteristics). The sacred texts have decided that delay would cause many hurdles.

Vīravikrama said :

25. O brāhmaṇa, I shall give you my daughter tomorrow.

This will not be otherwise. A man offering his right hand should not do (as) a mean man (would do).

Sūta said:

26-32. O brāhmaṇa, O sage, having called the brāhmaṇa (named) Kṛṣṇaśarman, his priest, he told him all (about) the agreement. "How do you give your daughter to a brāhmaṇa, (when) you desire to give her to a śūdra? Do not give her to an unknown person who does not belong to a good family." O ascetic, thus his relatives like his father etc. spoke to him. (They said): "O dear Vīravikrama, listen to our words. Men of our caste do not give their daughter(s) to a man whose family, country, race, so also wealth and character and age are not known." O best brāhmaṇa, he (i.e. Vīravikrama) said: "I have offered my right hand. Now I shall not at all be able to change (my words)." Speaking thus to them, he proceeded to offer his daughter to that brāhmaṇa. Seeing that all the kinsmen were very much amazed. O sage, hearing his truthful words, (Viṣṇu) holding a conch, a disc and a mace, mounted upon Garuḍa, suddenly came there.

The lord said:

33-34. Blessed is your family; blessed is your way of life; blessed are your mother and father; blessed is your truthful speech; blessed is your right hand; blessed is your deed; blessed is your existence. (A man like you) does not exist in the three worlds. With such a deed, O good man, you will emancipate your family.

Sūta said:

35-42 When Śrīkṛṣṇa was talking like this, an aeroplane made of gold, having attendants of Viṣṇu (in it), and Garuḍa-bannerded everywhere, came (there). The holder of a conch and a lotus (i.e. Viṣṇu) himself put all (the members of) his family with the cāṇḍāla and the priest into the chariot, O brāhmaṇa; and thus taking them all (with him) Viṣṇu went to his abode in Vaikuṇṭha. He remained there for a long time, enjoying rare pleasures. One who violates his words or his right hand (i.e. a promise), goes, to hell with his family. I speak the truth, the truth only. O brāhmaṇa, his manes and deities should not accept the food and water of (i.e. offered by) him. O best brāhmaṇa, (king) Dharma leaves his house through fear and goes (elsewhere). The foolish man, who, giving (i.e. creating) hope, later disappoints (a person), would go taking along with him a crore of his own people (i.e. members of his family) to hell. (King) Dharma violates (i.e. destroys) his (prosperity) through a king, or fire or thieves, who violates (i.e. does not keep) his promise. He, having heard (i.e. who hears) this (khaṇḍa) subsequent to the Svarga (khaṇḍa), being liberated while alive in this world, would (after death) go to the excellent abode, named Kṛṣṇa, beyond heaven.

V PĀTĀLAKHAṆḌA

(Section on the Nether World)

CHAPTER ONE

Rāma Sees Nandigrāma from Puṣpaka

Salutation to Śrī Gaṇeśa. Salutation to the family-deity. Salutation to the lotus-like feet of the preceptor.

1. After having saluted Nārāyaṇa and Nara, the best man, (so also) goddess Sarasvatī and Vyāsa, a man should recite Jaya.

The sages said :

2. O you glorious one, we have heard from you the entire charming Svargakhaṇḍa. O you long-lived one, tell us now the account of Rāma.

Sūta said :

3. Once the excellent sage Vātsyāyana asked the lord of serpents, the prop of the earth (i.e. Śeṣa to tell him) this very virtuous tale.

Śrī Vātsyāyana said :

4-8. O Śeṣa, (I have heard) from you all stories like the creation and dissolution of the world. So also (you have told me about) the settled rule about the terrestrial world, the celestial sphere, and about the cycle of the luminaries, so also about the products like the principles e.g. Mahat, and separate primary substances. O sinless one, you also told me the accounts of many kings. There is the wonderful account of the kings born in the solar race. In it is the story of the deeds performed by Rāma, which destroys many great sins. From you I have heard in brief the account of the horse sacrifice of (i.e. performed by) that hero Rāma. Now I desire (to hear) it in detail, which being heard or remembered, is said to destroy great sins to give the desired objects and to give joy to the heart of the devotee.

Śeṣa said :

9. O best brāhmaṇa, you whose mind longs like this for the honey of the two (lotus-like) feet of the hero in Raghu's family, are blessed.

10-15. All sages say that the company of the good is excellent. Since the story of Rāma would destroy sins, you have favoured me by reminding me of Rāma again. I am a mere (insignificant) gnat in the ocean of the story of Rāvaṇa's enemy (i.e. Rāma) whose feet are adorned with the lights of gems in the series of the crowns of gods and demons, being deluded by which even gods like Brahmā do not know them (properly)? Still, I shall tell you (the story) according to my capacity, (as) birds resorting to (i.e. depending upon) their own speed go (i.e. fly) into the very extensive sky. The story of Raghunātha (i.e. Rāma) has the expanse of a hundred crore (verses). As men have minds, so do they speak. The chaste fame of Raghunātha will purify my mind as fire by its contact purifies gold.

Sūta said :

16-17. Thus speaking to the best sage, he with his eyes closed in meditation, perceived the auspicious, extraordinary account, through his intellect. With his voice indistinct, and his body horripilated due to great joy, be again told the spotless story of Daśaratha's son (i.e. Rāma).

Śeṣa said :

18-19. When (Rāvaṇa) the lord of Laṅkā who caused affliction to gods and demons, who snatched away the beauty of the moons in the form of the lotus-like faces of the host of the celestial nymphs, was killed, all gods—Indra and others—became happy. Being pleased they, bowing (before Rāma) like servants, praised him.

20-26. Having placed the righteous Bibhīṣaṇa (on the throne) in Laṅkā Rāma resorted to (got into) the Puṣpaka (aeroplane) with Sītā. He was at that time accompanied by Sugrīva, Hanūmat, Sītā and Lakṣmaṇa. Bibhīṣaṇa too, pining away in separation, followed them with his ministers. He (i.e. Rāma) seeing Laṅkā with its ramparts and portals broken in many ways, (so also seeing) Aśokavana, the place of (the stay of) Sītā, (seeing the śiṁśapā trees having flowers and buds, crowded with the demonesses who were (now) dead through the fear of Hanūmat, fainted. Seeing all (that) in this way, Rāma, the best of the Raghus, hearing the loud sounds of the kettledrums of gods, pleasant to the ears, and being honoured by the dances of the celestial nymphs (i.e. by the celestial damsels with their dances) along with gods like Brahmā (who had got) into their own aeroplanes, showing Sītā on the way the holy places with hermitages, and the sages, their sons and their chaste wives, went to the city (of Ayodhyā).

27-29. Rāma showed her all the places where he, the intelligent one, had formerly stayed with Lakṣmaṇa. Thus showing her (all the places on the way) Rāma saw his own city (i.e. Ayodhyā), and also near it Nandigrāma where king Bharata, with many signs of the grief due to the separation from his brother (i.e. Rāma), lived doing righteous deeds.

30-36. He lay (i.e. lived) in a cave, he practised celibacy, had (grown) matted hair and (put on) bark garments. His body had become slim, he was afflicted with grief, and was repeatedly telling stories about Rāma. He did not eat even barley-food, did not again and again drink water. Looking at the rising sun, he used to say: "O you eye of the worlds, the lord of gods, remove my great sin. For my sake, even Rāmacandra, venerable to the world, went to the forest. Waited upon by Sītā of a delicate body, he went to the forest. Oh! that Jānakī, that Sītā, who was pained on finding a stalk in her bed of flowers, who, the chaste one, never received the heat of the sun, roams for my sake from forest to forest. That Sītā who was never seen even by hosts of kings with their eyes is indeed being seen by the mountaineers. Oh! that Sīta, who did not desire to eat even when fed with sweet food, today longs for wild fruits."

37-41. Thus this Bharata, the great king dear to Rāma, every morning, everyday says after waiting upon the sun. That king (i.e. Bharata) who was being spoken to by his ministers who were wise, who knew the right course, who were well-versed in sacred texts, and who had the same sorrows and joys as he had (i.e. who shared his sorrows and joys) said to them: "O ministers, why do you speek to me who am luckless and a mean man? For me my elder brother Rāma has gone to the forest and is sinking. O good ministers, by again and again respectfully remembering the feet of Rāmacandra, I, the unfortunate one, am purifying the sins of my mother. Sumitrā who gave birth to a hero (like Lakṣmaṇa), and who is dear to her husband, is extremely blessed (as) her son (Lakṣmaṇa) is everyday waiting upon the feet of Rāma."

42. Rāma saw that village, remaining in which, Bharata, affectionate towards his brother, was lamenting loudly.

CHAPTER TWO

Rāma Meets Bharata

Śeṣa said:

1-2. Then Rāma, with his heart being distressed by the eagerness to see him, repeatedly remembered his brother Bharata who was the foremost among the righteous persons; and removing the darkness with the moon-like lustre of his teeth that became visible, he said to the powerful Hanūmat, the son of Wind:

3-9. "O hero Hanūmat, hear my words which are impelled by my long-standing separation from my brother, and which are faltering and confused. O hero born from the body of Wind, go to that (my) brother whose body is emaciated due to separation from me and which he sustains forcibly (i.e. against his will). He puts on a bark-garment, he wears matted hair; being affected by separation from me, he would not even eat fruits. For him the wife of another person is like his mother, and gold is like a clod. My brother who knows the right way, would look upon his subjects as his own sons. Quickly sprinkle him whose body is burning with the flames of the fire of grief due to separation from me, with the shower of the water of the message of my arrival. Tell him that Rāma has come with Sītā, is accompanied by Lakṣmaṇa, and the lords of monkeys like Sugrīva and demons with Bibhīṣaṇa and that he is comfortably seated on a seat in the Puṣpaka (aeroplane), so that my younger brother quickly becomes happy due to my arrival."

10-13. Having heard these words of the intelligent Raghu-hero (i.e. Rāma), the obedient (Hanūmat) went to Nandigrāma, the abode of Bharata. Having gone to Nandigrāma, the intelligent one saw Bharata in the company of old ministers, afflicted with the separation from his brother (Rāma), and telling his old ministers the account of Rāmacandra; and full of the honey of the lotuses of his feet he saluted Bharata possessing the form of Dharma.

14-15. Seeing him who was fashioned with all portions of goodness only by the Creator, Bharata with the palms of his hands joined, quickly rose, and said: "Welcome to you; tell me about the safety of Rāma". The right hand of him who was speaking like this, throbbed. Grief went (away) from his heart, and his face was filled with tears of joy.

16-17. Seeing the king like that the lord of the monkeys spoke to him: "Know that Rāma, with Lakṣmaṇa, has reached the vicinity of the town." He, whose body was sprinkled over with the nectar of the message of Rāma's arrival, had flood of joy. I do not know whether he had a thousand faces.

18. He said (to Hanūmat): "I do not have what I could give to you. As long as I live, I am the servant of Rāma carrying out his order."

19-22. Vasiṣṭha too, taking the materials of worship, and the very much delighted old ministers, went to Rāma along the path shown by Hanūmat. From a distance (they) saw the delightful Rāma who had come there seated on a seat in the Puṣpaka (aeroplane) along with Sītā and Lakṣmaṇa. Rāma also saw Bharata walking (to him) and having matted hair and having put on bark-garment with a small piece of cloth worn round his privities. He also saw his ministers whose dresses were similar to that of his brother (Bharata) and who had matted hair, and whose forms were emaciated due to being afflicted by daily penance.

23-28. Seeing the king (i.e. Bharata) like that, Rāma too thought (to himself): 'Oh! this son of the intelligent Daśaratha, the king of kings, having matted hair and dressed in bark-garments is coming on foot to me. I, even when I was in the forest, did not experience so much grief as this one had due to separation from me. Oh! see Bharata, my brother, my companion dearer (to me) than (my) life, having heard that I have come in the vicinity, comes, accompanied by his old, very much delighted ministers and Vasiṣṭha, to see me.' The king (i.e. Rāma) honoured by Bibhīṣaṇa, Hanūmat and Lakṣmaṇa, and with his mind afflicted due to separation (from Bharata), and again and again saying, 'O (my) brother, O my brother', quickly got down from the (aerial) car, viz. the Puṣpaka (come down) from the wide firmament.

29-31. The intelligent Bharata, saw Rāma who was accompanied by gods, and who was afflicted due to his separation from his brother (i.e. Bharata himself), getting down from the (aerial) car. Shedding tears of joy, he saluted him like a staff (i.e. prostrated himself before Rāma). The chief of Raghus (i.e. Rāma) also, seeing him falling on the ground like a staff (i e. having prostrated himself), raised him, and full of joy and grief, held him by the arms (i.e embraced him). The hero, fond of seizing the lotus-like feet of Rāmacandra, and repeatedly weeping, did not get up, though strongly lifted (by Rāma).

Bharata said:

32-33. O great hero, O treasure of compassion, O Rāma, through kindness favour me who am of a bad conduct, who am wicked and sinful. O Rāma, just that foot (those feet) of yours which felt the touch of the hand(s) of Sītā to be harsh, wandered on my account in the forest.

34. Speaking like this, he, the dejected one, with his face full of tears again and again embraced (Rāma), and with the palms of his hands joined and his face full of joy stood before (Rāma).

35-36a. Raghunātha (i.e. Rāma), the abode of compassion, having embraced that younger brother (of him), having saluted the great principal ministers and having taken their leave, occupied with (his) brother Bharata a seat in the Puṣpaka.

36b-40. Bharata saw the praiseworthy Sītā, his brother's wife. He looked upon the daughter of Janaka, a chaste wife, like

Anasūyā, (the wife) of Atri, or like Lopāmudrā (the wife) of (Agastya) born from a pitcher, and saluted her. (He said to her): "O mother, forgive (me) the sin, which I, the ignorant one, committed. Ladies like you, devoted to their husbands, do good to all." The glorious Sītā also, respectfully looked at her brother-in-law, gave him blessings, and enquired after his health. All of them got into that aerial car in the wide firmament. In a moment (Rāma) saw his father's city (drawing) near.

CHAPTER THREE

Rāma Enters Ayodhyā

Śeṣa said:

1. Rāma, the intelligent hero, who, for a long time, desired to see the capital was delighted on seeing it where his own people lived.

2. Bharata too sent to the city his friend, minister Sumukha, to prepare the city for the festivity.

Bharata said:

3-12. The people should quickly celebrate the festival of Rāma's arrival. They should have gay pictures drawn in every house. The royal roads should be free from dust. They should be sprinkled over with liquid sandal. They should be furnished with abundant flowers. They should be crowded with delighted and rich people. All the big courtyards should be adorned with flags of various colours and painted. The fronts of the ridges of the thatched roofs should appear like the bow at the time of the arrival of the clouds (i.e. like the rainbow). The people should send forth agaru (sandal), seeing the smoke of which peacocks would dance sportively. They should paint with the minerals from mountains my elephants resembling mountains and well-controlled by the drivers. The horses having the speed of mind and painted should also look beautiful, seeing whose speed the heavenly horse gives up his pride. Beautiful virgins in thousands adorned with all ornaments and mounted on elephants, should scatter pearls. The married brāhmaṇa-women with vessels in their hands containing dūrvā (grass) and turmeric (powder) should wave lights before Rāma, the great king. May Kauśalyā who is afflicted by the information about the union with her son, and who very much longs for seeing him, be delighted. The delighted people should make such arrangements giving beauty to the city on the arrival of Rāma.

Śeṣa said:

13-21. Hearing these words from (i.e. uttered by) him, Sumukha who was best among the counsellors, went to the city to have in it triumphal archs erected for the festive occasion. That minister named Sumukha, having gone to the city (viz. Ayodhyā), informed the people of the great festival (to be celebrated) on the arrival of Rāma. The people who had formerly given up their enjoyments and pleasures due to separation from him, were (now) very much delighted on hearing that Rāma had come (back) to the city. Pure brāhmaṇas, rich in (the knowledge of) the Vedas, with darbhas in their hands, and covered with bright upper garments, went to the lord of the Raghus. So also many excellent kṣatriyas who were the bravest, who had held bows and arrows, who were brave in battles went to him. Similarly vaiśyas who were wealthy, whose hands were adorned with signet-rings, who had put on white garments went to the lord of men (i.e. Rāma). Śūdras who were devoted to brāhmaṇas, who practised their own course of conduct, who followed the code of conduct (as laid down) in the Vedas also went to the lord of the city. So also people who followed (various) vocations, and who were attached to their own duties went, taking their own things (i.e. presents), to king Śrī Rāma. Thus, people full of flood of delight, and (taking) with (them) many wonderful objects, approached by the order of the king (Bharata) the lord of men (i.e. Rāma).

Śeṣa said:

22-30. Raghunātha also, surrounded by all deities seated in their own cars, entered the city in which attractive objects were arranged. The monkeys, leaping and going along the aerial path, and with their bodies beautified followed (the king) to the best city. Rāma accompanied by Sītā and surrounded by his attendants quickly got down from the Puṣpaka, and got into a vehicle drawn by men. Then he entered Ayodhyā, in which triumphal arches were erected for the festive occasion, which was crowded with joyful and rich people, and which was fully adorned with gay objects. He looked very much pleased with the musical instruments like lutes (being played upon) and kettle-drums and other musical instruments being played upon and was praised by Sūtas, Māgadhas and other bards. Hearing the auspicious words, "Victory to Rāghava, to Rāma; victory to the ornament of the solar race; victory to the son of Daśaratha; may the lord of the world be victorious" uttered by the citizens who were delighted, and who looked graceful on account of horripilation produced on seeing Rāma, he entered (i.e. went to) the excellent path which was adorned with places where many roads meet, which was sprinkled over with sandal (mixed with) water, and which was furnished with flowers and leaves. At that time certain women in the city, desiring to see the form of Raghunātha, (and therefore) resorting to the holes of the latticed windows said (these words):

The women of the city said:

31-34. Oh! the bhilla-girls who in the forests drank with their lotus-like eyes the lotus-like face of Rāma, were lucky. They are very prosperous due to their good luck. See the blessed lotus-like face of Rāma having lotus-like eyes. See the blessed face, having lotus-like eyes, of Śrī Rāmadeva, the abode of bravery, which (face) gods like the Creator also saw. Oh! we are (indeed) very lucky. She this face which has a charming smile, which shines with a crown, which is extremely charming, which possesses lips the beauty of which has surpassed that of the bandhūka (flower), and which has a high nose.

Thus spoke those women, observing him with glances resembling lotus-petals. The lord of all, of a weak body, but delighted, entered his mother's house, which had great love (in store for him).

CHAPTER FOUR

Rāma's Consecration

Vātsyāyana said:

1-5. O great lord of the serpents, O lord capable of sustaining the burden of the earth, listen to one doubt of mine; and please explain (i.e. remove) it. Since the departure of Rāma to the forest she (Kauśalyā) lives with body but with a vacant mind. She is afflicted by separation from him; her body is emaciated; she is extremely unhappy. How indeed was she happy when she heard from Sumukha, the minister, that Rāma had come (back)? What happened (to her)? What were the marks (of her feelings)? What did she say to him who had brought the message of Rāmacandra? Remove this doubt of mine. Do me a favour and tell me who am listening, about the rich virtues of Raghunātha.

Śeṣa said:

6-7. Well asked, O you glorious one, O you who are in the forefront of best brāhmaṇas. Listen (now) attentively to it when I am actually telling it. She, having repeatedly drunk the nectar fallen from the lotus-like mouth of him (i.e. Sumukha), of (i.e. telling about) the arrival of Rāma, she became afflicted with her body becoming steady.

8-13a. She said: "Is it a dream of (i.e. seen by) me, a fool? Or do the words cause confusion? How can I, luckless that I am, see Rāma again? Due to having practised much penance I had obtained this my child—my son; but due to some sin of (i.e. committed by) me, he became separated from me. O good minister, is Rāma accompanied by Sītā and Lakṣmaṇa all right? Does he, moving in the forest, remember me, who am extremely pained?" Thus, she, who remembered Rāma, loudly wept. She fainted, and was not conscious of what belonged to her and what to others. Sumukha too, seeing (Rāma's) mother extremely unhappy fanned her with the ends of garments, and then she regained consciousness. Then he repeatedly spoke gentle and delightful words to the mother (of Rāma). He again made her happy by reminding her of the arrival of Raghunātha:

13b-19a. "O mother, know that Raghunātha with Lakṣmaṇa has come home. See Rāma with Sītā, and sprinkle them over with (i.e. give them) blessings." I do not know (i.e. I have not seen) such joy which she experienced on hearing the true words uttered by Sumukha. With her hair standing on end, she got up and reached (i.e. went to) the courtyard. With her body perturbed by joy, and shedding tears, she looked for Rāma. Just then Rāma, the lord of kings, and of a good conduct, and seated in a vehicle drawn by men, reached first the house of his mother Kaikeyī. Kaikeyī too, bent due to the burden of the sense of shame, did not say anything to Rāma standing in front of her. She was very much worried. Rāma, the banner of the solar dynasty, seeing his mother who was ashamed, said, consoling (i.e. to console) her, (these words) mixed with (i.e. full of) politeness:

Śrī Rāma said:

19b-21a. O mother, having gone to the forest, I did everything (as I was ordered to do). O mother, what should I do now by your order? I have done nothing despicable. Then, how (is it that) you are not looking at me? Greeting this Bharata and me with blessings, look at me.

21b-24a. Hearing these words of (i.e. uttered by) him, O sinless one, she, with her face hung down, slowly said: "Rāma, go to your (own) house." And Rāma, the best among men, having heard (these) words of his mother, saluted her, and the treasure of compassion went to the house of Sumitrā. The large-hearted Sumitrā, seeing Rāma with her son (Lakṣmaṇa), said, with (i.e. giving him) blessings: "Live long, live long."

24b-28. Rāmabhadra too having saluted the feet of his mother, and having, full of joy, embraced her, again said (these) words to her: "O you conceiving a gem (like Lakṣmaṇa), no (other) brother of me has removed my grief as this intelligent one (i.e. Lakṣmaṇa) has done. Sītā who was kidnapped by Rāvaṇa, was got back by me—O mother, know all that to be the working of Lakṣmaṇa." Accepting with his head (i.e. by bowing down his head), the blessing given by Sumitrā, the wise one surrounded by the wise went to the house of his mother (i.e. Kauśalyā).

29-33. Hari (i.e. Rāma) seeing his mother delighted and longing to see him, quickly got down from the vehicle and seized her feet. His mother, eager to see him and with her mind confused, repeatedly embraced Rāma and was delighted. Horripilation due to joy appeared on her body and she faltered while speaking. Hot tears of joy trickled down up to her feet. Polite Rāma, seeing his mother bereft of the two large ear-rings and having her body without ornaments (worn) on the hands and feet and delighted to a certain degree on seeing him, having an emaciated frame, and experiencing grief, thought that it was not the time for grief and said to her:

Śrī Rāma said:

34-39. O mother, I have not waited upon your feet for a long time. So forgive me who am unlucky for my fault. Those sons who are not eager to serve their mother and father should be looked upon as great insects born from semen, O mother. What should I do? I went to the Daṇḍaka forest by the order of my father. There too, due to your favourable glance, I crossed the ocean of grief. Rāvaṇa kidnapped Sītā, and took her to Laṅkā. By your favour I got her (back) after killing that lord of demons. This is Sītā my devoted wife who has fallen at your feet. Show regard for her who is timid, and who has set her heart on your feet.

Hearing these words of (i.e. uttered by) him, she greeted her daughter-in-law who had fallen at her feet, with blessings and said to that devoted wife (of Rāma). (Kauśalyā said):

40-44. "O beautiful lady, O Sītā, enjoy for a long time with your husband. Give birth to two sons. O you purifying one, purify your own family. Women like you, who are devoted to their husbands, and who experience pleasure and pain with their husbands, become unhappy. There is no truth in the three worlds. O daughter of Videha (i.e. Janaka), you who followed the couple of the lotus-like feet of Rāma to the great forest, have purified your family. What wonder is there that those men in whose house there are chaste wives desiring what is dear to their husbands, are like a hurricane to crores of enemies?" Saying so to Rāma's wife of curved eyes she remained quiet, with her hair standing on end due to great joy.

45-48. Then Rāmacandra's brother Bharata gave (back) to the intelligent Rāma, the great kingdom given to him by their father. The delighted ministers, invited astrologers, knowing sacred hymns, and, with great respect, asked them about an auspicious time; and being eager they consecrated Rāma on the great kingdom on an auspicious time on a good day united with an auspicious constellation. The great king, the lord of kings, stood on a beautiful (piece of) tiger-hide, after drawing on it (the picture of) the earth with its seven islands.

49-54. From that day only the hearts of the good men became joyful; the hearts of the wicked, tormenting others, became weary. Women due to their devotion to their husbands, were greatly attached to them. O sage, men did not even mentally commit any sin. Demons, gods, so also serpents, yakṣas, asuras, and great snakes remained on the right path. All they held Rāma's order with their heads (i.e. respectfully obeyed Rāma's order). People engaged in obliging others. They were happy as they followed their own course of conduct laid down for their caste. Auspicious moments of days and nights were passed in (getting) knowledge and diversions. Even great wind did not carry away even the small garments of those who remained on the roads. There was (absolutely) no talk about thieves. The kind Rāma, treasure of compassion, gave wealth to suppliants. With his brothers he always praised the preceptors and deities.

CHAPTER FIVE

The Coming of Sage Agasti

Śeṣa said:

1. Then the gods, with their minds delighted due to (Rāma's) killing the lord of demons called Rāvaṇa, humbly praised Rāma, consecrated (as the king).

Gods said:

2-10. Victory to you, O son of Daśaratha, O you who remove the sufferings of gods; victory to you who burnt the race of the demons; victory to you, O god, destroying the enemy whose hands were engaged in seizing the bevies of excellent women. The eager poets describe your destroying the lord of demons. O lord of the worlds, at the time of the deluge you again easily swallow the group of the worlds. Victory to you who are free from the causes of birth, old age etc. O mighty one, emancipate (us). Victory to you who have taken birth in the ocean of the family of the righteous, O you ageless, immortal and the fixed one. By means of (reciting) the names of you, the greatest god, even those who have committed great sins are purified. What then if good, foremost brāhmaṇas have obtained the human existence with a good body? The pair of your feet, praised by Śiva and Brahmā gives abundant things that are desired. We mentally desire it which is well arranged in the heart with the marks like those of pure barley (grains) etc. O you having the loveliness that excels Madana's frame, if you do not grant fearlessness to the world, then how can, O you compassionate and purifying one, the hosts of gods be happy? You take birth on the earth whenever the demons trouble us, O lord, though you are unborn and immutable, though you are the greatest lord. You who are the self-adorned one and you who are praised by those who approve of virtues, quickly enter (i.e. go back to) your own place, after having filled the earth with your superhuman good deeds like nectar to the dead and destroying sins. May the beginningless one, the foremost one, who takes the form of a god, who has put on a necklace and a crown, who looks like Cupid, who has forcibly killed his enemies, whose lotus-like feet are served by Cupid's enemy (i.e. Śiva), be victorious.

11. Speaking like this, all the gods led by Brahmā and Indra and pleased with the destruction of (their) enemy, repeatedly saluted the chief of the Raghus (i.e. Rāma).

12. Being extremely pleased by the praise, the very glorious lord of the Raghus, seeing the gods with their necks bent down, said to them:

Śrī Rāma said:

13. O gods, choose from me some boon which is extremely difficult to obtain and which some eager god, demon or yakṣa has not obtained.

Gods said:

14-16a. O lord, from you we have obtained the best thing, since you have killed our enemy, viz. Rāvaṇa. Whenever a demon troubles us, you should in this way destroy (that) enemy.

Saying, 'All right', the hero Raghunandana (i.e. Rāma), spoke again.

Śrī Rāma said:

16b-20. O gods, carefully listen to my words. The man, who again and again recites in the morning and at night the wonderful hymn of me (i.e. in my honour) composed by you and couched with my virtues will never meet with an extremely terrible defeat from his enemy. He will not experience poverty and will not suffer from a disease or a defeat. By reciting (the hymn) devotion to the pair of my feet will be produced in the joyful hearts of men.

Speaking thus, the crest-jewel of kings (i.e. the best king) remained silent. All the gods who were delighted went to their respective worlds.

21-27. Raghunātha (i.e. Rāma) also looked after his wise brothers like their father, and the lord of the world fondled the subjects like his own sons. When he was ruling, the people did not meet with an untimely death; in the houses there was no great discomfiture like a disease. The calamity of the season was not seen, so also there was no fear from enemies. The trees always bore fruits, and the earth yielded much grain. The life of people was blessed with sons, grandsons and attendants. Their depression was removed due to their wives' company. They were everyday eager to listen to the stories about the lotus-like feet of Rāma. They never employed their words in censuring others. Even artisans, apprehensive of a blow from the hands of Rāma, never even mentally committed a sin. People, with their eyes becoming steady on seeing the face of Sītā's husband, were always full of compassion.

28-45. He (had) the kingdom to which there was no rival, which was prosperous and had (in it) powerful elephants (or horses). It was charming on account of delighted and thriving sages and with ornaments of gold. It was well-nourished by those who always did the pious things like performing sacrifices and digging wells and doing other acts of charity. It was always rich with crops, had good wealth and fields. Its regions were good; subjects were good; it was self-abiding; it had ample grass, and a large wealth of cows. It was all around adorned by rows of temples. In it were villages adorned with ample wealth and prosperity. The lands in it shone with artificial gardens having good flowers, with trees having very sweet fruits, and with lakes having good lotus-plants. In the country only the rivers were *sadambha* (i.e. containing good water); the people were not *sadambha* (i.e. were not proud). There were families of many castes, well-born but not poor. In it *vibhrama* (i.e. amorous movement) was (seen) in women, but *vibhrama* (i.e. an error) was never seen in (i.e. committed by) the learned. Only the rivers flowed in a crooked way (*kuṭilagāminyaḥ*) but the subjects were not wayward in sex. The nights (only) were dark in the dark fortnights; but men were not full of darkness (i.e. ignorance).. Only women had *rajas* (i.e. menses), (but) people did not behave unrighteously. A man was neither *andha* (i.e. blind) due to wealth nor without rice (*āndhya*) in (i.e. while taking) his meal. Only a chariot took a wrong course and never a royal official. *Daṇḍa* (i.e. a handle) was to be seen in (i.e. attached to) an axe, a spade, a row of fans or an umbrella; but *daṇḍa* (i.e. punishment) was rarely due to a fault or disturbance. Except among the groups of those who played at dice, there was no repentence. Only the gamblers were seen with dice (*pāśa*) in their hands (and none else with nooses—*pāśa* in his hands). *Jāḍya* (i.e. frigidity) was seen in water only. The waists of women alone were weak. Only women were hard-hearted, and not men. There was the *kuṣṭha* (herb) only among medicines; but no *kuṣṭha* (i.e. leprosy) among men. A hole was seen in good gems; a pointed weapon was (seen only) in the hand of a man fashioning images. Tremor was due (only) to good feelings, never due to the fear of someone. Fever was due to sexual passion; there was poverty (i.e. scarcity) of the wicked (only). There was no want of a thing for a lucky person due to his good deeds. Only elephants were wanton in a war, and waves in a lake. Loss of *dāna* (i.e. 1. ichor 2. gift) was (seen) only in the elephants. Only thorns were sharp. Going away from the *guṇa* (1. string 2. virtue) was (seen) only in arrows; a compact utterance with a peculiar arrangement of words was (seen) only in a book. Abandoning friendship was present only in the wicked, and not among the kinsmen. Fondling the loved subjects he looked after that country. Like Yama to a wicked person he established righteousness in the country. When the lord was thus righteously protecting the country—the earth, a thousand and eleven years passed.

46-50. He who perpetuated the Raghu-family, on hearing (words) of dishonour about Sītā, and his own censure from a mean washerman abandoned her. By one order of him, the king who was protecting the earth righteously, Sītā who was (up to that time) well-protected, was abandoned. When once the highly intelligent one was seated in his assembly, the great sage, the best sage born from a pitcher (i.e. sage Agasti) came (there). Taking a respectful offering he got up; and the great king accompanied by Vasiṣṭha and people, honoured him who had dried the ocean and who had arrived there with a welcome, and enquired after his health. Then the descendant of Raghu (i.e. Rāma) spoke to the sage who had seated comfortably and who had taken rest.

CHAPTER SIX

Agastya Begins Rāvaṇa's Story

Śeṣa said:

1. The intelligent Rāma, the lord of all worlds, thus said to the sage, the treasure of celibacy and penance and pleased with the welcome:

2-6. "O you illustrious one, O you born of a pitcher, O you treasure of penance, welcome to you. All of us, with the members of our family are purified (by your arrival). I hope, your respect for the Vedas and sacred texts continues. On the globe there is none that would obstruct your penance. O glorious one, Lopāmudrā is your virtuous wife due to whose conduct as a devoted wife everything becomes auspicious. O you best sage, O you glorious one, O you piety embodied, O you treasure of compassion, tell me what thing should I do for you who are greedless. Everything takes place due to your penance, and you can have many things through your own penance, and you can have many things through your own desire. Yet, O best sage, just favour me, and tell me (what I can do for you)".

Śeṣa said:

7. Thus addressed by the intelligent Rāma, the lord of people, the king of kings, he spoke to Rāma, the lord of the world with more polite words.

Agastya said:

8-10. O lord, O king of kings, O treasure of compassion, know that thinking that to see you is extremely difficult, I have come here. You killed the demon named Rāvaṇa who troubled the world. Luckily gods are happy today; luckily Bibhīṣaṇa has become the king. O Rāma, today on seeing you indeed my sin has gone (away). O best god, the vessel of my mind is full of joy.

11. Speaking thus, (Agastya) born from a pitcher, with his mind perturbed due to joy on seeing Rāma, quickly became quiet.

12-15. Rāma again asked that sage well-versed in knowledge: "You know everything everywhere about the past, present and future in the world. O sage, tell it all in great detail to me who am asking you. Who was that Rāvaṇa, who troubled the gods and whom I killed. What is that Kumbhakarṇa? What is his species? O great sage, is he a god, or a demon, or a friend, or a goblin? O you omniscient one, tell me all that. You know all that in detail. Therefore, favouring me, tell me all that."

16-29. Hearing these words from him, that treasure of penance (viz. Agastya), born from a pitcher, began telling all that was asked by the king (Rāma) of the Raghu (family). "O king, Brahmā brought forth the creation. His son was Pulastya. From him was born Viśravas, conversant with the Vedic lore. He had two wives, who were of a chaste conduct. The name of one was Mandākinī, and the other one was known as Kaikasī. From the former (i.e. Mandākinī) Kubera, enjoyer of the pleasures of a regent of the quarters, was born; through Śiva's favour, he took his residence in Laṅkā. Three great sons were born to (Kaikasī) the daughter of Vidyunmālī: Rāvaṇa, Kumbhakarṇa, and the righteous Bibhīṣaṇa. O very intelligent one, due to being born from the womb of a demoness and due to being born at the evening time, the mind of the two was steeped in unrighteousness. Endowed with brilliance, he (i.e. Kubera), once, having got into the Puṣpaka aeroplane made of gold and having (i.e. adorned by) groups of small bells, and being praised by his attendants having many jewelled ornaments, went to see his parents. The son (i.e. Kubera), having come to his parents, and having for a long time fallen at their feet and being beside himself with joy and with his hair standing on end due to horripilation, said: "Today is a good day for me. There is the rise of the fruit of my great luck, since I saw your feet, seeing which gives great religious merit." Having praised them with such words of praise, he went to his own house. The parents also became delighted due to the son's affection (for them). Seeing him (i.e. Kubera), the intelligent Rāvaṇa, said to his mother: "Who is this man who having fallen upon my father's feet, has again gone (back)? Is he a god, or a yakṣa or an excellent man? He is the treasure of great luck. He is surrounded by his own attendants. Due to which penance has he obtained this aeroplane, which has the speed of the wind, and which is the best place of enjoyment having in it gardens and groves for sports etc.?"

Śeṣa said :

30-36. Hearing these words, his mother, displeased and overcome with anger, and with a slight change in her eyes said to her son: "O son, listen to my words full of great instruction. His birth, deeds etc. are superior due to his (good) thoughts and cleverness. He has taken birth (i.e. is born) from the womb of my co-wife, (and) has brightened the pure, great family of his mother; but you, who are born from my womb, are an insect, are a sinner, and fill your own belly (only). Like a donkey who does not know (i.e. has no idea about) the load (on his back) nor its quality, you appear to be learned but enjoy lying and sitting; your existence is like one that is asleep, gone away, or fallen. By means of his penance he who pleased Śiva, has obtained residence in heaven, an aeroplane having the speed of the mind, and royal glory. His mother is very blessed, very lucky and very prosperous, whose son has obtained the position of the great due to his merits."

37. Having heard these words angrily uttered by his unhappy mother, the most wicked one (Rāvaṇa), entertaining anger for himself and determined to (practise) penance, again said (these) words.

Rāvaṇa said :

38-43. O mother, listen to my words full of pride. You, who have three sons like us, are one who conceive gems. Who is that insect of that Kubera? What (i.e. how insignificant) is his small penance? What (i.e. how insignificant) is Laṅkā? What (i.e. how insignificant) is his kingdom having (but) a few servants? O mother, full of compassion, listen to my pledge taken through determination, and never taken (before) by any one, O very lucky Kaikasī. If by practising difficult austerities pleasing Brahmā, and by always giving up food, water, sleep and sport, I do not bring under my control the entire world, then I would incur the sin due to harming the world of the manes.

Accompanied by Bibhīṣaṇa, Kumbhakarṇa too took the pledge with Rāvaṇa and saying the same went to a mountain-grove.

CHAPTER SEVEN

Elimination of Rāvaṇa by Viṣṇu

Agastya said :

1-6. Then the demon practised a severe penance for ten thousand years. Looking at the sun with his eyes, he remained with his feet upwards. Kumbhakarṇa also practised a very difficult penance. The righteous Bibhīṣaṇa also practised penance. Then the lord, the god of gods, the lord of beings, served by the crowns of the gods, demons, yakṣas and others, was pleased, and gave him a great kingdom, shining in the three worlds; he also made his body charming and waited upon by gods and demons. Then he always tormented Kubera having a religious mind. He took away his aeroplane, and forcibly (captured) the city of Laṅkā. He tormented the entire world; the gods also went to heaven. He killed brāhmaṇa families, and cut off the roots of the sages.

7-9. Then the gods who were grieved, came with Indra to Brahmā and the magnanimous ones prostrating themselves (before him) like staffs praised him. All the respectful gods praised (him) with proper words. Then, the lord, who was pleased, said: "What should I do?" Then in front of Brahmā the gods narrated the trouble from Rāvaṇa and their own defeat.

10-15. Thinking for a moment, Brahmā went to Kailāsa with the gods. The gods led by Indra and full of surprise remained by the side of that mountain and praised Śiva. (They said:) "Salutation to Bhava; salutation to you—Śarva; salutation to you-Nīlagrīva; salutation you—the gross, the subtle, and the multiformed one." Śiva, having heard the words uttered from the mouths of the gods, said to Nandin: "Bring the gods near me." In the mean while, gods invited by Nandin, entered the city and looked with wonder-struck eyes. Brahmā came forward and saw Śiva who did good to the world, who was served by crores of delighted attendants who were naked, deformed, crooked, dusty and hideous.

16-17. Remaining in the front the grandsire along with the gods saluted and said to the highest lord of gods: "See the condition of the residents of heaven. Take pity, O great god, O you who are affectionate to those who seek your refuge. You (now) exert yourself to kill the wicked demon."

18-20. He (i.e. Śiva) too hearing their words full of dejection and sorrow came with all gods to the place of Viṣṇu. Along with gods, serpents and kinnaras all the sages praised him: "O Mādhava, victory to you. O lord of gods, victory to you. O you, who remove the afflictions of your devotees, victory to you. Look (at us), O great god. Look at your servants." In this way all gods led by Śiva loudly spoke.

21-28. Hearing what was said (by gods) Viṣṇu, the great lord of gods, seeing the grief of gods spoke as if pacifying their grief in a voice loud like (the thundering of) clouds, to the gods: "O gods led by Brahmā, Śiva and Indra, you should listen to (my) words intent on your good. I know the fear caused to you by Rāvaṇa. Today, taking an incarnation I shall destroy that. The city of Ayodhyā, an ornament to the earth, is protected by kings born in the solar family and doing good acts like (making) great gifts and (performing) sacrifices. It shines with silver regions. Daśaratha, the mighty king, who conquered the whole world, who is endowed with wealth (but) who is childless, now rules over the kingdom (and lives) in it. He, endowed with great power performed with a desire to have a son the sacrifice according to the rite through revered Ṛṣyaśṛṅga solicited for (performing) the sacrifice. Then, O gods, he first prayed to me through penance. I was born in four ways having the names Rāma, Lakṣmaṇa, Bharata and Śatrughna on his three wives. I shall fully eliminate Rāvaṇa along with his army and horses (or elephants). You should also by your own portions taking the form of bears and monkeys move on the entire earth."

29-36. Thus speaking in the heaven, he quickly ceased to speak. All the gods, having heard these great words, and with their hearts pleased, did what was told by the intelligent god of gods. They, taking the forms of bears and monkeys filled the earth with their portions. O great king, you yourself are that great god Viṣṇu, who destroys the misery of gods, and who has taken up a (human) form. O highly intelligent one, this Bharata, Lakṣmaṇa and Śatrughna are (born) from your portion. So also is Rāvaṇa who troubles the gods created. Due to the continuity of former enmity he kidnapped Sītā, O king. You killed that demon born in the stock of a brāhmaṇa demon. You overthrew that lord of demons, the son of Pulastya, who troubled the entire world. The whole earth has become happy. Today the brāhmaṇas have secured happiness and the ascetics have secured the power of (their) penance. All the holy places have (again) become auspicious, and all the sacrifices are well-established. O soul of the universe, O origin of the world, O best man, when you are the king, the entire world with gods, demons and men has become happy.

37. I have, according to my intellect (i.e. intellectual capacity) today told you everything—the birth and death (of Rāvaṇa)—as asked by you, O innocent one.

38. Hearing in this way the account about the family of the lord of demons, the great man of well-known prowess, the lord, the ruler, checking his tears trickling on his lotus-like face, fell on the ground in his assembly.

CHAPTER EIGHT

Agastya Advises Rāma to Perform a Horse-Sacrifice

Śeṣa said:

1-4. O best sage Vātsyāyana, well-versed in the Vedas, the story of the god of gods, the only protector of all righteous ways, destroys sins. Seeing Rāma (fallen) unconscious, Agastya, the treasure of penance, immediately wiped his tears slowly with his hand, and said: "O Rāma, revive quickly, why do you sink? You are the ancient Viṣṇu, the destroyer of the demons' family. Without you the world—the past, present, future, the immovable and the movable—does not go on. (Then) why have you fallen unconscious here?"

5-6. Hearing the words uttered by him who was born from a pitcher (i.e. by Agastya), the great king (Rāma), with his lovely face full of tears trickling on it, got up, and with his frame bending due to sense of shame, and averse to doing wrong to a brāhmaṇa, said very piteous, distinct words in detail.

Śrī Rāma said:

7-15. Oh! see the ignorance of me who am a fool and wicked-minded, that I, very eager through passion, killed (Rāvaṇa) born in a brāhmaṇa-family. (Though) I had the true knowledge of the Vedas and (other) sacred texts, I, void of intelligence and of a bad mind killed a brāhmaṇa, (destroyed) a brāhmaṇa-family. A brāhmaṇa never got a reproach in (i.e. from a member of) the Ikṣvāku family. (But) I, doing such a deed (as killing a brāhmaṇa like Rāvaṇa) have greatly stained it. Those brāhmaṇas who deserve worship by means of presents, honours and food, have been killed by me with strokes of volleys of arrows. Which worlds shall I go to? Even the unbearable (hell called) Kumbhīpāka (will be secured by me). There is no such sacred place as is capable of purifying me. There is no sacrifice, no penance, no gift, or no vow etc. that would purify and emancipate me who have wronged a brāhmaṇa. Those men who have angered a brāhmaṇa-family, go to hell, and after having reached hell repeatedly experience misery. For those who have the true knowledge of the castes and the stages of life, Vedas are the roots of religious practices. The brāhmaṇa-family is the root of all the prominent branches of the Vedas. What world shall I who through insolence cut off that root, obtain (i.e. go to)? What should be done today by which good would take place in my case?

Śeṣa said :

16. Agastya said these words to the lord of kings, the best among the Raghus, who had taken a human form through his divine power and who was very much weeping.

Agastya said :

17-23. O very wise, very intelligent king, do not be dejected. No (sin of) killing a brāhmaṇa would be earned by you, desiring the destruction of the wicked. You are the ancient man; you are actually the lord beyond Prakṛti. You are the author (of the world); you take it away; you are its protector; you are actually qualityless (but) possess qualities due to your desire, since by (merely) uttering your name, all, viz. the drinker of spirituous liquor, the killer of a brāhmaṇa, one who steals gold and one who commits a sin, are quickly purified. O you very intelligent one, this respectable lady Sītā is a great lore, merely by remembering whom those that become free (from the mundane existence) obtain beatitude. Rāvaṇa also was not a (real) demon. He was your servant in Vaikuṇṭha. O you killer of demons, he obtained demonhood due to the curse of sages. You have favoured that brāhmaṇa (viz. Rāvaṇa) and have not killed him. Thinking like this do not again grieve over (the death of Rāvaṇa).

Hearing these words from him, Rāma, the conqueror of his enemies' cities, spoke sweet words, uttering stammering sounds.

Śrī Rāma said :

24-26. Sin is said to be of two kinds, viz. deliberate and non-deliberate. Deliberate is that which is done with an intention. The non-deliberate is that committed unintentionally. The deliberate sin is exhausted only after experiencing (the fruit of that sinful) deed. The other one would perish through remorse. This is declared by the scriptural injunctions. The words of the good cannot be properly regarded as removing the grief of me who have intentionally committed the extremely censurable killing of a brāhmaṇa.

27-28. Tell me a vow, a gift, a sacrifice, a (visit to a) holy place, or some great worship like that, which would burn my sin, and by which my spotless fame will purify the people who are defiled by sinful conduct and whose lustre is taken away due to the killing of a brāhmaṇa.

Śeṣa said :

29-36. That treasure of penance (i.e. Agastya) spoke these words to Rāma whose feet were illumined by the gems on the heads of the gods and demons that saluted him and who had spoken thus: "O Rāma, O great hero, O you who does favour to the worlds, listen to words which I (shall now) speak for removing (the sin due to) killing a brāhmaṇa. He who would perform a horse sacrifice, overcomes all that sin. Therefore, O soul of the universe, you perform that auspicious horse-sacrifice. You who are wise, who are endowed with great glory, who are having great power, who are the lord of the earth should perform that horse-sacrifice which removes the sin of (i.e. due to) killing a brāhmaṇa, and which was performed by the great king Dilīpa, your ancestor. Indra, the best among men, having performed a hundred sacrifices, secured, in Amarāvatī, a position well waited upon by gods and demons. All these your ancestors—Manu and king Sagara, and king Marutta, so also (Yayāti) the son of Nahuṣa, performed (this) sacrifice and went to the (highest) place. Therefore, O lord of kings, perform (that sacrifice); you are fully capable (of performing it). Your brothers, the regents of quarters, are appreciative of it."

37. Having heard what the sage said, that fortunate Rāma, the best of the Raghus, afraid of having killed a brāhmaṇa, very much deciding to perform it, and (with his glory) sung by those who were conversant with past events, asked (Agastya) about the manner (in which it was performed).

CHAPTER NINE

Instructions in Religious Practices

Śrī Rāma said:

1. What kind of horse should be (used) there (i.e. in that sacrifice)? What is the manner in which he is to be honoured? How can it be performed? Which enemies are to be conquered in (i.e. while performing) that sacrifice?

Agastya said:

2-11. A horse that is having the colour of the water of Gaṅgā, that is auspicious in body, that is dark in ears (i.e. that has dark ears), that is red in face (i.e. that has a red face), that is yellow in the tail (i.e. that has a yellow tail), that has good characteristics, that has the speed of the mind, that can move everywhere, that resembles Uccaiḥśravas, that has auspicious marks is said (to be used) in a horse-sacrifice. Having worshipped the horse on the full-moonday of

Vaiśākha, having written (and having put) a note marked with one's name and power on his forehead, one should let him loose, carefully guarded by guards. The powerful guards should go wherever the horse to be sacrificed goes. The guards should forcibly bring him back from him who, with force, binds him due to his own heroism and power. The sacrificer should remain (practising) and should observe celibacy. Till two years pass while the man is observing the vow, the poor, the blind, and the helpless should be satisfied by (giving) them wealth etc. O venerable (Rāma), abundant food should be given, and much wealth (also) should be given. The intelligent one gives whatever (a suppliant) asks for. O you destroyer of your enemies, the sacrifice of him who does acts like this, when completed, destroys all sins. Therefore, you are able to perform it, to protect it and to honour it. O king, having had auspicious fame, purify other people.

Śrī Rāma said:

12. O best brāhmaṇa, now see my stable; see whether there are horses like that (i.e. as described by you), having auspicious marks.

13-19. Hearing these words, Agastya, the mine of compassion, got up and desiring to see the auspicious horses fit for the sacrifice, went with Rāma to the stable and saw there very strong horses of lovely bodies, and having the speed of the mind. While seeing them he wondered to himself as to whether they were the descendants of the king of horses that had come (down) to the earth, or were solidified mass of the fame of Raghu kings, or whether it was a great mass of nectar (that had come out) of the ocean. On one side there was an excellent row of horses with crimson bodies. At one place there were horses with dark ears and shining like musk. At one place there were horses having a golden splendour. At other place there were horses of blue colour. At one place (there were horses) surrounded by particular spotted horses. Seeing all of them, the sage, with his mind full of eagerness went to another place to see the horses fit for the sacrifice. There he saw hundreds of them having that colour and tied (within the stable). Seeing them, the sage, with his body delighted (i.e. having marks of delight), was amazed.

20-21. Seeing at one place horses with dark ears, with their bodies resembling milk, with yellow tails, red faces, having auspicious marks, fully spotless, resembling the streams of pure water, graced with the speed of the mind, bright like the heaps of spotless fame, the sage who dried the ocean and whose eyes and face were bright due to joy, spoke on seeing the beautiful horses to the lord of Sītā (i.e. spoke to Rāma).

Agastya said:

22-24. O best of the Raghus, the eyes of me who am seeing your many auspicious horses fit for the horse-sacrifice, are not today getting satisfaction. O illustrious Rāmacandra saluted by gods and demons, O great king, perform a big horse-sacrifice. O you prosperous one, performing all groups of sacrifices like (Indra) the lord of gods, drying like god Sun the ocean of your enemies, and having conquered the war in which the chief of the hosts of enemies is killed, make this earth full of pleasures and enjoyments.

25-30. He with all his senses fully delighted by the utterance of these words collected all excellent requisites for the (horse-) sacrifice. Accompanied by the sage, the great king came to the bank of Sarayū. There he ploughed a large (portion of) land with golden ploughs. Having plentifully scratched (i.e. ploughed) the land of the measure of four yojanas, the king constructed temporary halls for the sacrifice. He (got) prepared a basin with a womb and a girdle, decked with many gems and endowed with all charm. The best sage Vasiṣṭha, having a great penance (to his credit), got all that done according to the rules as laid down in the Vedic texts. That sage (i.e. Vasiṣṭha) sent (his) disciples to the hermitages of best sages. They (i.e. the disciples) told them that the best Raghu (i.e. Rāma) was ready (to perform a sacrifice).

31-35. Then all the sages, best among those who practised penance, were invited. They, being extremely eager to see the highest lord (i.e. Rāma) came (there). Nārada, (a sage) named Asita, Parvata, the sage Kapila, Jātūkarṇya, Aṅgiras, Vyāsa,

Ārṣṭiṣeṇa, Atri, Āsuri, Hārīta, Yājñavalkya, Saṁvarta, and (the sage) named Śuka—these and other sages went to (attend) the excellent horse-sacrifice of Rāma. The king (the descendant of) Raghu, of a magnanimous mind, honoured all of them by rising and saluting them and by making respectful offerings and offering seats to them. He whose valour was generally known, gave them cows and gold. (He said to them): "Today it is my great luck that I have seen you."

Śeṣa said:

36. O brāhmaṇa, when (the hall) was crowded on the arrival of excellent sages, there was discussion about the way of life well in conformity with the castes and the stages of life.

Vātsyāyana said:

37. What kind of discussion about the way of life took place there? What wonders (i.e. wonderful things) did they tell? What did the good (sages), through compassion for all people, say (there)?

Śeṣa said:

38. Rāma, the great son of Daśaratha, having seen the sages gathered there, asked them about all the ways of life proper for the castes and the stages of life.

39. They, on being asked by Rāma explained the very meritorious ways of life. I shall properly tell them to you. Listen to them.

The sages said:

40-47. A brāhmaṇa should always perform sacrifices, should engage in study etc. Having studied the Vedas and being free from passion he should not enter upon the householder's stage. A brāhmaṇa should always avoid serving low people. Even when he is in a calamity he should never live by following a dog's life. To approach his wife (i.e. to have intercourse with her) after the period of menstruation is the proper course for a brāhmaṇa; it is good for women. Or merely by remembering them he would desire a child. Approaching (their wives) by day by men is regarded as cutting short (the span of) life. An intelligent man should avoid (intercourse on) a śrāddha-day and all the parvan days. If he would cohabit with his wife through infatuation on these days he falls from the highest (position). That householder who has intercourse with (only) his wife after the period of menstruation, and who is devoted to his wife (alone) should always be known as a celibate. The period of menstruation lasts for sixteen days. Out of them four are extremely censured. Out of them (intercourse on) the even days causes the birth of a son and (on) the odd ones causes the birth of a daughter. He, being pure, and avoiding inauspicious (period of the) moon, so also (the constellations like) Maghā and Mūla, should cohabit with his wife, especially on (a night when) a male constellation (is predominant). She would give birth to a pure son who would help accomplish the (four) goals of human life.

48-62. The (gift of a) couple of cows that is spoken of in the Ārṣa form of marriage[1] is good. Even a small dowry for a girl causes a sin to the purchaser of the girl. Trade, serving a king, not studying the Vedas, a bad (i.e. improper) marriage, omission of the essential ceremonies of the Hindu religion, are causes of the downfall of the family. A householder (obtains) merit by giving food, water, fruits, roots and by giving a cow (to a brāhmaṇa) according to the proper rite. He, from whose house a guest goes unhonoured and disappointed, loses the merit that he has collected since his birth. A householder should eat the residue of the food after having given it to his manes, the deities and human beings. He who cooks for himself and fills his own belly only, eats sin (only). Sin enters oil on the sixth and the eighth days of the month, (while) it always remains in flesh. He should avoid a razor (i.e. shaving) and (coitus with) his wife on the fourteenth day and the new-moon day. He should not enjoy his wife when she is in her menses, and should not eat with her. (Only) with one garment (on his body) he should not eat, nor should he eat (by sitting) on a high seat. An excellent man, desiring lustre, should not see his wife while she is eating. A man should not blow into fire by his mouth; he should not see (his) wife when she is naked. He should not heat

1. Ārṣa Vivāha; A form of marriage derived from the ṛṣis; one of the eight forms of marriage in whtch the father of the bride receives one or two pairs of cows from the bridegroom.

his foot in fire; he should not put an impure thing into fire. He should not harm beings; he should not eat at both the twilights. He should not see a cow giving a suck (to her calf); he should not point out the rainbow (to others) by day or at night; he should not eat the fresh butter that has come up from curd. He should not salute his religiously wedded wife. at night he should eat till he is fully satisfied (i.e. till his belly is full). He should not love (i.e. take interest in) the union of song, dance or instrumental music; he should wash his feet in (a vessel of) bell-metal. He should not wear a garment or shoes worn by another person. He should not eat from a broken pot; nor should he eat polluted food. He should not lie with wet feet; with his hands and mouth uncleaned after having eaten food he should not go anywhere. He should not eat while lying down; with his hands and mouth uncleaned after having eaten food, he should not touch his head. He should not praise a human being, nor should he condemn himself. He should not salute him who has risen (in life) nor should he talk about the defects of others. Having thus resorted to the householder's stage, he should go to (i.e. take to) the hermit's stage of life with his wife or when the wife is dead; and then he should detach himself (from the worldly existence).

63. The great Rāma, desiring the welfare of the world, listened to these and other practices narrated by the sages at that time.

CHAPTER TEN

Rāma Appoints Śatrughna as the Protector of the Horse

Śeṣa said:

1-2. While Rāma was thus listening to religious duties (from sages) the spring season in which beginning of very great rites is made, set in. Seeing that season (had set in), the intelligent Vasiṣṭha, born from the pitcher, said to the great king Rāma, what was proper.

Vasiṣṭha said:

3-8. O Rāmacandra of mighty arms, for you the time when the horse fully honoured is let loose for the sacrifice, has come. Make preparations for it. Invite the best brāhmaṇas. May the lord worship the brāhmaṇas properly. May he give gifts that have come up to his mind (i.e. desired by him) to the helpless, blind and the miserable according to the proper rite after having worshipped and honoured them. Initiated along with the golden (image of your) wife, sleeping on the ground, being restrained, and avoiding excellent enjoyments, keeping the deer's horn on the waist, wearing a girdle, deer-hide, and a staff, you should make preparations for the (horse-sacrifice) with (all) the (required) things.

Hearing these significant and apt words of Vasiṣṭha, the intelligent (Rāma) spoke to Lakṣmaṇa words rich with various meanings.

Śrī Rāma said:

9. O Lakṣmaṇa, listen to my words (instructions); and having listened to them, quickly carry them out. Carefully bring a horse proper for the rite of the horse-sacrifice.

Śeṣa said:

10. Having heard the words of the lord of Raghus, Lakṣmaṇa, the conqueror of (his) enemies, said these words, describing (the horse) variously, to the commander-in-chief of the army.

Lakṣmaṇa said:

11-15. O hero, listen to these very sweet words of (i.e. uttered by) me; and having heard them, quickly carry them out according to the order of Rāma whose feet are rubbed by the crowns decorating the heads of the kings. Keep ready the army whose divisions are active due to the strength of the strong wind (generated) by the destroyer (of the universe), and having good chariots, elephants, foot-soldiers and good horsemen. Keep ready horses whose speed is like that of the wind, and whose plantings of their feet (i.e. steps) are charming like the rows of ripples, and which are mounted upon by good horsemen, holding many weapons and striking the enemy's army. Observe the elephants resembling mountains, which are (mounted upon) by the brave riders having darts and lances in their hands and having missiles, which exude profuse rut, which are intoxicated and are full of (i.e. have on them) all weapons and missiles. Let the groups of the charioteers take my chariots shining with extensive, large wealth, being yoked with horses having the speed of the wind, reminding (one) of the destruction of various foes, and with their topmost parts full with weapons and missiles. Let hundreds of foot-soldiers, having best weapons in their hands, exerting themselves in protecting the horse fit for the horse sacrifice, come to me.

16-30. Having heard these words of that magnanimous Lakṣmaṇa, the commander-in-chief Kālajit by name, made the (horse) ready. The horse adorned with ten stars, endowed with the charm of fine down, having faultless pearls round his neck, so also a gem round the extensive neck, having spotless beauty on the face, and blackish brightness on the ears, and with the mass of his reins held (by the commander-in-chief) with his hand, shone (there). The horse, with his face shining with (strips resembling) the digits (of the moon), adorned with bright gems, and beautified with necklaces of pearls, went out. At that time the lordly horse decorated with a white umbrella, adorned with a white chowrie, with his body surrounded (i.e. covered) by great loveliness, went out. Soldiers in front, in the midst, and in the rear, served him, as formerly gods waited upon Viṣṇu who deserved to be honoured. Then having called the entire army, very much crowded with hosts of elephants, horses, chariots and foot-soldiers, he issued orders to it. Then the noise produced by the army that had collected (there), was heard. Then in that excellent city there was (heard) the sound of the kettle-drums. Due to the great agreeable and sharp sound of the heroes the peaks of mountains trembled and palaces shook. O king, there was a big sound of the perplexed horses. The earth as it were, moved, when it sounded by the impact of the wheels of chariots. The earth was, all around, blocked up with the herds of elephants that were moving (along it). Dust moved there, and it screened the people (there). The great army full of men, being impelled by the commander-in-chief named Kālajit, moved out, covering the sun with its umbrellas. The best foot-soldiers, causing the battle-flurry, and ready for Rāma's (horse-)sacrifice, joyfully set out. All those (soldiers) having fragrant unguent of musk applied to their bodies, with their heads adorned with pure garlands of flowers, with their bodies adorned with the decorations of crowns and bracelets, and impelled by the king, set out. In this way, the excellent soldiers, holding bows, holding nooses and holding swords, and of loud steps, went to the great king. Thus the horse, marked for the sacrifice, scratching the ground with his hoofs, jumping in the sky (i.e. in the air), slowly reached the (sacrificial) hall.

31-42a. With his mind highly pleased on seeing the horse that had come (there), Rāma moved Vasiṣṭha to perform the (necessary) rite. Vasiṣṭha called Rāma along with (the image of) his wife made of gold, and made him perform the rite that would remove (the sin of) killing a brāhmaṇa. Rāma, the conqueror of his enemies' cities, practising the vow of celibacy, and holding a deer-horn got done that rite (through the brāhmaṇas). For the performance of the sacrifice he commenced (constructing) a basis furnished with a hall. The intelligent sage Vasiṣṭha, the old preceptor of Rāma's family, who was conversant with the Vedic concepts, became the preceptor there (i.e. at that sacrifice). Agastya, the treasure of penance, acting as the Brahmā-priest, performed the duties of that priest. The sage Vālmīki was the Adhvaryu-priest, and (the sage) Kaṇva (acted as) the doorkeeper. There were eight gates (to the hall) which were auspicious with ornamental arches. O brāhmaṇa, at each gate two brāhmaṇas, knowing the sacred hymns (were placed). At the eastern gate (were posted) the two best sages named Devala and Asita. At the southern gate (stood) the two great treasures of penance, viz. Kaśyapa and Atri. At the western gate (were) the two best (sages) Jātūkarṇya and Jābāli. At the northern gate (remained) the two ascetics—the two sages—Dvita and Ekata. O brāhmaṇa, having thus made the arrangement at the gates, Vasiṣṭha, born from a pitcher, started worshipping the best horse. Women whose husbands were alive, who were adorned with (beautiful) garments and ornaments, started worshipping the best horse with turmeric, sacred rice grains, sandal etc., O brāhmaṇa. Then after having worshipped him, they waved lights before him and offered incense of agaru. Then by the order of the brāhmaṇa (viz. Vasiṣṭha), the courtezans offered him wishes for prosperity.

42b-54. After having worshipped him like this, he tied a note, bright and fashioned of gold purified with fire, on his spotless forehead to which sandal was applied, which was very fragrant with saffron etc., and which was all beautiful. There (i.e. in the note) he wrote the bright valour and power of Daśaratha's son (Rāma): "The magnanimous Rāma, the crest-jewel of all heroes, the remover of the pride of the heroes of their power, and the descendant of Raghu, is the son of him who was the banner of the solar family, who was a great archer and a teacher initiating (pupils) in archery, and whom all gods along with demons saluted with (i.e. by bowing down) their heads having gems (on them). Rāma's mother is the one born from the womb of the wife of the king of Kośala. Rāma, his (i.e. Daśaratha's) son, who was the gem born from her womb, who is fearful to his enemies, who is well instructed by the brāhmaṇa (Vasiṣṭha), is performing a horse-sacrifice to remove the sin due to his having killed the best brāhmaṇa named Rāvaṇa. (For that sacrifice) he has let loose this excellent horse, best among horses and well-protected by the moats (in the form) of great army surrounding him. The protector of the horse is Rāma's brother, Śatrughna, who had killed (the demon named) Lavaṇa, and who is accompanied by the multitude of the army (consisting of) elephants, horses, chariots and foot-soldiers. Those kings who, through the pride of their strength, have the jealous anger (as): 'We are great archers, we are brave, we are mighty', should capture with force the horse adorned with jewelled necklaces, having the speed of the mind, going at will, (capable of) moving everywhere, and very bright. From them Rāma's brother Śatrughna will easily free him with points of arrows (i.e. pointed arrows) whetted on grindstones and discharged from his bow." The greatest sage wrote such and other things (in the note) and then let loose the horse with his glory shining due to the power of the arms of Rāma, the treasure of beauty, being extremely swift and having the speed of the wind, and having a special property of moving in the nether world and on the earth.

55-74. Rāma, the best among the wielders of weapons ordered Śatrughna: "Go after the horse moving freely for protecting him. O Śatrughna go along the path of the horse. May good fortune attend upon you. O you who torment your enemies, may your arms conquer the enemies. O brave one, those warriors who fight with you, should be warded off by you. On this great earth, you, united with your hosts of virtues, protect the horse. You should not kill those who are asleep, who have fled, who have lost their garments, who are very much frightened, who are polite, who have done good deeds, by doing which (i.e. when you do like this) they will approve of (your) deed. O Śatrughna, you who desire (to have) religious merit, should not kill those who are without (i.e. who have lost their) chariots, who are afflicted with fear, and who say (to you): 'We belong to you.' He who would kill him who is humble, who is mad, who is asleep, who is frustrated, who is affected by fear, and who says: 'I belong to you', goes to a mean position. You who are full of all virtues, should not long for others' wealth, or for other man's wife; do not show interest in a mean person. O you conqueror in a battle, do not first strike the old (i.e. do not strike the old before they strike you). Being endowed with compassion, do not violate (the rule of) worshipping the venerable. Salute a cow and a brāhmaṇa, and a devotee of Viṣṇu possessing righteousness. Wherever you go after saluting (these), you will obtain success. Viṣṇu is the lord of all, is the witness (observing everything), and possesses a body that occupies everything. O you of mighty arms, O you descendant of Raghu, they who belong to him (i.e. Viṣṇu), who move in his form, who remember Viṣṇu remaining in the hearts of all, should be regarded as having a form similar to that of Viṣṇu. Those devotees of Viṣṇu for whom there is none that belongs to them, none that is a stranger, and for whom the enemy is like a friend, purify a sinner in a moment. They, to whom the Bhāgavata (Purāṇa) is dear, to whom the brāhmaṇas are dear, are sent here (i.e. to this world) from Vaikuṇṭha for purifying the world. Even that cāṇḍāla in whose mouth there is

Viṣṇu's name, in whose heart there is the ancient Viṣṇu, and in whose belly there is the offering of eatables presented to Viṣṇu, is dear to Viṣṇu. Salute them that are here, to whom the Vedas are dear and not the happiness due to the worldly existence, and who are devoted to their own way of life. There is no difference between Śiva and Viṣṇu; so also between Śiva (or Viṣṇu) and Brahmā. I carry (on my body) the dust particles of their feet, which are pure and which destroy sins. Those men, for whom Pārvatī, Gaṅgā, Mahālakṣmī, do not exist separately, should, all of them, be looked upon as having come here (i.e. to this world) from heaven. He who, in order to please Viṣṇu, protects him who has sought his refuge, and gives respect and makes presents according to his capacity, should be known as the best devotee of Viṣṇu. He who is devoted to the pair of feet of him (the utterance of) whose name quickly burns the heaps of great sins, is the devotee of Viṣṇu. By saluting those whose senses are controlled, whose mind also thinks of Viṣṇu (only), a man should purify (himself) from birth to death. Abandoning another man's wife like a sword, be the ground of the ornament of victory and welfare. Thus following my command, you will obtain the highest position and a praiseworthy good contact (with the highest Lord)."

CHAPTER ELEVEN

The Aśvamedha Horse Is Let Loose

Śeṣa said:

1-3. Having thus ordered (Śatrughna), the glorious Rāma, the tormentor of his enemies, looked at the heroes and spoke to them with (i.e. using) good words: "Protecting from the rear my brother Śatrughna, protecting the horse, and obeying his orders, who would vanquish, with his multitudes of missiles, all the heroes that would come (to fight) the chief one (i.e. Śatrughna), let him spreading his very great fame on the earth take up the sword of (i.e. offered by) me."

4-9. When Rāma spoke like this, Puṣkala, the son of Bharata, took that sword from the lotus-like hand of the king of the Raghu-family. "O lord, O master, being ready, holding all weapons and missiles and a bow and arrows, I shall go, guarding everyday, Śatrughna's rear. Today the entire earth will be conquered due to your valour. O very intelligent Rāmacandra, these (soldiers) are (just) a means. By your grace I am capable of warding off the entire (army of) gods, demons and human beings, (if it) approaches (us) to fight (with us). The lord will know everything on seeing my valour. To protect Śatrughna from the rear, here I go." Praising Bharata's son, who was speaking like this, and approving of (his words), the lord Viṣṇu (i.e. Rāma) praised all the chief heroes among the monkeys, led by (Hanūmat) born from the Wind.

10-13. (He said): "O great hero Hanūmat, carefully listen to my words. Due to your favour I obtained this kingdom free from trouble. To bring about my union with Sītā, you crossed the ocean. O monkey, O lord of monkeys, I know all your adventures. Being, by my command, the guardian of my army, (please) go. You should protect Śatrughna, my brother, as (you protected) me. O you very intelligent one, you have to enlighten my brother Śatrughna whenever he has confusion of mind."

14-18. Hearing the great (i.e. important) words of the intelligent Rāmacandra, he accepted them with (i.e. by bowing) his head, and saluted him. Then the great king (i.e. Rāma) instructed Jāmbavanta, the lord of the monkeys, and the most lustrous among them, to serve Raghunātha (i.e. Śatrughna). (He said:) "(All of) you like Aṅgada, Gavaya, Mainda, so also the monkey Dadhimukha, Sugrīva—the king of the monkeys, the two monkeys viz. Śatavali and Akṣika, (so also) Nīla, Nala, having the mind's speed and a master born from the body of a monkey, should be ready. All of you, being adorned with elephants, good horses, with armours as ornaments made of gold, with helmets, should go quickly."

Śeṣa said:

19. Then having called the good minister Sumantra, Rāma, shining with strength and power said to him: "O chief of the

ministers, say, which men, capable of protecting the horse should be employed now?"

20-33. Hearing the words spoken by him (i.e. Rāma), he, the killer of the enemy's heroes said: "O Raghunātha, listen to (the names of) the nine powerful kings, who have assembled here, who are archers, who are very learned, who are proficient in (the use of) all weapons and missiles, and who (therefore,) are capable of protecting the horse. (They are:) Pratāpāgrya, Nīlaratna, so also king Lakṣmīnidhi, Riputāpa, Ugrahaya, and king Śastravid also. This Nīlaratna is a distinguished person; Mahāvīra, Rathāgraṇī (are also there). He, the fearless one, would alone protect a lakh (of soldiers) and would fight with a lakh of soldiers. Let him go with (an army consisting of) ten akṣauhiṇīs furnished with armours, and with my arms raised (to bless him). This Pratāpāgrya is one who destroyed the pride of his enemy. Best among those who know (the employment of) all missiles, he discharges the arrows with (both) the right and the left hands. Let this Daṇḍabhṛt, who is young and who is ready to destroy the enemy, and who holds a bow, go with (the army consisting of) twenty akṣauhiṇīs for the protection of the horse. In the same way, let this best king Lakṣmīnidhi who, having propitiated Indra studied (the employment of) missiles, go (with Śatrughna). He knows the employment and discharge of the missiles like Brahmāstra, Pāśupatyāstra, Garuḍa, and the one called Nāga, (so also) Mayūra, Nakula, Raudra, Vaiṣṇava, the one called Megha, Vajra, the one named Parvata, so also the one called Vāyavya. Let him, the crown (i.e. the best) of the brave, a hurricane to all the enemies, go with (soldiers numbering) one lakh from the army. Today let also this Riputāpa go, who is the foremost among archers, skilled in (the use of) all weapons and missiles, and a wild fire to the bamboos in the form of the enemies. Let him go with the army consisting of four divisions. Let these mighty kings hold on their heads (i.e. obey) the order of Śatrughna. This great king Ugrāśva also knows (the use of) weapons. Let all of them, quite ready, go as the protectors of your horse."

34-36. Having heard these words of the minister, he was delighted and ordered those soldiers mentioned by Sumantra. They, desiring to wage war for a long time, and maddened after it, were glad on receiving Raghunātha's (i.e. Rāma's) order.

Ready with armours etc., and with the movements of the weapons and missiles, they, impelled by Sītā's husband, went in the company of Śatrughna.

Śeṣa said:

37-46. Then, as told by the sage (Vasiṣṭha), Rāma honoured all the preceptors and sages (by giving them) presents as told (by Vasiṣṭha). To the preceptor Rāma gave an elephant sixty years old, a horse having the mind's speed and adorned with golden necklaces, a golden chariot which was adorned with gems and jewels, to which four horses were yoked, and which was furnished with all necessary equipment. (He also gave him) a lakh of gems, and pearls measuring a hundred tulās (each of which is equal to 100 palas), a thousand tulās of bright lustre of corals, a very rich village crowded with many kinds of people, producing various kinds of crops, having many temples. In the same way he gave (presents) to the Brahmā-priest and to the Adhvaryu-priest. The best of the Raghus, having given profuse gifts to the priests, saluted them. Being honoured, they (said) with various words and blessings: "O Rāmacandra, the descendant of Raghu, O great king, live long." The great one (i.e. Rāma) gave the gifts of maidens, of land, of elephants, so also of horses, of gold, of sesamum with pearls, of food, water, and the excellent gift of fearlessness, so also all the gifts of gems, to brāhmaṇas. Give, (again and again) give wealth; do not say 'No' to anyone. One should give food, one should give food endowed with all pleasures.

47-49. Thus the sacrifice, accompanied by presents, full of the brāhmaṇas and with all auspicious rites, of the intelligent Rāma, proceeded. Then the younger brother of Rāma (viz. Śatrughna) went to his mother, saluted her (and said to her): "O auspicious one, give me leave; I am going just for the protection of the horse. With your grace, I, having conquered the group of the enemies, shall come (back) endowed with charm and accompanied by great kings and the best horse (let loose for the sacrifice)."

The mother said:

50-54. O (my) son, O great hero, go; may your journey be happy. O you of a good mind, having conquered all the hosts of your enemies come (back). Take care of Puṣkala, the best among those who know the course of conduct, the mighty son of your brother, (and) still a child, with (i.e. indulging in) sport. O son, if you come (back), with Puṣkala, and endowed with good fortune, I shall be glad. Otherwise I shall be unhappy.

He said to his mother who was speaking like this: "Remembering the pair of your feet, I shall have good fortune. O auspicious one, having taken care of Puṣkala like my own body, and doing (things) befitting my name, I shall come back happily."

55-58. Speaking thus, the hero went to see the great Rāma dressed for the sacrifice and seated with the best sages in the sacrificial hall. The intelligent hero endowed with all grace, said: "O Rāma, give me leave to protect the horse." Raghunātha (i.e. Rāma) too hearing those words, said: "God bless you. Do not kill a child, a woman, a mad person or one without a weapon." Then Janaka's son and Sītā's brother Lakṣmīnidhi, having smiled and having slightly moved his eyes said to Rāma:

Lakṣmīnidhi said:

59-64. O mighty-armed Rāmacandra, devoted to all righteous ways, instruct Śatrughna in such a way that he would be extraordinary. Doing a deed which is befitting his family, and doing what his elder brother had done, he would go to the highest place endowed with lustre and power. O great king, you said: 'One should not belittle a brāhmaṇa;' (but) your father had killed a brāhmaṇa, greatly devoted to his father. You also performed a deed very much abhorred in the world, (since) you had certainly killed a woman who should not have been killed. (And) O great king, the great valourous deed, viz. cutting off the ears of the demoness (Śūrpaṇakhā), which was done by his elder brother (Lakṣmaṇa) was not done by any one else. By your instruction Śatrughna will do the same thing. If, O lord, he would do like that, it would be unbecoming to the family.

65-71. To him, who was speaking like this, Rāma skilled in all kinds of speech, smiled, and spoke with a voice deep like that of a cloud: "May the tranquil meditating saints hear, who look equally upon pleasure and pain and who know such things as how to cross fully this (ocean of) mundane existence which is difficult to cross. Those who are brave, who are great archers, who are skilled in (the use of) all weapons and missiles (alone) know the calling of war, and not (people) like you. Those who torment others and those who go astray, should be killed by kings who desire the good of all the people." Hearing these words spoken by the subduer of enemies (i.e. by Rāma) all those members of the assembly smiled. (Then Vasiṣṭha) born from the pitcher, let loose the horse that was worshipped and well adorned. Uttering this hymn, and touching the horse with the tip of his hand, Vasiṣṭha, born from a pitcher, let loose the horse, with a desire for victory: "O horse, move sportively over the entire earth. Since you are let loose for the (horse-) sacrifice, come back quickly."

72-75. The horse, that was let loose, and that was surrounded by all warriors skilled in (the use of) all weapons and missiles, went with the speed of wind towards the eastern direction. The entire army shaking the earth moved on. Even Śeṣa held the earth with his hood slightly bent. The quarters were all around bright. The earth was full of beauty. Breezes blew gently from behind Śatrughna. The right arm of Śatrughna who was ready for the march, throbbed indicating (something) auspicious and leading to victory.

76-83. Puṣkala (the son of Bharata) entered his charming house which was rich with white balconies, and which had a jewelled quadrangular open shed in the middle of its courtyard. There he saw his wife who was greatly devoted to her husband, who was delighted when he was partially seen and who was eager to see her husband. She was chewing piper-betal (mixed) with camphor with her mouth resembling a lotus. Her very beautiful nose was like a sharp blade (of a sword). There were fine bracelets (worn) on her arms resembling lotus-stalks. Her excellent breasts were like the kapittha fruits. Her round hips were charming due to the knot of the wearing garment. Her very delicate feet had (worn) anklets. She saw her good husband. Having embraced his dear wife, speaking in a faltering tone, and with her body filled with the embrace (pressing) her breasts, he said: "O auspicious lady, by Rāma's order I having a chariot and looking after the sacrificial horse, am going guarding the rear of Śatrughna. You should serve my mothers by gently rubbing their feet etc., eating (the food) left over by them and showing great regard for doing (things told) by them. All the auspicious ladies, devoted to their husbands, like Lopāmudrā, should not be insulted by you, O timid one. They are adorned by the strength of their own penance."

CHAPTER TWELVE

Ahicchatrā City, King Sumada and Kāma

Śeṣa said :

1-14. She, smiling a little and looking at him with great love, spoke in a faltering voice to her husband who had spoken thus: "O lord, may you be victorious everywhere in battles (i.e. in every battle). You should obey Śatrughna's order in such a way that the horse would be protected. Always remember (this) your servant, always following your foot (steps). O lord, my mind never goes away from you to any other (person). O dear one, you should never think of me in a great battle. When I am (lurking) in your heart, victory in the battle is doubtful. O you lotus-eyed one, you should act in such a way that Urmilā and others will not laugh at me and clap their hands on seeing me (and say:) 'This is the wife of the great coward, running away in (i.e. from) the battle. When the cowards fight, where can there be an opportunity for the brave? O you of mighty arms, act, while protecting Rāma's horse, in such a way that the wives of my brothers-in-law will not loudly laugh (at me). You are everywhere a warrior first. The ones who are behind you, and the mighty enemies should be made deaf with the twang of your bow (-string). The enemy's army should be speedily confused with fear due to the dread of the sword in your raised hand. By conquering your enemies you should adorn this great family. O lord, O you of mighty arms, go; may you have good fortune here (i.e. in your undertaking). Quickly take this bow which is adorned with a great string (and with a great virtue), and hearing the roar of which the host of the enemies becomes greatly frightened. O hero, tie up these two quivers which are full with tips of arrows (i.e. pointed arrows) capable of killing crores of enemies, so that happiness will take place. Put this armour on your body which is handsome like thunder-bolt and so is strong enough to remove darkness. O dear one, put on your crest (i.e. head) this beautiful helmet. Put on these two bright ear-rings decorated with jewels and gems."

15. Looking at the hero's daughter (i.e. brave lady) who spoke spotless words in this way, and looking at her body with his lotus-like eyes, he, the conqueror of enemies, capable of fighting, and extremely wise one, who had become extremely joyful, said:

Puṣkala said :

16-18. O dear one, I shall do all that you tell me. O Kāntimatī, you will have the longed-for fame as the wife of a hero."

Saying so the mighty one took all (the things like) the excellent armour and helmet, the bow, the two quivers and the sword given by (his wife) Kāntimatī. Having put on all those (things), the great hero endowed with great charm, and skilled in (the use of) all weapons and missiles, looked extremely handsome.

19-23a. That chaste wife Kāntimatī repeatedly waved lights in front of him who was endowed with the beauty of the missiles and weapons, adorned with a garland of (i.e. fit for) a hero and smeared with saffron, aguru (sandal), musk, sandal etc. and adorned up to his knees with garlands of various flowers. Having repeatedly waved lights before him and with tears trickling from her unsteady eyes, she embraced her husband. Having closely embraced her for a long time, he comforted her: "O Kāntimatī, wife of a hero, do not experience (grief due to) separation from me. O you beautiful and chaste lady, here I am near you."

23b-24. Speaking thus to his wife, he got into the excellent chariot. That lady (Kāntimatī), greatly devoted to her husband, looked with eyes, void of winking, at her best husband, who was going (away from her).

25-28. He (then) went to see his father and his mother beside herself with love. Going to the father and mother, he joyfully saluted them with his head (bent down). The mother, having embraced her son, put him on her lap; (and) shedding tears profusely, said to him: "May it be well with you!" He said to his father Bharata: "The great Rāma is performing the (horse-) sacrifice. The magnanimous Lakṣmaṇa and you have to take care of him." Commanded with joyful words by his mother and father, he went to Śatrughna's army adorned with great heroes.

29-31. The best horse (let loose) for the great sacrifice of (Rāma), the ornament of (the) Raghu (-family), surrounded by the brave warriors occupying chariots, foot-soldiers, good horses and horsemen gladly moved (ahead). Endowed with all charm, he went to the Pāñcāla country, the Kuru country, Uttara-kuru, Daśārṇa and Śrī Viśāla countries. Everywhere hearing about the entire glory of Rāma, which brought about the protection of his devotees by killing the demon Rāvaṇa (he went ahead).

32-35a. Rāma who also commenced the rite like the horse-sacrifice, spread his fame in the world and protected the people from fear. The great excellent Śatrughna gave them necklaces, various gems, great wealth and dwellings. Rāma's excellent minister, bright and proficient in all branches of knowledge, Sumati by name, followed Śatrughna. The great hero went with him to many villages and countries.

35b-38. Due to Rāma's valour, nobody snatched the horse. Many lords of countries who were very mighty and brave, who were accompanied by elephants, horses, chariots, foot-soldiers—(i.e. the army with) four divisions—took with them much wealth along with pearls and rubies, and again and again saluted Śatrughna who had come for the protection of the earth. (They said to Śatrughna:) "O descendant of Raghu, all this—this kingdom, this wealth, along with my sons, beasts and relatives—belongs to Rāmacandra, and not to me."

39. Having heard these (words) uttered by them, Śatrughna, the killer of the enemy's warriors, having made them recognize his command there, went with them along the path.

40-52. O brāhmaṇa, in this way gradually Śatrughna along with the horse reached Ahicchatrā city which was crowded with various people, which was full of brāhmaṇas and the twice-born (i.e. kṣatriyas and vaiśyas), which was decorated with different gems, which was adorned with golden and crystal mansions and town-gates, where, in all mansions, were seen ladies who had lotus-like faces, who excelled Rambhā (in beauty), and who were endowed with grace; where the heroes, graceful with good conduct, enjoying all pleasures like the followers of Kubera, with bows in their hands, proficient in taking aim with an arrow, delighted (their) king named Sumada. The lord (i.e. Śatrughna), saw, from a distance, the city like this. In its vicinity was a park, endowed with loveliness. Śatrughna, the killer of his enemy's soldiers, saw (that park) which appeared beautiful with punnāga, nāgacampa, tilaka, devadāru, aśoka, pāṭala, cūta (i.e. mango), mandāra, kovidāraka, āmra, jambu, kadamba, priyāla, and panasa (trees); so also with śāla, tāla, tamāla, mallikā, jāti, yūthi, nīpa, kadamba, bakula, campaka, madana and other trees. The horse entered that (park) adorned with tamāla, tāla and other (trees). The hero (i.e. Śatrughna), whose lotus-like feet were served by archers, just went after him. There he saw a wonderfully constructed temple, which was adorned with sapphires, lapis lazuli and emeralds, which was fit to be enjoyed by gods, which resembled the peak of the Kailāsa (mountain), which was adorned with golden pillars, and which was the best among temples. Having seen that excellent temple, Rāma's brother asked Sumati, his minister, the best among speakers:

Śatrughna said :

53. O best minister, tell (me), what this is; of what deity it is the abode; which deity is worshipped here; and for what purpose the deity has stayed here, O sinless one.

54-59. Having heard this, the omniscient minister said: "O hero, listen attentively to the full and proper (account). Know this to be the great seat, giving happiness to all, of Kāmākṣā, by seeing whom, O lord of beings, everything is secured, (and) by praising and saluting whom gods and demons have obtained all (their) glory. She is the giver of (the four goods of human life, viz.) Dharma, Artha, Kāma and Mokṣa; she is kind to her devotees. She, who was formerly implored by Sumada, the king of Ahicchatrā, and who removes the misery of her devotees, lives here and does everything (for her devotees). O Śatrughna, O you crest-jewel of all heroes, salute her. Having saluted her, you will quickly obtain the purity which is difficult to be got by gods and demons." Having heard those words of (i.e. uttered by) him, Śatrughna, the tormentor of his enemies, the best among men, asked (him) the entire account of men, asked (him) the entire account of Bhavānī.

Śatrughna said :

60-61. Who is (this) king Sumada? Which penance did he practise due to which the mother of all the worlds, that dwells here, is pleased? O great minister, tell me all that which is full of diverse things. O you very intelligent one, since you know it correctly, therefore tell it to me.

Sumati said :

62-70. (There is) the pure mountain Hemakūṭa which is adorned by all gods. There is a pure, holy place, very much frequented by hosts of sages. Sumada whose mother, father and subjects were killed by all his feudatory kings, his enemies, went to that (mountain) for (practising) penance. With his sight fixed on the tip of his nose, and remembering mentally the mother of the worlds, he, (standing) on one foot, meditated for three years. Eating dry leaves for three years, he practised very severe penance, very difficult to practise. For three years he plunged himself (i.e. remained)in water in the cold season. In summer he practised (the vow of) the five fires; and in rainy season he remained looking up to the clouds. The wise one, restraining the breath in his heart and remembering Bhavānī, did not look at anything (else) for three years. When the twelfth year passed, Indra, seeing his great penance, very much contemplated in his mind, and through fear, vied with him. He (then) ordered Cupid surrounded by his followers, properly accompanied by celestial nymphs, and eager for the victory of Brahmā, Indra etc.: "O Cupid, O friend, O you infatuating one, go and do what is agreeable to me. Act in such a way that there would be an obstacle in the penance of (i.e. being practised by) Sumada."

71. Hearing these important words of Indra, the lord (i.e. Kāma) himself, who was very proud of conquering everything, spoke, O descendant of Raghu:

Kāma said :

72-74. O lord, who is this Sumada? And how little is his penance? I disturb the penance of (even) Brahmā and others;

then what need I say of him? Formerly the Moon, completely disturbed by the power of my arrows, went to Tārā.[1] You too went to Ahalyā, and Viśvāmitra to Menakā. O lord of gods, when I, (your) servant, am (here), do not be worried. This I go to Sumada. O respectable one, look after the gods.

75-86. Having said so, god Cupid, accompanied by his friend Spring and groups of celestial nymphs went to Hemakūṭa mountain. There Spring quickly made all trees full of flowers and fruits and noisy with cuckoos and rows of bees. Very cool breezes, resorting to (i.e. coming from) the southern quarter, and full of (the fragrance of) the flowers of cloves (growing on) the bank of the Kṛtāmala river, were blowing. When the forest was like this, the celestial nymph named Rambhā, surrounded by her friends, came near Sumada. She who was proficient in playing upon many musical instruments like tabor, drum, and adorned with a (sweet) voice like that of a kinnara, started singing. Then on hearing her music, on seeing (that) charming Spring, and (on hearing) the charming notes of cuckoos, the wise king turned his eyes. Then seeing the king awakened (i.e. who had opened his eyes), Cupid, having flowers as his weapons, hastened, and, O innocent one, quickly made ready his bow from behind him. One celestial nymph with bud-like eyes shampooed the king's feet. Another nymph cast glances at him. Another one made (coquettish) gestures. Thus crowded by the celestial nymphs and with his mind afflicted by the passion of love, the intelligent one, the crest-jewel (i.e. the best) of those who have restrained their senses, thought: 'These are the excellent celestial nymphs, all sent by Indra, and creating an obstacle in my penance; they will do exactly (as they are ordered by Indra).' Thinking like this, he who was practising excellent penance, said to those excellent females: "Who are you? Where do you stay? What do you desire? A great miracle has taken place that you are seen. You who are difficult to be obtained by penance, have come (here) due to my penance."

1. Tārā—Name of the wife of Bṛhaspati, the preceptor of gods. She was on one occasion carried off by Soma (the Moon) who refused to deliver her up to her husband when demanded. A fierce contest then ensued and Brahmā had at last to compel Soma to restore her to her husband. Tārā gave birth to a son named Budha who became the ancestor of the Lunar race of kings.

CHAPTER THIRTEEN

Śatrughna Enters Ahicchatrā City

Śeṣa said:

1-8. Hearing these words of Sumada, the treasure of penance, the army of Cupid, i.e. the celestial nymphs like Rambhā, joyfully said to him: "O dear one, all of us, beautiful damsels, have come to you due to your austerities. Enjoy the wealth of our youth, and give up the fruit of your penance. This is the pleasing Ghṛtācī, having a body like campaka, and charming due to the fragrance of camphor. You may enjoy the nectar from her mouth. O illustrious one, O dear one, quickly enjoy her who has charming gestures, whose body is attractive, whose breasts are compact and large, who has come (to you) as a result of your severe penance; and give up all your unhappiness. Firmly embrace me who am adorned with priceless ornaments, whose breasts are graced with the garland of mandara flowers, and who am expert in thinking about many tales about sexual union. Drink the nectar coming out from my mouth; enjoy, having reached the peak of Sumeru resorted to by means of great religious merit, pleasures—the fruit of your good penance. Let Tilottamā adorned with youth and beauty, hold on your head two good chowries—removing heat—like two streams of Gaṅgā with a constant flow, O most handsome one. O you, listen to the charming account of Cupid; drink the nectar longed for by the hosts of gods etc.; O lord, having, along with excellent damsels, reached the garden called Nandana, amuse yourself (there)."

9-10. Hearing these words spoken by them, the very intelligent king thought: 'Wherefrom have they come? By means of my penance I have created these celestial damsels. (But) this has become an impediment. What should I do now?' The very intelligent king Sumada who was thus anxious, thinking in his mind (i.e. to himself), spoke to the celestial damsels:

11-14. "You remain in my mind in the form of the mother of the world. That whom I think of is also said to be of your form. The pleasures in heaven, which you described, are worthless and uncertain. My mistress, waited upon by me with devotion, will give me a boon. Due to her grace Brahmā reached Satyaloka and became great. She who puts an end to the miseries of her devotees, will give me everything. What is (the use of) Nandana? What is (the use of) the mountain well-adorned with gold? What is the use of nectar which is obtained with very little religious merit and which has given unhappiness to demons?"

15-16. Hearing these words of the king, Cupid struck him with various arrows, but could do nothing to him. The beautiful (celestial) damsels were unable to disturb his mind through glances, sounds of their anklets, embraces and through looking at him.

17. Having gone, as they had come, to Indra, they said: "The king is firm-minded." Hearing that, Indra was frightened (thinking that) his undertaking was fruitless.

18-22. Then (goddess) Ambikā, having seen the king who had conquered his senses, settled at her lotus-like feet, was extremely pleased and appeared before him. She, the beautiful one, was seated on the back of a lion; the excellent one had held (in her hands) nooses and goads; the mother, purifying those who purify the world, had a bow and arrows (in her hands). The intelligent one (i.e. king Sumada), having seen the mother lustrous like crores of suns, and holding a bow, arrows and hooks, was delighted. Having many times saluted by (bending down) his head the mother obtained through devotion, smiling, and repeatedly touching his body with her hand, the very intelligent king, with the functions of his mind full of devotion and with his body adorned with horripilation, praised her with a faltering voice:

23-30. "O goddess, O great goddess, victory to you, who alone are waited upon by the hosts of devotees, and O innocent one, you whose pair of feet is worshipped by the lords of gods like Brahmā, Rudra. O mother, this (world consisting of) the mobile and the immobile, is put in motion by a portion of you. All that does not exist without you. O auspicious mother, I salute you. The earth is settled by you through the strength of your prop. (So) it, adorned with mountains, rivers, gardens, quarter-elephants, does not shake. (Due to you) the sun, heating the earth with his sharp rays, shines in the sky; through your power he takes the water existing on the earth, and releases it (in the form of rain). Let the fire remaining within and without (you) cause happiness to the worlds due to your power, O great goddess, saluted by gods and demons. You are learning, you are the wonderful, divine power of Viṣṇu, who alone protects the world. O you fascinating one, through your own power you create this (world) and look after it. All gods obtain perfection from you and go to (i.e. secure) happiness. O you who bless (your devotees) with your grace, O you who are saluted (by them), O you, to whom your devotees are dear, look after me, protect me, O mother, who am your servant, and who am devoted to your feet, O you the ancestor of the great Puruṣa."

Śeṣa said:

31-33. The mother of the world, who was thus pleased, said to that devotee Sumada of an emaciated body: "Ask for an excellent boon." Hearing these words king Sumada who was extremely delighted, asked for his own kingdom which was (formerly) snatched away (from him) and the troublesome wicked persons in which were killed, and for inviolable devotion to the pair of feet of the great goddess, the devotion that would (cause) emancipation at the end of life and would help to cross the ocean of the mundane existence.

Kāmākṣā said:

34-44. O Sumada, get (back) your kingdom in which everywhere the troublesome persons were killed. Be one whose pair of the lotus-like feet is resorted to by gems of (i.e. excellent) women. O you called Sumada, may you not be defeated by your enemies. When Rāma, of great glory, will, after having killed Rāvaṇa, perform the horse-sacrifice, adorned with all requisites, and when his brother Śatrughna, the great hero and the killer of the enemies' soldiers will come here looking after the horse and surrounded by brave men, you will present to him your entire prosperous kingdom and wealth etc., will look after the horse, and will move everywhere on the earth along with your own warriors and pre-eminent archers, O you, very intelligent one. Then having saluted Rāma served by Brahmā, Indra and Śiva, you will obtain release difficult to be obtained by meditating saints having restraint as their means. I shall stay here till Rāma's horse comes here. After that, having emancipated you, I shall go to the highest position.

Saying so, the goddess, served by gods and demons, disappeared. Sumada too, having killed his enemies, became the king in Ahicchatrā. This king, though capable and possessing army and horses (or elephants), will not snatch your horse, (as) he is well instructed by (the goddess), the wonderful power (of the lord). O you omniscient one, having heard that the best sacrificial horse has come near the city, and (that) you also (have approached the city), the king named Sumada will now give everything to you, the very intelligent one, whose feet are served by great kings, due to the valour of the great king Rāmacandra.

Śeṣa said:

45-48. The intelligent, mighty and very glorious (Śatrughna), having heard this account of Sumada, said: 'Good, good' and was delighted. The lord of Ahicchatrā, surrounded by all his attendants and waited upon by many kṣatriyas, was happily seated in his assembly. Brāhmaṇas learned in the Vedas, and wealthy and prosperous vaiśyas waited upon king Sumada endowed with charm. The just and excellent brāhmaṇas blessed the king, the only protector of all the people, with Vedic learning and diversion.

49-51. At this time, someone came (there) and said to the king: "O you lord, I do not know whose horse, with a note (on his head) is (i.e. has come) near (the city)." Hearing that, he quickly sent a superior servant (i.e. officer): "Ascertain as to who the king is whose horse (has come) near my city." The servant having gone there and having ascertained from the beginning, reported it to the king, waited upon by great kṣatriyas.

52-54. The wise king who was everyday thinking about Rāma's horse, having heard (that he had come) ordered all people: "All my people who possess wealth and grains, should put up ornamental arches on their houses in the city. Let thousands of beautiful maidens, adorned with all ornaments, and mounted upon elephants, go forth (to great) Śatrughna."

55-57. Having ordered all like this the king himself surrounded by his sons, grandsons and queen went (to receive Śatrughna). Śatrughna, accompanied by many very great ministers, good warriors, saw the brave king named Sumada.

58-61. Then the great king, having come (there) joyfully saluted Śatrughna who was accompanied by elephants, foot-soldiers, the tormentors of enemies, and accompanied by horsemen, and horses that were adorned with brave soldiers and who was accompanied by heroes. (He said to Śatrughna:) "I am blessed, I am satisfied, my body is honoured. Quickly accept this kingdom, adorned with great kings, and well filled (i.e. furnished) with great wealth like large rubies and pearls. O lord, I have been waiting for a long time for the arrival of the horse. Everything that Kāmākṣā had told before, has now come about just as (she had told). See my city, and make the men (i.e. its citizens) blessed. O you younger brother of Rāma, O you very intelligent one, purify our entire family."

62-67. Saying so, he mounted (Śatrughna) on an elephant very bright like the moon, also (put up) Puṣkala (on the elephant), and he himself also mounted (upon the elephant). At that time, the sound of musical instruments like the kettle-drums, impelled by the great king Sumada, pervaded (the atmosphere). Maidens, employed by the lord (i.e. Sumada), having come to the great lord of kings viz. Śatrughna whose feet were waited upon by Indra and others, felicitated him with the heaps of pearls which were (held by them) in their hands. Having slowly come into the city, he who was joyfully glorified by people, reached the house that was decorated with ornamental arches etc. King Śatrughna, accompanied by the gem of the horse, graced by heroes, and led by king (Sumada) reached the house. Having honoured Rāma's younger brother with materials of worship etc. (Sumada) offered everything to the intelligent Rāmacandra.

CHAPTER FOURTEEN

The Cyavana Episode

Śeṣa said :

1. Then, the king, the best among men, longing to listen to the excellent account of Rāma, spoke to Śatrughna who was pleased with the reception.

Sumada said :

2-5. I hope Rāma who is the crest-jewel of the entire world, who has descended (on the earth) to protect his devotees, and who has favoured me, is happy. The people who with the cups of their eyes constantly drink the lotus in the form of Rāma's face and are delighted, are blessed in the city (of Ayodhyā). O you best among men, O you very intelligent one, my entire wealth and all my family, land etc. and my possessions are blessed. Formerly, Kāmākṣā, tender with kindness, showed favour to me. (She told me:) "With your family you will see the lotus-like face of Rāma."

6. When that hero, the best king Sumada spoke this, he told him all the exalted virtues of the lord of Raghus (i.e. Rāma).

7-11. Having stayed there for three nights, (Śatrughna) the younger brother of the lord of Raghus, and the highly intelligent one, decided to proceed further with the king. Then knowing that, Sumada, with the approval of the great king Śatrughna and of Puṣkala, quickly consecrated his son on the kingdom (i.e. consecrated his son as the king). The highly intelligent one gave garments, many jewels and various kinds of riches to the servants of Śatrughna. With his highly wise ministers, foot-soldiers, horses, elephants, good horses and crores of chariots he (i.e. Śatrughna) started to go (i.e. proceed). Śatrughna, having the valour of Raghunātha, then went smiling along the way with that Sumada, the holder of a bow (i.e. the archer).

12-15. The best horse after having reached the bank of Payoṣṇī went (further). All the warriors, the protectors of the horse, went after him. (Śatrughna) saw various hermitages of sages doing excellent penance. Everywhere he heard the excellent qualities of Raghunātha (being narrated by the sages). (The sages said:)

"Here goes the intelligent horse protected by Viṣṇu, so also repeatedly protected by monkeys devoted to Viṣṇu (i.e. Rāma), followed by excellent horses." The great lord (i.e. Śatrughna) hearing everywhere these words of (i.e. uttered by) the sages with feelings saturated with devotion (for Rāma), was pleased.

16-22. And he saw a holy hermitage crowded with people and (other) beings, removing by the sounds of Veda the entire inauspicious things (i.e. sins) of people that heard (the sounds of the Veda), purifying the entire atmosphere by means of the smoke of the perpetual domestic fire, and looking charming due to the sacrificial posts (put up) for the many sacrifices of (i.e. performed by) the excellent sages. There in that hermitage cows fit to be looked after, were looked after by a lion; in it the rats did not dig a hole through the fear of a cat; snakes constantly played with peacocks and mongooses. There (i.e. in the hermitage) elephants and lions, having become friends, always stay. The black antelopes (living) there showed interest in eating the rice growing wild, and being protected by groups of sages were not afraid of death. The cows there had udders like pitchers, and their bodies were like that of Nandinī (the daughter of the divine cow, Surabhi). They purified the earth with the dust raised by their feet (i.e. hoofs). Seeing the sages having sacred fuel fit for the religious rites in their lotus-like hands (Śatrughna said to) the all knowing minister of Rāma, viz. Sumati:

Śatrughna said :

23-25. O Sumati, of which sage is the place that appears before (us), that is resorted to by beings having no enmity (for one another), and is crowded with hosts of sages? I shall hear the account of the sages, and by means of their accounts and descriptions etc. I shall render my body pure.

Having heard this statement of the magnanimous Śatrughna, the minister of the intelligent Raghunātha (i.e. Rāma) told him:

Sumati said :

26-29. Know this to be Cyavana's hermitage adorned by great ascetics, crowded with beings free from enmity and full of the wives of the sages; and he who is the great sage (viz. Cyavana) obtained a portion of the oblation of the two physicians of gods (i.e. the Aśvins). He broke (down) the pride of Indra in the sacrifice of the Self-born (Brahmā). Nobody obtains the prowess of the great sage, rich with the power of penance and having the image of the Vedas.

(Śatrughna) Rāma's younger brother, having heard the things about the eminent Cyavana, asked everything including the breaking of Indra's pride (i.e. Indra's humiliation) etc.

Śatrughna said:

30. When did he receive the portion of the oblation of the two wonder-workers (i.e. the two Aśvins) in the rows of gods? What did the lord of gods do at the sacrifice performed by Brahmā?

Sumati said:

31-34. There was a famous sage named Bhṛgu in the family of Brahmā. Once in the evening he had gone (out) to collect sacred fuel. At that time a very strong demon, Damana (by name), came there and uttered these very fearful words: "Where is that so-called sage? Where is that innocent lady?" He, full of anger, repeatedly uttered these words. At that time, Fire, realising that danger was imminent from the demon, showed him the praiseworthy, pregnant wife of him (i.e. of Bhṛgu).

35-36. The demon snatched her who was crying like an osprey: "O Bhṛgu, protect me, O (my) lord, protect me; O (my) husband, O treasure of penance, protect me." The wicked one took her who was speaking like this and who was afflicted, and went out. He admonished that chaste (wife) of Bhṛgu with the strokes of (i.e. with abusive) words.

37-39. Then from her uterus the foetus of blazing eyes, afflicted with great fear, and as it were the fire born of (her) body, fell (out). He said: "O you of a wicked mind, do not go; be reduced to ashes quickly. Having touched the chaste lady, you will not obtain bliss." He, who was thus addressed, fell down with his body reduced to ashes. The mother, who was agitated, took the child and went to the hermitage (of her husband).

40-41. Bhṛgu, knowing all that was done by Fire, was full of anger, and cursed (him): "O you who gave a suggestion to the wicked enemy, be one who consumes everything." Then Fire who was (thus) cursed, was afflicted with grief and seized his feet. (He said to Bhṛgu:) "O lord, ocean of compassion, O you highly intelligent one, (please) favour me. I told a lie through fear, and not through malice against (my) preceptor (i.e. you). Therefore, O you crest-jewel of piety, be kind to me."

42. Then (Bhṛgu) favoured him. (He said:) "You will consume everything, (yet will be) pure." Thus the ascetic, wet with (i.e. soft due to) compassion, spoke to him.

43-45. The brāhmaṇa (i.e. Bhṛgu) who was very auspicious, who was pure, having darbhas in his hands, performed, according to the rule, the ceremony performed at the birth of a child, of the son that had fallen from the uterus. All the sages called him 'Cyavana' on account of his having fallen (from the uterus). Gradually he grew like the moon of the first night (of the month, waxing) in the bright half of (the month).

46-48. Surrounded by all his disciples who were endowed with the power of penance, he went to Revā, the only purifier of the world, to practise penance. The great one, having gone there, practised penance for a myriad of years. On his shoulders grew the kiṁśuka (trees) adorned with anthills. The eager deer, having come (to him) scratched (their bodies) against his body. Enveloped (i.e. engaged) in irresistible penance, he was aware of nothing.

49-56. Sometime lord Manu got ready for a pilgrimage. He, surrounded by a great army, went to Revā. There, having bathed in the great river, having gratified the manes and the deities, he gave gifts to brāhmaṇas to please Viṣṇu. His beautiful daughter (adorned) with ornaments of heated gold and accompanied by (her) friends, moved here and there in the forest. There she saw an anthill adorned with a great tree. She (also) saw some lustre, free from twinkling and winking (i.e. steadfast). Having gone there, she pierced it with small sticks. Seeing blood flowing (from it), the king's daughter was sad and extremely unhappy. Covered with the sin, she told about it neither to her mother, nor to her father. She, afflicted with fear, grieved to herself. O king, the earth quacked, and a meteor fell from the sky. All the directions became smoky, and the sun was surrounded by a halo. Then the king's horses perished, and many elephants died. Wealth, along with gems, perished; and there was feud among (the king's men) themselves.

57-59. Seeing that, the king (i.e. Manu) was afraid, and was slightly dejected. He asked his men. (He said:) "Somebody has wronged the sage?" Successively having come to know that act of his daughter, (and) being extremely unhappy, he went there with his army and horses. Having seen the treasure of penance endowed with great penance, he praised and pleased him (and said): "O best sage, be kind to me."

60-65. The best sage, having great penance, being pleased with him, said (to him): "Know that all that mischief is done by your daughter. O great king, your daughter burst (my) eyes. Profuse blood flew (out). (Though) aware of it, she did not say (anything) to you. Therefore, O great king, you should give her to me (i.e. in marriage) according to the proper rite. Then the calamity will cease. There is no doubt about it." Hearing that the king was grieved and gave his daughter, endowed with youth, beauty and good character, to the blind (sage). When the king gave the lotus-eyed daughter (in marriage to the sage), all the evil things caused by the sage's wrath, subsided. The king, grieved and full of compassion, having given his daughter to the sage, the treasure of penance, again went (back) to his city.

CHAPTER FIFTEEN

Cyavana's Penance and Enjoyments

Sumati said :

1-7. Then the sage went to his hermitage with Manu's daughter, his wife, endowed with yoga (abstraction), and with all sins destroyed was happy. That daughter of Manu, served, like her family-deity giving desired objects, her excellent husband who was blind, whose prowess was lost due to old age, and was excellent due to having intelligence like Viṣṇu. She who knew (his) internal thoughts, served her dear husband who was a treasure of penance, and the charming one became very much delighted like Śacī (i.e. Indrāṇī) diligent in serving Indra. The beautiful, slim princess, endowed with all (good) characteristics, and subsisting on fruits, roots and water, served his feet. She was always eagerly engaged in obeying his words (i.e. orders) and in serving him, and engaged in the welfare of all beings she spent her time. Having given up (i.e. free from) desires, religious hypocrisy, hatred, greed, sin and pride, and always careful and diligent, she pleased Cyavana. O great king, having, in this way, served him for a thousand years with words and physical acts, she entertained a desire.

8-9. Once the two physicians of gods (i.e. the two Aśvins) came to the sage's hermitage. Having well honoured them with a good reception, she worshipped them. The two handsome (Aśvins), with their minds pleased due to the worship, respectful offering, and water for washing the feet, offered by the daughter of Śaryāti, affectionately said to the beautiful lady: "Ask for a boon".

10-16a. The princess (Sukanyā), the best among the intelligent, seeing the two physicians of gods pleased, made up her mind to ask for a boon. Knowing the intention of her husband, the princess said (to them): "O gods, if you are pleased then give (back) the sight of my husband." Having heard these charming words of Sukanyā, and having observed her chastity, the best among the physicians said: "If your husband will give us a portion of (the oblations offered to) gods, then we shall now make his eyes endowed with a clear sight." Cyavana too said "yes" (i.e. agreed to) giving a portion to the granters of the boon. Then the Aśvins, being delighted, said to (him), the best among those who practise penance: "Go down into this pond fashioned by siddhas." Thus told by the Aśvins, he who was seized by old age, and (on whose body) the veins had stretched, got into the pond; the Aśvins also got down into it.

16b-20. Three men, very handsome and dear to women, came up (from the pond). They had golden necklaces and ear-rings (on their bodies). Their forms were similar and they had put on excellent garments. Not (being able) to recognize her husband, the chaste lady surrendered herself to the Aśvins. Pointing out her husband to her, and being pleased with her chastity, they took leave of the sage and went to heaven in an aeroplane. They had a hope of a portion being kept for them when a sacrifice was performed. After a long time, he, oppressed with passion of love, tenderly spoke, with words faltering due to love, to her who was lean and emaciated due to practising a vow.

21-24. "O beautiful young lady, I am today pleased with the great service done with exclusive devotion in your heart by you giving me respect. You did not look upon as praiseworthy (i.e. you did not care for) your body—that is very much loved by human beings—in wasting (i.e. when you wasted) it for my sake in serving me. Look, I shall give you all those favours which have been won by me, engaged in my own duty, and which are free from fear and grief, and which are agreeable due to your serving me at every step, from the Lord by means of my concentration, knowledge and abstract meditation. Then what about other objects created and falling from the stretched out eyebrow of the Lord of wide strides? You are endowed with supernatural powers; enjoy riches obtained by your righteousness, divine and difficult to be obtained by men due to displeasure of kings." Having looked at him, who was speaking like this, proficient in the lore of the entire wonderful power of women, she understood it; and with her face smiling and glittering due to her looking (at him) with a little bashfulness, she spoke in words perturbed due to respect and love.

Sukanyā said :

25-26. O best brāhmaṇa, O my lord, O mighty one, I know this is indeed achieved in the case of you, the lord of infallible wonderful power; I told you about the right time: Let there be coition with you, the great one; for chaste women a child is an excellence. Tell (me) in this case in accordance with the teaching (of the sacred texts), the act due to which you with a desire to enjoy me have been extremely emaciated. That would be accomplished. O you, being determined be kind to me, the bold one. Tell me what is proper about the abode of the lord.

Sumati said :

27-36. Desiring (to do what was) dear to his beloved, Cyavana resorted to abstract meditation; O king, then only he fashioned an aeroplane going at the will (of the occupant). It yielded all desires; it was charming; it was endowed with all gems; it had the collection of all objects; it was furnished with jewelled pillars; it was endowed with divine beds; it was comfortable in all seasons; it was adorned with variegated pieces of silken cloth and banners; so also with garlands and variegated wreaths and with sweetly humming bees; it was bright with various kinds of garments of silk and fine garments; it was beautiful with mats put separately in each one of the residences one above the other, and also with beds, fans etc. It was adorned at various places with craft-works done there. It was furnished with a slab of great emeralds and altars of corals. It shone with the threshold of corals at the doors. It had adamant door-panels. It was resorted to by (i.e. it had) golden pitchers on the sapphire-tops. It was furnished with variegated canopies with necklaces hanging from walls fashioned with bright best rubies. It had the cooing (sound) of the groups of swans and pigeons, who having climbed up (the walls) again and again found them to be artificial. It had been properly furnished with sporting places, causing wonder to oneself.

37-54. He, who knew the hearts of all beings, said to her who was thus looking at the abode with a heart that was not very much pleased: "O timid one, after having dived into this pond, get into this aeroplane." She, whose eyes were like lotuses, who had worn a dusty garment, whose hair was tied into a braid, whose body was covered with dust and mud, whose breasts were variegated, gladly entered that auspicious pond of water. In the lake lived one hundred and ten damsels in a mansion. All of them were young. They, having the fragrance of lotuses, saw her. Seeing her, the damsels got up, and with the palms of their hands joined said: "We are your servants, order us what we should do." O you who respect (others), they having bathed that high-minded lady with a costly bath, gave her new, spotless silken garments, and excellent, bright and costly ornaments. They gave her food possessing all excellences and drink like nectar and spirituous liquor. Then (she saw) in a mirror herself with a wreath and with a spotless garment. The maidens performed an expiatory rite averting an evil with great reverence for her. Her form was adorned with a costly necklace, and ornament for the neck; her form had an ornament on her breasts, bracelets and golden anklets that were jingling; she was adorned with a golden girdle, (decked) with many jewels, below her loins. Her brows were charming; her teeth were fine; her eyes with white loving glances, vied with the calyx of a lotus. Due to dark hair her face was bright. When she remembered her dear husband who was liked by the sages, she was there with the damsels where the lord of sages remained. (Seeing) herself in front of her husband and surrounded by a thousand damsels, and having heard about his knowledge of deep meditation, she was apprehensive. Then he, the devoted one and the killer of his enemies, put her who had taken a pure (i.e. a purifying) bath, who was freshly shining, who had her own (i.e. original, charming) form, whose charming breasts were covered, who was surrounded by a thousand vidyādharīs, and who had put on excellent garments, into the aeroplane. In that aeroplane, he, the very handsome one, with his greatness undiminished, accompanied by his dear wife, and with his body served by the vidyādharīs, shone like the moon in the sky, surrounded by stars, and with the multitudes of white lotuses blooming. He, the defender of those women and resembling Kubera, and praised by siddhas, enjoyed for a long time, in the troughs on the lord of the family-mountains, the place of the enjoyment of the eight guardians of quarters, charming with wind (i.e. the breezes), the friend of Cupid, and having charming sounds due to the falling into them of the celestial river. Pleased with the lady (i.e. Sukanyā) he enjoyed at (different places like) Vaiśrambhaka, the celestial garden Nandana, Puṣpabhadraka, Mānasa and Caitrarathya.

CHAPTER SIXTEEN

The Horse Goes to Cyavana's Hermitage

Sumati said:

1-4. Thus sporting with her everywhere on the earth, he did not notice the years counted in hundreds that rolled by. Then the brāhmaṇa, being aware of the lapse of his time, and realising that his excellent dear wife was full of (i.e. fully satisfied with) her desires (being satisfied), returned to his best hermitage which was situated on the bank of Payoṣṇī and which was crowded with foeless beings and people and resorted to by beasts. He, of an excellent penance, lived there with his disciples, endowed with (the knowledge of) the Vedas; and with his pair of feet being served (by his disciples etc.) everyday, he practised a great (i.e. severe) penance.

5-8. Then, sometime Śaryāti desired to perform a sacrifice in honour of deities. At that time he sent his servants to fetch Cyavana. Being invited by them, he, of a great penance went there along with Sukanyā, his religiously wedded wife, and greatly devoted to (proper) conduct. (The king) of a great fame, saw the best sage—a man with sun-like lustre—by the side of the sage's wife i.e. of his daughter. The king who did not give her blessings and whose mind was not very much pleased, said to his daughter who had saluted her father (i.e. him).

9-10. "What is this that you have desired to do? You who have abandoned your husband stricken by old age and are resorting to this paramour who is a wayfarer, have deceived the sage saluted by the world. How has your mind wrongly gone down (like this)? This is a family-bane to the child born in the family of the good. Since you, being shameless, are having a paramour, you are degrading the family of your father and of your husband to the lowest position."

11-14a. She, smiling a bright smile, said to her father who was speaking like this: "O father, this is your son-in-law, the son of Bhṛgu." She told her father everything about (Cyavana's) acquisition of youth and handsome form. The father, being amazed and very much pleased, embraced his daughter. A Soma sacrifice was got performed by the wise one, and he took a cup of Soma. Cyavana, endowed with power, made the Aśvins, who did not (up to then) drink Soma, have a cup of Soma.

14b-22a. Indra, (seeing) the two deities, allowed to sit in the line (of those who were served Soma), (though they were) not fit to be in the line, by Cyavana, took his thunderbolt to kill the best brāhmaṇa (viz. Cyavana). The intelligent sage, seeing Indra, holding his bolt and ready to kill him, gave out a 'hum' sound, and stupefied the arm of Indra. All men saw there Indra, whose arm was stupefied and who like a snake controlled by a charm, was breathing with anger. Indra whose arm was stupefied, praised the sage, the treasure of penance, and giving with a fearless heart a portion (of Soma) to the Aśvins, told (him): "O lord, give an oblation to the Aśvins; O Sir, I shall not prevent it; paradon me, a great sin I have committed." Thus addressed, the sage, the treasure of kindness, quickly gave up his anger. O best of men, at that time Indra's arm became free. Seeing this, all men, with their minds full of curiosity, praised the brāhmaṇa's power, difficult to be obtained (even) by gods etc. Then the great king gave much wealth to brāhmaṇas. He, the tormentor of his enemies, had the bath of purification at the end of the sacrifice.

22b-24a. Since I was asked by you to tell the great rise of Cyavana, endowed with penance and deep meditation, I have told you all about it. Having saluted this (Cyavana), an embodiment of penance, and having received (from him) blessings for victory, send him, along with his wife to the charming sacrifice of Rāma.

Śeṣa said:

24b-30a. When he was talking like this, the horse, imprinting the earth with the marks of his hoofs, due to his wind-like speed, reached the hermitage. He, eating with his mouth the dūrvā-shoots, moved into the great hermitage. When the sages had, after fetching darbhas, gone to the river to bathe, Śatrughna, the tormentor of enemies and liked by heroes, reached the extremely beautiful hermitage of Cyavana. The brave one (i.e. Śatrughna), having gone into the hermitage, saw Cyavana, being the (very) embodiment of penance, near Sukanyā; and announcing his own name, saluted his feet: "I am Śatrughna, the brother of Rāma and the protector of the (sacrificial) horse. For the appeasement of great sins, I am saluting both of you."

30b-39. Hearing these words, the best of the sages said: "O Śatrughna, O best among the heroes, may you attain prosperity. You who are protecting the (horse of the) sacrifice, will attain great fame. O brāhmaṇas, note the wonder; even that Rāma, by remembering whose name men having committed great sins and having had sexual intercourse with others' wives, destroy their sins and the free souls engaged in remembering whose name attain salvation, is performing the (horse-) sacrifice. Due to the touch of the dust rising from his lotus-like feet, the better-half of Gautama became at once one having an enamouring form. She (i.e. Ahalyā, Gautama's wife), full of love, by meditating upon that form of Rāma burnt all the heaps of her sins and became beautiful. By seeing his charming form in the battle (even) demons reached his changeless form. Those ascetics who are devoted to meditation, on meditating upon him have gone, being fully free from the fear of the mundane existence, to the highest position. Blessed I am that today I shall see Rāma's charming face, the corners of the eyes of whom resemble the cloud-water, which has a fine nose, beautiful eye-brows and which is well high. That is (really) the tongue that respectfully utters Rāma's name. The one other than this is like the tongue of a serpent.

40-46. Today I have obtained the merit of my penance; today my desires are fulfilled because I shall see Rāmacandra's face difficult (to be seen even) by Brahmā etc. I shall purify my body with the dust of his feet; I shall purify my tongue by means of very wonderful talk (with him)." With tears flowing and his words faltering he said "Go", when love for Rāma had increased by remembering Rāma's feet. In front of the sages, he, with his eyes full of tears said: "O Śrī Rāmacandra, O best among the Raghus, O you embodiment of righteousness, O you who take pity on your devotees, emancipate me from the worldly existence." Firm in his meditation he did not feel alien there, when he talked like this before the sages. Śatrughna said to the sage: "O lord, make very pure our best sacrifice by the dust of your feet. It is the great fortune of the lord of Raghus, that he, of mighty arms dwells in your heart". Thus addressed, and very much honoured by all people Cyavana, with his attendants and surrounded by all fires, and floating in the deep pool of joy, went there (near Śatrughna).

47. Seeing that devotee of Rāma, coming there on foot, Hanūmān, full of modesty, said these words to Śatrughna:

48. "O lord, if you tell me, I shall carry this very great and

extremely handsome devotee of Rāma, the best sage to your city."

49. Hearing these important words of the warrior-monkey, Śatrughna, ordered Hanūmat: "Go, take the sage (to the city)."

50. Hanūmān put the sage on his back, and, (moving) like Wind going everywhere, took the sage along with his family.

51-54. Seeing the sage, who had arrived (at Ayodhyā), Rāma, the best among the intelligent, being pleased and agitated through affection, offered him respectful offering and water for washing his feet etc. (Rāma said:) "Now I am blessed due to having seen you, the best sage. This sacrifice of me, which is equipped with all requisites has been purified." Hearing these words, the best sage Cyavana, extremely delighted, and with his body horripilated due to love, said: "O lord, O great king, the worshipping of fire by you, the knower of Veda, and the protector of the path of dharma, is but proper."

CHAPTER SEVENTEEN

Arrival of a Brāhmaṇa Ascetic

Śeṣa said:

1-3. Having seen the power of the penance of Cyavana, which was inconceivable, Śatrughna praised the brāhmaṇic penance which alone was adored in the world. (He said to himself:) 'Oh! see the perfection of abstract meditation in the best brāhmaṇa who just in a moment fashioned the aeroplane difficult to have. What a great disparity is there between the complete attainment of pleasure on the part of the sages of pure hearts and the desire for enjoyment on the part of human beings without the power of penance!'

4-7. Saying thus to himself, Śatrughna stayed in Cyavana's hermitage for a while, drank water and enjoyed comfort. The great horse, having the speed of wind, having drunk the water of (the river) Payoṣṇī having auspicious water, went along the way. Seeing the horse's exit, the soldiers went after him; some with elephants, some with foot-soldiers, some with chariots and some with horses. Accompanied by the best minister Sumati, Śatrughna followed him in a chariot drawn by a horse.

8-14. The horse that was moving on, reached the city called Ratnātaṭa belonging to a king called Vimala and crowded with happy and rich people. Having heard from his servant that the excellent horse of Rāma along with all soldiers had reached the vicinity of the city, he, along with seventy elephants having the moon's colour, myriads of horses, and a thousand chariots bright like gold, went forth to (greet) Śatrughna. Having saluted Śatrughna, and all great warriors that had come there, and having offered him riches, treasure and wealth and his entire kingdom to him, he stood before him and said: "What (should) I do?" The great king too with his arms closely embraced him who had bowed down to his feet and having entrusted his kingdom to his son and surrounded by many archers, went with him. Having heard Rāma's name, pleasing to the ears, all of them saluted the horse and offered him riches and great wealth.

15-20. With great joy Śatrughna honoured the king; and then, along with his army went after the horse. When he was thus going, he saw on his way an excellent mountain, which was adorned with crystal, golden and silver tablelands, which resounded with water-streams, the land of which had various minerals, which was adorned with good minerals like red chalk and colour of lac, where siddha-damsels having no fear from anywhere sported with siddhas, where gandharvas, celestial nymphs and nāgas were sporting with pleasure. Seeing the mountain served by cool breezes (that had been) in contact with the ripples of Gaṅgā, and charmingly graced with the sound of lutes, swans and parrots, Śatrughna, with his mind full of amazement on having seen it, said this (i.e. these words) to Sumati:

21-22. "What is this best among the great mountains? It astonishes my mind. This wonderful (mountain) having excellent tablelands of abundant silver, shines on my way. What deities dwell here? Is it the sporting ground of gods that excites my mind with the heaps of riches?"

23-37a. Hearing these words, Sumati who had set his heart on the lotus-like feet of Rāma, the abode of virtues which will be mentioned, then said: "O king, this is the mountain (called)

Nīla, which shines in front (of us) with great beautiful peaks and crystal tops on all sides. Those mean men, those sinful men, engaged in adultery, who do not realise the hosts of virtues of Viṣṇu, do not see this mountain. So also those men who having controversies and doubt in their minds, do not care for the way of conduct well settled by the good arising from the śrutis and the smṛtis, those who sell indigo, and those who sell lac do not see this (mountain). A brāhmaṇa who drinks spirituous liquor and sells ghee etc., so also he who would not give (in marriage) his daughter endowed with beauty to a man of good character and belonging to good family (do not see this mountain). (Similarly) a man who censures his wife coming from a good family and having a good character, who himself eats sweet (dishes, but) does not give them to his kinsmen (does not see this mountain). (In the same way) a man who discriminates in (i.e. while serving) food meant for brāhmaṇas, and the wicked one who does not offer mixture of rice and peas or rice boiled in milk to a suppliant (do not see this mountain). Those who torment guests (already) tormented by the sun's heat etc. (do not see this mountain). O great king, those who enjoy in the atmosphere and who are traitors, so also those who are averse to Raghunātha do not see (this mountain). This beautiful, auspicious, best mountain, adorned by Puruṣottama purifies all of us by its sight. Here lives Puruṣottama whose feet are honoured by the crowns of gods, who deserves to be seen by the auspicious ones, who grants religious merit, whom the śrutis saying 'Not this, not this' (i.e. this is not Brahman, that is not Brahman . . .) do not know, the dust of whose feet is sought after by gods like Indra and is extremely difficult to be secured, whom the wise know by means of the perfect statements of the Upaniṣads—that Puruṣottama along with Śrī lives on this Nīla-mountain. O king, having climbed it, having worshipped it with merit etc., and having eaten the offering of eatables presented to it, one becomes four-handed.

37b-48a. In this regard also they mention this ancient account. O great king, listen to it which is full of all wonder: What happened to king Ratnagrīva along with his family? (How) he obtained four hands etc. difficult to be got (even) by gods and demons? O great king, there was a city named Kāñcī, well known in the worlds. It was rich with great people and their attendants, and (had in it) army and horses (or elephants). In it lived best brāhmaṇas who were very much engaged in the six duties,[1] who were devoted to the welfare of all beings, and who hankered after devotion to Rāma. The kṣatriyas were fighters, and never fled away in a battle. They were averse to others' wives and to plotting maliciously against others. The vaiśyas conducted themselves well with lending money, agriculture and trade. They always took delight in (i.e. were greatly devoted to) the feet of Raghunātha. The śūdras passed their nights and days in serving brāhmaṇas etc. With the tips of their tongues they always uttered (the word) 'Rāma, Rāma'. No common man committed a sin (even) mentally. Charity, pity, restraint and truth always prevailed there. No sinless person even uttered words harming others. People did not show greed for the wealth of others, nor did they commit any sin. In this way, O great king, the subjects were looked after by Ratnagrīva. The king, free from greed, accepted only one sixth part[2] (of the income of each person), and nothing else (i.e. more). In this way, the king who righteously protected his subjects and enjoyed all pleasures, passed many years.

48b-58a. Once he said this (i.e. these words) to Viśālākṣī, his chaste and religiously wedded wife: "O Viśālākṣī, sons able to protect the subjects have been born (to us). I have many attendants free from distress. My elephants resemble mountains, and my horses are (swift) like the wind. I always have chariots yoked with great horses. Due to the grace of great Viṣṇu I have nothing wanting, but (still) there is one desire in my mind. O you extremely beautiful one, I have not as yet visited a great holy place capable of putting a stop to a stay in the womb (i.e. to birth) and adorned by Viṣṇu. I have become old with my body having wrinkles and grey hair. With reverence I shall resort to a charming holy place. That man who only fills his belly (i.e. eats to live) during his life and does not worship Viṣṇu, is said to be a bull. Therefore, O auspicious dear one,

1. Ṣaṭkarma—The six duties enjoined on a brāhmaṇa : 1. Reading (especially the Vedas), 2. Instructing, 3. Sacrifice. 4. Conducting a sacrifice, 5. Giving, 6. Receiving (gifts).

2. Ṣaṣṭhāṁśa—Cf. Manusmṛti, 7. 131ff.

with my family I shall go on a pilgrimage after having entrusted the entire responsibility of the kingdom to my son." Having resolved like this in the evening he, meditating upon Viṣṇu at night, saw a dream (and saw in it) a brāhmaṇa—an excellent ascetic. The great king, having got up in the morning and having offered the morning prayers etc., happily sat in the assembly with his ministers.

58b-65a. Just then he saw a brāhmaṇa ascetic of an emaciated body, wearing matted hair, bark-garments and a small piece of cloth worn over the privities and holding a staff in his hands, and with his body rendered auspicious due to visits to many holy places. The king of mighty arms, on seeing him, saluted him with (i.e. by bowing) his head. The king, with his mind pleased, offered him a respectful oblation and water for washing his feet. He asked (i.e. said to) the celebrated brāhmaṇa who had rested and was seated comfortably: "O lord, my bodily sin has today gone (away) due to having seen you. Great men go to the houses of the helpless ones through regard for them, to protect them. Therefore, O brāhmaṇa, now tell me, an old man, as to which god would bring about the end of (living in) the womb (i.e. the end of birth and death), and which holy place would be capable of (doing so). (People like) you move everywhere, are the greatest, are devoted to concentration and meditation and have become spotless and meritorious due to having plunged (i.e. bathed) in all the sacred places. O you, who well know (about) all the holy places, favour me and tell me in detail, who am listening and having faith."

The brāhmaṇa said:

65b-82. O best king, I shall tell you what you asked me about visits to holy places. By the favour of which deity would womb i.e. birth be kept off? That Śrī Rāmacandra who destroys the mundane existence, should be resorted to. He, the lord alone, called Puruṣottama, should be worshipped. I have seen many (holy) cities destroying all sins. Ayodhyā, Sarayū, Tāpī, so also the excellent Haridvāra, Avanti, Vimalā, Kāñcī and Revā going (i.e. flowing) into the ocean; so also Gokarṇa, (the holy place) called Hāṭaka, destroying crores of murders; so also the great mountain called Mallika, giver of salvation to those men who see it and where on the bodies the water would become dark or pure. I have seen this holy place which removes sin. I have seen Dvāravatī, which is resorted to by gods and demons, where flows the auspicious Gomatī, having Brahmanic water, where sleep is called absorption of the mind and death is said to be final liberation, and living where Kali would never be powerful. Where (i.e. there) the stones are marked with discs, and men also hold discs; beasts, insects, birds etc.—all have discs on their bodies; where the three-strided one (i.e. Viṣṇu), the only guardian of the worlds, would live (i.e. lives). Due to my great religious merit I saw that city. I saw Vārāṇasī which is made his abode by Viśvanātha and where they teach the hymn that emancipates (a person) and is called Brahman, having died where insects, moths, bees, beafts and others, and (even) gods, abandoning the pleasure due to the contact with their (i.e. as a result of their) deeds and overcoming grief go to Kailāsa. (Then there) is the holy place called Maṇikarṇi, in which the river flowing to the north cuts off the bondage of the mundane existence even of the sinners. All (of them) having matted hair, ear-rings, and adorned with serpents and excellent ones wearing the hide of an elephant live with their grief perished. There (the god) called Kālabhairava controls Yama. Lord Yama holding the (chastising) rod, does not talk about human beings. Kāśī, marked by (the presence of) Viśveśvara, was seen by me. O king, I also saw many holy places; but that great wonder which I saw on the mountain called Nīla, in the presence of Viṣṇu, was seen at no other place.

CHAPTER EIGHTEEN

A Miraculous Happening

The brāhmaṇa said:

1-10. O king, listen to the account (of the events) that took place on the mountain Nīla, believing which men go to the eternal Brahman. I who was wandering, went to that mountain called Nīla, the courtyard of which is repeatedly washed by the water of the ocean. There, on the top of the mountain, I saw bhillas, holding bows, having four arms and with their fatigue removed by eating roots and fruits. Then immediately a great doubt arose in my mind: 'How (is it that) these men are having four arms and they are holding bows and arrows? Their forms appear to be (like those) who have conquered their souls and live in Vaikuṇṭha. How have they obtained what is difficult to be obtained even by Brahmā and others?' They, with their hands shining with conches, discs, maces, śārṅga (bows) and lotuses, and with their bodies covered with sylvan garlands, and resembling the devotees of Viṣṇu were near (me). With my mind full of doubt I asked them at that time, O king, (I said:) "Who are you? How have you obtained this condition of having four hands?" Then they laughed much and said to me: "This brāhmaṇa does not know the wonderful importance of piṇḍa." Hearing this, I said (to them): "What is piṇḍa? To whom is it given? Tell it to me, O you most religious ones, having bodies with four hands." Then having heard my words, the magnanimous ones told me the entire account of the acquisition of four hands etc.

The kirātas said:

11-17. O brāhmaṇa, listen to the account: A child from amongst us everyday sported, eating jambu fruits etc. Once while playing and being surrounded by children on all sides he climbed up a beautiful peak of the mountain (Nīla). (The boy said:) "There I saw a wonderful temple of a deity. It was decked with the gems like emeralds and had golden walls. Like the sun it tore off (i.e. dispelled) the line (i.e. mass) of darkness with its lustre. Seeing it I was amazed (and thought): 'What is this? Whose abode is this? Going (into it) I shall find out whether the abode belonged to the great ones.' Thinking like this, I, due to my great luck, went inside the house. There I saw the lord of gods, saluted by gods and demons, and shining with crowns, necklaces, armlets and neck ornaments etc., so also having extremely pure and charming ear-rings, and lotus-like feet with bees intoxicated with the fragrance of tulasī (-blossoms).

18-24. (I saw the lord) the rich image (of the lord) whose

feet were served by a conch, a disc, a mace, a bow, a lotus which were embodied, and who was well served by Nārada and others. (There) some sang, danced and laughed; they pleased the great, very wonderful lord who alone was saluted by the entire world." O sage, my child seeing Viṣṇu, went there. O king, gods, after having majestically offered worship with incense etc., having made an offering of eatables for the dear (lord) of Śrī, so also having waved the lights, went, expecting his grace through great respect for him, to their own abodes. Due to the great luck (of the boy,) he got a particle of boiled rice that had fallen there, and that was difficult to be got by Brahmadeva and other gods and men. The child ate it; then he saw the image; and the very handsome child had four arms. Then we repeatedby looked at the boy who had come home, who had got four arms and who had held a conch, a disc etc.

25-30. We asked him: "What is this wonder that has taken place?" Then the boy told us all the great wonder: "I had gone to the eastern peak (of the mountain). There I saw the lord of gods. There I found the charming particle of boiled rice from the offering made to the deity. Just due to eating it, I have now become four-armed, and am amazed." Having heard those words of the boy, we, who were at once amazed, also saw the god, very difficult to be obtained. We ate there food etc. full of all tastes. Then due to the lord's grace we became four-armed. O best among the Kurus, go and have a sight of the lord. O brāhmaṇa, eating the particle of boiled rice (from the offering) you (will) be four-armed. O best brāhmaṇa, I have told you about the wonder, about which you had asked me.

CHAPTER NINETEEN

Ratnagrīva Goes on a Pilgrimage to Puruṣottama

The brāhmaṇa said:

1-5. Having heard the highly amazing words of the bhillas and thinking that it was a great wonder, I was delighted. Having bathed at the confluence of Gaṅgā and the ocean, with my body rendered auspicious, I climbed up the peak, variegated with gems and rubies. O great king, there I saw the god saluted by gods and others. I had become blessed by saluting him and by having eaten the food (from the offering). Due to having seen the lord Viṣṇu, I obtained the four-armed condition, marked with a conch, a disc etc. (and) did not enter a womb again (i.e. did not have rebirth). O king, you too quickly go to the mountain called Nīla, and make yourself blessed and free from the agony of remaining in the womb (i.e. being born).

6. Having heard these words of the intelligent best brāhmaṇa, he, with his body delighted, asked the sage, the manner in which the pilgrimage (was to be undertaken).

The king said:

7-8. O good one, O best brāhmaṇa, O sinless one, you have nicely described to me the greatness of the lord which destroys the sins of those who listen to it. Tell me the mode of the pilgrimage, along with (i.e. as told in) the scriptures. By which mode would men obtain the entire fruit?

The brāhmaṇa said:

9-16. O king listen, I shall tell you the auspicious mode of pilgrimage by means of which the god saluted by gods and demons, is obtained. Even if one's body is wrinkled (and) grey or one is endowed with youth, one should, realising death to be insurmountable, submit oneself to Hari. One should put one's heart into narration about him, listening about him, saluting and worshipping him, and not anywhere else like woman etc. Realising that everything is perishable and momentary and very painful, a man who somehow greatly worships Viṣṇu who is beyond birth and death, to whom devotion is dear, and who is infallible, (even) through anger, desire of carnal gratification, fear, hatred or greed, does not experience unhappiness. That Viṣṇu is reached through the sinless contact with the good. That which the good, with their attachment ceased and free from desire and greed, say, keeps one away from the worldly existence. Due to their grace men become free from unhappiness. At the holy places is found a good man highly devoted to Rāmacandra, whose sight is the fire burning the heaps of men's sins.

17-18a. Therefore, a man, afraid of the mundane existence, should always visit the holy places, having holy water and adorned with the rows of good people. The holy places, properly visited, destroy sins.

18b-20. O best king, listen to the mode (of visiting them). First a man should create in himself detachment from his wife and (other) members of his family. Knowing (all) that to be unreal, he should mentally recollect Viṣṇu. Having gone from there to a distance of a krośa uttering (the name) 'Rāma, Rāma', he should, knowing the (proper) way, having bathed at the holy places, get himself shaved.

21-23. The sins of men visiting holy places, go (with them) resorting to their hair. Therefore, one should get shaved. Then a man, free from greed and having put on the dress proper for a holy place, should hold a staff, a knotless garment, a pitcher and a piece of deer-skin. A special fruit is obtained by those men who go there according to the proper mode. Therefore, with all efforts a man should go through the rite of pilgrimage.

24-30. He whose hands, feet, and mind are well controlled, and who has knowledge, penance and fame, obtains the fruit of (a visit to) the holy places. The very lucky man, saying with his tongue 'O Hari, O Kṛṣṇa, O Hari, O Kṛṣṇa, O you to whom your devotees are dear, O you lord of senses, O you fit to be resorted to, O revered one, O Viṣṇu, protect me from the many (births in) the worldly life,' and mentally recollecting Hari, should visit a holy place on foot. A man going in a vehicle would obtain equal fruit. A man (going to a holy place) with his shoes on would obtain one fourth fruit, and the fruit obtained by killing a cow by going in a vehicle (to which) bulls (are yoked). A usurer obtains one third of the fruit, and a man gets one eighth by serving (i.e. one who serves others gets one eighth part of the religious merit). A man going to a holy place reluctantly would obtain half the fruit. A man should visit holy places properly. His sins perish, especially by observing the (proper) rites, There he should salute the good men by resorting to their feet etc. By that devotion to Hari, Puruṣottama, is secured.

31-33. Thus I have told you in brief and not in detail, the

mode of visiting the holy places. Resorting to this mode go to Puruṣottama (i.e. Viṣṇu). Acyuta (i.e. Viṣṇu) being pleased (with you), O great king, will give (i.e. bring about) devotion to (i.e. in) you, so that in a moment there will be the end of the mundane existence. O best man, having heard the mode of visiting holy places, which destroys all sins, a man is freed from all severe sins.

Sumati said:

34-35. The great one, having heard these words, and with his mind agitated through curiosity to see that holy place, saluted his feet, and ordered his minister, an excellent counsellor. Desiring to visit the sacred place, he decided to take all persons with him. (He said to the minister:)

36-38. "O minister, at my behest, advise all the citizens: 'The best men, who live in my city, who obey my orders, should move with me out of my city to please (Viṣṇu) by seeing the lotus-like feet of (that) Puruṣottama (i.e. Viṣṇu); but those sinful men, of irreligious intentions, who, violating my words (i.e. my order) stay (back) in their houses, should be punished with Yama's (i.e. capital) punishment.

39-42a. What is the use of that host of sons or those relatives of bad conduct who have not seen with their eyes Puruṣottama who gives religious merit? The birth of them whose sons and grandsons have not sought the shelter of Viṣṇu, is like that of a herd of pigs eating excretion. O multitudes of my subjects, quickly salute that god who by merely his name (being uttered) is capable of purifying all.'" Such charming words strung together with the virtue of the lord (were uttered by him).

42b-45. His chief minister Uttama, having the true name (i.e. true to his name), was much delighted. Having put (the announcer) on an excellent elephant he proclaimed by means (of the sound) of the drum: "Since it is ordered by the king desiring to go on a pilgrimage, all people should quickly go with the king to the great mountain. They should see there (the lord) having the name Puruṣottama and destroying sins. They should make (i.e. look upon) the entire ocean of the worldly existence (just as) a small puddle."

46-54. The minister, whose fatigue was removed by meditation upon the feet of Raghunātha (i.e. Rāma) made such a wonderful proclamation as ordered by the king. Hearing it, all the subjects swimming in the fluid of joy, decided to emancipate themselves by seeing Puruṣottama. Brāhmaṇas, well-dressed and accompanied by their disciples, and giving a blessing rich with boons to the king, then moved out. Brave kṣatriyas holding bows, vaiśyas graceful due to sale of objects, śūdras with their bodies delighted due to crossing the worldly existence, washermen, lovely shoe-makers, kirātas, wall-builders, those who lived on a needle (i.e. tailors), those who dealt in tāmbūla, those who kept musical instruments, those who subsisted on dyeing, the sellers of oil and the sellers of garments, bards, panegyrists, heralds full of delight and narrating old accounts moved out by the king's order. Those who knew the sweet taste of food, those who amused (others) with words causing laughter, magicians, vidyādharas, those who were proficient in intelligence, praising the great king went out of the city.

55-60. The king too, having finished the rites like the morning prayer, brought (there) the brāhmaṇa, the best ascetic and extremely pure. By his order the king went out of the city. The king, followed by people, shone like the moon with stars. He went over just a krośa, and getting himself shaved, held a staff and a water-pot, and wore an auspicious (deer-)hide. He had put on an auspicious dress and was engrossed in meditation on Viṣṇu. He, of a great glory, had his mind free from passion and anger. At that time the musicians repeatedly beat large kettle-drums, large military drums, and played upon other musical instruments, (blew) conches, and (played upon) lutes. People saying, 'O lord of gods, O you who remove grief, O you who are known as Puruṣottama, show me your body', went out (of the city).

CHAPTER TWENTY

The Importance of Gaṇḍakī

Sumati said:

1-11. Then, when the king, accompanied by all people proceeded (to Nīlagiri), he, the great king, heard on the way the narration of Kṛṣṇa, of Govinda, sung by distinguished singers, the devotees of Viṣṇu: "Victory to you, O Mādhava, O you Puruṣottama, who are fit to protect." On his way he visited many holy places and saw their greatness. From the ascetic brāhmaṇa he heard about their greatness. The king, with his mind amused with diverse accounts of Viṣṇu, made the singers sing about Viṣṇu on every path (that he took). The great, intelligent king whose senses were restrained, gave gifts to the helpless, blind, poor, lame persons, as desired by them. Very much devoted to the meditation on Viṣṇu, he, making himself auspicious and free from passion by means of visiting many holy places, went (on the pilgrimage) with his own people. The king while going saw ahead the river which destroys sins, which contained stones marked with discs, which was pure like the sages' minds, which was adorned with many rows of the hosts of many sages, which looked beautiful with the cooings of birds like the cranes. Having seen it, he asked the ascetic, the best brāhmaṇa who knew piety and who was full of the special knowledge of the significance of many holy places: "O lord, what is this auspicious river, resorted to by hosts of sages and making my heart full of joy?" Hearing these words of the intelligent king of kings, the learned (brāhmaṇa) commenced narrating the excellent significance of the holy places.

The brāhmaṇa said:

12-22. O king, this is river Gaṇḍakī which is resorted to by gods and demons, which is overflowing with holy water, and which destroys heaps of sins. She would burn mental sin by means of her sight (i.e. when she is seen), would burn the sin committed by means of deeds by to her touch, and would burn the heap of sins committed through words by means of her water being drunk. Formerly the lord of the beings (i.e. Brahmā), seeing all the beings to be sinful, produced this (river), the destroyer of many sins from the drops on his cheeks. Those men who, even though they have committed sins, touch this river having holy water and beautiful ripples, do not obtain a womb (i.e. are not reborn). The stones found in this river and adorned with the marks of disc, are actually great forms of the lord himself. A man who would everyday worship the stone with a disc (on it), would never enter the womb of a mother (i.e. would never be reborn). An intelligent man who would (like to) worship the excellent śālagrāma stone, must be of good conduct, and free from religious hypocrisy and greed. A man averse to the wife of someone else and to the wealth of others, should carefully worship the śālagrāma with the disc (on it). The disc born (i.e. found) in Dvārāvatī and the stone born (i.e. found) in Gaṇḍakī, destroy in a moment men's sins earned during a hundred existences. Even if a man would have committed a thousand sins, he would be purified by drinking the water of (i.e. flowing from) a śālagrāma. A brāhmaṇa, kṣatriya, vaiśya or śūdra householder, who is on the path of the Vedas (i.e. behaves according to the Vedic injunctions), would obtain salvation on worshipping a śālagrāma.

23-27. A woman should never worship a śālagrāma. If a woman who is a widow or whose husband is alive, who desires her well-being in heaven, touches through ignorance a śālagrāma, she would, even though she is endowed with good character and virtues, be deprived of her collection of religious merit and would quickly go to hell. The best brāhmaṇas say that flowers dropped from the hands of women on śālagrāma stones are more (powerful) than the fall of Indra's thunderbolt. The sandal offered to the lord by a woman would be like poison, a flower offered by her would be like Indra's thunderbolt, and offering of eatables made by a woman to the lord would resemble the deadly poison. Therefore, a woman should, by all means, avoid touching the (śālagrāma) stone. She who touches it, goes to (and lives in) the hell as long as fourteen Indras (rule).

28-38. Even a man of a sinful conduct or having (the sin of) a brāhmaṇa's murder goes to the highest position on drinking the water of (i.e. flowing from) a śālagrāma stone. Tulasī, sandal, water, a conch, a bell, a disc, a (śālagrāma) stone, a copper-pot and Viṣṇu's names are the nectar from (Viṣṇu's) feet. The tranquil sages, proficient in all sacred works, say that the nectar from (Viṣṇu's) feet (obtained) through these nine, burns the heaps of sins. O king, all the wonderful religious merit obtained by bathing at all places and by performing all (kinds of) sacrifices is present in each drop (of Gaṇḍakī). Within (a radius of) a yojana a crore of sacred places exist, where the śālagrāma stone is worshipped by best men. Even śālagrāma stones should be worshipped; not the double ones among the even ones. The uneven ones also should be worshipped; but not the triple among the uneven ones. (A śālagrāma with) a disc is (found) in Dvārāvatī, so also in Gaṇḍakī. Gaṅgā flows into the ocean where the two meet. The dry ones make man bereft of (long) life, prosperity and power. Therefore the glossy and of a charming form give prosperity. A man who desires a (long) life, so also a man longing for wealth (who) worships (them), obtains all (bliss) in the next world and in this world. O king, it is (only in the case) of a lucky person that he has Viṣṇu's auspicious name in his mouth, and the śālagrāma stone near him in his heart. (Even) at the time of the departing of the soul, he who has a sight of the śālagrāma stone even while relaxing, undoubtedly gets salvation.

39-44. Formerly the lord told the intelligent Ambarīṣa: "Brāhmaṇas, those who have renounced the worldly ties and smooth śālagrāma stones—these three are my forms taken by (the lord) that appear to destroy the sins of the sinners on the globe. Those sinners who (even) once censure the śālagrāma stone, are cooked in the Kumbhīpāka (hell) till deluge. The mother, the father, the groups of relatives of that foolish man who prohibits a man on the point of worshipping (a śālagrāma stone), rot in hell. He who tells (others), 'Offer the dearest worship to śālagrāma,' being blessed, quickly takes his ancestors to Vaikuṇṭha." In this case only the sages free from attachment and lust and anger tell an ancient (piece of) history:

45-54. Formerly in a country, void of piety, called Kīkaṭa, lived a man called Śabara, belonging to the pulkasa caste. He was always bent on killing beings; he again and again held his bow. He forcibly took away the life of those who desired to go on a pilgrimage. He killed many animals; he was always interested in others' wealth. He was always full of attachment etc. and of lust and anger. He who killed animals ceaselessly, roamed in a fearful forest. He was free in (i.e. he freely drew) the bow-string to which an arrow, to the tip of which poison was applied, was fixed. That hunter, dangerous to every being, and of a cruel mind, was once roaming. He did not realize that death had approached him. Yama's dark, fearful messengers, having red hair, long nails and long fangs, with nooses and mallets in their hands, holding iron chains and causing confusion, arrived (there). (They said to one another:) "(You may) fasten this sinner causing fear to every being. He never assisted any being even mentally (i.e. He never even thought of helping any being). He is always attached to others' wives, wealth, and is always given to cheating others." One said: "Therefore I shall draw out his big tongue." One said: "I shall take out his eyes" One said: "I shall cut off the hands of this sinner." Another said: "I shall cut off the ears of this wicked one."

55-61. Saying so, and gnawing their teeth, the furious messengers with weapons (in their hands) stood by the wicked one. Then one messenger took the form of a serpent and bit (him) on the foot. As soon as he was bitten, he was dead. Then those servants of Yama tied him with an iron chain, and angrily hit him with whips and struck him with mallets. (They said to him:) "O vicious one, O scoundrel, you never acted well even mentally. So we shall throw you in the Raurava hell. Fearful crows will angrily eat up your skin and flesh. (Right) from your birth you have not served Viṣṇu. You well maintained your wife and sons by cheating them. You never remembered Viṣṇu who removes sins. Therefore, by Yama's order we beating you very much shall take you (and put you on) an iron pike (or put you into) Kumbhīpāka and Raurava."

62-64a. When, after speaking thus, they desired to take him, a man, devoted to the feet of great Viṣṇu came there. That noble follower of Viṣṇu then saw the groups of the wicked (messengers of Yama) holding malicious weapons like nooses, mallets and staffs. They were ready to take (away) the pulkasa after having bound him with iron chains.

64b-70. They said (to one another): "Bind him, bind him, destroy him, tear him, break him, break him." Then that kind man, very much devoted to Viṣṇu, having seen him, made his heart extremely compassionate towards him. (He thought to himself): 'Let this very wicked one not suffer affliction in my presence. Today only I shall free him from Yama's messengers.' Thinking thus and being full of pity for him the best sage took a śālagrāma stone and went near him. Putting the water (flowing) from his (i.e. Viṣṇu's) feet and mixed with Tulasī-leaf, he put it into his mouth and muttered the epithets of Rāma into his ear. That devotee of Viṣṇu put the Tulasī(-leaf) on his head and the (śālagrāma) stone of great Viṣṇu on his chest, and said: "Let Yama's messengers, very much given to torture, go. Let the touch of the śālagrāma stone burn the great sin."

71-78. When he spoke like this, the very wonderful attendants of Viṣṇu came to the proximity of him whose sin had gone (away) by the touch of the (śālagrāma) stone. They who had put on yellow garments, who were adorned with conches, discs, maces and lotuses, came (there) and freed him from the unassailable iron chain. Having freed that pulkasa man who had committed great sins, he said: "Why have you bound this Viṣṇu's devotee who has a respectable body? Whose orders do you who act unrighteously obey? Release this devotee of Viṣṇu. Why have you held him up?" Hearing these words, the servants of Yama said: "By Yama's order we are ready to take (away) this sinner. He has not, even mentally, helped any being. This one, having a vicious body, committing great sins like killing animals, has plundered many people going on a pilgrimage. He is always interested in others' wives, and has done the largest number of sins. Therefore, we have come to take (away) this sinful pulkasa. Why have you got him released through warriors that have suddenly arrived?"

Viṣṇu's messengers said:

79-86a. A touch of the śālagrāma stone burns (just) in a moment all that sin due to killing a brāhmaṇa and due to the murder of a crore of beings. As a particle of fire burns cotton, in the same way the name of Rāma, even if casually heard, burns sins. He, on whose head there is a Tulasī (-leaf), on whose chest there is the charming (śālagrāma) stone, and who has Rāma's name either in his mouth or ear, is released just then only.

Therefore, formerly he had held Tulasī(-leaf) on his head; he was made to hear Rāma's name, and he well held the (śālagrāma) stone on his head. By that the heap of his sins was burnt, and his body has become auspicious. He will go to the highest position which is very difficult to be obtained by sinners. Having for a myriad years enjoyed all charming pleasures there, he obtains birth in Bhārata, and having worshipped the lord of the world, he will obtain the highest place difficult to be obtained by gods and demons. The importance of the (śālagrāma) stone of (i.e. representing) Viṣṇu is not known. When seen, touched or worshipped, it removes all sins in a moment.

86b-92a. Saying so all the attendants of Viṣṇu ceased (speaking) gladly. Those servants of Yama told that wonderful (account) to the king. The devotee of Viṣṇu, solely devoted to Raghunātha, became delighted. He, being free from Yama's noose, will go to the highest position. At that time a beautiful, very wonderful aeroplane, decorated with a number of bells, came (there) from the world of gods. Having got into it, he went to heaven resorted to by very auspicious (souls). Having enjoyed many pleasures (there) he went to (i.e. was born on) the earth. Having obtained a birth in a good brāhmaṇa family in Kāśī, and having worshipped the lord of worlds he went to the highest position. He, due to the company of the good, touched the śālagrāma stone, got free from great affliction, and went to the highest place.

92b-93. O king, I have narrated to you the important account of Gaṇḍakī. Having listened to it, a man is freed from sins and obtains pleasures and salvation.

CHAPTER TWENTYONE

Puruṣottama Appears to the King in the Guise of an Ascetic

Sumati said :

1-3. The best king having heard this matchless importance of Gaṇḍakī looked upon himself as blessed. Having bathed and having gratified all his (dead) ancestors, the great one was delighted. Having, according to the words of the brāhmaṇa, worshipped the śālagrāma, the best king took there twentyfour śālagrāma (stones) and with affection worshipped them with such means of worship as sandal etc.

4-5. Then the king, having given gifts there, especially to the poor and the blind, started to go to the temple of Viṣṇu. Thus, in due order, he reached the confluence of Gaṅgā and the ocean. Having brought it within the range of his sight (i.e. having seen it), he joyfully asked the brāhmaṇa:

6. "O lord, tell me, how far is the great mountain called Nīla which is the abode of Viṣṇu and which is saluted by gods and demons."

7-10. Having, at that time, heard the important words of (i.e. uttered by) king Ratnagrīva, he (i.e. the brāhmaṇa), full of amazement, respectfully said to the king: "O king, this is the region of the mountain Nīla which is adored. Why is it giving great religious merit not seen by you (i.e. why can you not see it)?" Again and again he said: "This is the region of the Nīla mountain. How is this (i.e. how can this), the place of the residence of Viṣṇu, not seen, (not be seen) by you? Here I had bathed properly. Here I had seen the bhillas. Along this way only I had climbed up the mountain."

11-16. Hearing these words of him, the king was mentally afflicted. Making his mind eager to see the Nīla-mountain, the king said (to him): "Tell us the means by which I shall see Viṣṇu, and I shall see the Nīla (mountain)." Then hearing the words of king Ratnagrīva, the ascetic brāhmaṇa, amazed by the king, said (these) words: "O king, having bathed at the confluence of Gaṅgā and the ocean we should remain here as long as the Nīla (mountain) is not seen. The (praise of) the great god called Puruṣottama, and destroyer of sins, will be sung. He who has the name 'Bhaktavatsala' (i.e. affectionate to his devotees) will quickly do favour. He, the crest-jewel of gods will not abandon (his) devotees. Many devotees have been protected by him. Therefore, O you very intelligent one, sing (the praise of) him."

17-19. Hearing these words, the king with his mind afflicted, bathed at the confluence of Gaṅgā and the ocean and observed a fast. "When Puruṣottama (i.e. Viṣṇu) will show favour by appearing (before me) I shall worship him and take food; otherwise I shall (follow) the vow of non-eating." Having made such a vow, he sang (songs praising) the multitude of virtues of Hari on the bank of the (confluence of) Gaṅgā and the ocean; and observed a fast.

The king said :

20-24. Victory to you who show compassion to the helpless; victory to you who remove misery, and who are called auspicious. Victory to you who destroy the suffering of your devotees; victory to you who have taken up a lovely form and who destroy the wicked. Seeing Ambarīṣa afflicted and with all his auspicious things destroyed due to the curse of a brāhmaṇa, you holding the Sudarśana disc in your hand protected him by living in his belly. He (i.e. Prahlāda) who was harassed by his father, the king of demons, was at once protected by you—when his father was seeing it having the form of Nṛsiṁha, by dropping spears, nooses, water and fire. Seeing the excellent lord of elephants whose foot had fallen into (i.e. was caught in) the mouth of an alligator and which was extremely afflicted, you, with your good heart wet with (i.e. full of) pity, mounted on Garuḍa. Then you abandoned (i.e. got down from) the bird (i.e. Garuḍa), took (your Sudarśana) disc; you whose speed causes a series of tremors in the sky are (i.e. were) sung (i.e. praised) by him (i.e. the elephant) with his life (i.e. sincerely). You liberated him from the alligator and instantly destroyed him (i.e. the alligator).

25-28. O lord, wherever your worshipper is oppressed, you take up a bodily form and protect your (worshipper) by means of your acts removing sins. O you who protect the helpless, O you whose feet are rubbed by the diamonds on the heads of the gods, O you to whom the devotees are dear, O you who burn crores of sins, O lord, grant me your vision. If this sinful person has come to your mind (i.e. if you think about him) then, show (yourself to him). We are yours O you who are worshipped by gods and demons, your destroying the stream of sins is not forgotten by us. Those who utter your pure name, cross the entire ocean of sins. If I have remembered you, then, let me reach you, O you who remove all sins.

Sumati said:

29-31. Thus the king, singing the merits (of the lord) at night and by day also, did not have rest or comfort even for a moment. Singing (the lord's virtues), going (to his image), invoking (him), standing (by his image), he day and night said this: "O lord of grace, O Puruṣottama, show me your body." Thus the king passed five days on the confluence of Gaṅgā and the ocean. Then the lord of the senses, the ocean of favour, thought through compassion:

32. 'This king has become free from sins due to singing my (virtues). Let him see my greatness honoured by gods and demons.'

33-34. Then the mighty lord, thinking like this, and with his mind full of compassion, put on the apparel of an ascetic, went near the king. O great king, having gone there after putting on the apparel of an ascetic, he reached him through compassion for the devotee and the ascetic saw him.

35-42. The best king, saying, 'Salutation to Viṣṇu', saluted him. With his mind devoted to Viṣṇu, he worshipped him with respectful offerings, water for washing his feet and with a seat; (and) said: "Matchless is my luck that I have seen you. Hereafter Viṣṇu will appear before me." Hearing these words of him, the ascetic said to him: "O king, listen to what I say. By means of my knowledge, I know the past, the future, and the present. Therefore, I (shall) say something. Listen with a concentrated mind. Tomorrow, at noon, Viṣṇu difficult to be seen even by Brahmā, will appear to you. With five kinsmen of you you will reach the highest place. (Those who will reach the highest place are:) you, (your) minister, your wife, the ascetic brāhmaṇa and the good weaver named Karamba (living) in your city. With these five you will go (to Viṣṇu), saluted by Brahmā and lord of gods and honoured by gods, on this best mountain Nīla." Speaking thus the ascetic disappeared, and was not seen anywhere. Hearing those (words of the ascetic) the king became glad and amazed.

The king said :

43. O lord, who is that ascetic that came and talked to me? He is not seen again. Where has he, giving delight to my mind, gone?

The ascetic said :

44-48. O king, due to great love for you, he, named Puruṣottama, the destroyer of all sins, with his heart attracted (by you) came (to you). Tomorrow at noon there will be (i.e. appear) a big mountain before you. Climbing it up and seeing Viṣṇu, you will be blessed.

With the torment in his heart destroyed by the flood of the nectar of these words, he obtained such (great) joy as even Brahmā did not know. At that time large kettle-drums were sounded. Lutes were played upon. Musical instruments were played upon. There was then great joy in the mind of the king of kings. Singing (the virtues of) Hari, stopping for a moment, laughing, chattering, talking, saluting, he obtained very great joy destroying all affliction.

CHAPTER TWENTYTWO

The Greatness of Nīla Mountain

Sumati said :

1-5. Then having passed the entire day with (i.e. in) the recollection and narration (of the glory of) Viṣṇu, at night he slept on the bank of Gaṅgā, giving a large fruit. In a dream he saw himself having four arms and holding a conch, a disc, a mace, and a bow, dancing in front of Viṣṇu with gods like Śiva with their pleasing bodies, with missiles like a disc, a mace, a conch and a lotus etc., (so also) with the excellent attendants of Viṣṇu having good bodies. Having seen (Viṣṇu) the lord of Śrī, the talk of the world, giving whatever is desired by the (devotees') mind, and called Puruṣottama, he was amazed and obtained very wonderful joy. The very intelligent one looked upon himself as worthy of his grace. In this way the best king saw the dream. When he got up in the morning he narrated the dream that he had seen to the brāhmaṇa.

6-7a. Having heard it the intelligent brāhmaṇa, who was amazed, told (the king): "O king, that Hari (i.e. Viṣṇu), called Puruṣottama, will give you (a body resembling) his own body marked with a conch, disc etc."

7b-10. Hearing this, Ratnagrīva, of a magnanimous mind, caused to give gifts to the poor as was thought fit by his mind. Having bathed at the confluence of Gaṅgā and the ocean, having gratified his ancestors (with oblations), he, singing the multitude of the virtues of Viṣṇu, waited to have his vision. Then in the noon, large kettle-drums, high-sounding, were beaten by the strokes of the hands of gods in the sky. All of a sudden a shower of flowers fell on the head of the king.

11-13a. "O best king, you are fortunate; see (the mountain) Nīla which is within the range of your sight." When the king heard these words uttered by the god, that great moutain, called Nīla which was wonderful and had greater brilliance than that of a crore suns, came within the range of the sight of the king.

13b-16a. On all sides it was shining with silver and golden peaks. 'Is it fire that is burning? Is it another sun? Is it the mass of lightning, which has suddenly obtained a steady lustre?' (Such were the reactions of those who saw it.) The ascetic brāhmaṇa having seen the very beautiful peak of the mountain told the king: "This is the auspicious great mountain." Hearing it the best king saluted (the mountain) by (bowing) his head.

16b-18. (He said:) "I am lucky, I am contented (that) (the mountain) Nīla has come within the range of my sight." O best man, the minister, the king's wife, the weaver Karamba also became glad on seeing Nīla. Hearing the big sounds of the large kettle-drums made by gods, the five went up the mountain at the triumphant time.

19-27. On the highest peak, adorned with variegated trees, he saw a matchless temple built in gold. Coming there always Brahmā worships Viṣṇu. Seeing an excellent, pure temple of

Viṣṇu at the place where he made an offering of eatables giving pleasure to Viṣṇu, he, surrounded by the five followers, entered it. Seeing there (the lord) charming with four arms, waited upon by the fierce and very fierce Jaya and Vijaya etc. and shining on the golden throne variegated with big gems, the king with his wife and accompanied by his servants, saluted him. The great king having saluted the best god and the highest soul, bathed him to the accompaniment of hymns proper for the bath and mentioned in the Vedas. The king with a pleased mind offered him an oblation and water for washing his feet. Then the king besmeared the lord's image with sandal, and offered two good garments. He offered (to the image) incense, waved a light and offered to the lord's image an offering of eatables fully sweet and charming. Having saluted him, he praised him by a number of hymns according to his intellect, in which a number of his virtues were strung by the ascetic brāhmaṇa.

The king said :

28-36. Puruṣa is actually one. The lord is beyond Prakṛti. He is different from effect and cause, and is worshipped by the principles like Mahat. Brahmā clever in creation was born from the lotus in your navel. Similarly, Rudra, the destroyer, was born from your eye. Ordered by you, he does all the activities about the world. The world, immovable, has come up from you, the ancient one. Having entered the power of consciousness you make him aware. O lord of the world, you do not have a birth (i.e. origin), nor do you have an end. O mighty one, growth, decay and change do not at all exist in you. Yet, for protecting your devotees and for establishing dharma, you do the acts like birth, having befitting excellences. Taking the form of a fish, you killed demon Śaṅkha. O Brahman, O ancestor of the great Puruṣa, you protected the Vedas well. Śeṣa does not know your greatness, nor does the great goddess Sarasvatī know it; then what about people like me of bad thoughts, O great Viṣṇu? (Even) this great goddess Vāk (i.e. Sarasvatī) does not mentally obtain you (i.e. is unable to conceive you). Then, O lord, how shall I be able to praise you?

Having praised him like this, he repeatedly saluted him by

(bowing) his head. His voice was faltering and his body was horripilated due to joy.

37. Viṣṇu, whose mind was pleased by means of this eulogy, said (these) significant words to the king :

The lord said :

38-40. O king of great intelligence, I am highly delighted by your praise. O great king, know me to be beyond Prakṛti. Quickly eat the charming offering of eatables. (Then) having obtained four arms, you will go to the highest position. I shall also make my appearance, giving enjoyments and salvation, to that man who will praise with the gem of eulogy (with which you praised me).

41-47. Having heard these words uttered by the lord, the king, along with his four dependents, ate the offering of eatables (made to the lord). Then an aeroplane, which was adorned with a mass of bells, which was waited upon by celestial nymphs, and which was full of all pleasures, came (there). The pious king, seeing (Viṣṇu) named Puruṣottama, saluted his feet (as) he was made the recipient of his (i.e. Viṣṇu's) favour. When he (i.e. the lord) was observing, he, with his wife, getting into the aeroplane, went to the wonderful Vaikuṇṭha in heaven. The king's excellent minister, very much devoted to piety, knowing all modes of behaviour, and waited upon by a bevy of women, went with (the king) by the aeroplane. The ascetic brāhmaṇa who had bathed at all the holy places obtained four arms and went with gods going in an aeroplane. O great king, Karamba too obtained the vision (of the lord) due to his merit (collected) through singing and reached the abode of the god, difficult to be reached (even) by all gods.

48-52. All (the five) having four arms, and holding conches, discs, maces and lotuses went to the very wonderful world of Viṣṇu. All of them had the splendour of clouds, were pure, had shining lotuses in their hands. With their bodies adorned with necklaces, armlets and bracelets, they went to the heaven. Seeing the rows of their aeroplanes, the people and the subjects made the sound of large kettle-drums in such a way that it may be perceived (i.e. heard) by ears. Then there was a brāhmaṇa, who loved the lotus-like feet of Viṣṇu. He, with his heart distressed by separation from them, went (after them), and became four-armed. The people, seeing that wonder, praised that great prosperity, and, having bathed in the water at the confluence of Gaṅgā and the ocean, went (back) to the city.

53-60. (They exclaimed:) "Oh, the (great) fortune of king Ratnagrīva, of a good mind! With this body (of him, i.e. without casting his body), he went to the highest place of Viṣṇu." O king, this Nīla mountain is honoured by Viṣṇu (himself). On seeing it (men) certainly go to Vaikuṇṭha, the highest destination. He who listens to this greatness of Nīla, is (indeed) fortunate. (He and) he who narrates it to people, both would go to the highest place. Having heard this a bad dream perishes just by remembering (it); and in the end Viṣṇu grants him (help to) cross the mundane existence. He who stays at the Nīla (mountain) is Rāma, Viṣṇu (himself). Sītā is actually the great Lakṣmī, the cause of causes. He whose name is prescribed in (i.e. as) the expiation for the murder of a brāhmaṇa, will, after performing the horse-sacrifice, purify the worlds. Now your horse has reached the vicinity of the Nīla mountain. O you highly intelligent one, salute god Viṣṇu; thereby we shall be sinless and shall go to the highest position. By his favour many have crossed this ocean of worldly existence.

61-63. When he was talking like this, the horse, striking against the earth with the speed of the wind, reached the Nīla mountain. Then the king also, going after him, reached and bathed at the confluence of Gaṅgā and the ocean. He sang (the praise of) Viṣṇu. That destroyer of the enemies, having praised and saluted the lord of gods, saluted by gods and demons, regarded himself as having become blessed.

CHAPTER TWENTYTHREE

Damana Fights with Pratāpāgrya

Śeṣa said:

1-4. The horse, having a chowrie (on his head), having the speed of mind, surrounded by a line of the heroes, bearing a note on his forehead, protected by the great hero Śatrughna, by king Lakṣmīnidhi, by Puṣkala, Ugravāha and Pratāpāgrya went to the city Cakrāṅkā protected by Subāhu. O lord, he was protected and followed by many crores of warriors. At that time his great (i.e. Subāhu's) son, Damana, who had gone ahunting, saw the horse with a note on his forehead and besmeared with sandal etc.

5-7. Seeing (the horse), he said to his servant: "Whose horse is seen by me? Why has he got a note on his head, so also a beautiful chowrie?" Hearing these words of the king, the servant then went from there to the place where the well-decorated horse with a note on his forehead stood. Having seized him, decorated with a jewelled necklace, by his hair (i.e. his mane) he took him in front of the king of the supporter of the Subāhu family.

8-12. He read the note having beautiful letters: "There was king Daśaratha, the powerful lord of Ayodhyā. Rāmabhadra, the crest-jewel of all the brave men, is his son. There is no other person having valour like his son. There is no other person having valour like him in archery on the earth. He has released his horse besmeared with sandal etc. Righteous Śatrughna, killer of the warriors of his enemy, is protecting him. Those (who think) 'We are brave warriors; we have bows in our hands' should forcibly seize the horse adorned with a jewelled necklace. Śatrughna, the crest-jewel of all heroes will free him. Otherwise let the archers bow down at his feet."

13-18. Knowing the import, the king's son said: "Rāma alone is an archer. We are not considered to be kṣatriyas! What is this great pride on the earth when my father is living on the earth? Let him obtain the fruit of his pride through the arrows discharged by me. Today let my sharp arrows really render Lakṣmaṇa like a blooming kiṁśuka tree with his body covered with wounds; and let my arrows split the temples of his elephants. Let them see the hundreds of horses covered with streams of blood. Let the groups of (the female attendants of Durgā called) Yoginīs drink the blood from the heads of men. Let the female jackals be pleased with eating the dead bodies of my enemies. Let his good (i.e. brave) warriors observe the great power of me, discharging crores of arrows released from my bow."

19-20. Having spoken like this, that prominent son of the king, named Damana, sent him to his own city, and said to his general: "To ward off the host of enemies keep ready for me a limited army, O you very intelligent one." When the fierce one made the army ready and stood facing the battle, (just) then the followers of the horse came (there).

21-28. They who were repeatedly confounded, asked one another: "Where is the great king's horse, marked with a note on his forehead?" Just then, the hero Pratāpāgrya saw in front of him the army that was ready and that was resounding with the sounds (made) by the heroes. At that time some people said: "O king, (your) horse is taken (away) by this one (i.e. by Damana). Otherwise, how would he, followed by the army of heroes stand facing (you)?" Hearing these (words), Pratāpāgrya sent his servant (to Damana). Having gone there, he asked (him): "Where is the horse of king Rāma? Who has taken it? Where has he taken it?. Does the fool not know Rāma, having made an offering to whom gods led by Indra have well bowed (before him). The large army of that righteous king, being angry, will fully destroy (him) if he does not salute him." Hearing (these words) spoken (by the servant), the mighty and wicked son of the king reproached with a mass of words.

29-32. (He said:) "I have brought the sacrificial horse adorned with such marks as the note etc. Those who are brave may free him by conquering me now with force." The servant, having heard those words, was full of anger, and he, laughing, went (back). He told the king as narrated properly (above). Hearing it, the very mighty Pratāpāgrya, with his eyes red due to anger, went to fight with the king's son, followed by great heroes. The mighty one went in a chariot made of gold, shining with four horses, having a good (i.e. strong) pole to which the yoke was fixed, and filled with all (kinds of) missiles.

33-36. Accompanied by a great army, he made the twang of his bow. Again and again he laughed loudly, causing tears to be shed through anger. The horse-riders, elephant-riders, with their hands glittering with swords followed that Pratāpāgrya whose eyes were full of tears due to anger. The elephants, the foot-soldiers in crores, ready for the fight, desired for a long time the fight waged by the hero. Then having come to know that the enemy's army was ready, the king's son, the best among the heroes, and surrounded by a huge army, advanced.

37-45. The young (prince), having taken a sword and a bow, sportively went to fight as a lion (approaches) a herd of elephants. Then the warriors, skilled in the act of fighting, being very angry, and desiring to kill one another, said: "Cut (him) off; break (him)". The foot-soldiers (fought) with the group of foot-soldiers; the elephant-riders (fought) with the warriors (on elephants); those who had got into chariots (fought) with those who were in chariots; the horse-riders (fought) with those who were seated on horses. The elephants were cut off, and were divided into two. The horses also were split up into two. The earth was filled with many human heads. Then that very mighty Pratāpāgrya who was very angry, having seen the prince ready to destroy his army, said to his charioteer: "Take the horses (i.e. the chariot) to that place where that great warrior, that prince, is engaged in the destruction of my army." Then the brave prince whose feet were bowed by the jewels of the heads of the heroes, confronted Pratāpāgrya. Pratāpāgrya's charioteer took his horses to that place where the hero Damana, the crest-jewel of all the brave, stood. Standing in the chariot nourished (i.e. adorned) with gold, and holding a bow he went to the prince ready to fight, and challenged him:

46-50. "O prince, O child, you have tied up the best horse. You do not know the great king (Rāma) who is served by all best heroes, whose wonderful valour even the lord of the demons (i.e. Rāvaṇa) could not bear. Having taken his horse, you went to your house. Know me, your enemy, of the form of death, who have come to your city. O child, leave the horse, and play a child's game. Whose son are you? Wherefrom do you come?

How have you—a short-sighted one—seized the horse? O child, pity for you has arisen in me." Having heard this, Damana, of a large heart, smiled, and, looking down upon the power of Pratāpāgrya, said to him:

Damana said:

51-52. I tied the horse forcibly, and took him to my city. O you very powerful one, I shall not give (back the horse). With life (i.e. if you live) fight (with me). About what you told me that I am a child and I should go and play, (I say), O great king, see my play in the battle.

Śeṣa said:

53-60. Speaking like this he took up his bow with the string. He, born from one having strong arms, discharged a hundred arrows on the chest of Pratāpāgrya. Having fixed a hundred arrows on his bow, the valourous one blew a conch. Due to that sound of the conch, the timid were frightened. He struck at his chest with a hundred arrows. Dexterous Pratāpāgrya cut off the good (i.e. sharp) arrows. Seeing the arrows cut off, and getting angry, the powerful son of the king discharged sharp arrows having heron feathers (attached to them). Curved arrows, bearing their names, and beautiful with sharp edge and falling (down), were seen in the sky and on the ground. The arrows sticking to his arms and chest produced many fire-particles and burnt the army. It was a great (tragedy). The very angry Pratāpāgrya, saying 'Wait, wait', struck him on the head with arrows, ten in number. Those arrows stuck into the forehead of the prince. O sage, they shone there like ten branches of a tree.

61-67. The high-minded one was not afflicted by being struck by the arrows, like a seven-year old elephant struck by sticks. Having fixed three hundred auspicious arrows with their feathered parts decked with gold, and resembling the fire of Śiva, on his bow he discharged them. Those arrows pierced the chest of Pratāpāgrya and being besmeared with blood, he went down like those who are averse to the devotion of Rāma. Pratāpāgrya got very much angry, and discharging thousands of arrows quickly, deprived Subāhu's son of his chariot that moment (only). With four (arrows) he killed his four horses; with two (arrows) cut down his flag. With one (arrow) he caused to fall down on the ground the charioteer's head from his body. Again with four (arrows) he struck the king's son. At that moment only he cut off with one (arrow) the bow along with its string. The large-minded one got into another chariot adorned with gems of horses and taking a bow in his hand he made it ready.

68-80. He said to Pratāpāgrya: "O good hero, you have shown a wonderful valour. Now see the superiority of my bow." Saying so, Damana took ten arrows; and with four (arrows) killed the four horses. With four he cut the chariot with its wheels into (pieces of the size of) sesamum (seeds). With one he pierced his chest, and with one he (pierced) his charioteer. Blowing his conch he roared and with the sound of the conch he honoured his deed (saying): "Well (done), O hero, O you of great power." Thus seeing the valour, Pratāpāgrya, with anger got into another chariot and went to fight with the prince. (He) said (to him:) "O hero, see my wonderful valour." Saying so he quickly discharged a volley of arrows with whetted joints. Everywhere, on (the bodies of) elephants and horses arrows were seen. Going into the space they occupied every place like the highest Brahman. The brave and great one, delighting his own hosts and making his enemies very much dejected, and (even) lose their life, quickly covering the prince with crores of sharp arrows, roared. The mighty and very powerful prince, seeing himself completely covered with masses of sharp arrows, got angry and he of an endless valour took up weapons; and he shaking the bow on his arms, and with his eyes red due to anger, discharging arrows, tearing the enemies, cut off all the missiles and weapons (of his enemy). Having destroyed that mass of weapons, the prince said to him: "O respectable one, if you are (really) brave, pardon me for this one stroke. O brave one, listen to my solemn declaration made by me through pride: "Let me have that sin, drowning me into the ocean of hell, of those arrogant ones, clever in disputation, who censure the Veda, if with this (one) stroke I would not knock you down from your chariot."

81-88. Speaking like this, he drew out from the quiver an excellent sharp arrow resembling death, full of a series of flames, and placed it on his bow. That arrow resembling in effulgence the destructive fire at the end of the world, and aimed at the chest (of Pratāpāgrya), was discharged by the excellent (son of the) king. It speedily reached him. Pratāpāgrya, seeing the arrow on the point of knocking him down fixed sharp arrows on his bow to cut off that arrow. That arrow cutting off all the arrows in the middle reached Pratāpāgrya's heart endowed with courage. The arrow stuck his chest and entered his heart. The king (thus) struck fell down on the ground. His charioteer, seeing him in a swoon and unconscious and fallen from the driving box on the ground, took him and carried him away from the battle (-field). There was a very loud wailing, the army was baffled and went where (their chief) named Śatrughna, surrounded by crores of brave men, stood. The king's son (i.e. Damana) having obtained victory after vanquishing Pratāpāgrya, waited for king Śatrughna.

CHAPTER TWENTYFOUR

Puṣkala Defeats Damana

Śeṣa said:

1-3. Śatrughna who was overpowered with anger, was grinding his teeth, shaking his hands, repeatedly licking his lip with his tongue, again and again asked them: "Who has taken (away) my horse? Who has vanquished Pratāpāgrya, the crest-jewel of all the heroes?" Then the servants said: "Damana, Subāhu's son, and the killer of his enemies, conquered Pratāpāgrya and has taken aways the horse."

4-10. Hearing this, viz. that his enemy Damana had taken (away) the horse, he speedily came to (the spot) where the battle had taken place. There Śatrughna saw (his) elephants that were (once) haughty due to rut, with their cheeks torn and merging in the water (i.e. pool) of blood. That very angry, brave Śatrughna saw his horses wounded and dead along with their riders. That killer of the enemies seeing his men, chariots and elephants completely vanquished was extremely angry as the ocean at the time of final deluge (is agitated). Seeing before him that pre-eminent Damana who had, after belittling his army, taken away the horse and had vanquished Pratāpāgrya, the king, with his eyes full of anger, said to his warriors: "Who is here (among the warriors) that would conquer Damana, wielding all (kinds of) weapons and missiles, and who, being fearless, will vanquish with a missile the brave prince skilled in fighting?"

11-17. Hearing these words, (Bharata's son) Puṣkala, the killer of (his) enemies, ready to conquer Damana, said these words: "O lord where is this Damanaka, and where is your unlimited army? (i.e. what a great disparity is there between the two?) Due to your valour I shall conquer (him); O highly intelligent one, here I go. When I the servant, remain (here) to fight (with the enemy), who will take (away) the horse? This valour of Raghunātha will do every act. O lord, listen to my solemn declaration which will give you joy. In the battle I shall conquer Damana skilled in fight. If I would not conquer Damana, let me incur that sin incurred by those who are deprived of the tasting of the honey from the lotuses in the form of the feet of Rāmacandra. I would have that sin which that son who (first) looking upon his mother's feet as a holy place (later) goes against her, if I do not conquer Damana. Today let the king's son (i.e. Damana), with his huge chest pierced by my arrow, adorn the earth by his lying (there) in the battle."

Śeṣa said:

18-24. Having heard this solemn declaration of Puṣkala, (Śatrughna) perpetuating the family of Raghu, was glad at heart; and the brilliant one ordered (him) to fight. Being ordered (by Śatrughna), he (i.e. Puṣkala) surrounded by a large army went there where the prince Damana, born in the family of the brave, stood. Knowing him to have come to the battlefield, the best among the heroes, surrounded by his army, went forth to him. The two seated in their chariots and looking graceful in them, encountered each other (and looked as if) Indra and a demon had come to the battlefield to fight. Puṣkala said to that very mighty prince: "O prince Damana, know me to be the mighty son of Bharata, and to have come to fight (with you) with (i.e. after having made) a solemn declaration; and O best one, know me to be known by the name Puṣkala and having the sweet vow of always serving the feet of Raghunātha. O you very intelligent one, I shall conquer you by means of a multitude of weapons. Be ready (to fight with) me)."

25-28. Having heard these words, Damana, the killer of enemies, an orator, fearless and one whose valour was noticed, laughed and replied: "Know me to be Damana, Subāhu's son, with my sin removed due to my devotion to my father, and to have taken (away) the horse of king Śatrughna. Victory is brought about by destiny. He whom destiny adorns, will have it. Observe my might in the battle." Speaking in this way, he fixed an arrow on his bow, stretched it up to his ear, and discharged sharp arrows that took away his enemies' life.

29-31. The arrows, getting darkish, covered the sky where the brilliance of the sun's rays was put off by the shadow of the arrows. The line of arrows that had stuck to the wall-like temples of the elephants adorned (them) like variegated colours of minerals. Men, horses, elephants and chariots, struck by the volley of arrows of (i.e. discharged by) the king, were seen to have fallen there.

32-39. Puṣkala, the killer of the enemies, having seen his valour and having seen the battlefield covered with the shadow of arrows fixed an arrow accompanied with hymns sacred to Agni on his bow. Having sipped water according to the proper rite, he discharged the arrow. Then there on the battlefield fire appeared. Touching the sky with its flames it rose like the fire at the time of the deluge. Then his army was tormented and was frightened on the battlefield. Being oppressed by the flames of fire, it took to heels. The (crescent) moon-like umbrellas of the archers were burnt and appeared to have the lustre of silver. The enemies' horses, burnt at their (i.e. with their) manes (burnt), ran away. The chariots also, along with good drivers' seats, were burnt. Camels, carrying gems like rubies, and troubled by series of flames as in a crematory, ran (away). At some places elephants died; at some place riders of horses perished; at places footsoldiers with their bodies burnt by fire perished.

40-45. All the arrows discharged by the prince perished. They were reduced to ashes by the arrows (discharged with the accompaniment) of (hymns sacred to) fire. Then, Damana, knowing the use of all missiles, with his mind full of anger, took the missile called Varuṇa, when his army was (thus) burnt. He discharged the missile (to the accompaniment) of (hymns sacred to) Varuṇa to pacify the fire. It submerged all his army full of chariots and horses. The chariots of the enemies were seen to be submerged in the water. Elephants also were inundated. His own (elephants) had become calm. The fire that was discharged through the 'fire-missile' had died. His own army, oppressed by the flames of fire, became peaceful. The enemies trembled and made sounds by drawing in breath due to the cold water, and struck by shower of hail and troubled by wind.

46-52. Then seeing his own army troubled by flood of water, and shaken, agitated, fled and removed by the Varuṇa (missile), Bharata's son Puṣkala, with his eyes red due to great anger, fixed a great arrow, the 'wind-missile' on his bow. Then there was great (i.e. strong) wind propelled by the wind-missile. It speedily, destroyed the dense army that was present there. The serpents shaken by the wind struct one another. The horses also along with their riders struck one another. Men shaken up by the wind, had their hair loose, were lustreless, and were seen to be falling like vampires that had come to the earth. The prince, seeing that his army was overpowered by wind on all sides, fixed the 'mountain-missile' on his bow. Then mountains fell on the heads of those who were fighting. They covered the wind; and it did not stir anywhere.

53-60. Puṣkala fixed (the arrow) called Vajra on his bow. Those (enemies) cut off by Vajra in a moment became reduced to the size of sesamum-seeds. (That missile called) Vajra reducing mountains to particles, and with its shafts accompanied by a hymn, heavily fell, with a loud sound on the chest of the prince. He the strong hero, with his mind confounded and struck on the chest and heavily wounded was pained and was very much dejected. The prudent charioteer, seeing the prince dejected in mind, took him away from there to a distance of a krośa. Then the prince's warriors fled and ran away. Having gone to the city, they told (people there) about the prince being in a state of dejection of mind. The righteous Puṣkala having thus secured victory in the battle and remembering the words of Rāma was not able to (i.e. did not) strike again. Then there was the loud sound of the large kettledrums. There was a huge cry of victory. Charming words like 'Well (done), Well (done)' proceeded there. Seeing Puṣkala victorious that Śatrughna was glad. Surrounded by ministers like Sumati, he praised (Puṣkala).

CHAPTER TWENTYFIVE

Subāhu Gets Ready with His Army in the Krauñca Array

Śeṣa said:

1-3. Then, seeing his warriors with their bodies covered with streams of blood, the king was not happy. He grieved; and asked them about the movements of his son (Damana): "Tell me his entire act. How did he take away the excellent horse? Tell me also how much army (the enemy has)? How many heroes came there to fight? How did my hero Damana, intent on fighting with the enemy's army, fight and someone, having conquered this invincible hero, destroyed him."

4-17. Having heard these words of the king, those servants of him, wearing garments wet with blood (oozing) from their bodies, said: "O king, having seen the horse adorned with marks like the note etc. I got it seized through pride and belittling the best of Raghus. Then the follower (i.e. the protector) of the horse, surrounded by a small army, came (there). And a fierce and thrilling fight took place with him. When your son, having, made him swoon with his own arrows, stood there, Śatrughna, surrounded by his large army came there. Then a great battle accompanied by (i.e. in which) weapons and missiles (were used), ensued. Your very mighty son became victorious many times. O king, now, having discharged a missile, the son of Śatrughna's brother has made your brave son swoon in the battle." Hearing these words, (the king) full of anger and grief had his body covered (with bravery) like the ocean on the parvan-day. With his lips throbbing due to anger, (gnawing) his teeth with this teeth, licking his lips with his tongue, and emaciated due to grief, he said to his general: "Keep my army ready in the vicinity (of Śatrughna's army). I shall fight with Rāma's brave soldiers who have harmed my son. Today I shall, with sharp arrows, overthrow him who has troubled my son, (even) if the great lord will protect him. The general, having heard these words spoken by the king of mighty arms, did like that (i.e. as he was ordered), and himself became ready. He reported to the king that the army which consisted of four divisions, and resembled the army of Death, had killed crores of wicked people. Having heard the words of his general, Subāhu, the killer of his enemies, went out to that place where Śatrughna who had troubled his son, stayed. (He went there) with elephants intoxicated by rut, with horses having the speed of mind, with chariots full of all weapons and missiles and conquering the enemy.

18-26. At that time, due to the great weight of the army, the earth quaked. As the army was moving on, there was a great hustle and bustle. Seeing the king to have moved out in a chariot with its parts made of gold, Śatrughna's army, (capable of) striking all enemies, became ready. His brother Suketu, skilled in mace-fight, and full of (i.e. endowed with) all weapons and missiles quickly came there by a chariot. The king's son, Citrāṅga, skilled in all (types of) battle, quickly went in his own chariot to the furious army of Śatrughna. His younger brother known as Vicitra, skilled in various (modes of) fight and afflicted by his brother's grief, went in his golden chariot. Other brave warriors, skilled in the use of all weapons and missiles, being ordered by the king, went to the battle full of warriors. King Subāhu angrily came to the battlefield. He (there) saw his son in a swoon (due to being) hit by an arrow. Seeing his unconscious son named Damana lying in the driving box, the king again and again became grieved and fanned him with twigs. The brave hero, knowing (the use of) great missiles, sprinkled with water and touched by the king with a delicate hand, slowly regained consciousness.

27-30. He got up (and said:) "Where is my bow? Where has Puṣkala, after having got ready (to fight) and being hurt by my arrow, gone after having left the battle?" Hearing these words uttered by his son Subāhu was extremely glad and embraced his own son. Damana with his body wounded by rows of missiles, on seeing his father, bowed his neck (i.e. head) and devoutly fell at his feet. The king skilled in (various) acts of fight put back his son into the chariot, and said to the general:

31-35. "Arrange the military array called Krauñca, invincible to the enemy, entering which I shall conquer the army of king Śatrughna." Hearing those words of king Subāhu, his general arranged the special type of military array called Krauñca, which the very mighty groups of enemy, holding hosts of weapons did not enter all of a sudden. At its mouth (i.e. entrance) Suketu stood; at the throat (a hero) called Citrāṅga remained; at the two sides stood two princes, and at the tail the king (himself) stood. In between his huge army looked splendid with its four divisions. Having made the Krauñca array, the general informed the king of having arranged it. The king, having seen his army that was ready (for the action), and the well-formed Krauñca-array, decided to fight with the warriors present in Śatrughna's army.

CHAPTER TWENTYSIX

A Fierce Fight Between Lakṣmīnidhi and Suketu

Śeṣa said:

1-2. Seeing that army like a cloud of a fearful size, and surrounded by many elephants, horses, chariots and foot-soldiers, Śatrughna spoke thus to Sumati in serious words. Waited upon by learned men knowing many words and ideas.

Śatrughna said:

3-6. O Sumati, whose city has reached my best horse? I see this army resembling the ripples of an ocean. Whose army is this which is endowed with four divisions, is very joyful, and appears before (me) standing with eagerness to fight? Properly tell all this to me who am asking you, knowing which I shall order my soldiers to take position for the fight.

Hearing these words, Sumati, of an auspicious mind, being pleased, said to Śatrughna, the tormentor of his enemies.

Sumati said:

7-11. O king, in the vicinity there is an auspicious city (called) Cakrāṅkā, in which there are sinless persons due to their devotion to Viṣṇu. This Subāhu, most familiar with the religious law, and the lord of that city, is present, surrounded by sons and grandsons, before you. He is always attached to his own wife and is averse to another man's wife. Viṣṇu's story revealing the highest object, dwells in his ears. The king does not take more than a sixth part of the wealth of another person (i.e. any person is his kingdom). He, the religious one, worships brāhmaṇas with the same devotion with which he worships Viṣṇu. Having the vow (of drinking) the honey from the lotuses of the feet of Viṣṇu, he is always engaged in serving him. He is devoted to his own duty; he is averse to another's way of life.

12-14a. The army of no other heroes is like his army. Hearing about the defeat of his son, he, being full of grief and endowed with his four-divisioned army, he is present (here) to fight. You also have these many heroes like Lakṣmīnidhi. With the host of their weapons, they will conquer the enemy. Order them who are well-disposed to you.

14b-21a. Hearing those words, Śatrughna said to his excellent heroes whose minds were full of great joy due to the battle having come near: "Subāhu's soldiers have today arranged the Krauñca array. His heroes have taken position at its opening and sides. Who, knowing (the use of) weapons, will break through it? He who has the power to break through it, or is eager for victory should take up this gauntlet from my lotus-like hand." Then the hero Lakṣmīnidhi took up (the gauntlet) to break the Krauñca(-array). He, surrounded by many heroes, knowing (the use of) all weapons and missiles, said (these) words: "O king, I shall go to break through the Krauñca(-array). Formerly, Bhārgava (i.e. Paraśurāma) broke through the Krauñca(-mountain). (Now) I (shall do) like (him)." Then he said to another hero: "Who will go with him?" Then Puṣkala made up his mind to go after him. Riputāpa, Nalaratna, Ugrāśva, Vīramardana—all (these) went by Śatrughna's order to break through the Krauñca(-array).

21b-27a. Great Śatrughna, seated in a chariot, having all (kinds of) weapons, and surrounded by many soldiers, followed him. At that time the two oceans with big waves and ready to destroy the world appeared to be agitated. Then big kettle-drums from both armies were beaten. At every place were heard the war-drums and sounds of conches. The horses neighed and the elephants trumpeted very much. The best heroes gave out 'hum' sounds. The fellies of the chariot-wheels made a sound. There on the battlefield many angry warriors who were brave and very proud of the might of their arms were seen saying (to one another): "Cut (him off); break (him)." When both the armies of Śatrughna and his enemy were thus ready to fight, Lakṣmīnidhi said to Suketu who was at the opening (of the array):

Lakṣmīnidhi said:

27b-31a. Know me to be the son of Janaka, known as Lakṣmīnidhi, skilled in (the use of) all weapons and missiles, and proficient in fighting. Release the horse of Rāmacandra, the destroyer of all demons. Otherwise, pierced by my arrows you will go to Yama's abode.

Hastening suddenly to the best hero who was speaking like this, Suketu made his bow ready and discharging arrows quickly became steady. Those arrows had sharp joints; had their feathered parts made of gold; they were difficult to be put up with; they were seen to pervade (everything) in the battle.

31b-40. Having speedily destroyed that volley of arrows, Lakṣmīnidhi stretched his bow and discharged at his chest six sharp arrows charming with whetted joints. Those arrows were seen to have gone down to the earth after having pierced the heart of the brother of the strong-armed one; they were smeared with blood and were stained. With his chest pierced by his arrows, Suketu, who was full of anger, struck him with twenty sharp arrows with their joints curved. Both were seen by the soldiers to have their bodies pierced with arrows, covered with blood like the kiṁśuka (trees) full of flowers. The two who were discharging crores of arrows, who were fixing (on their bows)quickly(-going) arrows, who were dexterous and mighty, were (i.e. could) not (be) distinguished by any one. They had coiled (i.e. bent) their good bows, they were showering (their enemy) with the stream of arrows, and were like new clouds executing Indra's order. Their arrows were just seen to behead elephants, horses and brave men, but were not seen when they were fixed on the bow or discharged. By them having bows and arrows in their hands and biting their lips through anger, the earth was filled with great warriors having diadems and rings. Between the two, knowing (the use of) all weapons and missiles, and fighting proudly, a fierce, great battle, causing wonder (even) to the gods, took place. A great battle, piercing crores of warriors, took place. Nobody at no place saw (i.e. could see) the sky in (i.e. due to) the net of arrows.

41-63a. At that time brave Lakṣmīnidhi who destroyed his enemies, fixed sharp, strong arrows, eight in number, on his bow. With four arrows the hero killed the horses of Suketu; and laughing he quickly cut off the very lofty flag (of his chariot). With one he knocked down on the ground the charioteer's head from his body. He, full of anger, cut off, with one (arrow) the (enemy's) bow along with the string. The swift king, with one (arrow) pierced the chest of Suketu. Seeing that wonderful deed, heroes were astonished. (Suketu) whose bow was cut off, who was without a chariot, whose horses and charioteer were killed, took up a big mace and approached (his enemy) with a desire to fight. Seeing him, skilled in mace-fighting, to have approached, he got down with a mace (in his hand) from (his) chariot. Lakṣmīnidhi, who was very angry, took a big mace fully made of iron and variegated with gold (i.e. bright) and full of all charm, hastily struck that mace resembling the fire of the thunderbolt on the chest (of Suketu). O great sage, that hero (though) struck by the mace, did not shake like an intoxicated elephant struck with garlands by a child. Then that best hero said to Lakṣmīnidhi: "O you tormentor of the enemies, if you are brave, (then) put up with one stroke of my mace."

Saying so, he heavily struck on his forehead with the mace. Being struck on the forehead with the mace, he vomitted blood, and was very angry, and struck on his head with the mace of the nature of death (i.e. the fatal mace). Suketu, knowing the ways of the world, also struck him on (his) shoulder. Thus the two, skilled in mace-fighting, being very much angry, fighting with maces, desiring to conquer each other, avoiding each other's strokes, were intent upon killing each other. In that war nobody would lose and nobody would win. The two very mighty and brave ones were wet with streams of blood on (i.e. flowing from) the head, the forehead, the shoulder, the chest, and all the limbs. Then Lakṣmīnidhi, getting angry, raised his mace speedily and he, the powerful one, went (forward) to strike the powerful younger brother of the king on his chest. Then the king's brother, seeing him coming, held his great mace, and went all of a sudden to kill him from (his) army to (Lakṣmīnidhi's) army. This one held (i.e. caught) in his hand the mace hurled by him; (and) the very powerful one struck him with the same mace. Then king Lakṣmīnidhi, seeing that he had taken (i.e. caught) his mace, desired to have hand-to-hand fight with the strongest one. Then the king's younger brother who was angry, who knew (i.e. proficient in) fighting of all kinds, and who was the best among the heroes, seized him with his arms. Then Lakṣmīnidhi struck on his chest with his fist. Then he too, raising his fist, struck him on his head. The two who were angry and were biting their bud-like lips, struck each other with terrible slaps with the hands resembling the thunderbolt. They indulged in boxing; they bit each other with their teeth; they seized each other's hair; they scratched each other with their nails.

63b-69. Thus the fight between the two was fierce and horripilating. Then the angry brother of the king seized the king's foot, swung him round and threw him on the ground. Lakṣmīnidhi seized the hand of the king's younger brother and swinging him round for a hundred times high up (in the air), overthrew him on the hip of the elephant. Then he fell on the ground; and then in a moment regaining consciousness, the brave one in the same way speedily whirled him in the sky (i.e. in the air). Then the two, who were fighting, again indulged in boxing. The two, desiring to kill each other, clung to each other—one's foot on the other's foot, seizing the hand (of the enemy) with his own hand, chest with chest, and mouth with mouth. Both were very valourous, both swooned. Seeing that (men) in thousands were amazed and praised (them): "O king Lakṣmīnidhi is blessed; blessed is the mighty younger brother of the king!"

CHAPTER TWENTYSEVEN

Killing of Citrāṅga

Śeṣa said:

1-3. Citrāṅga who was seated in his chariot and was at the neck of the Krauñca(-array), and was adorned with heroes, plunged into that army as a boar plunges into the ocean. Having stretched his very strong bow, resounding like thundering, he discharged sharp arrows burning crores of enemies. Great heroes with their entire bodies very much pierced with the arrows, lay (there) with the diadems and armours on their bodies and with their lips bitten.

4-8. When the battle proceeded like this, Puṣkala taking the bow that was variegated with gems and that very much tormented the enemies, went to fight. The forms of the two who had come together (to fight) looked very charming like the forms of Skanda and Tāraka in the Tāraka-battle in ancient times. That dexterous Puṣkala, quickly stretching his bow, quickly struck him with arrows having curved joints. Citrāṅga too, who was overpowered with anger, fixed sharp arrows on his bow and repeatedly discharged them in the front part of the battlefield. The taking (of the arrow from the quiver) was not noticed; the fixing (of the arrow on the bow) was not noticed; the discharge (of the arrow) was not noticed. Only the two (heroes) who had coiled (i.e. stretched) their bows were noticed.

9-13. Then that Puṣkala who was angry pierced the great, pre-eminent warrior on his chest with a hundred arrows.

Citrāṅga in a moment cut off all those arrows into (pieces of the size of) sesamum seeds; and with (his) arrows he struck Puṣkala on the limbs of his body. With his charming, deceptive missile Puṣkala whirled that divine chariot in the sky (i.e. air). It was indeed a wonder. That chariot, along with the horses, after having moved round in a circle (in the air) became steady; and with a great difficulty it remained on the battlefield. Seeing his valour, that intelligent Citrāṅga who was skilled in (the use of) all missiles, was angry, and said to Puṣkala:

Citrāṅga said:

14-19. You have done a good deed, appreciated by good warriors in the battle, viz. you whirled for a moment my chariot with the horses in the sky (i.e. air). (Now) see also my valour displayed by good warriors. You would be moving in the sky and (would be) honoured by gods.

He the best one among those familiar with the use (of weapons), and knowing (the use of) great missiles discharged with (i.e. from) his bow an extremely fierce missile. Being pierced in the battle with that arrow he alongwith his chariot, horses, flag and charioteer moved in the sky like a bird. (And) even before the best chariot quickly whirling in the sky (i.e. air) became steady, he discharged another arrow. The chariot, along with the charioteer, again whirled round (in the air). Seeing that act of his son, the king was amazed.

20-29. Puṣkala, the killer of the heroes on the side of the enemy, somehow became steady and struck his chariot, along with the charioteer and horses, with arrows. That hero, whose chariot was shattered, resorted to another chariot. That too was broken with his arrows by Puṣkala on the battlefield. When, after having got into another chariot he encountered him, he again shattered his chariot with sharp arrows. In this way that hero, Puṣkala, shining in the great battle, shattered ten chariots of the king's son. Then Citrāṅgaka, remaining in a variegated chariot, speedily came to fight with Puṣkala in the battle. In the battle he struck Puṣkala with five arrows. The son of Bharata (i.e. Puṣkala), being struck with those arrows, was extremely pained. He, being angry, raised his bow, and discharged ten great, sharp arrows with their feathered ends beautified with gold, at his chest. Those extremely fierce arrows drank his blood. Having drunk it, they fell on the ground like one's ancestors who were false witnesses. Then the angry Citrāṅgaka took five arrows and discharged them at the forehead of the very vigourous son of Bharata. He (i.e. Puṣkala) being struck with those arrows, fixed an arrow on his excellent bow and took a vow to kill Citrāṅga:

30-38a. "O hero, listen to my pledge regarding killing you. Knowing it, you should attentively fight here. If, with this arrow, I do not deprive you of your life, then indeed it is my pledge that I would have (i.e. go to) that world which is reached by those people governed by Yama, who have polluted a chaste woman graceful with good conduct." Having heard these best words, the killer of great heroes laughed. The intelligent hero spoke auspicious words to Puṣkala: "Death always and everywhere is certain in the case of beings. Therefore, O you crest-jewel of heroes, I am not sorry about my death. O hero, that pledge which you, endowed with valour, have taken, is certainly true. That sin which a man who breaks (i.e. changes) the mind of him who desires to go on a pilgrimage, or which a man who knows (i.e. values) any other vow than the lofty vow of Ekādaśī has, gets, will accrue to me who would violate my vow (i.e. if I violate my vow)."

38b-39. Speaking these words only, he became silent, and took up his bow. Then he, having taken out from his quiver an excellent arrow, spoke distinct words leading to the enemy's murder.

Puṣkala said:

40-48. If I have served with a mind free from wickedness the pair of Rāma's feet, then my words would come true. If I have enjoyed my own wife, and do not know (i.e. have not seen) any other woman (even) in a dream, then my words will come true.

Saying so he fixed on his bow an arrow resembling the destructive fire at the end of the world, and (capable of) cutting the heroes' head, and discharged it. The powerful son of the king, seeing the arrow that was discharged, fixed on his bow a sharp arrow resembling the destructive fire at the end of the world. That arrow cut off the arrow ready to kill him. There was a great wailing when that arrow was cut off. The hinder part of the arrow fell on the ground, and the forepart along with the blade cut off his neck in a moment like a lotus-stalk. Seeing him falling on the ground his soldiers wailed profusely and fled away. That excellent head along with the diadem and ear-rings fell on the ground and looked beautiful like the cresent moon (falling) from the sky. Seeing the hero fallen, Puṣkala, Bharata's son, plunged into the array, fully accompanied by all heroes.

CHAPTER TWENTYEIGHT

Subāhu's Defeat

Śeṣa said:

1-4. Then the king, having seen his pre-eminent son fallen dead (on the ground), was pained by the grief due to (the death of) his son, and wept very much. Being extremely afflicted, he struck on his head with his hands. Trembling very much, he shed tears from his lotus-like eyes. Taking the son who was fallen (dead), who was charming like the curved orb of the moon (i.e. like the crescent moon), who was wet with the blood (oozing) from the wounds caused by the arrows of Puṣkala, who looked charming by means of the ear-rings, whose pair of eye-brows was curved, who was the best, who had bitten his budlike lower lip, he kissed him with his lotus-like mouth and lamenting said these words:

5-7. "O (my) brave son, O hero, why do you not look at me, of an eager heart, with the pair of your clear eyes? Why are you without (i.e. not telling me) a story for my diversion? You indeed appear to have your mind plunging into the sea of anger. O son, tell me how (i.e. why) you are not laughing and not talking to me. (Why) are you not amusing me with your nectar (-like words) having a sweet taste, O son? O you very intelligent one, take Śatrughna's horse adorned with a white chowrie and possessing beauty on account of a golden leaf; (but) give up your sleep.

8-12. This Puṣkala, spotless with his valour, the best due to his valour, the tormentor of his enemies, the killer of enemies' heroes, appears having a bow (in his hand) before you. Ward him off by good, sharp arrows discharged from your bow. O hero, how do you, being unconscious, lie in the battlefield? The elephants, the foot-soldiers, so also those seated in chariots, being afflicted through fear, will surrender themselves to you. Look at them, O very intelligent one. O son, how, without you, am I able to bear the sharp arrows of Śatrughna, discharged from his fierce bow on the battlefield? Henceforth who is capable of protecting me abandoned by you? If you will abandon your sleep, then I am capable of (having) victory."

13-19. The king, lamenting very much like this, afflicted due to the grief (of the death) of his son, very much and repeatedly beat his chest with his hand. Then (his two sons) Vicitra and Damana seated in their own chariots saluted the feet of their father, and spoke what was proper for the occasion: "O king, when we are alive, tell us what grief you have in your heart. The death longed for by the heroes in a battle, becomes great. Indeed this lordly Citrāṅga who, with his diadem, with his lips bitten with his teeth, looks splendid on the heroes' ground, is fortunate. Quickly tell what work, desired by you, we should do today. We two shall today destroy the entire helpless army of Śatrughna. Today only we shall cause to fall down from the chariot, Puṣkala, the killer of our brother in the battle, after having cut off his head adorned with a crown. Give up your grief. O you very highly intelligent one, how do you appear to be very much afflicted with grief?"

20-24. Having heard these words of his two brave and highly honoured sons, the great king gave up his grief and decided to fight. They too, who were furious in the battle, and who longed for an opponent, went into the enemy's army, full of unlimited warriors. The two heroes, resembling clouds in the rainy season fought in the battle—Damana with Riputāpa, and the other (i.e. Vicitra) with Nīlaratna. The powerful king, holding a bow and remaining in his chariot, covered with gold, beautified with gems, rich in beauty on account of jewelled poles, and looking down upon great heroes skilled in archery, went to fight with Śatrughna surrounded by crores of heroes.

25-29. Seeing Subāhu, full of wrath, having come to fight with Śatrughna who had destroyed his son and had caused the killing of his entire army, Hanūmat having his nails as his weapon, making a loud sound, and moving by the side of Śatrughna ran to him. Subāhu, with his eyes full of anger, seeing that Hanūmat making a loud sound, coming to him, said laughing: "Where has Puṣkala gone after having killed my son in the battle? Today I shall quickly knock down his head with bright ear-rings. Where is Śatrughna, the protector of the horse? Where is Rāma? And where are the warriors? Let them see me who will snatch away their life in the battle to have come."

30-36. Hearing these words of (i.e. uttered by) him, Hanūmat spoke to him: "Śatrughna, the destroyer of Lavaṇa (the son of Madhu), is the guardian of the army. How would he fight in the battle, O king, when his servant is in the fore. O best of men, having conquered me in the battle you will go to him." He speedily struck with ten arrows on the chest of the monkey who spoke like this, who was very strong and who remained like the best mountain. He took in the cavity of his hands the arrows that came to him and pounded them, the sharp ones tearing (i.e. capable of tearing) the enemy, (to pieces as small as) sesamum seeds. The very mighty one having pounded those arrows and roaring like the thunder of clouds and having surrounded his chariot with his tail, took it high up (in the air). Then that best king, while remaining in the sky (i.e. in the air), repeatedly cut off his (i.e. Hanūmat's) tail with arrows of sharp end. He (i.e. Hanūmat) struck on the end of his tail with arrows with curved joints, abandoned that divine chariot spotted with gold.

37-45. When he (i.e. Subāhu) was released by him, he, with his eyes full of wrath, struck with sharp arrows, that best monkey, Hanūmat. Hanūmat, the lord of monkeys, pierced with arrows and covered with blood everywhere (on all the parts of his body), entertained great wrath against the king. Having seized with his large teeth his chariot along with the horses, he speedily pounded it. That was indeed a wonder. Seeing his own chariot being broken, the mighty king quickly resorted to another chariot and fought with the mighty (Hanūmat). The king, proficient in taking aim with an arrow and conversant with (the use of) great missiles, struck him on his tail, face, and chest and on arm and feet. Then the angry and best monkey (i.e. Hanūmat), jumped and struck with his foot on the chest of the king shining among good (i.e. brave) warriors. He, being struck with (Hanūmat's) foot fell unconscious on the ground; and vomitting blood from his mouth, he trembled with a flood of (i.e. heavy) breathing. Then Hanūmat who was very angry, speedily pounded the horses the heroes and (even) the elephants on the battlefield. Then his brother Suketu and king Lakṣmīnidhi—both, quite ready, came near (each other) to fight.

46-50. Men, wounded with volleys of arrows showered by Puṣkala, fled and went (away) on seeing the king who was unconscious. The king's powerful son, Damana, seeing his army being defeated, stopped it as a dam stops the high-going sea. Then the king who being struck with the stroke of his foot by the best monkey in the battle was unconscious, saw a dream: in a pavilion on the bank of Sarayū in Ayodhyā Rāmacandra was surrounded by many pre-eminent brāhmaṇa sacrificing priests. There gods like Brahmā and others, crores of universes, with the palms of their hands joined, repeatedly praised him with eulogies.

51-54. Nārada and others with their hands glittering with lutes sang (the praise of) the dark Rāma, of beautiful eyes and holding a deer's horn. Celestial nymphs like Ghṛtācī and Menakā danced there. Vedas, being embodied, stood by Rāghava, full of all charm, and giver of whatever things (i.e. everything), and giver of pleasures to his devotees. Seeing this and other (things), he whose knowledge was destroyed by the curse of a brāhmaṇa, while getting up, regained consciousness, and said: "What have I seen?"

55-58a. Having got up, he, having a retinue of a crore of servants, and surrounded by a crore of chariots went on foot to the feet of Śatrughna. Having called Suketu, so also Vicitra and Damana who were ready to fight, he, who was familiar with law, warded them off. The great, righteous king, endowed with piety said to them: "O brother, O sons, listen to my words possessed of virtue. Now immediately stop fighting.

58b-67. Great unfairness has taken place, since you, O Damana, seized the excellent horse of Rāmacandra. This Rāma is the highest Brahman and is beyond effect and cause. He is the lord of the mobile and the immobile world. He has taken up a human form. I have now perceived this knowledge of Brahman. I, the innocent one, was formerly deprived of the wealth of my knowledge due to the curse of Asitāṅga. Formerly I had gone on a pilgrimage with a desire to know the true nature (of Brahman). There I saw many sages most familiar with religion. With a desire to know (Brahman) I went to see the sage Asitāṅga. Then the brāhmaṇa, showing favour to me said to me: "He, who is the lord of Ayodhyā, is known by the term Para Brahman (the highest Brahman). She who is his queen Jānakī, is said to be actually full of pure intelligence. The meditating sages, desiring to cross the boundless ocean of the worldly existence, difficult to be crossed, directly wait upon him by means of restraints etc. He whose banner is Garuḍa, removes great sins, merely when he is remembered. That wise (man) who waits upon him, will cross the mundane existence." Then I laughed at the brāhmaṇa (and said): "Who is he? Rāma is just a man. Who is that queen Jānakī who is full of joy and sorrow? How can a birthless one be born? What here is the act of a non-doer, which is beyond birth, death and old age? O sage, tell it to me."

68-75. The best sage, getting angry with me who spoke like this, cursed me: "O meanest among the mean, not knowing the (true) nature of him, you are replying (i.e. speaking) to me. Laughing, you are censuring Rāma, (by saying that) he is a human being. Therefore, you who do not know the truth, are (just) feeding your belly (i.e. you are selfish)." Then I clasped his feet. Then he, the ocean of pity, seeing my modesty, spoke to me with kindness: "O king, when you will create an obstacle in Rāma's sacrifice, then Hanūmat will forcibly strike you (with) his foot. Then you will realise the truth, not otherwise (simply) due to your desire." Formerly he told me like this. Now I have seen (i.e. realised) it. When the angry Hanūmat struck me on my chest, I saw Ramā's (i.e. Lakṣmī's) lord, of the nature of the perfect Brahman. Therefore, the very mighty one should bring the horse, rich in beauty, so also wealth and garments. I shall give my kingdom (to Rāma). Seeing Rāma in the sacrifice giving great merit, I shall be blessed. Let them bring the horse. I like to hand him over (to Rāma)."

CHAPTER TWENTYNINE

King Subāhu Surrenders to Śatrughna

Śeṣa said:

1. They, the strikers (of their enemies), (too) hearing the words of their father, said joyfully, "Let it be so", to the great king longing to see Rāma.

The sons said:

2-9. O king, we do not know anything except the lotuses of your feet. Let that which you have in your mind, take place quickly. Let this horse, adorned with a white chowrie, very much beautified with a jewelled necklace, and smeared with sandal (-paste) etc. be taken there. Your kingdom has the fruit of your orders (i e. your orders are obeyed), O lord. Your treasures are very rich. Your garments are very costly, fine and excellent. There is (plenty of) sandal; so also there is camphor. Your horses are very charming. The elephants are haughty due to rut. The chariots have golden poles. There are a hundred thousand female servants who are adorned with many ornaments of various colours. There are very agreeable servants. There are gems resembling the sun. There are various jewels. There are white pearls produced from the temples of elephants. There are a hundred thousand corals. O you very intelligent king, give all those things which are very splendid, to Rāmacandra. O king, offer us, your sons and your servants (to Rāmacandra). O king, how is it that you do not make your throne over to him?

Śeṣa said:

10. Hearing these words of his sons the king became glad;

and he said to the brave sons who were ready to do his words (i.e. to obey his orders):

The king said:

11. Let all (the heroes) having put on (their armours), having weapons in their hands, and surrounded by many chariots, bring the horse. Then I shall go to the king.

Śeṣa said:

12-18. Hearing these words of the king the diligent (men), brave in battle, viz. Vicitra, Damana, so also Suketu, went by his order. The heroes went to the city and took in front of the king the horse which was adorned with a golden plate etc., was richly decorated with a jewelled necklace, was decorated with a variegated note, was well adorned with a mass of pearls, and was held by the heroes possessing great weapons and missiles and having all (kinds of) charm from the front and the back by means of a rope. On the head of the horse, a white chowrie appeared aloft. In front of him a couple of good chowries shone again and again. (They) took the horse of the good (i.e. auspicious) horse-sacrifice, which had wind's speed and was made fragrant with Kṛṣṇāgaru sandal, in front of the king. The intelligent king seeing the horse decorated with a jewelled necklace, having the speed of mind and a beautiful form brought (before him) was pleased.

19-23. The very righteous king adorned with royal insignia and accompanied by his sons and grandsons went on foot to Śatrughna. Thinking that wealth is perishable and gives pain to them whose hearts are attached to it, he went to make a proper use of the unsteady wealth. Then he saw Śatrughna adorned with a white umbrella and being fanned by servants standing before him, asking Sumati (to narrate) Rāmacandra's story free from any tidings causing fear, well adorned by heroes, crowded with crores of heroes who desired to protect the horse, and surrounded on all sides by thousands of monkeys.

24-26. Seeing the feet of Śatrughna, he was delighted; and thinking 'I am lucky', and with a concentrated mind uttering (the word) 'Rāma', he with his sons saluted the feet of Śatrughna. Seeing that pre-eminent and affectionate king, Śatrughna got up from his seat along with all his heroes and embraced him with his arms. The king, the killer of his enemies, having very much (i.e. devoutly) honoured Śatrughna, and being delighted, spoke with a faltering voice to Śatrughna.

Subāhu said:

27-31. Today I am blessed along with my sons, my family, my horses (and elephants) that I am seeing your feet praised by crores of kings. O you ocean of kindness, my ignorant son Damana had seized this best horse. (Please) forgive him this unfairness. He does not know (Rāma) the crest of the Raghus, the deity superior to all gods, the creator of the universe with ease, the destroyer and yet the protector also. (Take) this kingdom rich in all constituents and having mighty horses (and elephants). These treasures of me are full of wealth. These sons of me and I myself—all of us are Rāma's servants, obeying your commands. Take all (this) along with their effects. I have no superiority complex.

32-41. Where is that Hanūmat, the bee at Rāma's lotus-feet, due to whose favour I shall have the sight of the king of kings? What is not obtained on the earth in the company of the good? Seeing that great king (i.e. Rāma) having eyes like lotus-petals, I the ignorant one, have today overcome (the effect of) the brāhmaṇa's curse, and will obtain here the entire fruit of my existence, difficult to secure. Being very much separated from Rāma, I have passed a large (portion of my) life. Only a little (part of) it is left. How shall I see the best of the Raghus? Show me (that) Rāma who is proficient in the rite of sacrifice, and by the dust of whose feet (Ahalyā) the dear wife of sage (Gautama) who was turned into stone was purified. The crow—the bird—obtained the highest position due to his arrow's touch. Many in the battle went to (the best) position on seeing the lotus of his face. Those who respectfully take the name of this Raghunātha go to the highest place thought of by ascetics. Blessed are the people born in Ayodhyā, who having drunk with the cups of their own eyes the lotus of Rāma's face go to (i.e. obtain) happiness (and) great prosperity.

Having spoken like this to the king (i.e. Śatrughna) he offered the (sacrificial) horse, his kingdom and wealth (to Śatrughna) and said (to him): "O lord of the earth, I am (your) servant." Hearing these words of the king the eloquent Śatrughna who conquered the cities of his enemies and who was proficient in (using correct) words replied to the king:

Śatrughna said:

42-49. O king, how do you speak (like) this? You are old, (therefore) you are venerable to me. Let this Damana command your entire kingdom. It is the duty of kṣatriyas which enjoins a battle. By my order let all this kingdom and this wealth go back (to your son Damana). As Raghunātha (i.e. Rāma) is always adorable to me by means of speech and mind, similarly, O lord of the earth, you will also be adorable (to me). Having armed yourself, having put on an armour, having taken a sword, and with your elephants and horses, you should today be ready to go after the horse.

The lord of the earth who was highly respected by Śatrughna, having heard these words of Śatrughna, consecrated his son on his throne, and the king, a great warrior and a knower of the truth, surrounded by great heroes, having performed purificatory rites according to the sacred commands over his son killed on the battlefield by Puṣkala, grieved for a while from the point of view of the world (i.e. as commonly people do). Recollecting Raghunātha he destroyed his grief with knowledge. Being ready and seated in a chariot, he, led by great warriors and surrounded by a great army, came to Śatrughna.

50-53. The king (i.e. Śatrughna), having seen him having come with his entire army, made up his mind to go to protect the horse. The horse marked by a note on his forehead and released by him, took a turn towards the left and wandered towards many eastern countries. At every place respectable and very brave kings saluted him. Nobody seized him. Some brought variegated garments, some brought wealth, (others brought) people, and some brought (i.e. handed over) their kingdom and saluted him.

CHAPTER THIRTY

Janaka Releases Sinners from Hell

Śeṣa said:

1-7. Then the horse, adorned with the note, reached Tejaḥpura (city) in which king Satyavān truthfully protected his subjects. Then Raghunātha's younger brother (Śatrughna) with a retinue of a crore going after the horse went in front of (the king) the conqueror of cities. Having seen the beautiful city, adorned with variegated ramparts, shining with golden pitchers all round, adorned at every place with thousands of temples of deities (Śatrughna said to Sumati). "In it monasteries of ascetics, full of ascetics, look beautiful. Here flows the great goddess (Gaṅgā), remaining on the head of him having three eyes (i.e. Śiva), and crowded with swans and ducks, and resorted to by hosts of sages. O Sir, in every house of brāhmaṇas smoke produced from the sacred fire purifies those whose minds were overflowing with sins." With his mind amazed due to the joy produced on seeing that city Śatrughna, the subduer of his enemies, said to Sumati.

Śatrughna said:

8. O minister, tell (me), whose city this is, which being seen by me, gives joy to my mind as it is righteously protected.

Śeṣa said:

9. Hearing these words of king Śatrughna, Sumati told him everything properly and without exaggeration.

Sumati said:

10-13. O lord, being attentive, listen to the auspicious tales of Viṣṇu's devotees, hearing which one is freed from sins like the murder of a brāhmaṇa. Satyavān is a king who is liberated while living, is a bee resorting to the lotuses in the form of Rāma's excellent feet, knows sacrifices and their constituents, is a performer of sacrifices and a great protector, whom his father known as Ṛtambhara-famous in the world and very religious, obtained after having propitiated the cow by means of many vows. The cow, pleased (with him) gave him a son, adorned with many virtues and having a great charm, (called) Satyavān. Know that best king.

Śatrughna said:

14-15. Who is king Ṛtambhara? Why did he worship the cow? How did he have a son—a devotee and worshipper of Viṣṇu? Tell me all this account of the devotee of Viṣṇu. When heard, it removes the mountain of the great sins of beings.

Śeṣa said:

16-18. Hearing these very meaningful words of Śatrughna, he clearly told him the story about his origin. Formerly there was king Ṛtambhara who was childless. He had many wives, but did not have a child on (i.e. from any one of) them. Then he, intent on his well-being, asked the sage named Jābāli who had luckily come there, the cause of (i.e. leading to) the birth of a son.

Ṛtambhara said:

19-21. O lord, tell me, the childless one, the words leading to the birth of a son. Knowing from you that by doing which an excellent child (i.e. a son) holding (i.e. continuing) my family will be born to me, I shall certainly carry out these excellent words (of you). (I shall give) a gift, (I shall observe) a vow, (visit) a sacred place or (perform) a sacrifice, O best sage.

Hearing these words of the king longing for a son and bowing to him, the best sage told him words leading to the birth of a son.

He said:

22-30. O lord, there are three means for him who longs for a child: Viṣṇu's grace, grace of a cow or of Śiva. Therefore, O king, you offer worship to a cow having a divine body, in whose tail, mouth, horn and back gods live. When she is pleased, she will give what is longed for (and) is accompanied by righteousness. Knowing thus, O Ṛtambhara, offer worship to a cow. The ancestors of him and the deities also are always pleased with him who everyday worships a cow with grass etc. All the desires of him, of a pious vow, who gives a cow her daily measure of food, are really fulfilled. A thirsty cow tied at home, an unmarried daughter in menses (i.e. who has attained puberty) and a deity with faded flowers destroy the religious merit obtained before. The ancestors of him who forbids a cow that is eating her grass (i.e. grass meant for her), are on the point of falling (into hell). That foolish man who beats a cow with a stick, goes, bereft of his hands, to the city of Dharmarāja (i.e. Yama). The ancestors who have gone down (to hell), of him who wards off the gadflies, dance (saying): "This fortunate son (i.e. descendant) of me (of us) will emancipate us."

31-37. In this case they narrate this ancient account: the wonderful event of Janaka that formerly took place in the city of Dharmarāja (i.e. Yama). Once king Janaka gave up his life by means of abstract meditation. Then an aeroplane decorated with a mass of small bells came (there). Then the king, with his body being carried by servants, got into it, and went (to heaven). On his way he went near the city of Yama. Then sinners were being oppressed in crores of hells. Having received the wind (i.e. breezes blowing) from the body of Janaka they became happy. The affliction due to the tormentation in hell became joyful (i.e. bearable) for them. Due to the wind (i.e. breezes blowing) from Janaka's body, their great misery perished (i.e. disappeared) at that time. Then the beings oppressed due to sins, not desiring separation from him, lamented very much. They uttered piteous words to him: "O blessed one, do not go from here. We who are tormented, are happy due to the wind (i.e. breezes blowing) from your body."

38-39. Hearing these words, the very righteous king, filled with a flood of pity, thought in his mind: 'If the beings are happy here due to the touch of the wind (i.e. breezes blowing) from my body, I shall stay in this city only. This is charming heaven (for me).'

40-43a. Thinking like this, the king, with his mind being sympathetic, and causing happiness to beings, stayed there only in front of the hell. Dharma (i.e. Yama), causing severe torment to the sinners, came there at the door of hell. Then he saw king Janaka, doer of great meritorious deeds, full of pity, who had stood at the door (having come) in an aeroplane. The lord of the dead bodies (i.e. Yama), smiling, said these words to Janaka:

43b-53. "O king, why have you, the crest-jewel of piety, come here? This is a place for the wicked sinners who cause harm to the life (of others). O king, men like you, who do meritorious acts, do not come (to this place). Those men who are intent upon deceiving others, who are engaged in censuring others, and are intent on (grabbing) other's wealth, alone come here. That man who would abandon his wife who is religious and absorbed in serving him without her fault, would come here. He who, greedy through attachment for wealth, deceives his friend, comes here, and receives intense torment from me. Having bound the man who, a foolish one, does not remember Rāma mentally, with words or acts, through hypocrisy, hatred, or ridicule, I throw him among these and cause him to be boiled. Those who have remembered the lord of Ramā, leave my place and quickly go to Vaikuṇṭha. O very intelligent king, my servants, unable to look at (people) like you, bring those who are great sinners. Therefore, O great king, go, enjoy many pleasures. Having got into an excellent aeroplane, enjoy the (fruit of the) religious merit earned by you." Having heard these words of Dharmarāja (i.e. Yama), the lord of that (city), he, full of the flood of compassion, said to him:

Janaka said:

54-55. O lord, due to pity for (these) beings I (shall) not go (to Vaikuṇṭha). Comforted by the wind (i.e. breezes blowing) from my body, they are staying here. O king, if you release all these living in hell, then, being happy, I shall go to heaven resorted to by meritorious persons.

Jābāli said:

56. Hearing these words, he, pointing out to him each one of the many dwelling in hell, said to Janaka:

Dharma said:

57-65. This one cohabited with his friend's wife that confided in him. Therefore, I have roasted him on an iron-pale for a myriad of years. Then having thrown him—the defaulter—into the species of pigs, he, marked with the marks of a eunuch, would be cast down into the species of human beings. This one repeatedly and forcibly embraced the wife of another (man). Therefore he, is roasted in Raurava (hell) for a hundred years. This wicked one stole the wealth of others and enjoyed it. Therefore, having cut off his hands, I shall cook him in puss and blood. This one did not honour and welcome a guest oppressed with hunger that had come to him even by words. Therefore, he should be dropped into the Tāmisra (hell) full of fuel. Let him, troubled by bees, meet with torment for a hundred years. This one, being shameless, loudly reviled another person. This one too sending forth his ears (i.e. with great interest) listened that reviling many times. Therefore, these two have fallen into a dark well. This one who had deceived his friend being dejected, is very much roasted in Raurava hell. Therefore, making them eat the fruit of their sins, I shall release them. O best among men, you, accumulating a heap of religious merit (would please) go (to heaven).

Jābāli said:

66. Thus he pointing out the sinful beings became quiet. The devotee of Rāma with his eyes full of pity said:

Janaka said:

67. Tell me quickly how the miserable beings can be free from hell and doing what would they obtain happiness.

Dharma (*i.e. Yama*) *said*:

68-71. These have never propitiated Viṣṇu. They have never listened to his stories. How can (these) sinners (then) be free from hell? If, O great king, you (desire to) release them, even though they are great sinners, then give them that religious merit (of you about) which I shall tell (you now). Once, having got up in the morning, you meditated with pure heart upon this Śrī Raghunātha (i.e. Rāma) who is called the remover of great sins. Give them that religious merit which you collected when you uttered with pure heart the name Rāma, Rāma; by that their freedom from hell would take place.

Jābāli said:

72-77. Hearing these words of the intelligent Dharmarāja (i.e. Yama), the great king gave (them) the religious merit obtained by him from his birth. (He said:) "Let there be pleasing release of these from hell due to the religious merit earned (by me) from birth by the worship of Raghunātha." When he was speaking like this, the beings dwelling in hell that moment only became free from hell and became divine-bodied. They said to king Janaka: "O king, by your favour we have been in a moment freed from miserable hell, and will (now) go to the highest position." He intent on showing kindness to all beings, seeing those men resembling the sun freed from hell, was very much pleased in mind. All those, praising Janaka, the great king, the treasure of pity, went to heaven adorned by gods.

CHAPTER THIRTYONE

King Ṛtambhara is Blessed with a Son

Jābāli said:

1. When those men living in hell went (to heaven), king (Janaka) asked Yama, the best among those who know dharma.

The king said :

2-4. O Dharmarāja, you have said that men who commit sins and are not interested in religious discourses, come to your place. O you righteous one, tell me for what sin I have come here, and the cause of my sin, from the beginning.

Hearing these words of him, O you tormentor of the enemies,

Dharmarāja then told him (the cause of) his arrival to Yama's city.

Dharmarāja said :

5-12. O king, you have great religious merit. None else has like it on the surface of the earth. O you who have been observing the vow of (drinking) the honey from the two (lotus-)feet of Raghunātha, the celestial river in the form of your fame which gives great joy and emancipates the wicked, purifies all the sinners full of the dirt (of sin). Still, O you best king, there is a small bit of sin (in you), due to which you, full of merit, have come to my residence (Saṁyaminī). Once you prevented a cow that was grazing (from doing so). Due to the effect of that sin, you have seen the gates of hell. Now, freed from (that) sin and endowed with great religious merit, enjoy many many pleasures obtained through your religious merit. Raghunātha, the ocean of pity, taking away (i.e. desiring to remove) the misery of these, has sent (you) the devotee of Viṣṇu on this great route. O you of a good vow, how would they have been free from sin, if you had not come along this way? O very intelligent one, people like you who are afflicted by others' misery and who are the abode of kindness, thus remove the misery of beings.

Jābāli said :

13-15. Having saluted Yama, who was speaking like this, he went to heaven in a divine aeroplane adorned with the host of celestial nymphs. Therefore, cows are to be honoured; one should not even mentally censure them. One who censures them, remains in hell as long as the fourteen Indras rule. Therefore, O best among kings, worship a cow. Being pleased, she will quickly give you a son who is devoted to piety.

Sumati said :

16-20. Having heard it, he asked about the worship of a cow: How is she to be respectfully and carefully worshipped? What kind of man does she make him? Jābāli duly told him the worship of a cow. He who has undertaken the vow of (worshipping) a cow, should everyday go to the forest to graze her. He should make the cow eat barley-grains and should collect them from her dung. O king, one longing for a son should eat those barley-grains. He should drink pure water (only) when she drinks water. He should be seated (only) when she would sit on a high seat. Everyday he should ward off the gnats and should himself collect grass or fodder (for her). She gives a son devoted to piety to him who does like this.

Sumati said :

21-27. Hearing these words that pious Ṛtambhara, longing for a son, practised the vow. Worshipping the cow everyday, he pleased her with grass etc. The intelligent one, showing great care for her food (like) barley, warded off the gnats. Of him who was worshipping the cow grazing grass etc. in the forest and having fear from nowhere, auspicious days passed. Once that king, curious to observe the beauty of the forest, had cast his eyes on it, and was roaming all around. At that time a lion having come from the interior of the forest struck the cow that was yelling in many ways, that was helpless and that was afflicted due to the burden of the lion (on her body). Then the king, having come there and having seen his mother (i.e. the cow) struck by the lion, was very much distressed and cried. Being afflicted he came to Jābāli, the best sage, and asked him about the atonement for the sin of killing a cow.

Ṛtambhara said :

28-29. O lord, I had resorted, by your order, to the forest and looked after the cow. A lion not falling within the range of (my) sight (i.e. not noticed by me) came from somewhere and attacked the cow. What do (i.e. should) I do for the atonement of that sin, by your order? How can I fulfil the vow granting a son to me?

30-40. The best sage said to the king speaking like this: "O king, there are means for the atonement of a sin. There are expiations, O you very intelligent one, for all sins of one who has killed a brāhmaṇa, who is ungrateful and who drinks liquor. All the sins of him who observes the (vows) duly go away by means of vows like Kṛcchra, Cāndrāyaṇa (observed) along with restraints and controls. For two sinners who have committed heaps of sins, there is no expiation: for him who deliberately kills a cow and one who censures Nārāyaṇa (i.e. Viṣṇu). The meanest one who mentally desires (giving) pain to cows, resides in a place in hell as long as fourteen Indras (rule). Even that unfortunate man who just once censures Hari, would, surrounded by his sons and grandsons, see hell. Therefore, O lord of men, you should realise that he who censures Viṣṇu or causes pain to cows never gets release. There is an expiation if a cow is killed through ignorance. You (now) go to Ṛtuparṇaka, the intelligent devotee of Rāma. He looks equally upon all his foes and friends. He will quickly tell you the expiation for this killing of the cow. Formerly you had attached his countries, so he had abandoned them. Giving up enmity, go to Ṛtuparṇaka. Being composed, do quickly what he will tell you (to do), so that there will be the expiation of the sin committed by you."

41-48. Hearing these words of (i.e. spoken by) him, he went to Ṛtuparṇaka who was an excellent devotee of Rāma and who looked equally upon his foe and friend. He told him whatever, the killing of the cow etc., took place. He too thought of a means for the expiation of that sin. Having reflected for a moment, king Ṛtuparṇa who was intelligent and who knew dharma laughed and said to Ṛtambhara: "O king, who am I before (i.e. as compared with) the sages knowing the scriptures? Why have you, abandoning them, come to me, fancying myself to be learned? If you have faith in me, then I shall say something. O best of men, carefully listen to my words. By means of act, thought and words have recourse to Raghunātha. O you highly intelligent one, please the lord of the worlds without deceit. When pleased, he will grant (i.e. satisfy) all desires of your mind. He will destroy the sin of having ignorantly killed a cow. O you religious-minded one, O you best one, remembering Rāma, look after the cow. By giving gold to a brāhmaṇa, you will atone for the sin."

Sumati said:

49-57. Hearing those words king Ṛtambhara, with his mind purified, took to remembering Rāma, and observed the vow. Engaged in the well-being of all beings, and always remembering Rāma, he, looking after the cow, went to the forest as before.

Surabhi was pleased with him. When gratified, she said: "O king, choose a boon from me according to the desire of your mind?" Then the king said (to her): "Give me a son who is a devotee of Rāma, who is fond of his father, and who will follow his own duty." The merciful, desire-yielding, divine cow, being pleased, gave the boon to the king longing for a son, and disappeared. Then at the (proper) time he obtained a son—Viṣṇu's devotee and serving Rāma. His father (i.e. king Ṛtambhara) named him Satyavān. Having obtained the son (named) Satyavān who was greatly devoted to his father and comparable to Indra (only) in valour, the great king obtained great joy. The king, having obtained a righteous son, was full of joy and having deposited (i.e. entrusted) the kingdom with him, went to a forest for practising penance. There, with his mind full of devotion he propitiated Viṣṇu, and with his sins fully washed, he physically went to the place of Viṣṇu.

CHAPTER THIRTYTWO

Satyavān Meets Śatrughna

Sumati said:

1-9. O dear one, this king too who was well known by the name Satyavān pleased by means of his duty Raghunātha, the lord of the worlds. Being pleased (with him) the lord of Ramā (i.e. Viṣṇu) gave him unswerving devotion to his feet, difficult to obtain through crores of religious deeds by his worshippers. He, full of pity and not being fatigued, everyday told the purifying tale of Śrī Raghunātha to people. He beat with sticks, causing fear even to Yama, the man who did not worship Ragunātha (i.e. Rāma), the lord of Ramā (i.e. Viṣṇu). He made every man who would be above the age of eight till he would be eighty years old, observe the fast of Ekādaśī. To him Tulasī was dear; his neck never abandoned the excellent garland from the lotus-like feet of Raghunātha. He was venerable even to the sages.

How then was he not (so) to others? He loved remembering Raghunātha. His sins were washed. His misfortune was destroyed. He, knowing that the very wonderful horse of Rāmacandra has come, will come and give you the kingdom free from troublesome fellows. O king, I have told you the best (thing) that you have asked for. O lord, what more do you ask? Order it (and) I (shall) do it.

Śeṣa said :

10. The horse, possessing many wonders, went into the city. Seeing him, all the people went to the king, and reported to him.

The people said :

11-12. A certain horse, shining with a note on his forehead white like the water of Gaṅgā, has come.

Hearing those charming and pleasing words uttered by the people, the king laughed and said (to them): "Ascertain whose horse that is."

13-20a. They told him: "A horse, looked after by Śatrughna, has come from the city of king Rāma." He, having heard the very pleasing, two-lettered name of Rāma, marked with a faltering sound, was very much delighted in mind: "The horse of that Rāma, the lord of Ayodhyā, who is constantly thought by me has come with Śatrughna to my city. Hanūmān who serves the feet of Rāma and who never forgets Rāma in his mind, will also be there. I (shall) go there where there are Śatrughna, (Hanūmat) the son of Maruta (i.e. the Wind) and other men who serve the lotus-like feet of Rāma". He ordered his minister: "Quickly come, taking all the royal wealth with me. I shall go to look after the excellent horse of Raghunātha, and to do (i.e. to offer) service to Rāma's lotus-like feet, which is difficult to be had." Saying so he with his soldiers went out to Śatrughna.

20b-26. Just then Rāma's brother (Śatrughna) along with his soldiers reached the city. Mighty heroes roared; chariots produced big sounds; there were the sounds of the triumphant conches; everywhere there were the flute-sounds. King Satyavān, having come along with his ministers, saluted (Śatrughna's) feet and presented to him his very wealthy kingdom. Śatrughna, having recognised the king, observing Rāma's vow, gave his great kingdom to his son named Rukma. He, endowed with truth, and of great glory, having embraced the very glorious Hanūmat of mighty arms and also other devotees of Rāma, regarded himself blessed; and with Śatrughna, he was delighted in mind. Just then the horse well-protected by heroes went a long way off. Śatrughna along with that king and heroes went (after the horse).

CHAPTER THIRTYTHREE

Śatrughna's Army Gets Ready to Fight Vidyunmālin

Śeṣa said :

1-7a. When many excellent warriors like Śatrughna and all great kings having crores of chariots were going, there was all of a sudden, on the way, very fearful darkness in which kinsmen could not recognise their own man or a stranger. The sky was covered with dust and was full of lightning and thunder. In such a very fearful confusion clouds showered profuse blood with puss and (other) foul things. The heroes who were great enemies, became very much confounded. When the people were perplexed, the condition was: 'What is this? What is this?' The eyes of people of renowned vigour were pervaded with darkness. (A demon) who was well known as Vidyunmālin who was Rāvaṇa's friend, lived in the nether world and was surrounded by a line of demons took away the horse. He was seated in an aeroplane made of iron and going according to (occupants') desire.

7b-10a. He causing fear to all heroes took away the horse. In a short while the darkness disappeared and the sky became pure. Those heroes led by Śatrughna said: "Where is the horse?" Looking for the best horse, they saw one another; (but) when they did not see the horse, there was loud wailing. "Where is the horse of (i.e. intended for) the horse-sacrifice? Who, the wicked one, has taken it (away)?"

10b-12. They spoke such words. Just then that lord of demons who was surrounded by the best demons, seated in an excellent aeroplane, was seen by all the best warriors, seated in chariots and adorned with valour. There fearful demons, having bad faces, terrible mouths, long fangs, were seen ready to seize the army (of Śatrughna).

13-14. Then they informed Śatrughna, the best among kings: "We do not know (how) one, shining in an aeroplane, took away the horse into the sky. Having confounded us—the heroes, with darkness, he came, and seized the horse. O best king, do what is proper."

15-18. Hearing those words, Śatrughna was full of great anger. (He said:) "Who is this powerful demon that has seized my horse? Today let the aeroplane, struck by the volley of my arrows, fall down. Today let the head of my enemy fall down, (after being struck) by my arrows with sharp horse-shoe-shaped heads. Make ready all chariots filled with great weapons and missiles. Let (our) warriors go to strike back the horse-snatcher." Speaking thus, he, with his eyes red due to anger, said to his minister who knew justice and injustice and who was proficient in the affairs of a war.

Śatrughna said:

19-21. O minister, tell me who, that are diligent in killing the demon, are very brave, are having great weapons, are best among those who know (the use of) excellent missiles, should be appointed (to kill the demon). Think and quickly tell me. I shall do your words (i.e. I shall do as you tell me). Tell me about the heroes knowing (the use of) all missiles and capable of (fighting with) him.

Having heard this the minister spoke befitting words showing the heroes, bent quickly (before Śatrughna), capable of (fighting in) that excellent battle.

Sumati said:

22-31. Let Puṣkala, the tormentor of the enemies, and having great weapons and missiles and ready to get victory in the battle, go to conquer the demon. In the same way let Lakṣmīnidhi possessing a mass of missiles, go. Let him break his vehicle with his sharp arrows. Hanūmat of bold deeds is capable of fighting with the demons. O lord, let him strike the demon with his face and tail. So also let all the brave monkeys who are skilled in fighting and are prompted by your words, go to fight. Let the best ones (like) Sumaḍa, Subāhu, Pratāpāgrya, go to fight with the mean demons with their sharp arrows. May you too, seated in a chariot endowed with great weapons and ready to kill the demon, obtain victory in the battle. O king, this is my view. Let those warriors who are brave and capable of destroying him, go (to fight with him). What is the use of (sending) many other warriors?

When the minister, named Sumati, and best among the heroes, spoke like this, Śatrughna told the heroes skilled in fighting (as follows): "O heroes, let Puṣkala and others, who are skilled in (the use of) all weapons and missiles, state in my presence their pledge to destroy the demon. Let you, making a great solemn declaration befitting your valour and accompanied by the army, go into the battlefield."

32-33. Hearing these words, the mighty (heroes) of Śatrughna, who were endowed with lustre, made their own great solemn declarations. Then, first, the hero Puṣkala, endowed with great energy, having heard the words of the lord of the earth, made this (i.e. the following) solemn declaration:

Puṣkala said:

34-40. O best king, listen to my very wonderful solemn declaration made due to my valour in the presence of all people that are listening to it. If I do not make the demon overcome with a swoon and his face full of scattered hair, let me have the sin which he who enjoys his own daughter, gets, or which one gets by censuring deities. Let me have that sin if I falsify your words. O great king, listen to my pledge in case the very powerful soldiers (of the demon) do not fall on being pierced with my arrows. If I do not make my words true, let me have the sin of him who distinguishes between Viṣṇu and Śiva or Śiva and Śakti. These are all the words uttered by me (i.e. I had to say). That firm devotion which I have towards the lotus-like feet of Raghunātha, will itself make (my words) true.

Hearing that pledge of Puṣkala, king Lakṣmīnidhi, made a truthful solemn declaration, adorned with his valour.

Lakṣmīnidhi said :

41-43. If I turn back (from the battlefield), I would have that sin which a man gets if he keeps mum on hearing the censure of the Vedas, or being outcast from all religions, he mentally likes (the censure of Vedas); (I shall have the sin of) the brāhmaṇa who is wicked and sells liquor and lac etc., or who, the fool, being tempted by greed sells a cow; (or of him) who having drunk the water from the money of a mleccha, does not observe an expiation.

44-54. Having heard the pledge, Hanūmat, skilled in battle, said, after having remembered Rāma's feet, (the following) auspicious words: "My lord (Rāma) whom all gods along with demons salute by (bowing) their heads (adorned) with gems, should always be reflected on by meditating saints in their hearts. The glorious Rāma is the lord of Ayodhyā and is worshipped by the lord of the world. Those words which one would utter by remembering him will come true. O king, who (i.e. how insignificant) is this mean, weak demon, seated in (the aeroplane) moving according to (occupants') desire? Tell me quickly what should be done by me. Who would (i.e. is able to) knock me down? With my tail I (shall) lift up the Meru (mountain) along with the lord of gods. I (shall) dry up the entire ocean. I shall even drink up the Saṁvarta (cloud abounding in water). I have the favour of king Śrī Raghunātha and Jānakī. O king, there is nothing on the surface of the earth which would ever be unattainable for me. If, O king, these words uttered by me would be untrue, then at that time only I would be away from devotion to Raghunātha. If I falsify my words, then let me have the sin which a śūdra who would keep a tawny cow with the desire (to obtain) milk (from her), would have. If I speak false words, let me have the sin of that śūdra who infatuated by love has sexual intercourse with a brāhmaṇa woman. Certainly let me have that sin which a man greedy through the taste of the tongue would drink liquor by the smell of which a man would go to hell and by its touch would even go to Raurava (hell), if, due to Rāma's grace I shall not make my pledge true."

55-59. When this was spoken by the great heroes, the warriors quickly made a solemn declaration shining with their valour. Śatrughna also praising those heroes skilled in battle (with the words) 'Well (said), well (said)', made a solemn declaration when people were observing (i.e. in the presence of people): "In front of you, I shall declare my vow adorned with my energy. Let the magnanimous ones endowed with exertion for fight, listen. If I do not strike with my arrows and knock down on the ground from the aeroplane his head cut off and broken from his trunk, let me certainly have that sin which one would get by giving false testimony or by stealing gold or due to censuring the Vedas."

60-63. Hearing the good words of Śatrughna, those (warriors) honoured by heroes (said:) "O Rāma's brother, you are blessed. Who else but you would be (so) great? O lord of the world, you alone killed the very mighty Lavaṇa, Madhu's son, who caused misery to gods and demons. Who (i.e. how insignificant) is the demon? Where (i.e. of what importance) is his small army? O you very intelligent one, you will (just) in a moment destroy him." Saying so, the heroes became ready on the battlefield. Gladly they went to (attack) the demon to make their pledge true.

CHAPTER THIRTYFOUR

Vidyunmālin Killed in Battle

Śeṣa said:

1-7. With chariots having good horses (yoked to them), rich in charm and full of all weapons and missiles and endowed with various jewels, they went to (i.e. marched against) the mean demons. Seeing them the demon seated in a vehicle going according to (occupants') desire, as it were, repeatedly threatening them, said with a deep-sounding voice: "Let the brave warriors not go to fight. Let them go home. Let them not cast their life. I shall not release the excellent horse. I am well-known as Vidyunmālin, and am the friend of Rāvaṇa. I have come to atone for my friend who is dead. Where has that Rāma who has killed (my) friend Rāvaṇa, gone? Where also is his brother (Śatrughna) who is the crest-jewel of all the brave men? Having killed him—the younger brother of Rāma, and drinking his blood along with bubbles coming up from his neck, I shall atone for (the death of) him (i.e. Rāvaṇa)." Hearing these words Puṣkala, the best among the excellent warriors, said to him endowed with valour and bravery:

Puṣkala said :

8-11. Excellent warriors do not brag in the battle. By means of showering their weapons and missiles they show (their) valour. O you maddened one, he who killed Rāvaṇa is surrounded by his kinsmen. Where will you go by snatching his horse? You will fall (when struck) with Śatrughna's arrows discharged from his bow. Jackals will eat you fallen dead on the ground. O wicked one, do not roar when I, Rāma's servant, am (here). In a battle excellent warriors roar in the battle due to great accomplishment after conquering their enemy.

Śeṣa said :

12-21. The best demon hit strongly with a (missile called) Śakti, Puṣkala—the hero—who was speaking thus, and who was ferocious in battle, on his chest. That Puṣkala, seeing that great iron missile, attached (i.e. decked) with gold, cut it off with three very fierce and sharp arrows. Made lustreless by the arrows, it fell on the ground in three parts. While falling it shone like Viṣṇu's three missiles. Seeing the missile cut off the demon, the tormentor of his enemy, quickly took up a lance having three points and made of iron. The best demon discharged it having sharp points and resembling fire. He, called Puṣkala, made it into (pieces like) sesamum seeds with his arrows. Puṣkala, Rāma's servant, having quickly cut off the trident, fixed on his bow sharp arrows having the speed of mind. The arrows quickly sticking (i.e. striking) his chest produced anger, as the charming qualities of Viṣṇu produce love in the heart of a devotee of Viṣṇu. The very ferocious Vidyunmālin afflicted with pain due to being pierced by his arrow and ready to strike took up a fierce mallet. He whose name was Vidyunmālin, sent (i.e. discharged) that mallet. It struck the chest (of Puṣkala). It produced (blood) and made him foul. Puṣkala, the tormentor of his enemies and the hero struck by the mallet, shaking with tremour, fell in the middle part of the chariot.

22-28. In the same way his brother Ugradaṁṣṭra fought with Lakṣmīnidhi, with fatal weapons and missiles discharged in various ways. Ragaining consciousness just at that moment, he said to the demon: "O greatest among the demons, you are fortunate. Great is your valour. Now listen also to my great vow honoured by the brave. Today with sharp arrows I shall knock you down from the aeroplane." Speaking thus, he took up an arrow, which was sharp, difficult to be overtaken, burning, having the lustre of fire, and having great excellence. Just when he exerted to retaliate, a very fierce and sharp arrow got into his chest. Confused by the arrow and with his heart perplexed, the demon, losing his consciousness, fell on the ground from the middle part of the vehicle going according to the occupants' desire. Ugradaṁṣṭra saw his elder brother falling. Being afraid of the enemy, he took him into the interior of the vehicle.

29-37. With great anger he said to his enemy Puṣkala, the best among the mighty: "O wicked one, having overthrown my brother, where will you go? Having vanquished me in the battle (i.e. if you vanquish me in the battle then only), you will get excellent victory. When I am (alive), put an end to the hope of victory in your heart." He (i.e. Puṣkala), with his eyes full of anger, quickly struck with ten arrows on (i.e. discharged ten arrows into) the chest of the wicked one who was speaking like this. The wicked one, struck with ten arrows by the magnanimous Puṣkala, got angry in his mind, and started to strike him. Grinding his teeth in anger, he raised his fist and struck (Puṣkala). Causing in (others') hearts fear (like) the noise of the whirlwind (caused) by the fall of the thunderbolt, he roared. The hero Puṣkala, knowing (how to wield) great missiles, struck with a fist, desiring the destruction of the wicked-minded one, did not tremble. He discharged into his chest arrows very sharp like the teeth of a calf. The demon, pained (due to being struck) with those arrows, took up a trident which had three points, which was burning and which was extremely fierce due to lines of flames. The fierce one struck (i.e. hit) the chest of Puṣkala, the great hero. The best archer, struck by the trident, fainted. He suffered from a great mental depression and fell on the chariot.

38-51. Knowing him to have fainted, Hanūmat, the son of Wind, with his heart overcome with anger, spoke to the demon: "O you wicked-minded one, where are you going? With kicks I shall kill you who have come here to snatch away the horse." Saying so, and remaining in the air, he tore with the tips of his nails the great demons, the soldiers of the enemy seated in the vehicle. The son of Wind (i.e. Hanūmat) struck some with his tail, some with the soles of his feet, some with his fore-arms. Some, when struck, perished; some, being struck, fainted. Then (they) afflicted and frightened due to strokes with the feet, fled. The Wind's son (i.e. Hanūmat) killed there many very fierce demons; they were cut off, broken and divided into two pieces. The vehicle, going according to the will (of the occupants) and with its defences and gateways broken, was surrounded on all sides by the wailing demons. When the very brave Hanūmat was in the sky in a moment, on the earth the (next) moment, the unassailable vehicle moving according to the (occupants') will, would be seen here and there. The monkey, Wind's son, taking any form at will, would be seen striking (the enemies), wherever that vehicle (moved). When the great men (i.e. the demons) remaining in the vehicle, were thus distressed at that time, Ugradaṁṣṭra, the lord of demons, approached Hanūmat. (He said): "O monkey, you have done a great deed, viz. knocking down the warriors. If you stay for a moment, I shall deprive you of your life." Speaking thus, that wicked-minded one struck Hanūmat with a very sharp trident having the lustre of a blazing fire. The mighty one (i.e. Hanūmat) seized the trident coming to him in his mouth and reduced the entire one made of gold to powder. Having powdered that iron trident discharged by the demon, the powerful Hanūmat struck him with many blows of his open hands.

52-57. He (i.e. Ugradaṁṣṭra) struck here and there by the lord of the monkeys with the blows of his open hands, was afflicted and created an illusion, causing fear to the entire world. Then there was darkness in which none was noticed, in which (a soldier) belonging to one's own side or of the enemy did not recognise many men. Rocks resembling mountain-peaks fell upon the (bodies of) excellent warriors. Being struck by them all of them were perplexed. (Streaks of) lightning flashed; clouds thundered violently, showered puss and blood, discharged dirty water. Many trunks with the heads having ear-rings cut off, were seen falling from the sky. Everywhere naked, ugly, fierce, terrible, very hideous demons, with their hair very much scattered, were seen.

58-63. Then the people, distressed and full of fear of one another, took to their heels; a great portent was thought (to appear). Then the very glorious Śatrughna came (there) in his chariot, and having remembered Śrī Rāma, he fixed arrows on his bow. Having shaken off the illusion with the bewitching missile the powerful one, scattering streams of arrows in the sky, showered the demon (with them) in the battle. Then the quarters brightened up; the sun had its halo (of lustre), clouds went (away) as they had come; lightning subsided. Then the great vehicle, occupied by the demons, and full of words like 'Cut off, break' was seen in front; and thousands of arrows with their feathered ends adorned with gold, repeatedly fell on the vehicle remaining in the sky and going according to (occupants') desire.

64-68. Then the aeroplane, a portion of which was broken, did not appear (moving) high, (but) appeared like a portion of the city that is broken, on the earth. Then the demon, being very angry, fixed arrows on the bow, and roaring, he scattered (i.e. discharged) them on (Śatrughna) Rāma's brother. Those arrows in hundreds stuck to his body in many ways. They, the sharp and bent ones, causing streams of blood to flow, gave him great charm. Śatrughna, endowed with a great power, fixed on his bow a missile presided over by the Wind-deity and causing the demons to tremble. The demons, with their hair loose, and falling from the vehicle and the sky, appeared like groups of ghosts and vampires moving in the sky.

69-76. The demon's son, seeing the missile discharged by Raghunātha's brother, fixed on his bow a missile presided over by Śiva. From it proceeded vampires, ghosts, evil spirits and fiends, having skulls and swords and drinking profuse blood.

They difficult to ward off, and adorned with swords in their hands, gladly drank the blood of the heroes of Śatrughna even while they were alive. Seeing that missile pervading (everything) and destroying all the warriors, he discharged, to send it back, the missile called Nārāyaṇa. That missile, presided over by Nārāyaṇa, in a moment, checked all of them. All of them, impelled by the demon, met with destruction. Then that angry demon Vidyunmālin took a sharp, fierce and strong trident to kill Śatrughna. Seeing Vidyunmālin coming with a trident in his hand, (Śatrughna) struck (him) on his arm with arrows resembling the crescent moon. With his arm cut off with those arrows he prepared himself to strike (Śatrughna) with his hand. (He said:) "O Śatrughna, you are (now) killed. Go. Who will be your protector?"

77-81. When he was talking like this, (Śatrughna) quickly cut off with arrows the head along with the ear-rings of that mighty hero. Seeing him (i.e. Vidyunmālin) with his head cut off, the valourous Ugradaṁṣṭra started striking Śatrughna served by the brave with his fist; but Śatrughna cut off his head with an arrow with a sharp horse-shoe-shaped head. All the heroes skilled in the use of weapons and missiles ran on the battlefield. Except the lord of the demons all with their life remaining (i.e. saved) went (away). Having saluted Śatrughna they gave (back) the horse snatched (away by them). Then were heard all around the sounds of lutes, the sounds of conches and the charming cries of victory of the brave soldiers.

CHAPTER THIRTYFIVE

Dialogue between Lomaśa and Āraṇyaka

Śeṣa said:

1-5. King Śatrughna, along with Puṣkala, obtained great joy on obtaining the horse taken away by the demons. Those warriors, with their bodies sprinkled with blood, so also Lakṣmīnidhi praised the great king full of energy to fight. When that great demon Vidyunmālin, difficult to conquer, was killed, all gods, O sage, gave up their fear and obtained happiness. The rivers became clean; and the sun became clear. Breezes sprinkled with scented water blew. The great heroes, with spotless lustre and of clean bodies seated in the chariots, became ready. All of them endowed with the good luck of victory said to the king:

The heroes said:

6-8. O you very intelligent one, luckily you have killed the demon Vidyunmālin, due to whose fear gods were frightened and were driven out of the heaven. Luckily the great horse of Raghunātha has been got (back); luckily you have obtained victory everywhere on the globe. O lord, release this charming horse having the speed of mind. Let there be no delay now, O you very intelligent one.

Śeṣa said:

9-14. Hearing these words of the heroes which were proper for the occasion, he, having praised them (with the words) 'Well, well', released the best horse. He that was well-protected by chariots, foot-soldiers, best horses and those who were proficient in the use of all weapons and missiles, went, when released, to the northern direction. O Vātsyāyana, listen to the account of what took place (in the case) of Śatrughna, which burns heaps of sins. He reached Revā's bank resorted to by hosts of sages. Her water was the fluid of the heap of sapphires under the pretext of water. He (i.e. Śatrughna) waited upon by the brave, saluted the respective (i.e. everyone of the) sages and followed the gem of the horse going at will. He went to that old hermitage made of the leaves of palāśa, sprinkled with the waves of Revā and the refuge of those who remove sins.

15. Śatrughna who did all deeds bringing merit and worldly prosperity, on seeing it, said to Sumati who knew everything and was proficient in political wisdom.

The king said:

16. O Minister, O you who are best among those who think,

tell me who am asking you, to whom this hermitage, which appears auspicious belongs.

Śeṣa said:

17. Hearing these words, Sumati, showing his affection, said to the king, with words accompanied by a bright smile.

Sumati said:

18-24. O great king, having seen this best sage, absorbed in all scriptures, we shall indeed have our sins removed. Therefore, bow down before him, and ask him. He who is extremely greedy of the honey from the lotuses in the form of Rāma's feet, will tell you everything. (Bow down before him) known by the name Āraṇyaka, the servant of the feet of Rāma, full of very severe penance and proficient in the significance of all sacred texts.

Hearing these words augmented by religious significance, he went along with a few servants to see him. (They were) Hanūmat, the brave Puṣkala, the best minister Sumati, Lakṣmīnidhi, Pratāpāgrya, Subāhu, and Sumada also. Noble-minded king Śatrughna, surrounded by these reached the hermitage to salute that best brāhmaṇa Āraṇyaka. Having gone there he with all the heroes who had bent down their necks in modesty, saluted the best ascetic.

25-27. Having seen all those kings led by Śatrughna, he then offered them respectful offering and water for washing their feet etc. along with fruits and roots. He said to all the kings: "Where had you gone together? O sinless ones, how have you gathered here? Tell (me) all that." O brāhmaṇa, having heard those words of the best sage, Sumati, skilled in speaking (proper) words, said (to him):

Sumati said:

28-29. By all (these) the horse of the king belonging to Raghu's family is being protected. The hero (Rāma) will perform a sacrifice furnished with all ingredients.

Hearing those words of (i.e. uttered by) them the best sage, as it were dispelling the entire darkness with the lustre of his teeth, said:

Āraṇyaka said:

30-34. What is the use of other sacrifices furnished with all ingredients, giving (but) little merit and giving perishable positions? Foolish people worship other (god), leaving Hari, the Raghu hero (i.e. Ramā), the lord of Ramā, giving a stable glorious position. A foolish man torments (himself) by sacrifices, abstract meditations and vows by leaving him who, even when merely remembered, removes the mountain of sins. Oh! see the folly and illusion of people (that) a man leaving the easy worship of Rāma, would practise (i.e. he practises) difficult (things). It gives liberation to men and removes all sins merely by being remembered. It is reflected upon by the meditating saints having desires.

35-40. Formerly with a desire to know the reality and thinking much about (how to find) a wise man, I went to many holy places. But nobody taught me the truth. Then, due to my great luck I came across the sage Lomaśa who had come (down to the earth) with a desire to visit the holy places. Having saluted that great sage who had a great (i.e. long) life and whose couple of feet was served by great meditating saints, I asked him (about the truth): "O lord, today (i.e. now) I have obtained the human existence, which is wonderful and difficult to obtain. What should one who desires to cross the fearful ocean of the worldly existence, do? Having thought, tell me if there is a vow, a gift, a prayer to be muttered, a sacrifice, or a deity, that would emancipate me from the ocean of the mundane existence. O lord of reflective thinking (i.e. greatest mediating saint), O You who are the master of the significance of all the scriptures, tell me that knowing which I shall by means of the ocean of your grace cross the fierce mundane existence."

41-49. Hearing these words of (i.e. uttered by) me, the best sage said: "O brāhmaṇa, listen attentively and with great faith. There are gifts, holy places, vows, voluntary religious observances and restraints. So also there are many abstract meditations, sacrifices giving (i.e. taking one to) heaven. O magnanimous one, I shall tell you a great secret which removes all sins and helps (one) to cross the ocean of the worldly existence. Listen to it. It is not to be told to an atheist, or to a nonbeliever, so also to a censurer, or to a wicked man; it should not be given to the enemy (i.e. hater) of devotion. It (i.e. the secret) which is excellent and removes all misery, should be told to Rāma's devotee who is calm and free from lust and anger. There is no greater god than Rāma; there is no greater vow than (that in honour of) Rāma. There is no greater reflection than (on) Rāma; there is no greater sacrifice than (in honour of) Rāma. Having remembered him, having muttered prayers to him, and having worshipped him, a man gets the highest (position) and obtains great glory in this and the next world. When he is remembered, when he is mentally meditated upon, he who is the giver of all desired objects, gives (i.e. generates in the mind of the man) great devotion which helps him to cross the ocean of the mundane existence. Even a cāṇḍāla by remembering Rāma goes to (i.e. obtains) the highest position. Then what about those like you who are greatly devoted to the Vedas and (other) scriptures?

50-52. I have disclosed to you the secret of all the Vedas and (other) scriptures. Act as you would desire. Rāmacandra is the only god. His worship is the only vow. (Uttering) his name is the only hymn; and praising him is the only scripture. Therefore, worship the charming Rāmacandra by all means; so that the ocean of the mundane existence would be as trifling as a small puddle."

53-70. Having heard those words, I again put a question: "How is the god meditated upon by men? Or how is he worshipped by them? O you highly intelligent one, O you who know everything, tell me (all that) in detail, knowing which I shall be blessed in the three worlds, O best sage." Having heard these words of (i.e. uttered by) me, that Lomaśa, having reflected, told me everything preceded by the meditation on Rāma: "O best brāhmaṇa, O you sinless one, I shall tell you what you have asked me, as to how the lord of Rāma (i.e. Viṣṇu) burns (i.e. removes) the distress of the mundane existence. In the city of Ayodhyā, which is charming and adorned with a variegated pavilion, at the root of the desire-yielding tree giving all prosperity, one should meditate upon the charming Raghurāja (i.e. Rāma) seated upon an attractive throne, adorned with great emeralds, gold and jewels like the sapphire removing darkness by means of its lustre. (One should meditate upon Rāma) whose body is dark like dūrvā-blades, who is worshipped by god of gods, whose face condemns the beauty of the full moon on the full-moon night, whose forehead resembles the portion of the moon on the eighth day (of the month), who is rich with the beauty of dark hair, who is tinged with the jewels of his crown, who is adorned with beautiful ear-rings having the shape of crocodiles, who is beautified with lips shining with coral-like lustre, who is adorned with the row of teeth having the shape of the rays of the lord of the stars (i.e. the moon—i.e. having pointed teeth), whose mouth is beautified with a tongue sweet like the China rose, on which reside Vedas like the Ṛgveda along with sacred books ,who is adorned with a neck possessing the charm of a conch, who, the excellent one, possesses lofty and fleshy shoulders like those of a lion, who has long arms marked with armlets and bracelets hanging up to the knees and adorned with rings and diamonds, who has a very large chest beautified by the perfume of Lakṣmī and marked with beautiful marks like that of Śrīvatsa, who has a large belly with a large navel and adorned with a beautiful waist endowed with a jewelled girdle and special charm, who is adorned with spotless thighs and knees and with majesty, who is adorned with delicate feet marked with lines like a diamond-pin and a barley-shoot and fit to be reflected upon by the meditating saints. Having reflected upon and remembered him you will cross the ocean of the mundane existence. One worshipping him according to his own desire by means of sandal etc. obtains great prosperity in this world and the other world.

71. O great king, you asked me about the excellent meditation upon Rāma. I have told it to you. (With its help) cross the ocean of the worldly existence."

CHAPTER THIRTYSIX

Lomaśa Narrates the Deeds of Rāma to Āraṇyaka

Śeṣa said:

1. The best brāhmaṇa, having heard this very important (advice) from Lomaśa, again asked that sage, who knew everything and who was best among the meditating saints.

Āraṇyaka said:

2-4. O best of sages, O you very intelligent one, tell me (what) I am asking you. Preceptors are full of compassion, and explain everything to their servant(s). O magnanimous one, who is that Rāma who is reflected upon by you everyday? What are his deeds? O best brāhmaṇa, tell me. Why has he taken the incarnation? Why is he born as a human being? (Please) quickly tell me all that to remove my doubt.

Śeṣa said:

5-7. Having heard these very charming words of the sage, Lomaśa narrated to him the wonderful good conduct of Rāma. Knowing that people have been merged into hell, the lord of the lords of abstract meditation, the charming highest lord, the ocean of kindness—knowing thus, descended along with Śrī in four ways to spread his glory in the world, by means of which (a man) would cross the terrible (mundane existence).

8-10. Formerly when the Tretā age came, Rāma, the descendant of Raghu, the full incarnation, having lotus-like eyes, was born in the solar dynasty. That Rāma had Lakṣmaṇa as his companion and the young (boy) had side-locks of hair on his temples. Due to the promise of their father, the two youths (i.e. Rāma and Lakṣmaṇa), devoted to Viśvāmitra, were handed over (to Viśvāmitra) for the protection of his sacrifice by the king. They were restrained, (good) archers, brave, and were devoted to Viśvāmitra.

11-15a. To cause an obstacle to them a demoness named Tāṭakā met them in the fearful forest when they were going along their way. Rāma, the descendant of Raghu, sent by the sages' permission Tāṭakā (to face) the torture inflicted by Yama by means of his practice of archery. By the touch of the sole of his foot Gautama's wife Ahalyā (who had been transformed into) a stone due to Indra's contact, again got her own form. When Viśvāmitra's sacrifice proceeded well, (Rāma), the best among Raghus, killed with great arrows Mārīca and Subāhu. He broke Śiva's bow that was in Janaka's house.

15b-17. When Rāma was fifteen years old, he married, according to (the proper rite of) marriage, the charming Sītā not born from the womb. Having had Sītā (as his wife), Rāma then became (i.e. regarded himself) fortunate. Then for twelve years he enjoyed with her. In his twenty-seventh year, he prepared (himself) for the rank of (i.e. for being consecrated as) an heir-apparent.

18-23a. Then Kaikeyī asked king (Daśaratha to grant) two boons: "By one of the two Rāma, having matted hair, should go away along with Sītā and Lakṣmaṇa for fourteen years. By the second, my (son) Bharata should be (consecrated as) the heir-apparent." The king sent away Rāma accompanied by Jānakī and Lakṣmaṇa. For three nights he took (only) water (and) on the fourth day he ate fruits. On the fifth (day) Rāma prepared an abode on the Citrakūṭa (mountain). In the thirteenth year, O great sage, Rāma disfigured the demoness Śūrpaṇakhā in Pañcavaṭī. When he was moving in the forest along with Jānakī, the demon (Rāvaṇa), due to the ripening of his sins, came to kidnap her.

23b-27. Then on the eighth day of the dark half of (the month of) Māgha, at the time called Vṛnda, Rāvaṇa took away Sītā left (alone) without Rāma and Lakṣmaṇa. She, being taken away by him, wailed like an osprey: "O Rāma, Rāma, protect me who am taken away by a demon." As a hawk overcome with hunger would take a wailing quail similarly Rāvaṇa being under the influence of passion took away Janaka's daughter. When he was thus carrying away the daughter of Janaka, Jaṭāyu, the lord of birds, fought with the king of demons. Struck by Rāvaṇa he fell (down).

28-29. On the tenth day (of the first half of Mārgaśīrṣa) Sampāti told the monkeys about Sītā whom (he had seen) on the ninth day of the first half of Mārgaśīrṣa to be living in Rāvaṇa's house. On the eleventh day Hanūmat jumped from the Mahendra mountain and saw her the same night in Laṅkā. During the remaining (part of that) night Hanūmat had the sight of Sītā.

30-34a. On the twelfth Hanūmat stayed on the śiṁśapā tree. On the same night (he told) a story for (generating) confidence (in Sītā's mind). Then his fight with Akṣa and others took place on the thirteenth day (of the first half of Mārgaśīrṣa). On the fourteenth day the monkey (i.e. Hanūmat) was bound by Indrajit with the missile presided over by Brahmā. He burnt Laṅkā with fire set to his tail. On the full-moon day the monkey (i.e. Hanūmat) returned to the Mahendra mountain. (Having spent) five days from the first day of the second fortnight of Mārgaśīrṣa on the way, Madhuvana was burnt (by the monkey) after again having come back. On the seventh day (a token of) recognition (from Sītā) and full report (of the adventure) was given (to Rāma).

34b-35. Rāma set out on the eighth day when there appeared the Uttarāphālgunī constellation and the time was (the auspicious) Vijayā, and when the sun had reached the middle of the sky (i.e. at mid-day). Having made a solemn declaration, Rāma went towards the southern direction: (His solemn declaration was:)

36-38a. "Even having crossed the ocean, I shall kill the lord of demons." Sugrīva was the companion of Rāma who proceeded towards the southern direction. After seven days his army encamped on (the shore of) the ocean. Rāma, along with his army encamped on (the shore of) the ocean from the first day to the third day (of the first half of Pauṣa).

38b-40a. On the fourth day Bibhīṣaṇa joined Rāma. Consultations took place for crossing the ocean on the fifth day. For four days Rāma undertook fasting to death. Then he obtained a boon from the ocean who advised to make a joint effort.

40b-42. (The construction of the bridge) was begun on the tenth day, and was completed on the thirteenth day. On the fourteenth day Rāma encamped his army on the Suvela mountain. From the full-moon day to the third (of the dark fortnight) the army of the lord of the monkeys crossed the ocean and with Lakṣmaṇa besieged Laṅkā for (getting back) Sītā.

43-45. The encampment lasted for eight days, beginning with the third day and ending with the tenth. On the eleventh day Śuka and Sāraṇa came (to Rāma). On the twelfth day of the dark half of Pauṣa, the counting of (the soldiers in) the army was done. The lord of the best monkeys quickly described the army. For three days from the thirteenth day to the new-moon day Rāvaṇa assessed (the soldiers in) his army and showed inclination to fighting.

46-52a. On the first day of the bright half of Māgha Aṅgada went (to Rāvaṇa) as (Rāma's) envoy. Then Sītā was shown an illusory head of her husband (by Rāvaṇa). For seven days from the second of Māgha to the eighth (of Māgha), a confused battle took place between the demons and the monkeys. On the night of the ninth day of the bright half of Māgha Indrajit bound Rāma and Lakṣmaṇa with the serpent-noose. When the lordly monkeys were perplexed and were completely nervous, Pavana, on the tenth day, muttered into Rāma's ear his real form for freeing him from the serpent-noose. Then there was the arrival of Garuḍa on the eleventh day. On the twelfth day Dhūmrākṣa was killed (by Rāma). He himself killed Kampana in the battle on the thirteenth day. From the fourteenth of the bright half of Māgha to the first day of the dark half, Nīla (after fighting with Prahasta) killed him after three days.

52b-58a. From the second day of the dark half of Māgha till the fourth day, in the fierce fight that lasted for three days Rāma made Rāvaṇa flee the battlefield. From the fifth day to the eighth day Rāvaṇa woke up Kumbhakarṇa. Then he ate food for four days. After six days—from the ninth to the fourteenth—Rāma killed in the battle Kumbhakarṇa who had eaten up many monkeys. On the new-moon day there was a temporary cessation of hostilities due to grief. During the four days from the first day of the bright half of Phālguna to the fourth day five demons—Bisatantu and others—were killed. In the same way Atikāya was killed (in the battle that took place) from the fifth to the seventh. During (the battle that lasted for) five days from the eighth day to the twelfth day (the two demons) Nikumbha and Kumbha were killed. Then, after three days Makarākṣa was killed.

58b-59. On the second day of the dark half of Phālguna Indrajit won (the battle). There was a temporary cessation of hostilities for five days from the third day to the seventh day due to the soldiers being intensely occupied in fetching the herbs.

60-61a. Then, in the battle that lasted for five days (from the eighth day) to the thirteenth day Lakṣmaṇa struck Indrajit who was well-known for his power and valour. Temporarily ceasing the hostilities, on the fourteenth day Rāvaṇa took initiation (i.e. performed a sacrifice).

61b-70a. Rāvaṇa went to fight on the new-moon day. When from the first day of the bright half of Caitra to the fifth day Rāvaṇa was fighting for five days, there was a great killing of the demons. Mahāpārśva and others were killed (in the battle that took place) from the sixth day of Caitra to the eighth day. On the ninth day of the bright half of Caitra Lakṣmaṇa was pierced (i.e. struck) by a missile (discharged by Indrajit). Rāma who was full of anger made Rāvaṇa flee. The son of Añjanī (i.e. Hanūmat) brought the Droṇa mountain for (treating) Lakṣmaṇa (with the herbs on the mountain). The demons temporarily ceased fighting on the night of the tenth. On the eleventh day the charioteer Mātali sent by Indra devoutly presented Rāma in the battle with a chariot (sent by Indra). From the twelfth day (of the bright half) to the fourteenth day of the dark half i.e. for eighteen days Rāma fought with Rāvaṇa in a single combat in chariots. In the battle that was fierce Rāma obtained victory. During the eighty seven days of the war which began on the second day of the bright half of Māgha and continued up to the fourteenth day of the dark half of Caitra, there was a cessation of hostilities for fifteen days—thus the (actual) war took place for seventy-two days. The obsequial ceremonies of Rāvaṇa and others took place on the new-moon day. Rāma stayed on the battlefield on the first day of Vaiśākha.

70b-75. On the second day of Vaiśākha Bibhīṣaṇa was consecrated on the kingdom (i.e. as the king) of Laṅkā. On the third day took place the purification of Sītā and obtaining boons from gods. Having, after a long time, killed the lord of Laṅkā, he, the elder brother of Lakṣmaṇa, accepted the auspicious Jānakī, afflicted by the demon (viz. Rāvaṇa) and taking her (with him) with great love, he returned. On the fourth day of

Vaiśākha Rāma got into the Puṣpaka and through the sky again came back to Ayodhyā. When the fourteenth year was complete Rāma along with his group stayed in Bharadvāja's hermitage on the fifth day of Vaiśākha. On the sixth day he met Bharata at Nandigrāma. On the seventh the descendant of Raghu (i.e. Rāma) was consecrated (as the king) in Ayodhyā.

76-79a. Maithilī (i.e. Ṣītā) lived without Rāma in the house of Rāvaṇa for eleven months and fourteen days. Rāma ruled (i.e. was consecrated as the king) when he was forty-two years old. At that time Sītā had completed thirty-three years. That lord Rāma being delighted entered the city Ayodhyā at the end of the fourteenth year and with his brothers ruled there.

79b-83. When he is thus ruling, Agastya born of a pitcher, the priest best among the eloquent, will come to the lord of the Raghu (dynasty). At his words (i.e. suggestion) he will perform a horse-sacrifice. O you of a good vow, his horse will come to your hermitage. His delighted warriors will (also) come to your hermitage. In front of them you will narrate pleasing tales about Rāma. O best of brāhmaṇas, along with them you will go to Ayodhyā. Seeing Rāma having eyes like lotuses in Ayodhyā, you (will) be just at that moment crossing the ocean of the worldly existence."

84-86a. Having thus spoken to me, that best sage Lomaśa, (most) intelligent of all, said: "What do you want to ask (now)?" Then I spoke proper (words): "Due to your grace I have known all the wonderful deeds of Rāma. By your favour I shall obtain the lotus-feet of Rāma." The lord of sages saluted by me went (his way).

86b-92. By his favour I have secured the worship of the feet of Rāma. That I (i.e. such as I am, I), everyday, repeatedly remember Rāma's feet. Being careful, I shall again and again sing his deeds. I shall purify other people by the enchanting song. With a desire to see him and repeatedly remembering the sage's words I shall be delighted. On the earth I am fortunate, I am blessed, I am lucky (that) I shall have a desire to see Rāma. Therefore, by all means that charming Rāma should be worshipped, for he (alone) should be saluted by all with a desire to cross the ocean of the mundane existence. Therefore, (tell me) why you have come here. Which king, a religious-minded one, will perform the great sacrifice, viz. the horse-sacrifice? You should tell me all that now; and should go to look after the horse. You should, repeatedly remembering Rāma's feet, remember them (constantly).

93. Hearing these words of the sage, they were wonderstruck. Remembering Raghunātha, they said to sage Āraṇyaka.

CHAPTER THIRTYSEVEN

Sage Āraṇyaka Goes to Viṣṇu's Heaven

Śeṣa said:

1. By the best sage they were asked (about) the wonderful deeds of Rāma. Regarding themselves as blessed and fortunate they spoke with respect.

The people said:

2-5. On seeing you we are now purified, since by (telling us) the account of Rāma you are purifying people (like) us. Listen to the true statement. You are the best among the brāhmaṇic sages. We shall tell all that you have asked us. By the words (i.e. at the suggestion) of Agastya Rāma is performing a very great sacrifice furnished with all ingredients for removing (the sin due to) the killing of a brāhmaṇa. We who all look after him have come along with the horse to your hermitage. O very intelligent one, know it.

6-11. Hearing these pleasant words, an elixir of life, the brāhmaṇa, devoted to Rāma was highly delighted. "Today the tree of my desire for glory has become fruitful. Today my mother who gave me birth, is blessed. Today I have obtained kingdom free from troublesome fellows. The treasures are very rich today. Today the gods are very much pleased. I have today obtained the fruit of maintaining the sacred fire to which oblations were offered, that I shall see the pair of the lotus-like feet of Rāmacandra.

That extremely charming lord of Ayodhyā, who is everyday meditated upon in my heart, will indeed be seen by me. Hanūmat, embracing me, will ask me about my well-being. The best one, on seeing my great devotion, will be pleased."

12-13. Hearing these words, Hanūmat, the best of the monkeys, clasped the pair of the feet of the sage Āraṇyaka. "O lord, O brāhmaṇa-sage, I am (Rāma's) servant standing before you. O lord of sages, know me, Rāma's servant, resembling a dust-particle."

14-17. When he was speaking like this, the sage, who was highly delighted, embraced Hanūmat adorned with his devotion to Rāma. Both were full of love, both were bathing with nectar (as it were). Covered (by each other) they appeared as it were drawn in a picture. They sat there and told very pleasant stories. Their minds were full of love for the lotus-like feet of Raghunātha. Hanūmat said various charming words to that excellent sage Āraṇyaka who was full of the thought about the feet of Rāma:

18-24. "O lord, this is the great diamond-like offspring of Daśaratha's family. He is Rāma's brother; is very brave. This Śatrughna salutes you. He killed Lavaṇa who was fearful to the entire world; and he made all sages, of excellent penance, happy. This is (Bharata's son) named Puṣkala, who is served by very great heroes and who now conquered many great heroes on the battlefield. Know this one of many merits and of great power to be Rāma's minister, dear to Raghupati (i.e. Rāma) like his own life, knowing everything and proficient in dharma. This is Subāhu, who is very fierce, who is a conflagration to the families of the enemies, and is a bee (howering) round the lotus-like feet of Rāma. This one of great fame salutes you. This Sumada too, who, due to service of Rāma's feet given (i.e. assigned) to him by Pārvatī, has now achieved the great crossing over the ocean of the mundane existence. This Satyavān who having heard from his servant that the horse (of Rāma) had come, offered his kingdom (to Rāma). He is saluting you (by prostrating himself) on the ground."

25-29. Having heard these words, sage Āraṇyaka, having embraced (them) with respect, welcomed them by offering fruits etc. They, very diligent ones, being delighted, having performed their daily morning rites in Revā, stayed in the hermitage of the excellent sage. Having put the sage with his servants in a man-drawn vehicle, Śatrughna reached Ayodhyā where Rāma had taken his abode. He (i.e. the sage) seeing from a distance the city in which the king of the solar dynasty lived, quickly (got down from the vehicle and) went on foot with a desire to see the lord of Raghus. He reached the beautiful city of Ayodhyā adorned with people. A thousand of desires got (into his mind) for seeing Rāma.

30-32. There on the bank of Sarayū adorned with a pavilion, he saw Rāma who was dark like dūrvā-blades, whose eyes had the beauty of lotuses, who was holding on his waist a charming deer-horn endowed with beauty, was surrounded by hosts of sages led by Vyāsa, was well-served by the brave (soldiers), was surrounded by Bharata and Sumitrā's son (Lakṣmaṇa), was giving to the groups of the poor whatever they asked for.

33-36. Having seen him, (the sage) called Āraṇyaka regarded himself as blessed. "My eyes, resembling lotus-petals, are seeing Rāma. Today my knowledge of all sacred texts has become very significant, since, knowing Śrī Rāma, I have reached this city of Ayodhyā." He, delighted, saying these and many other words, and shining with his body very much delighted on seeing the feet of Rāma, went near Ramā's lord who was extremely inaccessible even to other lords of deep meditation, devoted to reflection. "Today I am lucky (that) Rāma's feet will come within the range of my sight (i.e. will be seen by me)". Saying these charming words (he stood) seeing Rāma.

37-40. Rāma too, seeing the best brāhmaṇa glowing with his own lustre, having the form of penance, got up. The great Rāmacandra saluted his feet for a long time. "O brāhmaṇa god, you have today purified my body." Saying these words, the lord, before whose feet (the lights of) the gems on the crowns of gods and demons bending before him were waved, fell at his feet. The best brāhmaṇa, of a great penance, held the best king between his arms, and embraced the dear lord.

41-46. The son of Kauśalyā (i.e. Rāma), the lord, having put him on a high jewelled seat, washed his pair of feet with water. And Hari (i.e. Rāma) himself took (i.e. put) that water, used for washing the sage's feet, on his (own) head, saying: "Today with my attendants and (members of) my family I am purified. Having smeared him with sandal (-paste), he gave him a milch cow; and he, served by the lord of gods, said (these) charming words: "O lord, I would perform the sacrifice called Vāji-medha (i.e. horse-sacrifice). That will be today fully completed due to the arrival of your feet. Today, sacrifice (called) Aśvamedha (i.e. horse-sacrifice), purified by your feet, will destroy my sin due to the killing of a brāhmaṇa." To him, served by the lord of kings the sage Āraṇyaka smilingly spoke thus in sweet words:

47-58. "O lord, O king friendly to brāhmaṇas, your words are proper. O great king, the brāhmaṇas who have mastered the Vedas, are (but) your forms. O king, when you will perform the auspicious act like worshipping brāhmaṇas, all the (other) kings will worship a brāhmaṇa. O great king, the words which you uttered, viz. "I shall perform a pure sacrifice to remove (the sin of) a brāhmaṇa's murder" are but laughable. (Even) a fool void (i.e. ignorant) of all sacred texts, would go to the highest position after having crossed the ocean of all sins (merely) by remembering your name. It is clear that the essential meaning of all the Vedas and old narratives is that Rāma's name is remembered to overcome sins. O Rāmacandra, as long as your name is not distinctly uttered, sins like those of brāhmaṇa murders, roar. O great king, having heard your name, the elephants in the form of great sins run away with a desire to find a place somewhere (to hide themselves). Therefore, O Rāma, O you whose sight is meritorious, how can there be a killing by you? A men, having heard your good (i.e. auspicious) account, instantly becomes pure. Formerly in the Kṛta age I heard the words from the mouth of (i.e. uttered by) sages knowing ancient accounts and residing on the bank of Gaṅgā: 'As long as men do not utter the charming name of Rāma, there are fears for those very sinful cowardly men'. Therefore, now I am blessed; O Rāmacandra, the destruction of my mundane existence has now become easy due to my having seen you." He worshipped the sage who was speaking like this. All the sages uttered the words, 'Well, Well'.

Śeṣa said:

59-67. O Vātsyāyana, best among the sages, and greatly devoted to Rāma, a great wonder took place there. Listen to it when I am telling (it to you). When he saw the great king Rāma (just) as he had seen him in his meditation, he, who was extremely delighted, said to the best sages: "O best sages, listen to my very pleasant words. Who will be (i.e. who is) so very lucky like me on the earth? There is none like me; there was none born like me; there will be none like me, since Rāmabhadra having saluted me inquired about my (i.e. offered me a) welcome. He the dust of whose feet is always sought for by the scriptures has today after drinking the water (flowing) from my feet regarded himself pure." When he was speaking like this, Brāhmaṇic (lustre) burst out (from his body) entered (the body of) the lord of the Raghus. (The sage) when all people were watching in the pavilion on the bank of Sarayū, obtained absorption (into the deity, viz. Rāma), which (absorption) is difficult to be secured by the meditating saints. In the sky there was at that time the sound of musical instruments. There was (also) the sound of lutes. Shower of flowers fell in front of them who were watching the interesting wonder. The sages also, having seen it, praised the best sage (saying): "The best sage is fortunate, since he has secured residence in the body of Rāma."

CHAPTER THIRTYEIGHT

Getting Back the Horse from the Possession of an Under-Water Female

Sūta said:

1. Having heard this account, the noble-minded Vātsyāyana obtained great joy and said to the lord of the serpents.

Vātsyāyana said:

2-5. O lord of the serpents, I who listen to the story of Raghunātha who is famous for destroying the affliction of his devotees, am not (at all) satisfied. The great sage Āraṇyaka possessing (the knowledge of) the Vedas, who cast his perishable body after seeing Raghunātha, is blessed. From there where did the king's horse go? By whom was he restrained? How was the glory of the lord of Rāma produced there? O lord of serpents, tell me all the truth, since you are omniscient. You hold the body of Viṣṇu; you actually possess his form.

Vyāsa said:

6. Hearing these words, he, with his heart delighted, narrated Rāma's deeds highlighting his so many (innumerable) virtues.

Śeṣa said:

7-16. O brāhmaṇa sage, you are well asking about Raghunātha's virtues by expressing a desire to hear them, by regarding them as not having been heard, though you have repeatedly heard them. From there the horse, surrounded by many soldiers, went out to the charming bank of Revā resorted to by hosts of sages. Then all the soldiers, skilled in fighting and carefully watching the path of (i.e. taken by) him, proceeded wherever the horse (moved). Then the horse holding a golden note on his forehead and with his body worshipped, went to a pool of water in Revā full of unfordable water. Then the excellent horse of Rāmacandra plunged into water. At that time all the great heroes were wonder-struck. They just said to one another: "How can the horse be regained? Who will go into the water to bring the horse of great splendour?" When, thus dejected, they were consulting one another, the lord of the Raghu (family) arrived there with hundreds of heroes. Seeing all of them dejected, the crest-jewel of the brave called Śatrughna, asked them with a voice deep-sounding like that of the clouds: "Why do you all today stay in groups in the water? Where is Raghunātha's horse adorned with the golden note? Has it been drowned into the water? Or has it been snatched by some haughty person? Tell me that quickly as to how you are confused."

Śeṣa said:

17. Having heard these words of the best (descendant of) Raghu, the king, the heroes told everything to the crest-jewel of the brave.

The men said:

18-22. O lord, we do not know. For a while he was in the water. Then he plunged (into the water). Your charming horse did not come (up). You yourself (should) go there, and bring the horse quickly. O you very intelligent one, we would go there with you.

Hearing these words of the soldiers, the descendant of Raghu (i.e. Śatrughna) was dejected on seeing the men ready to swim in the water. He said to the chief minister: "What should we do hereafter? Tell (me) how the horse will (i.e. can) be brought (back). Which brave ones should be employed to find out the horse in the water? Tell me who will bring back the horse and by what means."

23-26. Hearing these words of the king, Sumati, the best minister, said, as it were delighting Śatrughna, what was proper for the occasion: "O lord, you, of wonderful deeds, have glorious power. It is clear, you have the power to go to the nether world through water. Another thing is: Puṣkala the magnanimous one, has also the power. So also Hanūmat engaged in serving the feet of Rāma (has the power). Therefore, you three (should) go and certainly bring the horse from the place where the sacrificial horse of the intelligent Raghunātha might be."

Śeṣa said:

27-32. Hearing these words, Śatrughna, the killer of the enemy's warriors, himself, along with Hanūmat and Puṣkala entered the water. When he entered the water, he saw a city. The city was rich with the beauty of many gardens and immeasurable. He saw there Rāma's horse well adorned with the golden note, and tied to a golden pillar decked with rubies. There excellent ladies having attractive forms were waiting upon a beautiful lady comfortably seated upon a couch. Seeing them all the ladies said to their queen: "These (individuals) of a small height, young and with well-nourished bodies will be the best object of your food. The blood of these men when they die (i.e. when they will be killed) will be sweet."

33-36. Hearing these words of her female servants, that

sinless beautiful lady, gesticulating her face with her eye-brow; laughed a little. At that time the three shining with the beauty of their armours, having helmets, and endowed with valour and bravery, reached there. O brāhmaṇa, seeing there the ladies endowed with the wealth of beauty, they expressed their amazement: "What is this great thing being seen?" With the feet (of the lady) shining with the lustre of the gems in their crowns, all the magnanimous ones saluted the divine, excellent, ladies.

37-39. That beautiful young lady, the greatest of all, asked those men: "Who are you that have come here? How is it that you men are holding bows? My place is greatly deluding and is inaccessible to all gods. No one that has come here ever returns. To which king does this horse belong? How is it that the horse is fanned with chowries? (How is it) rich in beauty with the golden note? You should tell (everything) to me."

Śeṣa said:

40-43. Having thus heard her words full of deluding manner, Hanūmat, with his fear gone and smiling, said: "We are the servants of the king, the crest-jewel of the three worlds. This group of the three worlds salutes (him) the crest-jewel of all gods. Know the horse to belong to Rāmabhadra who is proceeding to (perform) a horse-sacrifice. Release our horse. O you beautiful lady, how (i.e. why) has he been tied? We are skilled in (the use of) all missiles; we are proficient in (the use of) all weapons and missiles. Killing those who obstruct (our) horse, we shall forcibly take (back the horse)."

44-49. Hearing these words of the monkey (i.e. Hanūmat), that excellent lady, seated in a hollow, proficient in (using proper) words, laughed, and said: "Nobody is able to free this horse brought by me, even (if he fights) with sharp points of arrows that are blazing up, (even for) a myriad of years. But I am the servant of the lotus-like feet of Rāma. I do his work. I shall not seize the horse of that intelligent king of kings. I, who took away the good horse, have committed great rudeness. Let that Rāmacandra, the protector, who loves his devotees, pardon me. You, the men of him, the protector, are afflicted for that horse. O best one, ask for a boon difficult to be secured even by gods, so that the best man would forgive me the severe harm (done to him). Giving up all bashfulness, choose the best boon."

50-52. Hearing her great words, Hanūmat said to her: "Due to the grace of Raghunātha everything that we have is excellent. Still, I ask for an excellent boon. Give that one, desired by my mind: Let Raghunātha be our lord in every existence, and let us be his servants doing his work." Hearing these words of the monkey (i.e. Hanūmat), that lady laughed and said sweet words, honoured for their merit:

53-63. "O servants of the lord of (the) Raghu (family), whatever is desired by you, which is difficult to be obtained by deities, will take place. There is no doubt. Yet, I who slighted (Rāma) shall give (you) a boon to please Ragunātha. My words would come true. Later king Vīramaṇi, accompanied by great heroes and protected by Śiva, will seize your horse. O you very powerful ones, take a great missile from me to conquer him. You, great Śatrughna, should fight with him in a single combat in chariots. When, in the battle, you will discharge this missile; he, being purified by it, will again realise the true nature of Rāma. Realising him, and giving the horse (back to you) he will fall at your feet. Therefore, take from me the missile destroying the enemy." Hearing that (i.e. those words), Rāma's brother (i.e. Śatrughna), facing the north, and with his body purified, received that wonderful missile given by that female devotee. Having received that missile, he became one with great might, destroyer of the enemies, difficult to be assailed and propitiated, and a hook to drive the elephants in the form of his enemies. Having saluted her, Śatrughna, the best among the descendants of Raghu, took the best horse, and from the water went (up) to the bank of Revā, fit for comforts. Having seen him, all the soldiers, with their bodies delighted and full of joy, praised him (as): "Well (done), well (done)!" and asked him about the coming out (i.e. as to how the horse came out of the water). Hanūmat told them about the great (i.e. important) coming (out) of the horse, and also about having received the boon. They too, hearing (it) were delighted.

CHAPTER THIRTYNINE

The Seizure of the Horse by Vīramaṇi's Son

Śeṣa said:

1-8. When everywhere the tabors were sounded and when everywhere there were the sounds of lutes, the horse was released. From there he (went) to Devapura fashioned by gods, in which men's houses laughed, as it were, (i.e. were bright) by means of the constructions of crystal walls at the spotless Vindhya mountain resorted to by elephants. Even the houses of the subjects (i.e. ordinary people) were made of silver here (i.e. in this city). Here the ornamental ruby gateways were girdled by variegated gems; in every house there were attractive, most beautiful women that with side-glances attracted the hearts of men. Here, O brāhmaṇa, in every house rubies were seen to have been fixed in the good (i.e. beautiful) floors, as it were, to vie with the lips of the women. In every house the pleasure-mountains fashioned with sapphires produced the hope of (the arrival of) clouds in (the minds of) the peacocks having plumages. In this city swans, restrained on the crystal-floors in the houses were not afraid of a cloud and did not remember the Mānasa lake. (In it) at the abode of Śiva darkness was always dispelled by the moonlight; (so) the men there did not distinguish between the bright half and the dark half (of the month).

9-11. There the great king Vīramaṇi, the chief among the righteous (kings), ruled over a large kingdom full of all enjoyments. His very brave and powerful son named Rukmāṅgada (once) went to a forest to sport with women of charming bodies. The sound of their anklets and also the sound of their bracelets attracted the mind of Cupid (himself); then what to say about others!

12-16. He (i.e. Rukmāṅgada) went to the great forest which was full of trees with good flowers, where Sadāśiva had made his abode, and which shone with the six seasons. In it the many campaka trees adorned with blooming buds caused affliction in the hearts of passionate men, when they were seen by the men. (There) the mango trees, having crores of sprouts, were bent with fruits etc. (There were) the nāga (trees), the punnāga trees, the śāla (trees), the tāla (trees) and the tamāla (trees). In it the cooings of cuckoos were heard. The good jasmine (creepers) had always lost their sleep (i.e. were blossoming) due to the humming of bees. (There) the groups of the pomgranate (trees) were linked to the karṇikāra (trees); the rows of the sylvan trees shone with the ketakī and kanakī trees.

17-20. With his mind full of joy, singing sweetly and indistinctly, and having a body—the abode of charm—he, with women on all sides having a strong desire to talk sweetly and having raised breasts, entered the forest through passion and free from fear. Some pleased him with their knowledge of dancing, some (pleased) him with their singing arts, some with clever words; others, being intoxicated, pleased him with the signs (i.e. knittings) of their eye-brows. The women made him happy with their skill in embracing. Having collected flowers with them he, having Cupid's body, praising them with tender words, adorned those women.

21-23. When the intelligent king of kings was passing his time like this, that extremely charming horse went to that region of the forest. The women seeing him, on whose forehead was arranged (i.e. put) the golden note, who resembled Gaṅgā (in colour), whose body was tawny due to the reddish saffron, who was uniform in speed which excelled that of the wind said (the following) to their lord. The women had a tawny complexion like the interior of a lotus. They had set back the beauty of corals afraid of their red lips, with their red lips. Their faces were beautiful due to the laughter meted out by the rows of their teeth. They were lustrous due to their seductive eyes resembling Cupid's arrows.

The women said:

24. O darling, who is this great horse adorned only with the golden note? To whom does he, endowed with loveliness, belong? Seize him with your might.

Śeṣa said:

25-26. Hearing those words spoken (by the women), he having charming and sportive eyes, easily seized the horse with only one hand resembling a lotus. Having read the golden note having clear letters, he seized him, and again said these words to the women.

Rukmāṅgada said:

27-32. On the earth there is none else like my father in valour and wealth. How can that king Rāma show haughty disregard of him? Let my very mighty father whom Rudra, the holder of the trident, always protects, whom gods, demons, yakṣas salute with their heads having jewels (bowed), perform the horse-sacrifice. Let this (horse) go to the stable. Let my soldiers tie him.

Hearing these words, the charming women had their faces joyful, and embraced their lover. The great son of king Vīramaṇi, seizing the horse, entered with his wives the city with great enthusiasm. When the sounds of the tabors that were beaten, were loud, he, being praised on all sides by the bards, went to the great house (i.e. palace) of his father.

33-37. He told him about his having seized Rāma's wonderful horse released for the horse-sacrifice, moving freely and protected by Śatrughna endowed with great power. The great, very intelligent king Vīramaṇi, having heard his words, did not very much approve that deed of him. Taking the seizure of that horse which was brought (to him by his son) like a thief's act and bringing him (to Śiva) he told lord Śiva, of wonderful deeds, having a lady (i.e. Pārvatī) as the half (part) of his body, having the moon for decorating his body. The great king Vīramaṇi honoured by the great, having condemned the deed done by his son, consulted him.

Śiva said:

38-44. O king, your son who took away the great horse of the intelligent Rāmacandra, has done a wonderful deed. Today a great war deluding gods and demons, with the great king Śatrughna, the only protector of a crore of heroes, appears (imminent). Your son has carried away (the horse)—the constituent of the sacrifice—of that Rāma who is held by me in my heart, and who is spoken (about) with my tongue (by me). But in the battle there will be a great gain, since we shall see the lotus-like feet of Rāma, which are waited upon by me. Now a great effort must be done to protect the horse. They will forcibly take this horse, though protected by me. Therefore, O great king, with modesty you should (first) give along with the kingdom, the horse and food and then see the pair of his feet.

Having heard these words of Śiva, the best king said to him, whose pair of lotus-like feet were adorable (even) to Indra and others.

Vīramaṇi said:

45-50. This is the duty of kṣatriyas to preserve valour. He is eager to surpass it by the sacrifice called horse (-sacrifice). Therefore whosoever is possessed of self-respect, has to maintain his own valour, by doing, as is possible, a deed, (even) spending (i.e. harming) his (own) body. Everything is done by (my) son since he has seized the horse. He has angered king Rāma. (So) O lord, do what is proper for the occasion. It would certainly not be an act to be done by kṣatriyas that he (i.e. a kṣatriya) overcome with fear, should all of a sudden, salute the feet of his enemy. The enemies laugh at him (and say): "This mean king is a coward. He is insignificant; he, the mean one, being overcome with fear like a common man, has bowed (before me)." Therefore, when the fight is imminent, you should think and do whatever is proper and should protect your devotee.

Śeṣa said:

51-56. Hearing these words, Śiva laughed, and spoke words in a voice deep-sounding like a cloud, and infatuating his mind: "Even if the thirty-three crore gods are present, who would take the horse from you when I am your protector. If Rāma comes and shows himself to me, then I shall salute his very delicate feet. One should not fight with one's lord. (Doing so) is said to be a very evil course. Other heroes are (insignificant) like blades of grass. They are not capable of doing anything. Therefore, O best of kings, fight when I, your protector, am well-settled. Who would take (away) the horse even if the three worlds come together."

Śeṣa said:

Hearing those great words of Candracūḍa (i.e. Śiva) the king who took pleasure in fighting was very much delighted in his mind.

CHAPTER FORTY

Śatrughna Resolves to Fight Against Vīramaṇi

Śeṣa said :

1-7. Looking for king Rāma's horse the great king's soldiers endowed with great power (or army) came (there). (They said:) "Where is the horse? Who has taken him? How is it that he is not seen? Who, a very dull one, will go to Yama's city after having (i.e. because of his having) taken the horse?" While the soldiers of Raghu were searching the course of the horse, the great king surrounded by a large army came (there). He asked all his servants: "Now where is my horse? How is it that the horse, adorned with the golden note is not seen?" Hearing these words of (i.e. uttered by) him, the servants who were following the horse, said: "The horse having the mind's speed has been snatched away by someone into the forest. Therefore, even though we know the path well, the horse is not noticed. Therefore, O lord, an effort should be made now to get (back) the horse." Hearing their words, Śatrughna, the killer of his enemies, and having a fascinating form, asked Sumati:

Śatrughna said :

8. Which king stays here? How did he secure the horse? How much is the power (or army) of the king, who has today taken away my horse?

Sumati said :

9-12. O king, this is Devapura fashioned by the lord himself. It is like the Kailāsa (mountain) inaccessible (even) to hosts of the army, well joined together. In it rules the very brave and valourous king Vīramaṇi, protected by Śiva, and he is ruling justly. He, Śiva who is the destroyer of the whole universe, (but) who always lets loose (his) partiality for his devotee, is won over (by the king) by means of his devotion. So if the horse is taken, there will be a great war. Let the good ones, being careful, protect the army.

13-16. Hearing this, that Śatrughna, the very glorious one, and the crest-jewel of all kings, waited (i.e. got ready to fight) after arranging the army. When he having consultations with his good minister (Sumati), waited comfortably, the divine sage (Nārada), eager (to see) the battle, came there. Having seen the sage, the abode of austerities, that had arrived there, Śatrughna got up (from his seat) and seating him on a seat, offered him a respectful offering. He, skilled in speaking, pleasing Nārada the best sage, with words, said to him pleased with the welcome (offered to him):

Śatrughna said :

17-19. O highly intelligent brāhmaṇa, tell me where my horse is. My servants, experienced in their duty, cannot trace his course. Tell (me the name of) that insolent kṣatriya who has taken (away) my horse. O you abode of penance, how will the horse be got (back by us)?

Hearing these words of Śatrughna, Nārada, sounding the lute and repeatedly singing Rāma's account, said:

Nārada said :

20-24. O king, this is Devapura. Vīramaṇi is the great king there. His son, who was in the forest, has seized your best horse. Today you will wage a very fierce battle (against him). Here (i.e. in this battle) soldiers having might and valour will fall. Therefore, O very powerful one, you should remain here with great effort. Make an array to which access is difficult for the enemy's soldiers. O king, in it you will have victory over the best king with difficulty. Who would defeat Rāma even on the entire earth?

Speaking like this, the brāhmaṇa disappeared, and remained in the sky watching the very fierce battle like the one between gods and demons.

Śeṣa said:

25-26. Then king Vīramaṇi, the crest-jewel of all brave men, asked his general, very eminent and brave among the enemies, to proclaim loudly by beating the war-drum; and told him with deep sounding words:

Vīramaṇi said:

27-31. O general, give the order (with the beating) of the war-drum in my beautiful city. Hearing it, let my well-equipped (heroes) march against Śatrughna.

Hearing the words of Vīramaṇi, the general at that time made the proclamation with the war-drum making a great sound. In every house and on the road the sound of the war-drum was heard: "Let all the heroes present in the capital march (against) Śatrughna. Those who looking upon themselves as brave disobey the order of the king, even though they may be sons or brothers, should be killed by the king's order. Let the heroes listen to the sound (which is produced) when the war-drum is beaten. Having heard it, they should, without delay, perform their duty."

Śeṣa said:

32-34. The best heroes, having heard the sound of the war-drum, with their bodies decorated with golden armours and with the interior of their hearts delighted by the festival of fight, went to the best king. Some, having put on beautiful helmets on their heads, and very charming due to the armours, and (thus) crores of them well adorned, went (to the king). The furious ones, as a result of the king's message, went (to the king), in chariots to which two horses looking beautiful due to gems and gold were yoked.

35-45. All of them obeying the command of the king went riding very charming horses to the king's abode. Rukmāṅgada also, who was well adorned with a distinguished golden armour and a helmet, got into his chariot having mind's speed. His younger brother Śubhāṅgada, having put on his body an excellent armour full of (i.e. decked with) big gems, went to (participate in) the festival of fight. The king's brother Vīrasiṁha, proficient in the use of all weapons and missiles went there by the king's order, for that was a royal order. The king's sister's son also who was known as Balamitra, equipped with an armour and a sword, went to the king's palace. His great general Ripuvāra, making ready the army with its four constituents, reported to the king. Then king Vīramaṇi got into the best chariot full of all weapons and missiles and high due to having high wheels made of gems. Then in the ocean of the heroes the sound of conches, as if well impelling the cowardly warriors to fight, was heard. Kettle-drums sounded by auspicious musicians were beaten on all sides. The troops of him who proceeded to fight, stood there. All (the soldiers) had averted the evil by recitation of hymns; all were adorned with all ornaments. All fully equipped with missiles and weapons went to the battlefield. The mountains and caves were filled with the sounds of kettle-drums and conches. Is it that their sound went to call those who stayed in heaven?

46-48. When that din took place, the great king Vīramaṇi, full of enthusiasm to fight, went to the battlefield. When, after arriving at the battlefield full of chariots and foot-soldiers, he remained there, his army went there like the ocean to wash away the (enemy's) men from that place. Having seen that army full of warriors fighting from chariots, proficient in (the use of) weapons, and making a great noise, the king (i.e. Śatrughna) said to Sumati:

Śatrughna said :

49-50. The powerful Vīramaṇi who had seized our horse, has again come with a great army having four divisions. How should the battle be fought? Who, fierce with might, will fight? Show all those heroes to me, and (show me also) how the desired victory would be had.

Sumati said :

51-54. O lord, that great king, endowed with devotion to Śiva and surrounded by a huge army, has come to fight. Now, let the hero Puṣkala knowing the use uf great missiles fight. Let other warriors like Nīlaratna, proficient in fighting (fight). O innocent one, you should fight with Śiva or with the king. He, of a great power and valour, should be conquered in a single combat. In this way, O king, you will be victorious. O very intelligent lord, later you should do what you like.

Śeṣa said:

55-57. Hearing these words Śatrughna, the killer of the heroes of his enemy, having determined to fight, ordered his good warriors: "All the kings with their armies proficient in (the use of) weapons, should quickly exert themselves in such a way that I get victory." Hearing it, those (kings) proficient in fighting, full of great energy, went with their soldiers to fight (against the enemy in order to obtain) victory for the descendant of Raghu.

CHAPTER FORTYONE

Rukmāṅgada Is Defeated by Puṣkala

Śeṣa said:

1-7. Those very powerful heroes of Śatrughna, endowed with valour and quite ready to fight, went into the army of Vīramaṇi. The men discharging arrows, piercing many soldiers, holding bows were seen standing in the battlefield. Many elephants were killed there. On the battlefield were seen jewelled chariots shattered with their horses. Having heard about their destruction the mighty Rukmāṅgada, standing in a jewelled chariot, came there to fight with the soldiers. He fixed arrows on his bow and had two inexhaustible quivers. That mighty Rukmāṅgada, full of great anger and with blood in his eyes, making thousands of brave men terrified with his arrows causing wailing (in the enemy's camp), went (to fight). The mighty prince challenged Śatrughna and Bharata's son Puṣkala like himself in fame and glory.

Rukmāṅgada said :

8-15a. You who perform brave deeds and whose power and valour are great; come to fight with me, the strong and lustrous prince. O brave one, what is the use of frightening and killing others, crores of men? Having fought a great battle with me, obtain victory.

The mighty Puṣkala laughed and quickly struck him who was speaking like this on his large chest with sharp hooks. Not bearing it, the prince fixing arrows on his great bow struck with ten arrows Puṣkala in his chest. Both excited while fighting, both desiring victory, shone in the battle like Kārtikeya and (the demon) Tāraka. Fixing very sharp arrows ten in number on his bow Puṣkala, the hero, made the prince chariotless. With four (arrows) he knocked down his four horses; with two (he knocked down) his charioter; with one (he knocked down) his flag and with two (he knocked down) the guards of his chariot. The swift one pierced the prince with one (arrow).

15b-17. Seeing that wonderful act all heroes were very much delighted. He whose bow was broken, who had lost his chariot, whose horses and charioteer were killed, became extremely angry and got into another chariot. Standing in the excellent chariot adorned with gems of horses, he took a big strong bow furnished with a string.

18-19. Rukmāṅgada said these words to the brave Puṣkala: "O you tormentor of the enemies, having done (a) great (act of) valour where are you going? Today see my valour brought about by might. O hero, stand carefully; I shall take your chariot to the sky."

20-22a. Saying so he fixed a very fierce arrow on his own bow. Then enchanting the 'bhrāmaka' missile (i.e. the whirling missile), he discharged that sharp arrow adorned with gold at the feathered part into Puṣkala's chariot. By that arrow his chariot was taken to a distance of a yojana. With difficulty it was held in check by the charioteer; the chariot roamed on the earth.

22b-24. Puṣkala, who knew the (use of) great missiles, getting back his position with difficulty, and fixing an arrow on his bow said (these words) to him: "O best among the heroes, reach heaven resorted to by all gods. O best king, people like you are not fit for (living on) the earth. They are fit for the assembly of Indra. Therefore, go to the abode of gods."

25-28. Speaking thus he discharged a great missile reaching the sky. (Struck) by that arrow the chariot straightway went into the sky. Going beyond all worlds it went to the sun's orb. By its flame the chariot, along with the horses and the charioteer, was burnt. With his chariot greatly burnt by its rays, he being extremely pained, fell, keeping in heart Śiva, the destroyer of the impious ones. With his body burnt by the rays, he fell there on the ground. He became extremely unhappy; and swooned on the battlefield.

29-33. When the prince dropped unconscious on the ground, there was a great wailing on the battlefield. The enemies led by Puṣkala got victory; (while) the enemies who had preserved the horse, were intent on fleeing. Then king Vīramaṇi, seeing the swoon of his son (i.e. seeing that his son was unconscious), was full of anger, and marched against Puṣkala who stood in the battlefield. At that time the earth, along with the mountains and excellent forests, trembled; the brave ones were delighted, (while) the cowards were oppressed with fear. Holding a great bow and two inexhaustible quivers and breathing heavily due to anger, he challenged his enemy.

CHAPTER FORTYTWO

Vīramaṇi Is Defeated

Śeṣa said:

1-4. Seeing him challenging king Puṣkala in the ocean of the great army, even Hanūmat, the lord of monkeys, having with a sound raised the tail of his big body and having made a sound like that of a cloud, ran to him. When the best heroes stood in the battlefield, the lord of monkeys went to the best king. Seeing Hanūmat coming the mighty hero Puṣkala looked at him with his eyes full of much blood (i.e. very red) due to anger towards his enemy with a deep-sounding voice like (the sound of) a cloud and filling the battlefield with his sound Puṣkala who knew (the use of) great missiles, spoke to that Hanūmat:

Puṣkala said:

5-10. O great monkey, how (i.e. why) have you come to fight in this battle? How much is the 'great' power of the king Vīramaṇi? It is very little. When the three worlds coming together stand before you, (even) then you may or may not desire to go to fight. Who is this king Vīramaṇi (before you)? How much is his power? It is battle. O hero, your fierce arrival (i.e. the arrival of you, the fierce one) here is not considered (necessary). By virtue of the side glance in the form of the grace of Raghunātha I shall come out after overcoming him who is difficult to be subdued. O lord of monkeys, do not have a mind to fight. With the heap of Rāma's grace you crossed the ocean in the form of demons. Similarly by remembering Rāma well I shall overcome this one difficult to be subdued. There is no doubt that the ocean of the miseries of them who after having encountered a difficulty remember Rāma, gets dried.

11. Therefore, O mighty hero, O powerful one, go near Śatrughna. I shall just come, after having vanquished king Vīramaṇi in a moment.

Śeṣa said:

12. Having heard these courageous words uttered by Puṣkala (Hanūmat), the killer of the heroes of the enemy, again spoke (these) words to Puṣkala.

Hanūmat said:

13-16. O son, do not act rashly towards king Vīramaṇi. He is a donor, a protector and is endowed with might and valour. You are young, (while) the king is old and the best among those who know (the use of) all weapons and missiles. In a battle he has conquered many heroes adorned with (i.e. characterized by) bravery. Know that by his side is protector Śiva, won over by means of devotion and living in his city with Umā (i.e. Pārvatī). Therefore, O Puṣkala, I will fight with this king only. Having vanquished other heroes, obtain great fame.

Puṣkala said:

17-23. Having won over Śiva through devotion he has installed him (i.e. his image) in his city; but the great lord does not directly live in his heart. That Rāma, having propitiated whom Sadāśiva reached the highest position, does not go to any other place after leaving my heart. The entire immobile and mobile world remains where Rāma remains. Therefore, I shall conquer king Vīramaṇi in the battle. O monkey, go to fight with other kings who are very haughty, in the battle. Do not be worried (about me), O lord.

Having heard these courageous words, Hanūmat went to fight with Vīrasiṁha, the younger brother of king (Vīramaṇi), in the battle. Lakṣmīnidhi, fought in a single combat in chariots with his son named Śubhāṅgada who knew the use of great weapons and missiles. Prince Sumada, distinguished by his own valour and might, (equipped) with weapons went to fight with Balamitra.

24-25. Seeing the king and challenging him, Puṣkala, skilled in a single combat in chariots, seated in a chariot decked with gold went to him. The king who spoke well, seeing Puṣkala, skilled in fight, to have come (there), said (to him) with fearless words on the battlefield.

Vīramaṇi said:

26-30a. O child, do not march against me who am angry and fierce and irascible in a battle; go (back) with a desire for (i.e. in order to save) your life. Do not fight with me. Kings like me favour children like you. They do not strike them. Therefore, go out of the battlefield. I was eager (to fight with you) till I had not seen you with my eyes. Now my mind does not desire to strike you. All that great act of you, having (but) a child's intelligence, viz. that you pierced my son with arrows and caused him to swoon, is forgiven by me.

Hearing these words, Puṣkala said to him:

Puṣkala said:

30b-33. (You say) I am a child, and you are very old, proficient in (the use of) all weapons and missiles. But the view of kṣatriyas is: Those alone who have a superior power are old and not those who are old in age. I made unconscious your son who was proud of his valour and might. Now I shall knock you down with (my) weapons in the battle. Therefore, O king, stand with care in the battle. Nobody (even if) he remains at Indra's position, can conquer me, a devotee of Rāma.

34-45a. Hearing these words of Puṣkala, the best king, seeing (i.e. knowing him to be) young, laughed, but again became angry. The furious son of Bharata, having seen him to be angry, struck the king in his chest with twenty sharp arrows. The king, seeing those arrows, discharged by him (i.e. Puṣkala) coming to him got very angry and cut them off in many ways with sharp arrows. Seeing the arrows being cut off he, the prince named Puṣkala and the son of Bharata, was very angry at heart, and struck the king on his forehead with three arrows. Stuck there, they shone as if they were the three peaks of the Trikūṭa (mountain). The king afflicted by the arrows and full of great anger, struck the hero Puṣkala, in his heart with nine arrows. By these arrows profuse blood was quaffed from the body of the son of the younger brother of Rāma, as (it were) angry poisonous snakes had clung on his body. Puṣkala who was extremely angry, again quickly pierced the king with a hundred arrows of sharp joints. By the arrows his armour was cut off. His crown along with the helmet (was broken). His chariot (was) broken. His great bow which was made ready, was also cut off due to the flood of (i.e. profuse) anger. Wet with the blood and with his body pierced with arrows the king getting into another chariot marched against the son of Bharata. (He said to Puṣkala:) "O hero, O bee (howering round) the lotus-like feet of Rāma, you are blessed. Today you have done a great feat that I was deprived of my chariot. Now, O hero, protect your life when I am fighting (with you). For you, (to save) your life is not easy when I stand (before you) in the form of death."

45b-56a. Speaking like this, he, proficient in (the use of) many weapons, struck (him) with innumerable arrows. On the earth and in (every) direction (only) his arrows (were seen) there. On all sides he pierced and cut into two the chariots along with the warriors (in them). On the battlefield flowed a river having the stream of blood, where the intoxicated elephants looked like peaks of mountains, the hair on the heads of beings again and again appeared like moss. Many arms of the heroes, which were beautified with rings and which were smeared with sandal, appeared after they were cut off like serpents. The heads of the best heroes had the resemblance of turtles. There the flesh of the great heroes was (i.e. looked like) mud. When such an incident took place, hundreds of witches drank, with vessels, the blood of the creatures falling in the battle on the battlefields. With joy and eagerness they enjoyed the flesh. Having drunk the blood and having eaten the flesh, the furious (witches) danced, laughed and sang loudly on the battlefield. The goblins there on the battlefield with their bodies intoxicated, holding with their hands the heads of creatures, were engaged in sounding them like musical instruments made of bell-metal. The furious jackals, causing fear to cowards, having eaten much flesh of those that fell on the battlefield roared. The cowards who were frightened got into the hollows of aśvattha trees. They were eaten up by the witches. Sinners survive nowhere.

56b-64. Seeing this destruction of his army, Puṣkala, the best among the heroes, also, brought about destruction on the battlefield. The heads of elephants were cut asunder, pearls fell (from their heads). That river (of blood) full of hair, appeared like the Tāmraparṇī (river). The arrows discharged by Puṣkala and stuck into the bodies of men destroyed the life of the heroes on all sides. On the battlefield, all the excellent warriors with their bodies wetted with blood, with their bodies pierced appeared like the kiṁśuka (trees). At that time Puṣkala who was angry and full of wrath, having spoken (a few words) to the king, struck him with many arrows. The king with his body pierced by his arrows and with his armour shattered, regarding him as very powerful, struck him with crores of arrows. Due to those arrows profuse blood discharged from the armour flowed (down). His body in the grip of the cage of arrows, became brilliant. That son of Bharata, remaining in the cage of arrows and with his mind afflicted, was not able either to take or to fix his arrows. Remembering Rāma, and holding tightly the great bow in his hand, he discharged sharp arrows keeping off the hosts of his enemies.

65. O best of sages, having shaken off the net of those arrows with those arrows, and having blown his conch, he with his fear gone said to the king in the battle.

Puṣkala said:

66-70. O hero, you have done a great feat by putting me, a great warrior and tormentor of heroes, into the cage of arrows. Due to your old age you are venerable to me; (but) O king Vīramaṇi, today, now, see my great act of valour on the battlefield. O hero, if with three arrows I shall not make you unconscious, then listen to my pledge deluding all the heroes: O hero, if I do not cause you to fall into a swoon in the battle, let me have the sin of him who, a great sinner and of very foolish deeds, even after reaching Gaṅgā that removes sins, censures her and does not plunge into her (water). Be ready, O king.

71-78. Hearing these words of Puṣkala, the best king (Vīramaṇi) was angry, and being very much afflicted fixed sharp arrows (on his bow). Those arrows went (off) after piercing the great chest of the son of Bharata and fell down on the earth like those who are averse to the devotion to Rāma. Then he aiming at his large expansive chest, discharged a sharp arrow, bright like fire. The lord of the earth cut it into two with his arrow; and burning like the orb of the sun it fell into the chariot. He fixed another auspicious arrow through (i.e. remembering) his devotion to his mother. He too cut it off with a big arrow. Then dejected in heart and remembering Rāma, the destroyer of his affliction, as to what to do (then), the knower of (i.e. he who was proficient in the use of) great missiles discharged (an arrow). The arrow resembling a serpent and burning with the sun's radiance, stuck into his chest, and made him unconscious. Then all wailed and were intent on fleeing. When the king became unconscious, Puṣkala obtained victory.

CHAPTER FORTYTHREE

Defeat of Puṣkala and Śatrughna

Śeṣa said:

1-7. Hanūmat having come to Vīrasiṁha, said these words: "O brave one, stop; where are you going? In a moment I shall conquer you." Hearing these powerful words of the monkey, he burning with a flood of (i.e. great) anger sounded his bow having the sound of clouds and discharging sharp arrows shone on the battlefield. Hanūmat, Añjanī's son, seeing those sharp arrows firmly stuck to his body, (and therefore looking) charming as in a heavy downpour of rain from a cloud in Āṣāḍha, became extremely angry in his heart. With his fist having adamantine strength he struck (Vīrasiṁha) on his chest. The hero struck with the fist fell on the ground. Seeing his uncle fainting, Śubhāṅgada (came to the battlefield). Rukmāṅgada also abandoning his swoon, went to the battlefield. Both of them showering arrows, loudly thundering like two clouds and causing great destruction, marched against the monkey (i.e. Hanūmat).

8-11. Seeing that the two heroes had come the lord of monkeys having encircled with his tail the two holding bows along with their chariots, broke them (by throwing them) on the ground (and) they became unconscious just at that moment only. With their bodies tinged with blood the two became motionless. Balamitra fought with Sumada for a long time and made him unconscious with (i.e. by striking him with) arrows having very sharp joints. In a moment Puṣkala led him to a swoon (i.e. made him unconscious) which was (characterized by) loss of sensation. Śatrughna's army destroying the (enemy's) warriors got victory.

12-20. At that time Śiva seated in an excellent chariot and stretching his divine bow ran (i e. rushed) to these warriors. The great one carrying the crescent moon in his twisted hair and having as ornaments serpents touching at will, took up his bow. The great god, the remover of the afflictions of his devotees, seeing his own men unconscious, went along with mighty troops to fight with these warriors of Śatrughna. With his attendants and followers he causing the earth to tremble came there to protect his devotees as he formerly came to Tripura. The trident-holder saluted by gods, the author of deluge, having eyes very red due to anger, saw very intelligent soldiers (there). Seeing the great god who had come there, the powerful younger brother of Rāma went to the battlefield to fight with the crest-jewel of all gods. Seeing Śatrughna having come (there), the holder of the trident, held a bow with the string (stretched), and being very angry said: "Puṣkala, the servant of Rāma's feet, who went to the battle after having killed my devotee, has done a great feat. Today where is that Puṣkala knowing (i.e. proficient in the use of) great missiles? Killing him who troubled my devotee in the battle, I shall get happiness."

Śeṣa said:

21-28a. Saying so he sent Vīrabhadra to Puṣkala. "Go to fight with Puṣkala who is troubling my servant in the battle." He sent Nandin to (fight with) the very mighty Hanūmat. He sent Bhṛṅgin of mighty arms to (fight with) Kuśadhvaja. He ordered his own attendant by name Caṇḍa to (fight with) Sumada. The large-minded Puṣkala seeing that the great attendant of Mahārudra (i.e. Śiva) had come went to fight (with him). In the battle Puṣkala struck him with five arrows. With his body wounded by those arrows he directed the trident (towards him). The very strong one, having cut off the trident in a moment, roared. O brāhmaṇa, seeing his trident cut off the mighty follower of Rudra quickly hit Bharata's son on his head with (the missile called) Khatvāṅga. That great warrior, hit with the Khatvāṅga, became unconscious for a moment. That good warrior Puṣkala knowing (i.e. proficient in the use of) great missiles, giving up his swoon (i.e. regaining consciousness) that moment only cut off with his arrows the Khatvāṅga in his hand.

28b-42a. Vīrabhadra, with the Khatvāṅga in his hand cut off became extremely angry and shattered the warrior's chariot. Having broken the chariot of the warrior and having (thus) made him a foot-soldier, he fought with the magnanimous Puṣkala in a close fight. That very mighty Puṣkala abandoning the chariot shattered to pieces by him (i.e. Vīrabhadra), hit Vīrabhadra with his fist. They hit each other with fists, thighs and knees. They were eager to kill each other. They desired to conquer each other. Thus (the fight) between the two powerful ones lasted for days, going on day and night. None lost in it and none of the very powerful ones won it. When the fifth day came, the very mighty Vīrabhadra seized the great hero Puṣkala and jumped into the sky. There a great fight, attracting (even) the gods, took place between the two, with fists, strokes of feet, arms and excellent hoofs (i.e. feet). Then Puṣkala who was extremely angry seizing Vīrabhadra by the neck struck (i.e. threw) him on the ground. The very mighty Vīrabhadra distressed by that stroke seized Puṣkala by the foot and repeatedly shaking him and throwing him on the ground the very mighty one cut off his head with blazing ear-rings with his trident. The very strong Vīrabhadra having killed Puṣkala roared. That roaring follower of Śiva frightened great warriors. When Puṣkala fell in the battle, there was a very great wailing. All the very proficient men became frightened on the battlefield. They informed Śatrughna that Puṣkala killed by Vīrabhadra, the attendant of Śiva, had fallen on the battlefield. The great hero, the mighty (Śatrughna) having thus heard about Puṣkala's being killed in the battle, was very much grieved and due to great grief trembled.

42b-47a. Knowing that Śatrughna was distressed Rudra spoke to him who was grieving for the hero (viz. Puṣkala) when Puṣkala was killed in the battle: "O very powerful Śatrughna, do not be distressed on the battlefield. The fall of heroes in a battle is said (to lead) to fame. The hero named Puṣkala who fought for five days with Vīrabhadra who causes great destruction and who in a moment killed Dakṣa that insulted me, and who in a moment killed the demons, the soldiers of Tripura, is blessed. Therefore, O lord of kings, O very powerful one, giving up your distress fight; When I—the warrior—am standing (before you), stand (i.e. wait) carefully, O best among the heroes.

47b-54. The brave Śatrughna, having abandoned his grief got angry with Śaṅkara, and making his bow ready he covered the great god with arrows. Those arrows, it was a great wonder, did not produce any wound on the body of the lord of gods who had come there for the protection of his devotees. Those arrows (of Śatrughna) and also the arrows of Śaṅkara remained in the sky, pervading this entire universe of the sage (i.e. Brahmā) working wonders. Everywhere (people) on seeing that war of arrows thought it to be the deluge, destroying the world and deluding everyone. Those (gods) who had remained in their own cities having come to see it by resorting to (their) divine cars, praised very much that (fight) of the two: "This one is the author of the destruction and the creation of the three worlds. This one is also the younger brother of the great king Rāmacandra. What will be this (i.e. what will it lead to)? Who, on the earth, will be victorious? Which hero will meet with a defeat on the battlefield?" The fight between the two thus continued for eleven days.

55-62. When the twelfth day came, the king (i.e. Śatrughna) full of anger discharged the missile called 'Brahmā' to kill Mahādeva. Knowing that (his) enemy Śatrughna had discharged the great missile he laughed and absorbed it and discharged the great (missile called) Brahmaśiras. Being very much astonished (he thought) what should be done hereafter? Into the chest of him (i.e. of Śatrughna) who was thinking like this, the crest-jewel of gods (i.e. Śiva) quickly struck an arrow resembling fire. (Being struck) by that arrow Śatrughna became unconscious on the battlefield. The entire army served by the warriors, wailed. All heroes, led by Subāhu, Sumada, and proud of the strength of their arms, were knocked down on the earth by the attendants of Śiva. Seeing Śatrughna pained by the arrow and fallen unconscious and Puṣkala being put in a chariot by the servants to protect him, the angry Hanūmat, wagging his dreadful tail, remembering Rāma, and delighting his own (colleagues) came to fight with Śiva, the author of destruction.

CHAPTER FORTYFOUR

Hanūmat on the Droṇa Mountain

Śeṣa said :

1. The hero Hanūmat, desirous of killing the lord of gods, came near Rudra on the battlefield and said (to him):

Hanūmat said :

2-5. O Rudra, what you are doing is against religious merit.

Therefore, I desire to punish you eager to kill Rāma's devotee. Formerly I heard it said variously by gods and sages that Rudra, the trident-holder, always remembers Rāma's feet. All that has become (i.e. proved) false in your case, who are fighting with Śatrughna. My brave (hero) Puṣkala is killed and Śatrughna also has become unconscious. Therefore, I shall today knock you, ready to destroy the three worlds, down. O Śarva (i.e. Śiva), you who are averse to Rāma's devotion, stand carefully.

Śeṣa said :

6-9. That great lord said to the monkey speaking like this: "O best hero, you are fortunate. What you say is not false. This Rāmacandra saluted by gods and demons is my lord. Śatrughna, the killer of his enemy's heroes, brought his horse. Inspired by devotion to him (i.e. Rāma) he came to protect him. The duty (of the lord) is that his devotee, his own soul, must be protected on any account. Let the great Raghunātha look upon me who am shameless by showing pity for me who was a little angry due to the great grief of my devotee."

Śeṣa said :

10-16. When the lord of Caṇḍī was speaking like this, Hanūmat, extremely angry, took a big stone and hit it at his chariot. His chariot, hit with the stone was broken to pieces along with the charioteer, horses, flag and banners. All the deities in the sky praised the lord of monkeys; "O lord of monkeys, you are blessed; you have done a great feet." Seeing Śrī Śiva without a chariot Nandin ran to him. He said to the great god: "Sit on my back." Hanūmat was extremely angry with Śiva who was seated on (the back of) the bull (i.e. Nandin). Drawing out a big stone he then quickly hit it on his chest. Hit with it the lord of the beings (i.e. Śiva) took a sharp, bright, spear, having three points and resembling the flames of fire. Seeing that great trident, bright like fire, that came to him, he (i.e. Hanūmat) took it in his hand and in a moment quickly broke it into (pieces as small as) the sesamum seeds.

17-21. When the lord of the monkeys quickly in a moment broke the trident, Śiva took in his hand the (missile called) Śakti entirely made of iron. That Śakti discharged by Śiva stuck to (i.e. hit) the chest of the intelligent (Hanūmat) (and) in a moment the lord of the monkeys became afflicted. In a moment having overcome that pain he seized a strong tree and hit it on (Śiva's) chest adorned with great serpents. The lordly serpents struck by the hero were frightened. Leaving him and going here and there they speedily went to the nether world. Śiva seeing the tree discharged (by Hanūmat) and (hitting) his chest got angry and took a terrible pestle in both his hands.

22-29a. (He said): "O mean monkey, you are (now) killed. Flee and go (away) from the battle. In a moment I shall destroy your life with (this) pestle." Seeing the pestle discharged by the angry Śiva the monkey remembering Viṣṇu (i.e. Rāma) avoided it very speedily. That pestle made of strong iron and discharged by Śiva, fell down. Having torn off the entire earth it went to the nether world. Hanūmat, the servant of Rāma, was extremely angry at that time. Taking a mountain in his hand he hit it on the chest (of Śiva). While the lord of Satī (i.e. Śiva) was thinking of cutting off the mountain he was struck by the lord of monkeys with a tree having many branches. When he (i.e. Śiva) was intent on cutting it off, he was hit with rocks (by Hanūmat). The persevering Śiva made up his mind to break those rocks. Just then he showered him (i.e. Śiva) with trees and mountains. Having encircled the protector of the beings (i.e. Śiva) with his tail he struck him again and again with stones, mountains, trees and strokes of his tail. Nandin was very much frightened, and even the moon was reduced to pieces. The very angry great god got very much confused.

29b-32. He said to the lord of monkeys who every moment made him very much disquieted: "O follower of the protector of Raghus, you are blessed. You have today done a great feat, so that I am very much pleased with you. O you, having a great speed, I am not easily obtainable by means of charity or sacrifice or a little penance. Therefore, ask for a boon from me."

Śeṣa said :

33. Hanūmat laughing (i.e. smiling) and speaking in fearless words, spoke to that very much delighted great god (i.e. Śiva) who was speaking like this:

Hanūmat said:

34-40. O great god, by Ragunātha's grace I have everything. Yet I ask for a boon from you who are pleased with the battle. This our (hero) named Puṣkala has fallen down dead. So also Śatrughna, Rāma's younger brother, became unconscious in the battle. Many other heroes wounded with arrows have also fallen. Some are unconscious, some have sunk; (please) protect them along with your own attendants. Do that by which big ghosts, vampires and fiends, so also foxes and others, will not take them away and eat them up; and (do that by which) their bodies will not be split. By all means preserve all of them, till, having conquered the attendants of Indra, I bring (either) the Droṇa mountain or the herbs thereon, and bring back, per force, to life these heroes kept under (your) control. Here I go to take that Droṇa mountain on which life-restoring herbs exist.

41-47. Hearing these words (Śiva) said to him: "All right. Quickly go to that mountain. I shall preserve your dead warriors." Having heard those words of the lord, he went to the mountain Droṇa. Having crossed all islands he went to the milky ocean. Here (i.e. on the battlefiled), great Śiva, with his very strong and brave attendants took care of the corpses. Hanūmat having reached (the mountain) Droṇa and having put that great mountain called Droṇa on his tail quickly started for the battlefield. O brāhmaṇa, when he was engaged in carrying it, the mountain shook. Seeing it shaking the hosts of deities protecting it wailed and said: "What is this happening on the mountain? Who is this hero of great power and valour that is taking away this (mountain)?" Doing (i.e. saying) so all the gods together saw the monkey. Saying to him, "Leave it" they struck him with crores of weapons and missiles.

48-55. Seeing them all striking (him) Hanūmat was very much angry. In a moment the hero struck them all as Indra had struck the demons. Some of them were struck (by him) with his feet; some were crushed with his hands. Some were struck with his tail and some were hit with the peak (of the mountain). All of them struck by the monkey, perished in a moment. Some wet with blood, fell on the ground. Some trembled due to the fear of the monkey (and) went to Indra, the lord of gods. Seeing them disturbed with fear and wet with blood, Indra, the best of all gods, being dejected said to the gods: "How (is it that) you are shaking with fear? How (is it that) you are wet with blood? By which demon or by which mean goblin have you been struck? Tell me the whole truth, so that knowing it I shall go to (i.e. march against) him; and having struck and bound him, the mad one who struck you, I shall come (back)." Hearing these words the best gods spoke in piteous words to Indra saluted by gods and demons.

Gods said:

56-61. We do not know (we are not sure, but) someone, taking the form of a monkey, came here and was intent upon taking that mountain after encircling it with his tail. When he decided (i.e. was about) to go back, all of us gathered together and being well-equipped and showering him with all weapons and missiles, fought with him. He, the powerful one, vanquished all of us in a battle. Many excellent gods, struck (by him) there fell on the ground. We with our bodies quite wet with blood and afflicted with the wounds and (i.e. but) alive due to our religious merit, have come here.

Hearing these words of the gods Indra ordered all gods endowed with great power: "Go to the great mountain Droṇa to bind the very mighty monkey. Binding him who has committed a great sin against the gods, bring him (here)."

62-67. Thus ordered, they went to the best mountain Droṇa, where the mighty hero, Hanūmat, the best monkey, stood. Having gone there all of them spoke to Hanūmat. They were struck by Hanūmat with fists and slaps. In a moment, they with their bodies having bloody wounds fell there. Others intent on fleeing went to the lord of heaven. Hearing it (i.e. the account) angry Indra, the best of gods, directed all the best gods towards the great hero, the lord of monkeys. Ordered by him they went where the mighty lord of monkeys (stood). Having seen all of them come there the best of the monkeys said: "O heroes, do not go to (i.e. march against) me in the battle. I shall now forcibly take you near the city of Yama."

68-72. Though told like this, all of them endowed with great power, got ready and struck the monkey with weapons and missiles discharged in various ways. Cruel due to anger some of the best gods struck the mighty one with various (weapons and missiles like) lances, hatchets, swords, spears with sharp edges, pestles and śaktis. He quickly struck all the best gods with rocks. Some fled to Indra and told (the account) to him. Hearing the words told by them the lord of the gods was frightened. Having gone near (i.e. to) Bṛhaspati, the head and the counsellor of the residents of heaven, the excellent preceptor of gods, and having saluted him, he asked him:

Indra said :

73. O lord, who is the monkey that has come to carry Droṇa (mountain)? Who (i.e. he) has killed my heroes, the gods, holding weapons.

Śeṣa said :

74. Having heard these words uttered by him, the great Āṅgirasa (i.e. Bṛhaspati) spoke to Indra, the lord of gods, who was dejected with fear.

Bṛhaspati said :

75-80. He is the servant of him (i.e. of Rāma) who killed Rāvaṇa in the battle and burnt (i.e. destroyed) Kumbhakarṇa and who killed all the enemies. Know him to be Hanūmat who with the fire (set) to his tail burnt Laṅkā along with the Trikūṭa mountain and who killed Akṣa. He killed all (the gods). He is intent upon (taking) the Droṇa (mountain). The great king (Rāma), the best one among the mighty, is performing the horse-sacrifice. The great king Vīramaṇi, Śiva's devotee, took away his horse. Then a battle fascinating the gods, took place. In the battle Śiva killed many heroes of Rāma. To revive them this very mighty one will certainly take the Droṇa (mountain). (Even) after fighting with him for hundreds of years he, the powerful one, will not be vanquished by you. Therefore, propitiate the monkey. Give him the herb thereon.

CHAPTER FORTYFIVE

Śrī Rāma Appears on the Battlefield

Śeṣa said:

1-2. Having heard the words of Bṛhaspati, the Supreme Being, the enemy of Vṛṣaparvan, having come to know that Wind's son (Hanūmat) had come there on Rāma's mission gave up the fear in his mind that was due to the monkey and was delighted and said to Bṛhaspati.

Indra said:

3-8. How shall we manage, O master of gods, if this Droṇa (mountain) is taken (by Hanūmat)? Tell me further, how can the gods survive? Now properly propitiate the son of Wind. Rāma will be very much delighted, and the gods would have happiness.

Hearing the words of the lord of gods, Bṛhaspati, putting Indra in the front and surrounded by all gods went there where the fearless monkey, Hanūmat, stood. Having forcibly conquered the happy gods he was roaring. They, led by Bṛhaspati, went near him and having saluted the feet of the son of Wind fell (at his feet). Bṛhaspati, the best among the eloquent being urged on by the lord of gods, the master of the world, spoke to the hero.

Bṛhaspati said:

9-11. Not knowing your valour the gods have done (this) act. O you highly intelligent one, you are the servant of Rāma's feet. What for is this undertaking, and how have you come here? We who are bent before you, will carry out what you say. O you son of Wind, having a body causing fear to the demons, give up anger and regard the lord of gods with favour.

Śeṣa said:

12-15. Hearing these words of the preceptor of gods he of a great fame, spoke to all gods and to Bṛhaspati: "In the battle with king Vīramaṇi, Śiva killed many warriors. To bring them back to life I shall carry the Droṇa mountain. Those who, proud of their power and valour, will stop it (i.e. the mountain from being carried by me) will be sent to Yama's abode by me. Therefore, give me either (the mountain) Droṇa or the herb on it, by which I shall revive the heroes who died on the battlefield.

Śeṣa said:

16-21. Hearing these words of the magnanimous son of Wind they all bowed before him and gave him the reviving herb. The gods had given up their fear and were delighted and the residents of heaven being happy went (back) keeping the lord of gods in front (i.e. led by the lord of gods). Hanūmat took the medicine and came to the battlefield. He was praised by all the hosts of gods eagerly watching that feat. Even all the enemies having seen the monkey who had come (back), praised him (with the words), "Well (done), well (done)", and looked upon the monkey as wonderful. The monkey (i.e. Hanūmat), full of great joy, came there and went near the dead warrior Puṣkala, the heart of Rāma, protected by Śiva on the fierce battlefield. Having called Sumati, the minister honoured by the great, he said (to him): "I shall bring back to life all the heroes, that died in the battle."

22-27. Saying so, (he put) the medicine on the great chest of Puṣkala, and joining his head with his body, spoke (these) auspicious words: "If I recognise (only) lord Rāghava (i.e. Rāma) by the deeds of my mind, body and speech, then let him quickly revive by means of the medicine." When he was saying these words, Puṣkala got up on the battlefield and he, the crest-jewel of the brave, gnawed his teeth in anger: "Where has that Vīrabhadra, making me unconscious on the battlefield, gone? I shall instantly knock him down. Where is my excellent bow?" To him who was speaking like this the lord of the monkeys said: "O hero, you who are talking about him on the battlefield, are blessed. You who were killed by Vīrabhadra, have been again brought back to life by the grace of Raghunātha (i.e. Rāma). Come on, let us go to Śatrughna who is unconscious."

28-35. Saying so he went to the front of the excellent battle. (There) Śatrughna afflicted by Śiva's arrow, was breathing (i.e. was alive). Having gone there near the magnanimous

Śatrughna Hanūmat put medicine on his chest that had come to (i.e. started) breathing, and said to him: "O best Śatrughna, revive. O you of great might and valour, why (i.e. due to what) did you become unconscious on the battlefield? If I being diligent (i.e. diligently) keep celibacy till (the end of) my life, then let this hero Śatrughna revive in a moment." No sooner did he utter these words than Śatrughna came back to consciousness in a moment. (He said:) "Where is Śiva? Leaving the battlefield where has Śiva gone?" Śrī Rudra, the trident-holder had killed many heroes in the battle. The magnanimous lord of the monkeys revived them all. Then all of them were well-equipped; their minds were full of anger. Seated in their own chariots they with their bodies wounded marched against their enemies. Puṣkala marched against Vīrabhadra; Kuśadhvaja against Caṇḍa; the hero Hanūmat against Nandin; and Śatrughna against Śiva in the battle.

36-52a. The king marched against Śatrughna who was the best among the mighty, who had stretched his bow, and who had stood after calling (i.e. challenging) Śiva in the battle. The heroic king Vīramaṇi and the mighty Śatrughna fought in the battle with each other a fight causing wonder to the sages. O brāhmaṇa, king Vīramaṇi in a moment shattered to (pieces like) sesamum seeds more than a hundred chariots of Śatrughna, the lord of kings. Then Śatrughna who was very angry on the battlefield, discharged the Āgneya missile (i.e. the missile presided over by Agni) to burn him along with his army. The king seeing that great burning missile discharged by Śatrughna got very angry and took up the Vāruṇa missile (i.e. the missile presided over by Varuṇa). Seeing that (fire) cooled by the Vāruṇa missile the strong younger brother of Rāma discharged at him the Vāyavyāstra (i.e. the missile presided over by Vāyu). Due to it great (i.e. strong) wind was produced. The clouds struck by the wind moved in all directions. They roamed here and there and the army (of Śatrughna) became happy. Seeing his army afflicted by the wind the great king Vīramaṇi took (i.e. fixed) the mountain-like missile eradicating the enemy on his bow. The wind was checked by the mountains and did not blow on the battlefield. Seeing it the younger brother of Rāma (i.e. Śatrughna) took up the missile like the thunderbolt.

All the mountains struck by the Vajrāstra were reduced to pieces like sesamum seeds and were powdered in the battle honoured by the heroes. The heroes with their bodies shattered by the Vajrāstra (i.e. the thunderbolt-like missile) were adorned with blood on the battlefield. The battle was interesting. Then the great king Vīramaṇi who was very angry fixed on his bow the wonderful Brahmāstra (i.e. the missile presided over by Brahmā) burning the enemies. Śatrughna took an arrow and remembered the very charming missile given by that female devotee and deluding all enemies. The Brahmāstra, which left his hand came to the enemy. Just then he, named Śatrughna, discharged the deluding missile. In a moment the Brahmāstra was cut into two by the Mohanāstra (i.e. the deluding weapon) and quickly stuck into the king's chest and made him unconscious. Hundreds of arrows were discharged by king Śatrughna. And all the brave attendants of Śiva that had become unconscious lay so on the ground near the feet of Śiva.

52b-60. The very angry Śiva seated in his chariot went to the king. Śatrughna at once went to fight with Śiva on the battlefield. Making his bow ready and drawn out he fought. Between the two a fight breaking the enemy, took place. It brightened up the atmosphere by means of the weapons and missiles discharged in various ways. Such a battle due to (i.e. involving) killings by missiles and counter-missiles and strikings and counter-strikings did not take place even between gods and demons. At that time Śatrughna was very much afflicted in the battle with Śiva. On the advice of the son of Wind (i.e. Hanūmat) he remembered his lord (i.e. Rāma): "O lord, O brother, the very fierce Śiva is snatching away my life. Raising your bow protect me on the battlefield. O Rāma, many crossed the ocean of grief by (uttering) your name. O Rāma, O Rāma, the cloud of kindness, lift me who am in misery." When he was speaking like this, Rāma who was dark like the blue lotus, whose eyes were like lotuses, having (tucked) a deer's horn to his waist, and who had the body of (i.e. like that of) an initiated person, was seen on the battlefield. Seeing him on the battlefield, Śatrughna was amazed

CHAPTER FORTYSIX

Vīramaṇi Surrenders the Horse to Śrī Rāma

Śeṣa said:

1-4. Seeing his brother Śrī Rāma destroying the affliction of him who had saluted him to have come (there) Śatrughna became free from all unhappiness, O best brāhmaṇa. The confused Hanūmat seeing with joy Rāma's feet saluted him who had come (there) for the protection of his devotees and said: "O lord, it is (but) proper for you to protect your devotees, since you freed everyone vanquished and tied with a noose in the battle. O you descendant of Raghu, we are now blessed that we shall see your feet. In a moment only we shall conquer the enemies by your grace."

Śeṣa said:

5-17. O brāhmaṇa, seeing Rāma who was within the scope of (i.e. known by) meditation of the meditating saints, who gave fearlessness to those who saluted him, who had come there, Śiva fell at his feet, and said: "You are the only Puruṣa (i.e. the Supreme Being) actually rising above Prakṛti (i.e. Nature). With a portion of you, you create and destroy the universe. You who are formless, are the highest cause of the entire world. Endowed with Māyā you who are only one, take up three forms: At the time of creation (you exist) in the form of Brahmā, In protecting (the world) you are full of your lustre; and at the time of the final destruction of the world (you are) known as Śarva (i.e. Śiva). O highest lord, your act of performing the horse-sacrifice for removing (the sin of) the murder of a brāhmaṇa, is (but) a wonderful mockery. Wherefrom can sin (come to) you, the spotless water from whose feet called Gaṅgā I carry inside (i.e. on) my head to pacify my sins? Certainly I did the act to hurt you much. O you kind one, forgive (me) about it which obstructs you. What do (i.e. can) I do? I did this for maintaining truthfulness. Knowing your prowess I came (here) for the protection of my devotee. This (king Vīramaṇi) formerly bathed in the river called Śiprā and practised wonderful penance in the temple of Mahākāla at Ujjayinī. Then, I who was pleased, said to the king: 'O great King, ask for (your desired object).' He chose a wonderful kingdom. I said to him: 'Your kingdom (i.e. rule) will be in Devapura. I shall diligently dwell for your protection in your city till Rāma's sacrificial horse comes (to your city)'. O Rāma, I who granted such a boon, am really your servant. I am now pitied (by you). The king will give back (i.e. restore) the horse along with his sons and beasts; and he will offer service to (your) feet."

Śeṣa said:

18. Hearing these words of Maheśa (i.e. Śiva), the best of Raghus (i.e. Rāma) with his eyes full of pity spoke with a grave voice:

Rāma said:

19-22. It is but the duty of the gods to protect their devotees. You have done an auspicious deed, since you have now protected your devotee. O Śiva, you are in my heart (and) I am in your heart. There is no distinction between us. (Only) the wicked-minded fools see (the distinction, i.e. they look upon us to be different). Those men who make distinction between us who are indeed of the same nature are roasted for a thousand kalpas in (the hell called) Kumbhīpāka. Those who are your pious devotees were (i.e. are) my devotees only; and my devotees also salute you with great devotion.

Śeṣa said:

23-36. The lord (i.e. Rāma) having heard these words of Śiva revived the unconscious king Vīramaṇi by touching him etc. The able lord and god along with Śiva, also revived other unconscious sons of king Vīramaṇi, who were afflicted with arrows. Making the king ready, the lord of the beings (i.e. Śiva), made him, surrounded by his sons and grandsons, salute Rāma's feet. Blessed was king Vīramaṇi who saw the best Raghu, difficult to be secured by meditating saints devoted to deep and abstract meditation even after myriads (of years). O best brāhmaṇa, having saluted Raghunātha (and thus) having their bodies rendered blessed, they became most venerable even to Brahmā etc. The king (Vīramaṇi) gave (back) the best horse to Rāma who was praised by Śatrughna, Hanūmat and (other) great warriors like Puṣkala. The king Vīramaṇi urged on by Śiva then gave (Rāma) everything along with his kingdom and with sons, beasts and kinsmen. Then Rāma was praised by all his enemies and servants, and especially by Śatrughna and others, who were very much eager. Seated in a jewelled chariot he then disappeared. When Rāma disappeared, all were amazed. Do not look upon that Rāma who alone is saluted by the world, as a human being. Being in water or on the land he is always present everywhere. At that time the heroes were thoroughly delighted and embraced one another. A great festivity with (the sound of) musical instruments and auspicious instrumental music, took place. Then all the heroes who were pleased and amazed, and who were proficient in (the use of) all weapons and missiles, followed the horse that was released. Having directed that servant (viz. Vīramaṇi), telling him to seek the refuge of Śrī Rāma, the only one difficult to be obtained in the world, Śiva, of a truthful vow, and the author of the deluge and creation, disappeared there. Adorned with (i.e. accompanied by) his servants, Śiva went to Kailāsa.

37-38. King Vīramaṇi meditating upon the lotus-like feet of Śrī Rāma and accompanied by his army, went along with the mighty Śatrughna. For those excellent men who listen to this story of Rāma, there is never the misery due to the mundane existence.

CHAPTER FORTYSEVEN

The Sacrificial Horse Develops Stiffness

Śeṣa said:

1-6. Then, O brāhmaṇa, the horse went to Hemakūṭa close to Bhārata. The horse with chowries tied (on to his body) was protected by thousands of warriors. That Hemakūṭa was (many) yojanas in expanse and length on all sides and had myriads of silver and golden peaks. There was an excellent garden adorned with trees (like) śāla, tāla, tamāla, karṇikāra, himtāla, nāga-punnāga, kovidāra and bilva, also campaka, bakula, megha (a kind of fragrant grass), madana, kuṭaja and others. It was also adorned with creapers like jātikā, yūthikā and navamālikā (varieties of jasmine), so also with mango-trees, vines with sweet grapes, and pomegranates. It was noisy with many birds; it was resounding with (the humming of) bees. It had the sounds of peacocks' notes. It gave joy in all seasons.

7-13. Accompanied by Śatrughna the horse which had mind's speed and had a charming golden note on his large forehead (came there). While that horse (let loose) for the horse-sacrifice, was (thus) going, suddenly a wonder took place. Listen to it, O best brāhmaṇa. His body became stiff, and he did not move, but (just) stood on the path. The best horse became immovable like the Hemakūṭa. Then all the guards of the horse gave him strokes with whips. Even though he was (thus) beaten (i.e. whipped) the horse with his body having become stiff, did not move (on). The guards of the horse, having approached Śatrughna, cried: "O lord, we do not know what has happened to (our) excellent horse. O you very intelligent king, when the excellent horse having mind's speed, was proceeding, there was a sudden stiffness in his body. We whipped him, but he did not move. O best king, having considered this, take whatever action (you deem proper)."

14-21. Then the king who was amazed, went along with his soldiers near the great horse. Puṣkala seized his feet with his hand, and lifted (i.e. tried to lift) him up from the ground. But he did not move from it (i.e. from the ground). Though attacked by the strong one the horse did not move at that time. Large-hearted Hanūmat decided to lift him up. The best among the powerful ones encircled him strongly with his tail, and with (great) might dragged (i.e. tried to drag) him. Yet he did not move. Then, Hanūmat, the best monkey, being amazed said to Śatrughna, the greatest among the mighty, when the heroes were listening (i.e. in the presence of the heroes): "(Encircling) Droṇa with my tail, I now (i.e. recently, had) lifted it up easily. But it is a great wonder now that this (comparatively) small horse does not move. The excited, strong heroes have in this case realised the general cause: Even though dragged, he did not move from his place as much as (the measure of) a sesamum seed." Having heard the words of the monkey Śatrughna, the best among speakers, said to Sumati, the best of the ministers.

Śatrughna said:

22. O innocent minister, why is there the stiffness in the body of the horse? Why (for what cause) is there stiffness in the horse's body, O innocent one? What remedy should be employed here, so that the horse can move?

Sumati said:

23. O lord, some sage proficient in all (branches of) knowledge should be looked for. I know only what actually occurs in a region and is perceptible but do not know what is concealed from the senses.

Śeṣa said:

24-29. Hearing these words of Sumati he, the knower of dharma, looked, along with his servants, for an auspicious sage. All the soldiers going everywhere looked for a sage, a knower of dharma. But, nowhere did they find the best sage. But one diligent follower (of the horse) went as far as (the distance of) a yojana in the east. There he saw a great hermitage where all beasts and men also had no enemies, (as) the very charming ones had all their sins destroyed due to a bath in Gaṅgā, where many (sages) practised penance with fire. With their faces hung down, they filled their bellies with (i.e. subsisted on) smoke, leaves and air; where the smoke rising from the sacred fire always purified (everything). It was happy with many sages and was excellent due to creepers with their leaves taken off.

30-32. He, coming to know that the charming hermitage belonged to the sage Śaunaka, reported it to the king with his heart full of wonder. Hearing that Śatrughna along with his servants became extremely glad. Along with Hanūmat, Puṣkala and others he went to that hermitage. Having seen there the best sage who had properly offered oblation to the fire, he saluted (prostrating before him) like a staff, his feet destroying sins.

33-36. Seeing king Śatrughna, best among the mighty, coming (there), he offered him materials of worship and water for washing the feet; and became glad on seeing him. The best sage seeing him comfortably seated and resting said to the king: "O lord, why are you wandering? Your wandering is great. If, kings like you do not roam over the entire earth, then the wicked will harass the good who are free from affliction. O king, Śatrughna, the best among the mighty, tell me (why you are wandering like this). May all your wandering etc. be for our good."

Śeṣa said:

37. The king with his body delighted replied in a faltering tone to the brāhmaṇa who was speaking like this.

Śatrughna said:

38-41. Not far away from your abode all of a sudden a wonder took place in the case of Rāma's horse having the mind's speed. O best among the wise, hear (about) it. The horse by chance went into your garden rich in beauty. In its skirt there developed stiffness in his body (just) in a moment. Then my mighty heroes like Puṣkala, fierce with madness, forcibly dragged the horse. Yet he did not move. Due to our good fortune you who are known to be a boat for us who are drowned into the boundless ocean of misery, are seen by chance. Tell us the cause (of the stiffness of the horse's body)

Śeṣa said:

42-43. The best and very intelligent sage, when asked like this, mentally conceiving the horse along with the cause (of its stiffness), thought for a moment. Having in a moment known it with his eyes dilating with amazement, he said to the king who was grieved and full of doubt.

Śaunaka said:

44-55. O king, listen, I shall tell you the cause of the stiffness (of the body) of the horse, hearing which you will be free from misery. Such is the strange account. In the Gauḍa country in a great forest adorned by the bank of Kāverī, a brāhmaṇa named Sāttvika practised a great (i.e. severe) penance. One day he drank water. One day he ate (i.e. subsisted on) air. One day he did not eat anything. In this way he would pass three days. When he was thus engaged in the vow Death himself seized him with his fangs; (and) the observer of the great vow met with death. Playing with celestial nymphs in a divine car, rich in all (kinds of) beauty and adorned with all gems, he went to the peak of Meru. There was a great Jambu tree, the fluid from which was enjoyable. (There was) a river called Jāmbavatī, full of golden water. In it, sages, meritorious due to many (kinds of) penance, and having all pleasures, sported eagerly according to their desires. There he (i.e. Sāttvika) joyfully playing at his will with the celestial nymphs, being arrogant due to pride on account of his high opinion about himself, acted disagreeably with them. Then he was cursed by the sages: "Be a hideous demon." Then, he being extremely afflicted said to the sages, rich in knowledge and penance: "May all you kind brāhmaṇas favour me." He was then favoured by them: "When you will speedily stiffen (Rāma's) horse, you will hear Rāma's account. After that you will be free from this very fierce cause." O lord, that brāhmaṇa thus addressed by the sages became a demon. He has stiffened Rāma's horse. Free him by narration (of Rāma's account), O sinless one.

CHAPTER FORTYEIGHT

The Horse Is Relieved of Stiffness

Śeṣa said:

1. He who killed the enemy's heroes, having heard what the sage told, was amazed at heart, and said to Śaunaka:

Śatrughna said:

2-3. The way of fate is mysterious, due to which that (brāhmaṇa) named Sāttvika, though he had reached heaven (i.e.

had become divine), was made a demon by his deeds. O lord, O great sage, tell me about the path (i.e. the consequence) of deeds, and which hell is (obtained by beings) due to the result of which deeds.

Śaunaka said:

4-36. O best among the descendants of Raghu, you are blessed that you have such a good thought. Though you know (it) you are saying (i.e. asking about) for the good of the people. I (shall) tell (you about) various results of various deeds. O great king, listen to them. Hearing (about) them one would obtain salvation. He, of a wicked mind, who forcibly seizes the wealth of others, the child of another person, and another's wife for the sake of enjoyment, is dropped after being tied with Yama's noose into the Tāmisra hell for a thousand years. There the arrogant servants of Yama beat him up. Then tormented by the fruition of his sins, he goes to (i.e. is born in) the species of pigs. Having experienced great misery there he goes to human species (i.e. is born as a human being) which is characterised by diseases etc. and which acquaints him with his infamy. He engaged in (committing) sins, deceives (other) beings, and feeds his own family only. He would fall into (the hell called) Andhatāmisraka. Those men who kill beings here (i.e. in this world) wrongly fall into (the hell called) Raurava and are eaten up by ruru (deer). He who, for (filling) his own belly, plainly kills (other) beings, is, through Yama's order, dropped into (the hell called) Mahāraurava. He, the sinner, who hates his own father or a brāhmaṇa, (is dropped) into the vicious (hell called) Kālasūtra extending over a myriad yojanas. He who hates cows is roasted for as many years as the hair on (the bodies of) the beasts by Yama's servants. That king who would, on the earth, punish him who does not deserve punishment or that greedy king who gives physical punishment to a brāhmaṇa, is harassed by Yama's servants having faces like those of pigs. Then for being free from (his) sins he is born in wicked stocks. Those men who through their might foolishly snatch or destroy the little wealth of brāhmaṇas or the means of subsistence of cows, are oppressed very much, and are thrown into (the hell called) Andhakūpa in the other world. He who being greedy brings and eats all alone sweet food, and intent on tasting (i.e. enjoying) it does not give it either to a deity or to his friend, certainly falls into the hell called Kṛmibhojana. That man who, when not facing a calamity, would snatch away gold etc. or the wealth of a brāhmaṇa, would fall into the very vicious hell (called) Sandaṁśa. The fool who nourishes his own body (only) and does not know (i.e. care for) anyone else, is dropped into the very terrible hell (called) Kumbhīpāka hot with oil. The servants of Yama make the man who would, through folly, desire an unapproachable lady to be his wife, embrace her metallic image (in hell). Those who, insolent through their might, violate the propriety of conduct as laid down by the Vedas, fall into Taraṇī and become eaters of flesh and blood. He who having made a śūdra woman his wife would lead the householder's life with her, is full of great misery and certainly falls into the Pūyoda (hell). Those fools, those rogues who practise religious hypocrisy for cheating people, are beaten by Yama and fall into Vaiśasa hell. Those fools, those sinners who make their wives of the same caste drink their semen, are engaged in drinking semen in a stream of semen. Thieves, those who set fire, those who are wicked, those who administer poison, those who plunder villages, being full of sins, are thrown into Sārameyādana (hell). A man who, full of sin, forcibly snatches the wealth of others, falls with his face downwards into Avīcinaraka. Having experienced much misery there he would go to (i.e. would be born in) the most sinful stock. The servants of Yama make him, the foolish man who through (sheer love of) taste drinks liquor, drink liquid iron. That man who through the pride of his knowledge and conduct, would disregard his elders, is after death thrown with his face downwards into the Kṣāranaraka. Those men who deviating from righteous conduct commit treachery, are thrown into the hell (called) Śūlaprota full of many torments. That wicked man who inflicts pain on all men through his words, falls into the Daṇḍaśūka (hell) and is bitten by snakes. Thus, O king, there are many hells for the sinners. Having committed sins they go (to them); and these (sinners) experience terrible agony. Those who have not listened to the story of Rāma or have not obliged others, have all (kinds) of miseries in hell. It is said that he who has happiness here, would have it in heaven. Those who are miserable and diseased, have come from hell.

Śeṣa said:

37-39. Hearing this the king, trembling every moment, again asked the brāhmaṇa to get all his doubts removed. (He said:) "O great sage, tell (me) the characteristics of the respective sins. Due to which sin, and having which characteristics, is (a man) born on the earth?" Hearing those words of him, the sage said to the king: "O king, listen, I shall tell (you) the characteristics of the sinners."

Śaunaka said:

40-69. One who drinks liquors and one having black teeth is born in hell. One who eats what is prohibited, is born as one having chronic enlargement of the spleen. He who eats (food) seen by a woman in her course, is born as one who has worms in his belly. Having eaten (food) touched by a dog, a cat etc. a man would be of (i.e. give out) foul smell. A man who eats (food) without offering (it) to gods etc. has a disease in his belly, is unhappy, and is troubled by a great malady. By creating obstacles in the food of others (i.e. by spoiling their food), indigestion takes place (in the body of the man who spoils others' food). He who though he has wealth (i.e. though he can afford to give good food), gives bad food, has slow digestion. A man who gives (i.e. administers) poison, gets vomitting sickness; he who kills (a person) on the way, has a disease in his feet. A wicked man is born as one suffering from asthma and cough in hell. A rogue would suffer from epilepsy; and he who torments others would suffer from colic. He who causes forest conflagration would suffer from dysentery. He who would throw dung into a temple or into water, would suffer from a very terrible disease of the anus (as) a manifestation of his sin. The diseases caused by miscarriage are consumption, urinary diseases and dropsy. A man who breaks the image (of a deity), does not have stability (in life). One who speaks wickedly becomes maimed; one who censures others becomes bald-headed. A man who laughs at what others say becomes squint-eyed; he who steals gold of a brāhmaṇa has bad nails. He who steals copper becomes corpulent. He who steals bell-metal becomes a leper. A man who snatches tin has his hair tawny. A man who takes away lead suffers from headache. A man who steals iron becomes a blockhead. A man who steals hide is surrounded by (i.e. full of) fat. A man who steals honey smells like a goat. By stealing oil a man is extremely troubled by itch. By stealing raw food a man becomes toothless; and by taking away cooked food he would suffer from a disease of the tongue. By copulating with his teacher's wife a man suffers from strangury. By copulating with his sister he becomes a leper. So also by cohabiting with his daughter he suffers from leprosy. By cohabiting with his brother's wife he suffers from leprosy called gulma-kuṣṭha. By cohabiting with her who is approachable only by his master, he suffers from leprosy with red spots on the cheeks. By cohabiting with the wife of his confidant he suffers from ring-worm. By having sexual intercourse with his father's sister he would have boils in the right side of his body. By cohabiting with his maternal uncle's wife he would have boils on the left side of his body. He has leprosy on his waist by cohabiting with the wife of his paternal uncle. By having sexual intercourse with his friend's wife he becomes one whose wife dies (i.e. becomes a widower). By having sexual intercourse with a woman of his own family he suffers from fistula in the anus. One who cohabits with a famale ascetic suffers from urinary disease. By having sexual intercourse with the wife of a learned brāhmaṇa he suffers from ulcer in the nose. By cohabiting with the wife of him who is initiated a man has a flow of defective blood. He who cohabits with the wife of his kinsman suffers from the ulcer of the heart. He who has sexual intercourse with a woman of a higher caste suffers from the ulcer of the head. By cohabiting with a beast he suffers from a urinary disease. There is no doubt that men suffer from these diseases in hell. Women also suffer from these diseases by having sexual intercourse with the respective men. Thus, O king, the characteristics of great sinners are narrated. The sin would perish by means of religious merit due to charity, by hearing Rāma's deeds, or by (practising) penance. The river of the narration of the deeds of Viṣṇu would wash all the sins—the mud—of the sinners. There should be no doubt about this. (Even) Gaṅgā does not purify him who despises Hari. Even very meritorious holy places are not able to purify him. He who being weak in knowledge (i.e. being ignorant) laughs at the deeds being narrated, does not get freedom from hell even at the end of the world. O king, go with your followers for freeing the horse. Relate the deeds of the lord of Śrī, so that the horse would move.

Śeṣa said :

70-76. Having heard this, Śatrughna, the killer of the enemy's heroes, became delighted and accompanied by his servants saluted him, and turning back went (back). Having, with Hanūmat, gone to the side of (i.e. near) the excellent horse, he narrated Rāma's deeds destroying terrible misfortunes. "Go (in) to the divine vehicle due to the religious merit obtained by the narration (of the deeds) of Rāma. Move freely in the world. Be free from the bad birth." When after having these words Śatrughna stood by, he saw an excellent (man) borne in a divine car. He said: "By listening to the narration (of the deeds) of Rāma, I have become free. O very intelligent king, I (shall) go to my abode. Give me leave to go." Saying so the divine one seated in his divine car, left. At that time, the followers (of Śatrughna) along with Śatrughna were amazed. Then the horse was free from the stiffness and the ground; and wandering through that forest full of birds proceeded.

CHAPTER FORTYNINE

King Suratha Seizes the Horse

Śeṣa said :

1-3. Seven months passed as the horse easily roamed over Bhāratavarṣa full of kings. He going round all the excellent Bhārata (country) was honoured by excellent kings. Surrounded by excellent warriors and mighty soldiers like Śatrughna he roamed over many countries near the Himālayas. Taking into consideration Rāma's might nobody seized him.

4-11. Praised by the kings of Aṅga, Vaṅga and Kaliṅga the horse went to the beautiful city of Suratha. The city was named

Kuṇḍala, where the ear-rings fell from Aditi's ears trembling with joy and fear. There no man ever violated religious laws. The people there remembered Rāma everyday. There everyday men, Rāma's servants, free from sins, worshipped Aśvattha and Tulasī. There everyday men of pure hearts, free from fraud, worship charming temples having Rāma's idols. There is the name of Rāma (told) in words and never the account of a quarrel. In the heart he alone is meditated on, and no memory of sex finds a place. There men whose bodies are purified by the story of Rāma and who have assiduous devotion to truth, never indulge in gambling. In it lives the mighty and righteous (king) Suratha whose mind is delighted by recollecting Rāma's feet, and is very mad (after Rāma).

12-17. How shall I describe the excellent servant of Rāma, viz. Suratha, whose all virtues spread on the earth purify sins? Once the servants of that king saw, while they were wandering, the sacrificial horse smeared with sandal (-paste). When they saw the note (on the forehead) of the horse, which had clear letters, they were amazed. Knowing that the horse which was charming to the eye, was released by Rāma, they were delighted; and being eager they told (about him) to the king who was in the assembly: "O lord, there is the city Ayodhyā. Its lord is Rāma. The horse which is fit for a horse-sacrifice and which is released (by Rāma), has, while wandering, reached along with the servants the vicinity of your city. O great king, seize that very charming horse."

Śeṣa said :

18. Hearing these words uttered by his (servants), the king, being full of joy, said to his strong heroes in a voice grave like (the thundering of) the clouds:

Suratha said :

19-20. We are blessed that with our servants we shall see the face of Rāma. I shall seize his horse surrounded by a crore of warriors. I shall release the horse when Rāma would come. The object of me, the devotee, always engaged in meditating (on Rāma) will be fulfilled.

Śeṣa said :

21-24. Saying so, the king ordered his servant: "Forcibly seize the horse. The horse should not be released. He (should be kept) within sight. By this, I think I shall have a great gain in that I shall see Rāma's feet, difficult to be obtained by Brahmā, Indra and others. He, one's relative, or son, or kinsman, or beast or vehicle, alone is blessed, by whom Rāma would be obtained. Therefore, seizing the sacrificial horse which has the speed he desires, which is charming, and which is adorned with a golden note, tie him in the stable."

25-26. They who were thus addressed, went and quickly seized Rāma's horse and gave him whose entire body was auspicious, to the king. The king, the destroyer of the demons and proficient in righteous deed, gladly received him, and said to his mighty servants:

27-35. "O very intelligent Vātsyāyana, listen attentively. No man in his (i.e. Rāma's) country was attached to another man's wife. No man was attracted to another man's wealth, and no one was lustful. No man was attached to (things liked by) the tongue, and went along a wrong path; (everyone) would narrate (nothing else) but (the deeds of) Rāma." The king said to his servants: "You skilled in religious deeds have come to serve; tell (me) your movements. (In my country) men have the vow of having one wife only (i.e. were loyal to their wives). They do not crave for others' wealth. They are not attached to censuring others. They have not gone away from the course laid down by the Vedas. The warriors everyday do recollection etc. of Rāma. I who am angry towards Yama, keep them for service to Rāma. I do not allow those wicked, sinful men, behaving in the opposite way, to reside in my country." In his country did not live the most sinful ones who mentally committed sins. (There lived people whose) all sins were destroyed by meditation on Hari and were full of joy. When the country was like this and the king was religious, all the men that died (i.e. after death) obtained bliss. In the city of Suratha there was no entrance for the servants of Yama.

36-38. Then Yama taking up the form of a sage came to the king. He having put on garments of the barks of trees and with his head adorned with matted hair, saw Suratha, the servant of Viṣṇu, in his assembly. He had the Tulasī (-leaf) on his head and uttered the great name of Hari. He always made his people listen to (i.e. narrated to his people) the accounts dealing with religious deeds. Then the king, seeing the sage who was, as it were, penance incarnate, saluted his feet and gave him water for washing his feet etc. The best king said to the sage who was comfortably seated and who was resting:

39-41. "Today my existence is blessed; today my house is blessed. Tell me various excellent stories about Rāma, hearing which the sin of the hearers perishes everyday." Hearing these words uttered (by the king) the sage, showing all his teeth, laughed very much and clapped his palms. (The king) said to the sage who was laughing: "What is the reason for your laughing? (i.e. what made you laugh)? Kindly tell me so that my heart will be pleased." Then the sage said to the king:

42-54. "O king, listen attentively to the excellent reason for (my) laughter. You told me: To me narrate the glory of Hari (i.e. Viṣṇu). Who is Hari? Whose glory (should I narrate)? All men are influenced by their deeds (i.e. fate). Due to deeds heaven is obtained; due to deeds (one) would go to hell. Due to deeds alone, all (things) like sons and grandsons would (be had). Indra after performing a hundred sacrifices went to the highest position. Brahmā also obtained the wonderful world called 'Satya' due to his deeds (i.e. his fate). Many gods like Maruts who became successful due to their deeds enjoy, being served by the hosts of celestial nymphs, pleasures. Therefore, perform sacrifices etc. and indeed worship deities, so that you will have spotless fame on the earth." Hearing these words of him he, with his mind agitated with anger and with his heart fixed on Rāma alone, spoke to the brāhmaṇa skilled in (various) acts: "Do not say (anything) about the account of deeds giving a perishable fruit. You who are condemned by the world, go out of my city. Indra will quickly fall down. Brahmā also will fall down, but men eager for Rāma's worship will not fall. See Dhruva, Prahlāda and the wonderful Bibhīṣaṇa. So also others who are Rāma's devotees never fall. These servants of Yama will beat with iron mallets and by binding with nooses, those wicked ones who condemn Rāma.

O mean brāhmaṇa, I do not punish you due to your brāhmaṇa-hood (i.e. because you are a brāhmaṇa). Go, go away from my sight; otherwise I shall beat you."

55-63. When the greatest king called Suratha, his servants were eager to drive him out by holding him with his arm, then Yama taking up his own (i.e. original) form, adorned by people, said to the king: "O servant of Viṣṇu, I am pleased; ask for (what you want). O you of a good vow, though I tempted (i.e. tried to lead astray) you with many words, you, served by the good, did not swerve from service to Rāma." Then the king, seeing Yama very much pleased, said: "If you are pleased, then grant me an excellent boon. Let me not meet with death till I meet Rāma. O Yama, let me never have fear from you." Then Yama said to the king: "This will take place in your case. The chief of the Raghu (family) will truly do everything desired by you." Saying so Yama praising the deeds of him who had set his heart on the devotion to Rāma, vanished and went to his own city. That righteous king, the servant of Rāma, seized the horse with great joy and said to the servants of Viṣṇu: "I have seized this horse of Rāma, the lord of the earth. All of you, skilled in fighting, should be ready everywhere."

64-69. Thus told, all the very powerful soldiers of the king became ready in a moment, and being eager (i.e. eagerly) went to the assembly. The king's ten brave sons were: Campaka, Mohaka, Ripuñjaya, Durvāra, Pratāpin, Balamodaka, Haryakṣa, Sahadeva, Bhūrideva and Sutāpana. These ten sons of the king became ready on the battlefield. Full of great enthusiasm they desired to march (against Śatrughna). The king too called his bright chariot fashioned with the beauty of gold and adorned with horses having excellent speed. The king having enthusiasm to fight, surrounded by the entire army, stood directing all his servants in the assembly.

CHAPTER FIFTY

Aṅgada Delivers Śatrughna's Message to Suratha

Śeṣa said:

1-6. Then the younger brother of Rāma came (there) and asked his servants: Where is the very charming sacrificial horse?" At that time those very mighty heroes said (these) words to Śatrughna: "We do not know. Some warriors took the horse and went into a city; and all of us were despised by the mighty servants of the king. You are now the authority as to what should be done now." Hearing those words of them, Śatrughna became very angry and the hero gnawing his teeth and repeatedly licking (his lips) with his tongue said: "Snatching my horse where will you go? Now (only) I shall ruin with (my) arrows (your) city with the people (i.e. the inhabitants)." Saying so, he said to Sumati: "Whose city is this? Who is its lord that took away my horse?"

Śeṣa said:

7-12. Hearing these angry words of the king the minister spoke in a sweet voice words with distinct syllables: "Know this to be a very charming city named Kuṇḍala. The righteous, mighty kṣatriya Suratha lives here. He is always given to religious conduct and is the servant of the couple of feet of Rāma; he is Rāma's servant like Hanūmat by thought, deeds and speech. There are hundreds of (good) deeds of this righteous (king) Suratha who is all-good, has a retinue of very strong (soldiers). If the best horse is snatched away, there would be a great war here. Many heroes skilled in fighting will fall (in the battle)." Having heard (the words) thus spoken, Śatrughna, the killer of the heroes of his enemy and the best among the eloquent, again said these words to (his) minister.

Śatrughna said:

13. How should we act here if he has snatched away Rāma's horse? He does not come to fight with (our) army which is strong and served by heroes?

Sumati said:

14-16. O great king, an eloquent messenger should be sent to the king, by (hearing) whose words the best among the strong will come along with his army. Or, the horse might have been carried away through ignorance by some proud (person). He will give us (back) the excellent, auspicious, sacrificial horse.

Hearing these words of (i.e. spoken by) him, the intelligent and powerful Śatrughna said these polite words to Aṅgada.

Śatrughna said:

17-19. You (please) go to Suratha's great city which is nearby. Having gone (there) as a messenger say to the king: "You have taken away knowingly or unknowingly Rāma's horse. Give him (back); or go in for a fight along with your warriors." O you, who are endowed with the greatest might and who are intelligent, act as a messenger in the same way as you acted as the messenger of Rāma to Rāvaṇa in Laṅkā.

Śeṣa said:

20-22. Hearing these (words) and saying, 'Yes' to the king, Aṅgada went to (Suratha's) assembly full of groups of warriors. He saw (there) king Suratha holding Tulasī-sprouts and telling (about) Rāma to his own servants. The king too seeing the monkey having a charming body and knowing him to be Śatrughna's messenger and Vālin's son, said to him.

Suratha said:

23. O lord of the monkeys, how and for what purpose have you come here? Tell me the full reason so that knowing it I shall do that (what is proper).

Śeṣa said:

24-29. The lord of the monkeys very much wondering in his heart said to the king who was speaking like this and who served Rāma: "O best king, know me to be Vālin's son, the lord of the monkeys. I have been sent to you as a messenger by Śatrughna. O king, some of your servants came and have now suddenly and unknowingly taken away my horse, (and thus) have done an unjust act. Go gladly to Śatrughna and having fallen at his feet quickly give the horse (back to him) along with your kingdom and sons. Otherwise, with your body wounded and deprived of your head by the arrows discharged by Śatrughna you will lie adorning the surface of the earth. Where will you go by snatching the sacrificial horse of him who easily in a moment destroyed the lord of Laṅkā?

Śeṣa said:

30-35. The lord of the earth, replied to him (i.e. to Aṅgada) who was speaking like this. "You are saying everything that is proper. Your words are not untrue. But listen to my words, O servant of Śatrughna's feet. I have seized the great horse of the intelligent Rāmacandra. Through the fear of Śatrughna and others I will not at all release him. If Rāma himself will come and appear before me, then (only) I with my sons will, after saluting his feet, give him my entire kingdom, much wealth, corn and army. If Rāma would not come, I shall now even in a moment conquer the great warriors like Śatrughna and bind them in my house."

Śeṣa said:

36. Hearing this, the intelligent Aṅgada laughed at the king; and said very important words with great courage.

Aṅgada said:

37-48. You, being devoid of understanding due to your old age, are speaking (like this)! That (i.e. understanding) has left you, since you, strengthened by your devotion (to Rāma) are despising Śatrughna who easily killed the demon Lavaṇa, the enemy of king Māndhātṛ, who killed many very strong and insolent warriors in battles. You are binding (i.e. thinking of binding) that lord of warriors who killed Vidyunmālin seated in (a vehicle) moving according to the occupant's desire. You appear to me to be devoid of wisdom. Śatrughna's brother's son Puṣkala is very mighty and knows (the use of) great missiles. Śatrughna has very much pleased Vīrabhadra, the attendant of Rudra. How can I describe his great valour earned through his might, resembling whom in might, fame or glory, there is none on the earth? Near him remains Hanūmat who has (set) his heart on the lotus-like feet of Rāma, whose (i.e. of Hanūmat) many deeds will be heard (i.e. known) by you, who in a moment forcibly burnt the demon's (i.e. Rāvaṇa's) city (Laṅkā) along with the Trikūṭa mountain, who killed Akṣa, the son of the wicked lord of demons, who repeatedly brought the mountain Droṇa along with the deities in it on the tip of his tail for reviving the soldiers. Rāma (alone) knows his uprightness. None else who is a dunce, knows it; him, the lord of monkeys, his servant, Rāma does not forget (even) a little from his heart. All the lordly monkeys like Sugrīva who live on the earth, serve king Śatrughna. They are eager to see (the horse). (So also there are others like) Kuśadhvaja, Nīlaratna, Riputāpa knowing (the use of) great missiles, (and) Pratāpāgrya, Subāhu, Vimala and Sumada. (So also) king Vīramaṇi, full of truth (i.e. truthful), is the servant of the king. These and other kings serve him.

49-50. There (i.e. among them), who are you (but) a mosquito in the ocean, O hero? Realising that, go (i.e. march) with your sons to the kind Śatrughna. Having given (back) the horse you will go to the lotus-eyed Rāma (and) seeing him you will make your limbs and your existence blessed.

Śeṣa said:

51-56. The king said to the messenger who was speaking in various ways: "You (will) immediately show them (to me, as) I do not know all (of them). O messenger, the might of Hanūmat who, taking Rāma on his back went to protect the sacrifice, is not as (great) as my own. If with devotion I worship Rāma mentally, with words and deeds, then he will quickly show me his body. Otherwise, let the heroes led by Hanūmat endowed with devotion bind me, and take (back) the horse speedily. (You) go to (my) enemy Śatrughna and tell him what I said. Let (your) good warriors be ready. This I, powerful one, am going to the battlefield. On the battlefield he will after thinking (properly) do what is proper. Let them free the great horse or give him to me."

Śeṣa said:

57. Having heard this and having smiled the hero went where the king (stayed), and having gone to him told him (everything) as was told by Suratha.

CHAPTER FIFTYONE

Hanūmat Frees Puṣkala from Campaka

Śeṣa said:

1-7. On hearing the words of Suratha from the mouth of (i.e. through) Aṅgada all (the soldiers) proficient in fighting and seated in their chariots became ready (to fight). There was the sound of the war-drums, so also of kettle-drums. On the battle-field the sounds of the roars of the soldiers arose. All the world was full of the sounds of the chariots and the trumpets of the elephants. The great sound (even) reached the sky. The soldiers skilled in fighting and full of enthusiasm for fighting made various sounds which scared the timid ones. When such a din took place, the king named Suratha surrounded by his sons and soldiers went to the battlefield. Pervading fully the earth with elephants, chariots, horses and hosts of foot-soldiers, and inundating it as the ocean (inundates it), he was seen with (or by) soldiers. Seeing that army resounding with the sounds of conches and also with cries of victory, and ready to fight, the king said to Sumati.

Śatrughna said:

8. The king surrounded with a huge army has come. O you very intelligent one, tell (me) what we should do now.

Sumati said:

9-10. Now many very fierce warriors like Puṣkala skilled in fighting and proficient in (the use of) all weapons and missiles, should fight. The very strong, very brave son of Samīra (i.e. of

Vāyu, viz. Hanūmat), very proficient in fighting, should fight with king (Suratha).

Śeṣa said:

11-18. When the great minister was speaking like this, the haughty sons of the king indeed stretched their bows on the battlefield. Seeing them, the very strong, respected soldiers like Puṣkala who were furious in battles and who had bows and arrows in their hands and who were seated in their chariots, went (to fight). The great warrior Puṣkala knowing the (use of) great missiles, fought in a single combat in chariots with Campaka protected by a great hero. That Kuśadhvaja, son of Janaka, fought with Mohaka. Vimala (fought) with Ripuñjaya, Subāhuka with Durvāra. Pratāpāgrya (fought with) Pratāpin, and Aṅgada with Balamoda. Nīlaratna fought with Haryakṣa, and Satyavān with Sahadeva. The powerful king Vīramaṇi fought with Bhūrideva. Ugrāśva, endowed with might, fought with Asutāpa. (Those warriors) skilled in fighting, fought a great single combat in chariots. All of them were skilled in (the use of) weapons and missiles and were proficient in fighting. O best sage, when the fight with Suratha's sons thus started, there took place great destruction.

19-21. Puṣkala said to Campaka: "O prince, what is your name? You who have come (to fight) with me in the battlefield, are lucky. Now wait; why do you go? How would you live (now)? O you proficient in (the use of) all weapons and missiles, come to fight with me." Hearing these words of (i.e. spoken by) him the mighty son of the king said to Puṣkala with a tone grave like the (thundering of) the clouds:

Campaka said:

22-25a. Fight here will not take place with (i.e. depending upon) name or family. Yet I shall tell you my name preceded by (i.e. with) my might. My mother is lord Rāghava; my father is said to be Rāghava. My brother is Rāmacandra; and my kinsman is Rāghava (i.e. Rāma). My name is Rāmadāsa (i.e. Rāma's servant). I am ever Rāma's servant. Rāma who favours his devotees, will save me in the battle. Yet following the belief of the people (i.e. convention) I shall now describe (myself) to you.

25b-28. I am Suratha's son; and Vīravatī is my mother. My name is that (i.e. Campaka) which makes all lovely in the spring season. The bees attracted by honey abandon the abode of my juice drunk in the spring. In complexion I resemble gold. I have a mark in the centre. O hero, know me as having the attractive name which is the name (of that tree). Fight with me with arrows. Nobody is able to conquer me in a battle. I shall now show you my wonderful valour.

Śeṣa said:

29-31. Hearing these great (i.e. important) words Puṣkala was glad in heart. Taking him to be difficult to be conquered he discharged arrows in the battle. He went (i.e. marched against) Puṣkala who was discharging arrows in crores. (And) then Campaka, full of anger, made his bow ready. He discharged sharp arrows which destroyed the hosts of enemies, which were marked by his name, and which had golden-feathered ends.

32-37. The great hero Puṣkala discharging arrows sharpened on (whet-) stones and causing darkness everywhere with arrows, cut off those (arrows) on the battlefield. Seeing his arrows being cut off by the hero, Campaka, full of anger, challenged the mighty Puṣkala. Saying "Leaving the battlefield, do not go (away)" he again quickly pierced Puṣkala at his chest with ten arrows. Those arrows of a sharp speed came and stuck very much (i.e. very deep) into the chest of Puṣkala, and quaffed the powerful blood. Afflicted by those arrows the hero too, through great anger, took five arrows, holding them like mountains. These powerful arrows, and the arrows of him, arranged in the sky, were cut off in a hundred ways by the king's son.

38-41. The mighty son of Suratha having cut off the very sharp arrows, took up a hundred arrows and struck Puṣkala on the chest. Those arrows cut off into a hundred ways by the magnanimous Puṣkala and opposed by the speed of (his) arrows fell in the vicinity of the battlefield. Seeing that very great feat the mighty son of the king clearly struck him on his chest with a thousand arrows.

42-44. Puṣkala knowing (the use of) great missiles, quickly cut them off too; but he again immediately fixed a myriad arrows on his own bow. Puṣkala knowing (the use of) great missiles cut them off too. Then being very angry he sent a shower of arrows. Perceiving that shower of arrows (coming to him), the destroyer of heroes, viz. Campaka, praising Puṣkala (with the words) "Well (done), well (done)", struck him. Seeing Campaka possessing great valour Puṣkala who knew (the use of) all weapons, fixed the missile of (i.e. presided over by) Brahmā on his bow.

45-48. The great missile discharged by him set ablaze the ten directions; and having pervaded the sky, the heaven and the earth, it was on the point of causing universal destruction. Campaka, proficient in (the use of) all missiles, seeing that missile discharged, discharged the same missile to kill his active enemy. People looked upon one of the two lustres as the final destruction of the world. The best missile united with the other one, destroyed it. Seeing that wonderful feat, Puṣkala saying, "Wait, wait", angrily struck Campaka with infallible arrows.

49-52. The magnanimous Campaka not caring for the arrows discharged (by Puṣkala), discharged the terrible missile called Rāmāstra towards Puṣkala. When he saw the missile discharged by the noble Campaka, and decided to cut it off, he was struck by an arrow. He was bound by the brave Campaka and was again put into his own chariot. The noble-minded one decided to send him to the city. When he named Puṣkala was bound there was great wailing. The warriors intent on fleeing, went to Śatrughna.

53-56. Seeing them routed, Śatrughna said to Hanūmat: "Which hero has completely defeated my army adorned with heroes?" O king, then he said: "This hero Campaka, firm in his position, is taking (away) the hero after tying him up." Hearing such (i.e. these) words of him, Śatrughna full of anger, said to Vāyu's son (i.e. Hanūmat): "Quickly free (him) from the king's son (i.e. Campaka) who, the very mighty one, has tied up (our) warrior Puṣkala, O best among the heroes, free him (i.e. Puṣkala) from him (i.e. Campaka). How do you delay in the battle?"

57-67a. Hearing these words, and saying "Yes", Hanūmat went to free Puṣkala from the hero Campaka. Seeing Hanūmat to have come to free him he, the very angry one, struck him with hundreds and thousands of arrows. He broke the arrows discharged by the noble one (i.e. Campaka). The mighty one was again quickly discharging arrows at him. He pounded all those arrows discharged by the enemy. Taking a śāla (tree) in his hand he struck the king's son (with it). The strong one made the śāla discharged by him like (i.e. of the size of) sesamum-seeds. Hanūmat discharged an elephant on the head of the prince. He too was struck by Campaka, so he died and fell on the ground. Hanūmat knowing (the use of) great missiles, discharged rocks. By means of a mechanism controlling arrows Campaka greatly pounded all the rocks; O brāhmaṇa, it was a great wonder. Seeing that all the rocks discharged by him were pounded, Hanūmat thinking that he was very powerful, was very much angry at heart. The monkey (i.e. Hanūmat), seized him in his hand, and jumped into the sky. Campaka fought with that Hanūmat. The best monkey was very much beaten by him in a close fight. The hero, terrible on account of a mountain of (i.e. great) pride, was angry in his mind.

67b-71. Seizing Campaka by his foot, he dashed him on the ground. Struck by the lord of monkeys, the speedy one got up in a moment and seizing Hanūmat by his tail whirled him round. The lord of the monkeys seeing his power and laughing again seized him by his foot. Having whirled him for a hundred times he dropped him on the haunch of an elephant. That Campaka, the son of the king, fell on the ground. Adorning the battlefield rich due to being embellished by heroes, he fainted. At that time the men, the followers of Campaka, wailed. (Hanūmat) freed Puṣkala who was tied up from the noose of Campaka.

CHAPTER FIFTYTWO

King Suratha Wins the Battle

Śeṣa said :

1-4. Seeing Campaka fallen Suratha, the mighty kṣatriya, with his body filled with grief, went, seated in a chariot (to the battlefield). Suratha who was very powerful, was angry and heaving heavy sighs, called (i.e. challenged) the monkey. Seeing the king challenging him the very brave hero, the lord of monkeys, having great speed, went to (i.e. marched against) him. King Suratha with his beautiful voice deep-sounding like (that of) the clouds, seeing Hanūmat who despised great heroes coming, said:

Suratha said:

5-8. O best monkey, possessing great might and valour you who performed a great feat for Rāma in the demon's city, are blessed. You are the devoted servant of Rāma's feet. You, the hero, overthrew my mighty son Campaka. Now having tied you up I shall go to my city. O best among the lordly monkeys, wait carefully. I have told (you) what I thought to be the truth.

Hearing these words of Suratha the lord of the monkeys said with a grave voice (to him) on the battlefield adorned only by warriors.

Hanūmat said:

9-10. You remind (us) of Rāma's feet. We are the servants of Rāma's feet. If you bind me forcibly, my lord (Rāma) will free me. O hero, make true (i.e. carry out) the pledge that you have in your heart. (A man) who remembers Rāma goes to the end of (i.e. destroys) his misery. The Vedas say this.

Śeṣa said:

11-18a. Suratha having praised Vāyu's son (Hanūmat) like this, pierced him with many fierce arrows sharpened on a whetstone. Not minding those arrows discharged (by Suratha) and causing bloodshed, Hanūmat seized (Suratha's) bow ready with arrows with his hand. The angry monkey holding the bow in both his hands broke it; and shouting (i.e. with his shouts) he scared the warriors and tore them with his nails. Seeing that his bow with the string attached was broken by him (i.e. by Hanūmat), he took another bow adorned with a great (i.e. strong) string. The monkey angrily seized that bow also and broke it. He (i.e. Suratha) took another bow. The mighty (Hanūmat) broke that (also). When that bow was broken, he took another bow. He (i.e. Hanūmat) having a great energy, quickly broke that bow also. Making great sounds in many ways every moment through great anger, he thus broke to pieces eighty bows of the king. Then (the king) getting very angry took (the missile) called Śakti.

18b-23. The hero (i.e. Hanūmat) struck by the Śakti fell down. (Then) in a moment being anxiously desirous (to defeat Suratha) he got up and, being very angry, seized the king's chariot. Seizing it he flew with a great speed toward the sea. Seeing him flying Suratha, the killer of his enemies, struck the active Hanūmat on his chest with iron-clubs. He dropped the chariot from a distance and in a moment it was shattered to pieces. Getting into another chariot he (i.e. Suratha) speedily went (i.e. rushed) to (Hanūmat), the son of Vāyu. Encircling the chariot along with the horses and the charioteer and with the banners, Hanūmat shattred it on the battlefield. Getting into another chariot, the very powerful king went (to attack Hanūmat). Hanūmat with his body getting strength violently broke it.

24-27. Seeing the chariot shattered Suratha got into another (chariot). He forcibly broke it along with the horses and the charioteer. In this way Hanūmat shattered fortynine chariots. Seeing that feat the king too along with his soldiers was amazed. Being angry he said to the lord of monkeys: "O son of Vāyu, acting bravely (like this) you are blessed. No one (but you) has done or will do this feat. O son of Vāyu, O bee (hovering round) the lotuses of the feet of Rāma, wait for a moment till I make my bow ready."

28-34. Saying so, and stringing the bow he, full of anger, fixed on his strong arrow the missile called Pāśupata (i.e. presided over by Paśupati). Then ghosts, friends, goblins, led by witches, frightening Hanūmat, suddenly appeared (there). The monkey was bound by the Pāśupata missiles. He was seen by the people (bound by the missiles). While they were wailing, the son of Vāyu remembering Rāma in his mind broke them in a moment. With his body freed he at once fought with king Suratha. Seeing him with his body freed Suratha, knowing (the use of) great missiles, taking him (i.e. Hanūmat) to be very strong, took the missile known as Brāhma (i.e. presided over by Brahmā). The strong Māruti laughed and swallowed the Brāhma missile. The king, the protector of the earth, seeing that (the missiles was) swallowed by him, remembered Rāma. Remembering Rāma, the son of Daśaratha, he fixed the Rāma-missile (i.e. the missile presided over by Rāma) on his bow, and said these (words) to him: "O best monkey (now) you are bound."

35-39a. Having heard those words, when the hero Hanūmat, Rāma's servant, would go ahead, he was bound on the battle-field by the king with the Rāma-missile. To the king Hanūmat said: "O king, what do (i.e. can) I do now? You have bound me with the missile of (i.e. presided over by) my master, and not with any ordinary one. I respect it; O king, take me to your city. That abode of kindness, my master, will come and release me." When the son of Wind (i.e. Hanūmat) was bound, the angry Puṣkala went to (i.e. marched against) the king. He pierced that Puṣkala who had come (like that) with many arrows. The mighty one struck the king with thousands of arrows.

39b-46. The king cut off many of his arrows on the battle-field. When that great warrior Puṣkala was thus angry in the battle, the entire world—immobile and also the mobile—was filled with arrows. Seeing their firm resolve to fight, the soldiers of gods were perplexed. Then what to say of (i.e. what can be said about) men who got scared in a moment! With the discharges of missiles and counter-missiles a fierce, thrilling battle took place among the warriors. Then the angry king took an arrow. But it was cut off by the arrows angrily discharged by Bharata's son (Puṣkala). When that arrow was cut off, the king took another. When he (i.e. Puṣkala) cut off (i.e. tried to cut off) that arrow, he was wounded on chest (with it) which stuck to (i.e. struck) his chest. Having fought a very great (i.e. fierce), wonderful battle with the king, the very lustrous and very intelligent Puṣkala fell into a swoon. When Puṣkala had fallen, Śatrughna who tormented his enemies, got angry with Suratha and seated in his chariot went (to him).

47-58. The very mighty brother of Rāma said to king Suratha: "You have done a great feat that you have bound the son of Wind (i.e. Hanūmat). You have overthrown even the great hero Puṣkala and so also my other very mighty and brave warriors in the battle. Now wait. O king, where will you go by overthrowing my soldiers on the battlefield? Now put up with my arrows." Hearing these words of the hero, the mighty Suratha having in his mind the charming lotus-like feet of Rāma, said: "In the battle I have knocked down your warriors waiting for Hanūmat. Now I shall overthrow you also on the battlefield. Recollect Rāma who, the hero, (will) himself come and protect you. Otherwise, O you tormentor of the enemies, you will not live before me." Saying so, the king struck him with thousands of arrows. He put the great Śatrughna into the cage of the volley of arrows. Śatrughna (trying to) avoid the volley of arrows, discharged a missile to burn the arrows with bent joints. The great king Suratha, seeing that missile discharged, destroying it with the Varuṇa missile (i.e. the missile presided over by Varuṇa), pierced him with crores of arrows. Then he fixed on his bow the wonderful missile given by the female devotee which deluded all heroes and made them sleep. The king seeing that great deluding missile remembered Viṣṇu and said to Śatrughna: "This one is proficient in (the use of) all weapons and missiles. No other delusion seems to be causing fear and tormentation to me who am deluded by the recollection of Śrī Rāma."

59-65. When the hero spoke like this, he discharged the great missile. Cut off by the arrow it fell on the battlefield. Seeing that the great missile was fruitless against the king, he being extremely amazed, fixed an arrow on his bow. The destroyer of great demons fixed on his bow that fierce arrow resembling fire in lustre with which Lavaṇa was killed. Seeing that (arrow) the king said: "This arrow sticks to (i.e. strikes) the chest of the wicked. It does not even remain in front of the devotee of Rāma." When he was saying like this, Śatrughna struck him with that arrow and pierced him in his chest (with it) resembling flames of fire. The tormentor of the enemies, afflicted by the arrow and full of great agony became unconscious for a moment in the interior of his chariot. Having in a moment overcome that agony he said to his enemy before him: "Endure one stroke of (i.e. given by) me. Where will you go from my presence?"

66-69. Speaking like this in the great battle he fixed on his bow an arrow full of flame of fire and having golden feathered ends. That arrow that was discharged from the bow and that remained on its way, though cut off by Śatrughna with the upper part of his (sword's) blade, fell upon his chest. Being rendered unconscious by that arrow, he fell on the chariot. The entire army that was defeated wailed and fled away. Suratha, the servant of Rāma, obtained victory in the battle. Then heroes rendered unconscious by his ten sons, fell somewhere.

CHAPTER FIFTYTHREE

Rāma Frees the Bound Heroes

Śeṣa said:

1-11. Seeing the army defeated and also seeing his master (lying) unconscious, Sugrīva went to fight with the king. "Come, O king, where are you going after rendering all the warriors unconscious? O you proficient in fighting, quickly fight with me." He possessing power saying so uprooted some huge tree with branches and struck it on his head. Due to that stroke the very mighty, very brave king looked at Sugrīva and angrily fixing sharp arrows (on his bow) struck them on his chest. Sugrīva laughed and at once foiled all those arrows. He, the very powerful one, struck Suratha on his chest. Tearing Suratha with his nails he violently struck him with mountains, peaks (of mountains), trees and bodies of elephants. With the very terrible missile called Rāma (i.e. presided over by Rāma) he quickly bound him also. The best monkey (i.e. Sugrīva) took Suratha to be a servant of Rāma. He became like an elephant which, having an iron chain hanging from his feet, cannot do anything. Putting all the warriors into his chariot he went to his own city. Going to his assembly, the very great one said to Hanūmat who was bound: "Remember the kind Raghunātha, the protector of his devotees, so that he of the best mind will instantly release you. Otherwise, even after a myriad years I shall not free you from bondage."

12-13. Having heard these words Hanūmat seeing himself tightly bound and the warriors unconscious and afflicted with the strokes of the enemy, remembered for freedom from the bondage Śrī Rāmacandra born in Raghu's dynasty, husband of Sītā and having eyes like lotus-petals. With all his senses free from grief he remembered the kind one for his own freedom from bondage.

Hanūmat said:

14-17. O lord, O best among excellent men, O kind one, O lord of Śītā, O you whose face is charming on account of beautiful hair, O you who burn (i.e. destroy) the affliction of your devotees, O you having an attractive form, release me at once from the bondage. Do not tarry. O abode of pity, you freed (beings) like the excellent elephant, so also gods who were being profusely burnt by the fire of the family of demons, and you untied the hair-bonds on the heads of their beautiful wives. (Please) remember me. You are engaged in the performance of a sacrifice along with the best sages; you give a thought to religious merit, O you whose feet are praised by kings. O god, O Supreme Being, today I have been firmly tied with a noose by Suratha; quickly release me. If in spite of my remembering you very much, O you whose lotus-like feet are worshipped by excellent gods, you would not release me, then the manifested world would laugh at you; therefore do not delay in this matter; quickly release (me).

18-27. Hearing this (prayer), the Raghu-hero (i.e. Rāma), the lord of the world and the abode of kindness, quickly came by the Puṣpaka (aeroplane) to release his devotee. The monkey (i.e. Hanūmat) saw him who was well accompanied by Lakṣmaṇa who followed him, and Bharata, and who was accompanied by hosts of sages led by Vyāsa. Seeing his lord having come (he) said to the king: "O king, see Hari who has kindly come to free his own (devotee). Formerly, merely by being remembered he freed many votaries of him. In the same way he has come to free me tied with a noose." Seeing Śrī Rāmabhadra (who had) come there, that Suratha, full of the flood of devotion, in a moment saluted him hundreds of times. Śrī Rāma having four arms, embraced him with his arms; and, repeatedly sprinkling his devotee with tears of joy, he said: "Your body is blessed. You have done a great feat. You fully tied the powerful lord of monkeys—Hanūmat." Śrī Rāma freed the excellent monkey from the bondage. He looked at all those unconscious warriors and (merely) by (his) glance he revived them. They gave up their swoon (i.e. they regained consciousness). They were seen by Rāma serving gods. They got up and saw the charming Rāmacandra. They saluted the lord of Raghus. He enquired after their well-being.

28-32. Then Suratha, having seen Rāma to have come there for favouring his votary, gladly presented to him his entire kingdom along with the (sacrificial) horse. He pleased Śrī Rāma with (i.e. by giving him) many excellent garments. He said (to Rāma): "O Rāghava, I did an unjust act; (please) forgive me." Then Śrī Rāma said: "You have protected the (sacrificial) horse. It is the duty of kṣatriyas to fight along with the lord. You have done a good deed. The warriors are highly pleased on the battlefield." (The king) along with his sons (then) worshipped Viṣṇu in a human form (i.e. Rāma). Having stayed (there) for three days and having dismissed him with a blessing, the mighty Śrī Rāma along with the sages went back in the divine car (i.e. Puṣpaka) moving according to (the occupants') will. Seeing him (going like that) all of them were amazed and told (one another) charming stories about him.

33-37. The powerful and very mighty Suratha, having placed (his son) Campaka in his city, decided to go with Śatrughna. Śatrughna, having got (back) his horse, caused the kettle-drums to be sounded. He (also) caused the various sounds of conches to be produced everywhere. The hero along with Suratha let loose the sacrificial horse. He roamed in foreign countries. (But) no powerful (man) seized him. Wherever the wandering horse went there Śatrughna along with great army and with Suratha also went. Once he (i.e. the horse) went to the excellent hermitage of Vālmīki which was resorted to by excellent sages and was marked with smoke in the morning (and which was situated) on the bank of Gaṅgā.

CHAPTER FIFTYFOUR

Lava Binds the Sacrificial Horse

Śeṣa said:

1-5. Jānakī's son Lava surrounded by sages' sons went to bring sacred fuel fit for the rites in order to perform the rites. There he saw the sacrificial horse marked with a golden note and made fragrant with the divine perfume of saffron, agaru (sandal) and musk. Seeing (the horse) and with curiosity aroused he said to the sons of the sages: "Whose horse having mind's speed has fortunately come to my hermitage? Come with me; observe (him); do not be afraid." Saying so that Lava quickly went near the horse. He born in the family of Raghu and standing near the horse, holding a bow and an arrow, stood invincible like Jayanta near the horse.

6-11. Having gone (there) with the sons of the sages he read the excellent note, shining with lines of distinct letters, and placed on the (horse's) forehead. "There is the great family of Vivasvat which is well-known in all the worlds; in which there is no one that is dependent or none that is greedy of another's wealth. To the family belongs Daśaratha who is the banner of the solar dynasty, who is a (great) archer, who is great, who is a teacher initiating (one) in (the science of using) a bow, whom all the deities with gods salute with their heads having (ornaments of) jewels (bent down). The noble Rāmacandra, descendant of Raghu, crest-jewel of all the brave, removing the pride of the might of the warriors, is his son. His (i.e. Rāma's) mother is the daughter of the king of Kośala, the producer of a jewel. From her womb was born a jewel of a son, Rāma who causes fear to his enemies, who is well-trained by a brāhmaṇa, is performing a horse-sacrifice to remove the sin due to his having killed the best brāhmaṇa, viz. Rāvaṇa.

12-17. He has let loose this sacrificial horse, chief among horses, surrounded by a large army and well-protected by moats. My brother Śatrughna, the killer of Lavaṇa, surrounded by an army consisting of the groups of elephants, horses, chariots and foot-soldiers, is his protector. Let that king who has, through his conceit, the pride that he is great, or let those who think that they are brave, they are best among the archers or that they are mighty here (i.e. on the earth), seize forcibly the horse adorned with a jewelled necklace, having the velocity of mind and moving at his will, and very bright due to his movement everywhere. From him (who has seized the horse) hurt by the arrow discharged from (Śatrughna's) bow, my brother Śatrughna will easily and forcibly free him. Let those kṣatriyas born from a kṣatriya girl (i.e. woman) or born in good families having good wives, seize him. Those of wrong bodies (i.e. those that are not proper kṣatriyas) should, after presenting their kingdom to Raghu (i.e. Rāma), salute him."

18-21. Having read like this, Lava, wielding a weapon and a bow, got angry, and with words faltering through anger said to the sons of the sages: "See quickly the audacity of that kṣatriya king who has written this in the note on the (horse's) forehead about his valour and might. Who is this Rāma? Who is Śatrughna? They are (but) insects having very little might. They are born in the family of kṣatriyas, and not we, the excellent ones? He does not have as his mother Sītā who has given birth to a hero—who has given birth to Kuśa, who had in her womb a gem called Kuśa, as the piece of wood (called Araṇi) used for kindling the sacred fire has fire (in it).

22-24. I shall now show on all sides my being a kṣatriya etc. If he is born of a kṣatriya and if he is killer of his enemy, he will take (back) this horse fit for the sacrificial rite, which is bound by me. Otherwise, he will abandon his kṣatriyahood and will worship Kuśa's feet. Now, with the arrows discharged from my bow he will lie down. So also the other great warriors, ornaments of the battlefield (will lie down)."

25-28a. Uttering these words, Lava, the best one, holding a bow and arrows, despising all kings, seized the horse. Then the sages' sons said to Lava who desired to seize the horse: "Rāma, the king of Ayodhyā, is very mighty and brave. Even Śakra (i.e. Indra), insolent through his power does not (dare) catch his horse. Do not seize him. Listen to these words of me (i.e. of us) which are beneficial." Hearing these words he said to the brāhmaṇa-sons:

28b-34. "O best brāhmaṇas, you do not know the power of kṣatriyas. Kṣatriyas are proud of their valour (while) brāhmaṇas have food (only). Therefore, going home, you eat (whatever) is brought by your mothers." Thus told they remained quiet and watched the valour of that Lava. Those sons of sages remained away and out (of the range of the imminent fight). When this incident took place, the servants of that king (i.e. (Śatrughna) came (there, and) seeing the horse bound, they said to Lava: "Who has bound the horse? Oh, with whom is Yama angry? Who, being in the midst of volleys of arrows, will get (i.e. suffer from) a great agony?" Then Lava quickly said: "I have bound this excellent horse. With him who releases (i.e. tries to release) him, (my) great brother Kuśa will be angry. What will even lord Yama himself, after coming over here, do? Being very much pleased with the shower of arrows, he will salute (Kuśa) and go (back)."

Śeṣa said:

35-37. He holding the bow in both his hands discharged arrows with sharp horse-shoe-shaped heads at those servants of Śatrughna who had on hearing these words come there to release Rāma's horse that was bound and who said, "This is a child". They with their arms cut off went to Śatrughna through grief, and when asked (by him), they all told about the cutting off of their arms by Lava.

CHAPTER FIFTYFIVE

The Observation of the Spies

Vyāsa said:

1. Having heard this charming account of the powerful Lava the sage entertaining a doubt again asked the serpent (i.e. Śeṣa) having a thousand faces.

Śrī Vātsyāyana said:

2-3. Formerly you had said that Rāma due to the censure by a washerman and ardently longing for fame abandoned Sītā all alone in the forest. Where were the two sons born to Jānakī (i.e. Sītā)? Where did they learn archery? How did they learn the science which enabled them to take away the horse of Rāma?

Vyāsa said:

4. Hearing these words of the sage, the very intelligent serpent Śeṣa praised the brāhmaṇa and narrated to him the wonderful deeds of Rāma.

Śeṣa said:

5-8. Protecting according to dharma a part of the earth, along with his wife Rāma ruled in Ayodhyā with his brothers. Sītā retained his semen (i.e. Sītā conceived), and five months had passed (i.e. her pregnancy was five months old). The queen shone very much like the triad (of Vedas) holding the Supreme Being. Some time Rāma asked (Sītā) the daughter of Videha (king Janaka): "What is your cherished wish? I shall fulfil it." The chaste lady, getting abashed, was asked in private only. With her words faltering through abashment she said these nectar(-like) words to Rāma:

Sītā said:

9-17. By your grace I have enjoyed everything and shall enjoy good (things). O dear one, no cherished wish remains in my mind. She whose lord is like you whose good feet are praised by gods, has all excellent (things). Nothing remains (to be secured). You are asking with persistence about the cherished wish present in my mind. (So) O you charming lord, I tell the truth to you. O lord, a long time has passed since I saw the chaste ladies like Lopāmudrā. O lord, my mind becomes eager to see those beautiful ladies. With you I obtained the kingdom and lived happily. I am ungrateful (as I have not seen them). Desirous of saluting them some time, I, having gone (to them) shall honour them, the treasures of penance, with garments etc. I shall also offer them bright gems and ornaments, so that the chaste ladies gratified by me will give me pleasant blessings. This, O dear one, is the longing in my mind. (Please) fulfil it.

Hearing these very charming words of Sītā, Rāmacandra

who was very much pleased, said to his beloved (i.e. Sītā): "O Jānakī, you are lucky. In the morning you will go, and having seen those ladies with penance as their wealth, (and thus) having made yourself blessed, you will come back near (i.e. to) me."

18-26. Hearing these words of Rāma she was extremely pleased. (She thought): 'In the morning I shall certainly see the female-ascetics.' The spies who were sent to ascertain his fame that was reported (by others) slowly went to him at night. Everyday listening to very charming stories about Rāma, they had that day gone to the large house of a rich man. Seeing a lamp burning and noticing (i.e. hearing) human voices, the spies remained there for a moment, and heard the great glory (of Rāma). There a certain beautiful lady pleased with her child sucking her breasts, said these pleasing words to it: "O son, drink (i.e. suck) as much pleasing milk of me as you like. O my son, later it will be difficult for you to have it. Rāma, shining like the petals of a blue lotus, is the lord of this city. Therefore, the people living in the city will not be reborn. How can there be the drinking (i.e. sucking) of milk in the absence of birth? Therefore, thinking in your mind that the milk is (later) difficult to obtain, drink (suck) it repeatedly. For them also who will remember Śrī Rāma, meditate upon and talk about him, there will certainly be no drinking (i.e. sucking) of (the mother's) milk (i e. they will not be reborn)."

27-38. Hearing these words—the nectar of Rāma's glory, they being delighted went to another house—a great house of a fortunate person. Just then, another spy, thinking that it was a pleasant house, remained there for a moment with a desire to listen to Rāma's glory. There a beautiful lady, chewing tāmbūla, affectionately offered it to her husband, seated on a couch. She, abounding in beauty, fumigated with camphor and agaru (sandal), seeing her husband, and with her eyes moving said with her bangles making a jingling sound to him having the form of Cupid: "O lord, you appear to me like the lord of Raghu (family) having an extremely handsome and very delicate body, a pair of eyes with their corners resembling lotuses, an attractive and expansive chest, and arms with armlets—you are to me actually Rāma." He, handsome like Cupid, having heard these very pleasant words of his wife, dancing (i.e. moving) the corners of his eyes, said: "Listen,

O darling, you, a chaste lady, have spoken very pleasant (words). It is proper for the loyal wives that their husbands are just like Rāma to them; but (see), where am I, the luckless one, and where is that great, fortunate Rāma? (i.e. there is a great disparity between Rāma and me). Where am I, small like an insect, and where (is Rāma) worshipped by gods like Brahmā? Where is the fire-fly, the gem of the sky, and where is the low moth? Where is the lord of beasts (i.e. the lion), the enemy of the elephants, and where is the dull-witted hare? Where is that respectable Gaṅgā, and where is the water on the street flowing the wrong way? Where is Meru, the abode of the gods, and where is a small heap of the guñjā fruits? Similarly, where am I, and where is Rāma, by (the touch of) the dust of whose feet the lady who was reduced to a stone, became in a moment one having the form that enticed (even) Brahmā?"

39-45. With passion produced in her, taken away by love for him, and making her eye-brows like bows dance (i.e. knitting her eye-brows), she embraced her husband who was speaking these words. Hearing words like these, the spy went to another house. Just then another spy heard words full of glory. Some lady making ready all (things) like a bed with flowers (strewn over it), sandal with camphor, fit for love-making, said (these) words to her husband: "O my lord, lie on the bed with flowers (strewn over it) and fit for enjoyment, also have smearing with sandal etc., so also enjoyment in various ways. People like you alone deserve enjoyment, and not those who are averse to Rāma. Enjoy properly everything that is obtained through Rāma's grace. A loving (wife) like me, sandal removing torment, a bed with flowers arranged over it—all (this) is due to Rāma's grace. Those men who will not worship Rāma are deprived of garments, enjoyments etc. and are not able to fill their belly (i.e. to maintain themselves)."

46-51. To the lady who was speaking like this, the husband who was delighted, said: "You are telling the truth; I have everything due to the grace of Rāma." The spy, hearing about Rāma's glory, went (away). Just then a spy, remaining in someone else's house, heard (these) words. A certain lady engaged in playing upon the lute with her husband on the bed, to whom her husband was singing the glory of Rāma, said to her husband: "O lord, we in whose city lord Śrī Rāma himself is the king and protects his subjects like his own sons, are most fortunate. The great feat, difficult to perform, which he performed, is not easy to do: He controlled the ocean and built a bridge over it; he having killed his enemy Rāvaṇa, after having shattered it with (the help of) the monkeys, brought (back) Sītā. Thus he performed a great act."

52-56. Hearing this speech containing very sweet words, the husband smiled, and again said these words to her: "O innocent, beautiful lady, this is not a great feat of Rāmacandra, viz. the killing of Rāvaṇa etc. or controlling the ocean etc. He, the great one, requested by Brahmā etc. easily came (down) to the earth and performed good deeds which remove great sins. Do not look upon Rāma who gives joy to Kauśalyā, as a human being. He who sportively obtained humanhood (i.e. was born as a human being), creates, protects and destroys the world. We are lucky that we see Rāma's lotus-like face which is difficult to be seen by gods like Brahmā."

57-67. He heard the deeds of Rāmacandra, giving delight to the ears. The spy that stood at the door repeatedly heard such words. Another spy having gone to another house stood there to listen to Hari's (i.e. Rāma's) glory. There also he heard the splendid glory of Śrī Rāmabhadra. A very beautiful lady, playing with dice with her husband, as it were causing her bangles to dance, spoke (these) sweet words: "O dear one, I have speedily won everything; what will you, having a mind to win, do (now)?" Saying these words in jest she joyfully embraced her husband. The husband said: "O you of a beautiful body, O you very charming one, I alone have won. I, who always remember Rāma, do not have a defeat anywhere. Remembering Rāma, the charming one, I shall just now vanquish you, as formerly the gods after remembering him, vanquished Diti's sons (i.e. the demons) in a moment." Saying so he turned over the dice. Just then he won; being delighted he said these words: "What I said has come true; I have defeated you, O young lady. One who remembers Rāma has never any fear from one's enemy." Speaking like this they who longed for each other, tightly embraced each other. Then the spy went home. Thus the five great spies, having heard the glory of the king and praising one another gladly went home. One, the sixth spy, having seen the houses of artisans, went there desiring to hear (about) the glory of the king, the lord of the earth.

68-73. A washerman, with his eyes red due to anger and full of anger kicked his wife who had stayed at another's house, and despised her: "From my house, go to the house of him where you stayed for a day. I shall not accept you who violate my commands." Then his mother said to him: "Do not abandon her who has come (back) to (our) house, who has not committed any fault, and who is free from bad acts." The angry washerman said to his mother: "I am not as great as Rāma as to accept (my wife) who stayed in another's house. Whatever that king does, might by lawful; (but) I will not accept my wife who has stayed in another's house." He again and again said these words: "I am not king Rāma who protected Sītā that had stayed in another's house."

74-79. Having heard these words, the spy was full of anger. He took a sword in his hand and decided to kill him (i.e. the washerman). He (then) recollected Rāma's words: "None of my subjects should be killed." Realising this, he, of a noble mind, wrathfully withdrew (his sword). On hearing (the washerman's words), he was very much afflicted with grief, and being angry and breathing out and in repeatedly (i.e. repeatedly sighing) he went where the five spies stood. They met one another there, and told (one another) the deeds of Rāma honoured by all people without an exception, and heard by them. Having heard his words they told one another: "This censure uttered by a wicked man should not be reported to Raghunātha (i.e. Rāma)." Having thus spoken to one another, the eager ones went (home) and slept, after having mentally decided: 'In the morning, we shall tell the king'.

CHAPTER FIFTYSIX

Rāma Seeks Bharata's Advice

Śeṣa said:

1-9. Having performed the daily morning duties, having duly gratified the brāhmaṇas, the most learned in the Vedas, with presents of gold, he went to the assembly. All men went to the assembly to salute Raghunātha, the king looking after all the subjects like his own sons. Lakṣmaṇa had held an umbrella over the king's head. Bharata and Śatrughna had at that time held the chowries. Sages led by Vasiṣṭha attended there (upon Rāma). Ministers led by Sumantra who did justice, (were present) there. When the time moved on like this, the six well-adorned spies came to salute the king seated in the assembly. Seeing them desirous of speaking, the best king, being eager, entered the interior, private chamber in the assembly. The good-minded king asked all the spies in private: "O spies, O you who restrain your enemies, tell me correctly how people talk about me; how (they talk) about my wife; in what way do they talk about the acts of my ministers?" Hearing these words the spies spoke in a grave tone like that of the (thundering) clouds to the lord of the Raghus who was asking them.

The spies said:

10-17. O lord, now your fame purifies all people in the world. We heard it, being told by men and women in every house. You the Supreme Being, went to the earth to adorn the great family of Vivasvat. You have largely spread your fame. (In that family) many famous and very mighty (kings) were (born) but they did not have that fame as you have. You, the lord, have made blessed all the subjects that do not have an untimely death and trouble from disease. As the moon, or as the river Gaṅgā illumines the earth, your good fame illumines the earth. Having heard (about) your fame, Brahmā and others are very much ashamed. O lord, everywhere your fame now purifies the people. We all who are your spies, O lord, are most blessed, (since) every moment we see your charming face.

Having seen (i.e. heard) these words of the five spies, he asked the sixth one whose face was marked with abashment.

Rāma said:

18-21. O you very intelligent one, tell me truly what you have heard (being talked) in the commingling (i.e. crowd) of people. Tell all that to me as it is. Otherwise you are a sinner.

Again and again, and fast, Rāma asked him in detail. Yet he did not tell Rāma the words of the people (i.e. popular scandal). Then Rāma said to the spy with an abashed face: "I swear you with truth. Tell me everything properly." Then a spy slowly said (these) words to the spy: "You have to tell what was said by the artisans, even if it is not fit to be told."

The spy said:

22-30. O lord, except that your wife stayed in the demon's house, your fame due to your having killed Rāvaṇa has (spread) everywhere. But an artisan—a washerman—despising his wife who had stayed in another's house, beat her at night. His mother said to him: "Why do you beat this innocent one? Accept the woman (i.e. your wife); do not censure her; follow my words (of advice)." Then the washerman said: "I am not king Rāma who accepted Sītā that had stayed in the demon's house." O lord, (the washerman further said:) "Every act done by a king is proper. The act of others, even though they perform meritorious deeds, is improper." Again and again he said: "I am not king Rāma." I got angry. (But) just at that time I remembered your words (viz. 'Do not kill a human being'). (I also thought:) 'Cutting his head I (should) at that time knock him on the ground.' Then I thought: 'Where is Rāma and where is the washerman? (i.e. there is a great disparity between Rāma and the washerman). This wicked one is telling a lie. He is not speaking the truth'. O Rāma, if you order I (shall) kill him now. Due to your persistence, I told you about the analogy, though (really) it should not have been told. The king is the authority here (i.e. in this matter). Let him think (what is relevant).

Śeṣa said:

31-32. Hearing these words which were like the great thunderbolt, (Rāma) heaving and breathing repeatedly fell unconscious. Seeing the king (fallen) unconscious, the spies full of grief fanned him with the end of their garments to remove (Rāma's) grief.

33-40. The king who regained consciousness after some time, said to them: "Go and quickly send Bharata to me." The spies carrying messages and grieved, quickly went to Bharata's house and told (him) Rāma's message. The intelligent Bharata, having heard Rāma's message went to the assembly. Learning that Rāma was in the private (chamber), he quickly came to him, and the noble-minded one said to the door-keeper: "Where is that Rāmabhadra, (that) treasure of kindness, my brother?" The hero went to the house charming with gems, indicated by him. Seeing Rāma tired out, he became afraid in his mind: 'Is this Rāma angry? Or is it the grief of the lord?' Then he said to the king, heaving repeatedly: "O lord, how is that your face which is easily pleased, is hanging (like this)? Your face, due to the tears appears like the moon eclipsed by Rāhu. Tell me the full and true cause. What do (i.e. should) I do for you? O great king, give up your grief. How can you be the receptacle of grief?"

41-46. The righteous hero Rāmacandra, who was thus being spoken to by his brother, spoke to him in a faltering voice: "O brother, listen to my words. (Listen to) the cause of my grief. O very intelligent one, this morning remove it. In the family of Vivasvat no king was (ever) hurt by infamy. My fame today has become foul; Gaṅgā has been joined by Yamunā. The life of those kings only is good on the earth who have fame. The life of those who are wounded by infamy is like (that of) the dead. Those who would have fame on the earth, go to eternal worlds. Those who are bitten by the female serpent in the form of infamy, would go down. Today my fame, the divine river in the world, has become turbid. Listen to the words which the washerman said about me.

47-52. In this city a washerman today uttered certain censurable words about Jānakī (i.e. Sītā). Then, O brother, what should I do on the earth? Should I abandon myself (i.e. should I commit suicide) today: or should I abandon my wife Jānakī? Which of the two should I do? Tell me what is proper." Speaking like this Rāma, the crest-jewel of Dharma shedding tears and with his body shaken with horripilation, fell on the ground. Seeing his brother fallen, Bharata, full of grief, having examined him carefully, slowly brought Rāma (back) to consciousness. Having seen Rāmacandra who was very much grieved, to have regained consciousness, he spoke very charming words to remove his grief: "Who is this washerman? Which censurable words did he utter? I shall cut off the tongue of him who censures Jānakī."

53-60. Then Rāma told the words that came out of the washerman's mouth (i.e. that were uttered by the washerman) and that were heard by the spy, to the magnanimous Bharata. Hearing them, Bharata said to his brother who was afflicted with grief: "Brahmā said: 'She is pure'. Your father Daśaratha also (said the same thing). (Then) how should she respected by the world, be abandoned merely on (the strength of) the washerman's words? Your fame praised by Brahmā and others, purifies the worlds. How will it be turbid today due to the words of the washerman? Therefore, give up the great grief due to the censure of Sītā. Look after the kingdom along with her—the very fortunate one—who is pregnant. How do you wish to abandon your charming body? Without you who remove our grief, we all are doomed today. That very glorious Sītā will not live without you (even) for a moment. Therefore, with (that) loyal wife enjoy ample glory." Hearing these words of Bharata, the righteous (king), the best among the eloquent, again spoke these words to him:

61-64. "O brother, whatever you say is all just. But by my order, carry out the words which I utter. I know that she is purified in fire, is chaste and is honoured by the world. (But) I am afraid of public scandal. (Therefore) I (shall) abandon my (wife) Jānakī. So, taking in your hand a sharp and very fierce sword, (either) cut off (my) head, or abandon (my) wife Jānakī in the forest." Hearing these words of Rāma, Bharata, with tremor in his body and tears (in his eyes), fell unconscious on the ground.

CHAPTER FIFTYSEVEN

The Washerman's Former Birth

Vātsyāyana said:

1-2. O you of a good vow, tell me how the lord received the utterance of the censure of Jānakī having pure, excellent fame in the world. O Śeṣa, do that by which my mind shall have very splendid happiness, so that I who drink the nectar coming out from your mouth, shall be satisfied, and by which my worldly existence will be cut off.

Śeṣa said:

3-11. In Mithilā, a great city, there lived a king by name Janaka. Pleasing his subjects, he ruled righteously. When that Sīradhvaja (i.e. Janaka) was ploughing the field, an extremely beautiful girl came out from the long, first furrow. Then king Sīraketu (i.e. Janaka) became extremely glad. He named her, the fascinating one, the glory of the world, Sītā. When she, extremely charming, was playing in the grove of the garden, she saw a pair of a male and a female parrot that delighted her mind. The parrots were extremely delighted and lustful, and affectionately talking to each other in pleasant words. That pair, enjoying (each other's company), quickly flew in the sky, settled on the lap of a mountain, and spoke (to each other): "On the earth, charming Rāma will be the king. His wife will be (a woman) by name Sītā. The intelligent, powerful king, vanquishing (his enemies), will rule (over the earth) along with her for eleven thousand years. Blessed is that queen Jānakī, and blessed is he, named Rāma, who having approached each other, will gladly enjoy."

12-16. When the couple of parrots was conversing in this way, Maithilī, observing their words and realising that this was a divine couple and thinking, 'this couple of parrots is telling charming tales about me, (so) I shall catch the couple, and will ask about all the words, the meaning of which is already expressed', she said to her friends: "Slowly catch this charming pair of the birds." The friends just then went to the mountain, and caught the excellent pair of the birds, and with a desire to do what was dear to their friend (Sītā), reported it to her. Seeing the pair uttering many words in various ways, she comforted it, and said to it these words.

Sītā said:

17-18. Do not be scared. Who are you two, the charming ones? Where have you come from? Who is Rāma, and who is Sītā? Wherefrom did you have the information about them? Tell me all that quickly. Let your fear of me go away.

The pair of birds said:

19-26. There is a very great sage Vālmīki who is the best among those who know dharma. That sage made his disciples sing the future adventures of Rāma. He, engrossed in the well-being of all beings, everyday remembered its words. All those future adventures of Rāma, being sung repeatedly, were heard by both of us; they came to us (i.e. were mastered by us) due to repetition. Listen to them. In the end we shall tell who that Rāma is and who that Jānakī is and what will happen to her with Rāma of a playful nature. Glorious Viṣṇu, good stories about whom are sung by celestial women, will, having divided himself into four, come up at the sacrifice performed by Ṛṣyaśṛṅga. He, having a bow in his hand, will come along with Viśvāmitra and his own brothers to Mithilā. Then there seeing a bow difficult to be taken (i.e. wielded) by other kings, he will break it, and will obtain the very charming daughter of Janaka. O excellent one, we have heard that with her he will rule over a large kingdom. O you of a beautiful body, we who had flown there, heard this and other (things) about you, told by those who lived there. Release us who desire to go.

27-40. Grasping (i.e. hearing) these words very pleasant to the ears, she again spoke (these) words to that pair of birds: "Where would that Rāma be? Whose son (will he be)? In what way will he marry her? What form will the excellent man have? Tell me exactly all this that I have asked you. Later I will do all good things liked by you." Hearing those (words), the female parrot, seeing Jānakī and realising in her heart that she was oppressed by love, then said to her: "There will be an intelligent mighty king having a line of chariots, and the scion of the solar dynasty, having resorted to whom gods will be fully victorious. He will have three wives, having forms that will fascinate (even) Indra. On them (i.e. from them) four children (sons) lofty on account of might, will be born. Rāma will be the eldest of all. Bharata is said to be (born) after him. After him (i.e. Bharata) Lakṣmaṇa (will be born), and after him (will be born) Śatrughna, powerful everywhere. The large-minded one (i.e. Rāma) will go by the name Raghunātha. They will have endless names; O friend, the face of the powerful Rāma will be charming like the calyx of a lotus. His very long (i.e. large) eyes will have the beauty of lotuses. His nose will be raised, large and charming. His eyebrows will be lovely and charming due to their being harmonious. His lovely hands will be hanging up to his knees. His very small neck will be charming like a conch. His chest will be plain and expansive and charming. His chest will be pure and will have a mark. Endowed with the beauty of charming thighs and waist, he will have a pair of knees, pure and naturally adored. His lotus-like feet will always be worshipped by all his (votaries). The very charming Raghupati (will be like this). Rāma possess a form like this. Who am I to describe him? Even one having a hundred mouths cannot describe him. Then what about birds like me? Seeing his form, (even) Lakṣmī, charming and having a beautiful body, was enticed. (Then) which (lady) is there on the earth that will not be enticed? He has great power, great valour, and has a very enticing form. What power do I have to describe Rāma endowed with all glory and virtues?

41-53. Lucky is that queen Jānakī (i.e. Sītā), having a very attractive form, who will gladly enjoy with him for a myriad years. O beautiful lady, who are you? What is your name that you cleverly and respectfully ask me to narrate (the account) of Rāma?" Hearing these words, Jānakī, telling the couple of birds about the charming and enticing (story of) her birth, said to them: "I am that Jānakī, the daughter of Janaka, whom you mentioned. I shall truly release you when that very charming Rāma comes to me; not otherwise—being (just) allured by your words! I shall caress you. You, having (i.e. speaking) sweet words, stay happily (with me)." Hearing these words they trembled and were frightened. They were mutually (i.e. both) afraid; (and) said this to Jānakī: "O good lady, we are birds, living in forests and resorting to trees. We wander everywhere. We would not get happiness (merely by staying) at home. I am pregnant. Having gone to my place and having given birth to sons (i.e. young ones) I shall come (back). I have told you the truth." (Though) thus addressed by the female parrot, she did not release her. Then her husband (i.e. the male parrot), eager, and with his face hung down spoke to her: "Sītā, release my wife. How do you keep this my beautiful wife? We shall go to the forest and shall happily move in the forest. My charming wife would be (i.e. is) pregnant. Having performed her (i.e. after her) delivery I shall come to you, O lovely one?" Thus, addressed, she said to him: "O you very intelligent one, you can gladly go. I shall keep this happy one, doing what is dear to me, near me." Thus addressed, the bird was unhappy; and full of tenderness, he said to her: "Those words which are uttered by the meditating saints are true: (The words are:)

54-56. 'One should not speak, one should not speak. One should remain by resorting to silence. Otherwise, due to the blemish in one's utterance, the mad one would be fettered.' Had we not talked (to each other) on this tree, how would we have been bound? Therefore, one should resort to silence." Saying so, he spoke to her: "O beautiful lady, O Sītā, I shall not live without this wife of me. Therefore, O you charming one, leave her."

57-66. Though admonished with various words, she did not release her. The (parrot's) wife, who was angry, and miserable, then cursed Janaka's daughter: "As you are separating me from my husband, in the same way you will be, when pregnant, separated from Rāma." When she, the afflicted one, was repeatedly saying like this, her life departed due to misery, full of the distress of her husband. For her who was repeatedly remembering Rāma and uttering (the name) Rāma, a divine car properly arrived. The female parrot became luminous when she had gone to heaven. When she died, her husband, that lord of birds, was extremely angry, and being distressed, fell into Gaṅgā: "In Rāma's city, full of people, I will be born as (a śūdra so) that due to my words she will be dejected, and extremely unhappy due to separation (from her husband)." Saying so, he who was distressed, angry, frightened and shaking due to separation from her, fell into the water of Gaṅgā graced with eddies. Due to his being angry, due to his being distressed, and due to his having insulted Sītā, he obtained very (mean) śūdrahood (as he was born as) a washerman named Krodhana. That best bird (or best brāhmaṇa) who, doing ill to the great, abandons his life through anger, obtains śūdrahood after he dies. That took place. Due to the words of the washerman she was censured and separated. On account of the curse of the washerman, she was separated (from Rāma), and she went to the forest.

67. O brāhmaṇa, I have told you what you had asked about (Sītā), born in Videha. Listen to the further account here (i.e. regarding Sītā). I (shall) narrate it.

CHAPTER FIFTYEIGHT

Lakṣmaṇa Leaves Sītā in the Forest

Śeṣa said:

1-8. Seeing Bharata unconscious, Raghunātha who was very much afflicted, said to the door-keepers; "Bring Śatrughna quickly to me." Hearing these words, (the door-keeper), in a moment brought Śatrughna where his brother Rāma remained with Bharata. Seeing Bharata unconscious and Rāma afflicted, he who was grieved, saluted (Rāma) and said: "What has this frightful (incident) come about?" Then Rāma, with his face hung down with a piteous voice and with his words faltering and with tremor, told Śatrughna, the servant of his feet, the words of the śūdra—the popular censure: "O brother, listen, and quickly and carefully do what I tell you, so that my fame will go (i.e. flow) like Gaṅgā on the earth. Having heard the words unequalled in the world, uttered about Sītā by the śūdra, I indeed decided to abandon my body or Jānakī." Hearing these words of Rāma, Śatrughna, the killer of his enemies, being afflicted fell down with a termor on the earth. Having regained consciousness after some time, he said to Raghunātha:

Śatrughna said:

9-13a. O lord, why are these horrible words being talked about Jānakī? Are the sacred texts, censured by the wicked-minded heretics, outcast from all religions, not to be accepted by the brāhmaṇas? Does Gaṅgā that destroys the sins of all the people and that removes calamities, not deserve to be touched by the good, since she is touched by sinful men? In the world the sun rises to give light to the world? What is lost if he is not liked by the owls? Therefore, you (please) accept this (your) wife, (though) censured by a śūdra. O Rāmabhadra, kindly do what I say.

13b-16. Having heard these words of the high-minded Śatrughna he again and again said what he had told Bharata. Hearing those words of his brother, Śatrughna, full of the flood of grief, fell unconscious on the ground like a tree with its roots cut off. Seeing his brother Śatrughna fallen (unconscious), he (i.e. Rāma), being very much afflicted, said these words to the door-keeper: "Bring Lakṣmaṇa near me." He, having gone to Lakṣmaṇa's house, told him these words (i.e. this message).

The door-keeper said:

17-19a. O lord, Rāma has summoned you quickly.

Hearing that summons (made) by Rāma, the sinless one quickly and speedily went where his brother (Rāma) was. Seeing Bharata unconscious, also seeing Śatrughna unconscious, he said (these) words to Śrī Rāmacandra, who was afflicted with grief:

19b-23a. "O king, what is this frightful (scene) like swoon etc. Therefore, O sinless one, tell me the entire main cause." To Lakṣmaṇa who was talking like this and was full of the flood of grief, the king quickly told the entire account from beginning. Hearing those words arising from the deserting of Sītā, he, sighing again and again, had his body as it were stupefied. Seeing his brother with his body stupefied, and repeatedly trembling, and not talking anything, he, afflicted with grief, said:

23b-27a. "Marked with infamy, what shall I do by being (i.e. living) on the earth? I, being afflicted, will abandon, through the fear of the world, this my glorious body. My brothers were always eager to do what I had told them; but, now unfortunately (for me) they are also doing opposite of what I tell them. Where should I go? Whom should I approach? Kings on the earth will laugh at me marked by infamy, as handsome men laugh at a leper. (When) formerly kings were born in Manu's race, they were born with superior qualities. (But) now when I am born that has become false."

27b-33a. Seeing Rāmabhadra speaking like this, he checked his profuse tears, and spoke in a weakened tone: "O lord, do not be dejected. How is it that you are deprived of your understanding? Who are you, learned one (i.e. How does a learned person like you) to abandon Sītā? I shall call the washerman, and ask him: 'How did you censure that Jānakī, the best among ladies?' In your country no small person is forcibly harassed. Therefore, act towards him as there is the conviction about him in your mind. Why do you (unnecessarily) abandon the timid one who is loyal to her husband (i.e. you)? The daughter of Janaka does not know anyone else (but you) mentally or by speech (i.e. she does not think or talk about anyone else). Therefore, accept her; do not abandon Jānakī. Having shown favour to me, resort to (i.e. do) it quickly."

33b-34. To Lakṣmaṇa who was speaking like this, Rāma, who was overpowered with grief and who was determined to abandon Sītā, advising Lakṣmaṇa with words of righteousness, said to him:

Rāma said:

35-41. How do you tell me: 'Do not abandon her?' Though I know her to be sinless, I am abandoning her due to public censure. For the sake of my fame I shall give up my unhappy body. I shall even forsake you, my brother, (if you are) condemned by public censure. Then how much more about other (member of my) family, sons, friends, and splendid wealth? For the sake of my fame, I shall give up everything, indeed Sītā also. To me my brother, my wife, my kinsmen, are not so dear as my beloved, spotless fame, known in the world. Certainly now the washerman is not to be questioned. In course of time the minds of people will be fully satisfied. A disease, as long as it is unripe (i.e. not properly developed), cannot be diagnosed on the earth, but goes away (i.e. is cured) after it has aggravated by means of medicine. Similarly this will take place (i.e. people will be satisfied) in course of time. Now do not delay. Leave this chaste lady in a forest, or kill me with a sword.

42-44. Hearing these words uttered (by Rāma), the great one was pained. Lakṣmaṇa, overpowered with grief, thought in his mind (i.e. to himself): 'Jamadagni's son (Paraśurāma), killed even his mother by the order of his father. The order of an elderly person, whether it is proper or improper, is not at all to be disobeyed. Therefore, with a desire to do what is dear to Rāma, I shall leave her (in the forest).' Thinking like this in his mind (i.e. to himself), he said to his brother:

Lakṣmaṇa said:

45-47. What ought not to be done should even be done. An elderly person's order should not be violated (i.e. disobeyed). Therefore, I shall carry out your words that you speak to me, O you of a good vow.

To Lakṣmaṇa, who was speaking like this, he said: "Good, good, O very intelligent one, you have pleased my mind. Tonight only, under the pretext of (fulfilling) Sītā's cherished wish to see the female ascetics, put her into a chariot and leave her in the great forest."

48-54. Hearing these words, he, with his mouth fully parched, weeping, shedding tears, went to his own house. Having called Sumantra, he said these words to him: "Make ready my chariot, adorned with good horses." He, having heard these words, then brought the chariot. Seeing the chariot that was brought Lakṣmaṇa overpowered with grief, was very much distressed; and he, the servant of his brother (Rāma), got into the excellent chariot, and sighing, went to Sītā's abode, and having gone into the harem and heaving and full of grief, said (these) words to the daughter of Mithilā: "O mother Sītā, Rāma has sent me to you. To fulfil your cherished wish you (can) go the female ascetics." Having heard these words of (i.e. spoken by) Lakṣmaṇa, Sītā who was very much delighted, said to Lakṣmaṇa:

Jānakī said:

55-63. I, Maithilī, who remember Rāma's feet and to fulfil whose cherished wish he sent Lakṣmaṇa, am blessed. Today I shall salute the female ascetics living in the forest, and looking upon their husbands as deities I shall honour the charming ones with (presents of) garments.

Saying so, Raghunātha's wife (Sītā), in order to do what was dear to her, took (with her) charming garments, costly ornaments, gems, spotless pearls, camphor etc. having fragrance, so also various things like sandal in thousands. Repeatedly accepting these (things) from the hands of the female servants and then going to Lakṣmaṇa, Sītā tumbled at the threshold. Not minding it through curiosity, she said to Lakṣmaṇa who did good to her: "Where is the chariot in which you will take me (to the forest)?" Heaving he along with Sītā got into the golden chariot. He said to Sumantra: "Drive the horses having the speed of mind." At the words of Lakṣmaṇa he looking at Lakṣmaṇa's face full of tears called the chariot, well-yoked (with horses). The horses, struck by kim with a whip, fell on the path. When the horses did not move, he said to Lakṣmaṇa:

Sumantra said:

64-78. O lord, though driven with effort, the horses do not move. What should I do? I do not realise the cause of their fall.

To him who was speaking like this, Lakṣmaṇa said in a faltering voice after mustering courage to the charioteer: "Strike these with whips etc." Hearing these words, the charioteer somehow drove them. Then Sītā's right eye, indicating trouble, throbbed. Just then in her heart grief, indicating misfortune, was produced. Just then only, auspicious birds turned round. Seeing these, Sītā said to her brother-in-law: "How is it that I have a desire to go to see the female ascetics. May well-being come to Rāma; so also to his younger brother, Bharata; so also to his subjects everywhere. Let misfortunes not come to them." That Lakṣmaṇa with his throat chocked and full of tears, did not say anything to Sītā who was speaking like this. She (while) going saw deer turning to the left and causing multitudes of miseries.

She said (to Lakṣmaṇa): "It is laid down that since today the deer are turning to the left, it is not proper that I am going after abandoning Rāma's feet. The highest duty of women is to serve their husbands' feet. So, whatever would happen to me who am going after leaving him, (must be said) to be proper only." When the queen (Sītā) was thinking like this on the way, she actually saw Gaṅgā which was resorted to by groups of sages only, in which waves of water resembling milk were seen, in which waves having the form of a staircase to heaven were seen. By the touch of the drops of her water the heap of great sins not finding any place all around, runs away. Having reached Gaṅgā, Lakṣmaṇa shedding tears said to Sītā, seated in the chariot: "Sītā, come down to the ground from the chariot." Having heard his words Sītā with her arms held by him, in a moment got down and on the way tumbled on thorns.

CHAPTER FIFTYNINE

The Birth of Kuśa and Lava

Śeṣa said:

1-8. Then Lakṣmaṇa, having made Sītā cross Gaṅgā in a boat to the other bank, took her by hand and went to the forest. On the way she who was marked with her face parched up, walked. Her good (i.e. delicate) feet were hurt with thorns. She tumbled at every step. At that time Lakṣmaṇa carrying out the order of Rāghava took her into the very fearful forest causing misery, in which there were fierce dense trees like barbula, khadira śleṣmātaka, ciñciṇīka, which were dry due to wild fire. Serpents living in the hollows of trees and getting very angry, hissed. Owls causing fear to the minds of people, cried. (In the forest) artless, very wrathful, tigers, lions, foxes, and elephants, eaters of human beings were noticed. Buffaloes, hogs which were wicked, which were marked with two fangs, afflicted the minds of beings. Sītā seeing such a forest suffered from grief through fear. With her feet pricked by thorns she said (these) words to Lakṣmaṇa.

Jānakī said:

9-12. O hero, I do not see (here) hermitages resorted to by sages and giving joy to the eyes. Nor do I see their wives having a great treasure of penance. I am only seeing fearful birds and dry trees. This entire forest is being burnt by wild fire. I notice you too with your eyes full of tears. At every step I am experiencing a thousand ill omens. Therefore, O best hero, tell me whether I of a wicked heart, am abandoned by the noble Rāma. Tell it to me quickly.

13-18. Hearing these words, Lakṣmaṇa, overpowered with grief, and with tears (flowing) on his face checked, then said nothing. She, afflicted with grief and moving with Lakṣmaṇa in that forest only looked at his face and again spoke to that hero; yet, he, desiring to see something, did not say anything to her. Then, (when) she asked him, she very much insisted (on getting a reply). When Lakṣmaṇa was asked by Sītā persistently, he with his throat choked and repeatedly repenting, told her the reason why she was deserted. Hearing those words like (the fall of) the thunderbolt, she, (though) free from any disease, became like a good creeper with its roots cut off. Just then the Earth did not take (back) this daughter (i.e. Sītā) of her, since she believed that Rāma would not abandon sinless Sītā.

19-24. Seeing Sītā fallen down, Lakṣmaṇa, eager (to revive her) revived her by means of breezes produced by (the movements of) the tips of sprouts. Having regained consciousness, she said, "O brother-in-law, do not joke. How does the descendant of Raghu abandon me who am sinless?" Having thus moaned much, she, having seen Lakṣmaṇa full of grief, being fully distressed, fell unconscious on the ground. Having regained consciousness after a while, she full of grief and hurt by sorrow, (and) remembering Rāma's feet, said: "How does that very intelligent, great Raghunātha who along with the monkeys restrained the ocean for my sake, abandon me? How will that great hero abandon me by (relying) upon the words of the washerman? Now, my destiny is unfavourable."

25-32. Saying so the daughter of the Videha(-king) again swooned. Seeing her unconscious he wept in a tone affected by emotion. Having regained consciousness she who was very much distressed, looked at Lakṣmaṇa who was afflicted with grief and whose throat was choked, and said to him: "O Lakṣmaṇa, go to Rāma, the (very) image of Dharma and the treasure of glory, and tell him these my words in the presence of the treasure of penance: 'Even knowing me to be sinless, you abandoned me. Does it behove your family, or is it the fruit of your knowledge of the sacred texts? You abandoned me who was always attached to your feet, who always ate what was left over by you. For all that my destiny is the cause (i.e. is responsible). O best among excellent warriors, may you have welfare everywhere. Remembering you mentally, in deeds and speech, I shall just hold my breath (i.e. live) in the forest. All others were mentally abandoned by me, O you born in the family of Raghu. O lord of the earth, you alone should be my husband in every birth: I who remember your feet, have all my sins destroyed and have become the best chaste lady.'

33-39. O best of the Raghus, convey all my message to my mothers-in-law. 'I (though) sinless, have been abandoned in the very fierce forest. I remember your feet in the forest, full of herds of deer. The very noble Rāma abandoned me (though) pregnant in the forest.' O Lakṣmaṇa, listen to my words. May well-being come to you. Now preserving well Rāma's semen (in my womb), I would give up my life. As you are proving true Rāma's words, you will have prosperity. One serving the lotus-like feet of Rāma, and depending upon another, has to do it. I should be favoured, and be remembered at times." Saying so, she fell unconscious on the ground in front (of Lakṣmaṇa). Seeing Jānakī unconscious, Lakṣmaṇa became afflicted. Saumitri (i.e. Lakṣmaṇa) fanned her with the ends of his garment, and having saluted her who had regained consciousness, he repeatedly consoled her with sweet words.

Lakṣmaṇa said:

40-43a. This I (i.e. I Just) go to Rāma; and will tell him everything. Near you, there is the great hermitage of the sage Vālmīki.

Speaking thus to her, he being afflicted and full of tears, turned round, and shedding tears, sorrowfully went to king

Rāma. Seeing her brother-in-law going, Jānakī with amazed eyes (said): "This my noble brother-in-law is joking. How (is it that) Rāghava abandoned me who was dearer to Rāma than his own life!"

43b-50. Thinking like this, she looked at him with unwinking eyes. Realising on his having crossed Jāhnavī (i.e. Gaṅgā) that her desertion by Rāma was a fact, she fell down, was in a very great peril, and fainted. At that time swans brought water from all places and sprinkled (it over her). Sweet fragrant breezes blew. Elephants with the tips of their tongues full of (i.e. wet with) water, washed as it were, her body covered with dust. Deer came near her with their eyes full of wonder. At that time, trees were full of flowers, without the spring (i.e though it was not the spring season). When this was the time (i.e. when so much time passed), the chaste lady regained consciousness and being very much afflicted with grief, and saying 'Rāma, Rāma', moaned. "O lord, O friend of the poor, O good treasure full of pity, how do you abandon me in the forest without my fault?" She talked like this; she wept again and again. She looked here and there; and she again and again became unconscious.

51-55a. At that time revered Vālmīki had come to the forest. At that time he heard weeping with piteous words. He then said to his disciples: "Find out from the interior of the forest who is weeping in a distressed tone in the forest." Ordered by the sage, they went to the place where Jānakī saying 'Rāma, Rāma' and full of a flood of tears, was sitting. Seeing that they eagerly came back to the sage Vālmīki. Having heard the words uttered by them, the sage then went (there). Seeing that heap of penance (i.e. Vālmīki), Jānakī who looked upon her husband as a deity, (said):

55b-58. "My salution to the sage, the image of the Vedas, the ocean of religious acts of austerity." He greeted that Sītā who was saying like this with blessings. "Live long with your husband; obtain two bright sons. Who are you? Why have you come to the fearful forest? Why are you like this? Tell me everything, I would (like to) know the cause of your sorrow." Heaving and with tremor produced in her body, Rāma's wife then spoke with piteous words to the sage:

59-63. "Listen to my significant words—the cause of all my sorrow. Know me to be the servant of king Raghunātha. I have been abandoned without a fault. I do not know the reason for that. By Rāma's order Lakṣmaṇa left me here and went (back)." Vālmīki, consoling Sītā having lotus-like eyes and lotus-like face full of tears, and who had said like this, spoke to Sītā: "Know me to be the sage Vālmīki who is your father's preceptor. O Vaidehī, do not be afflicted, come to my hermitage. O you who look upon your husband as a deity, suppose that your father's house is (situated) at a different place. In such an act (i.e. when such an act is done), let me be angry with the king (i.e. Rāma) (i.e. I would be angry with Rāma, and not with you)."

64. Hearing words like these, Jānakī who looked upon her husband as a deity, who was full of affliction, and whose face was full of tears, was a little happy."

Śeṣa said:

65-68. Having consoled her whose eyes were full with the flood of grief, Vālmīki took her to his auspicious hermitage full of the groups of female ascetics. She, going after Vālmīki, the treasure of penance, shone like a charming star going after the moon. Having reached his hermitage full of sages, Vālmīki told the female ascetics about Jānakī who had come to his hermitage. Vaidehī, of a noble mind, saluted all the female ascetics. Being very much delighted, they embraced one another.

69-72. That treasure of penance, Vālmīki, said to his disciples: "Construct a beautiful hut of leaves for Jānakī." Hearing these very pleasant words of Vālmīki, they constructed an attractive hut with leaves and (pieces of) wood. Waiting upon Vālmīki and eating (i.e. subsisting upon) fruits, Vaidehī, a chaste wife, lived in it. Jānakī who looked upon her husband as a deity muttering 'Rāma, Rāma', (both) mentally and in words, passed her days there.

73-80a. At (the proper) time Jānakī gave birth to two sons, having charming bodies, and having the likeness of Rāma and like (the two) Aśvins. Hearing about the birth of the two sons of Jānakī, the sage was delighted; he who knew the sacred prayers, performed the purificatory rites like the ceremony performed at the time of the birth of a child. Vālmīki performed (these) rites with darbhas and the hair of a cow's tail. So the two sons have well-known names Kuśa and Lava. Vālmīki also performed the auspicious rites where she free from menstrual excretion (i.e. who had given birth to a child) remained, in such a way that she having lotus-like eyes, was very much delighted in her heart. The same day, Śatrughna, with a few soldiers, had, after killing Lavaṇa, come to Vālmīki's pleasant hermitage at night. At that time Vālmīki had directed Śatrughna: "Do not tell Rāma about Jānakī's sons. I shall (later) tell it (to him)." The attractive sons of Jānakī grew there (i.e. in Vālmīki's hermitage). Vālmīki brought up the two joyful excellent (boys) with bulbs, roots and fruits. The two, very charming like the moon of the first day of the bright half (of a month), were purified (with rites) in due course.

80b-86. The two charming ones were initiated into sacred study (by Vālmīki). Having initiated them into sacred study, the sage taught the two boys the Vedas with their six limbs. He taught them the science of archery with its secrets and Rāmāyaṇa. Vālmīki gave them two bows well adorned with gold; (the bows were) unbreakable, had strings, and were best in warding off the groups of enemies. (He gave them) two inexhaustible quivers full of arrows, and two swords. He (also) gave to Jānakī's two sons, shields that could not be pierced through. The two archers who had mastered the Vedas, gladly moving in the hermitage, shone like the two bright Aśvins. Seeing (her) two excellent sons holding swords and shields, Jānakī was very much delighted and gave up (the grief) due to her desertion (by Rāma). O brāhmaṇa, I have told you this account of the birth of Jānakī's sons. Hereafter listen to the cutting off of the arms of the soldiers that took place.

CHAPTER SIXTY

Lava Defeats the Army and Kills the General

Śeṣa said:

1-4. Seeing his soldiers with their arms cut off, Śatrughna getting very angry and biting his lower lip with anger, said to them: "O you, which hero has cut off your arms? I shall cut off both the arms of him, (even though he is) protected by gods, O soldiers. The great fool does not know (anything about) the great might of Rāmacandra. Now through my valour I shall show (him) my might. Where is that hero? Where is the charming hero? Which fool, not knowing the valour, would seize sleeping serpents?" When the heroes were told (like this) they were amazed and much afflicted.

5-10a. They told (him) about the child that had the likeness of Rāmacandra. He on hearing the seizure of the horse by the boy, had his eyes red due to anger and willing to fight he ordered his general Kālajit: "O general, by my order array the entire army. We have to encounter a very mighty and brave enemy. This is not a child who has seized the horse. He might be Viṣṇu or he might be Śiva. My horse could not have been taken away in any other way. Certainly a great destruction of the mighty army will take place. The boy with a fearless mind, is playing (doing) acts according to his own will. We difficult to be conquered by our enemies, should get ready and go there."

10b-14a. Hearing these words of Śatrughna, that general of the army made ready that army which was arranged in (such) a way that it would be hard (for the enemy to dislodge it) and which had four divisions. Śatrughna, having seen that excellent (complete) army with four divisions made ready, ordered it to go to that place where the boy who had seized the horse, stood. Then the army moved with the four divisions causing that part of the earth to quake and scaring by its might the enemies. The generl saw that boy having a form (like that) of Rāma. Thinking (i.e. finding) him to be the likeness of Rāma, he spoke to him beneficial words:

14b-21a. "O boy, leave the best horse of the powerful

Rāma. I am the ferocious general, named Kālajit, of the king. Seeing you resembling Rāma, pity is produced in my heart. Otherwise, you will not live due to the suffering caused by me." Having heard these words of the warrior of Śatrughna (i.e. of Kālajit), the boy laughed a little, and with a little wrath said (these) wonderful words: "Go, you are free; report to that Rāma the seizure of the horse. O brave one, I am not afraid of you by means of (i.e. though you have uttered) words of political wisdom. I do not care (even) if crores like you (encounter me). Due to the grace of my mother's feet, they are to me (as light) as cotton. That your name which your beautiful mother gave to you, is only due to complexion and not due to valour, like the ripe bimba fruit (having red colour but no efficacy). Now, characterised by (i.e. on) the strength of your name (Kālajit), show me your valour. You will prove your name to be true vanquishing me who am your death."

Śeṣa said:

21b-25a. He, the crest (i.e. the best) of excellent warriors, disturbed by the words like thunderbolt, got very angry in his mind, and again said (these) words: "O boy, in which family are you born? What is your name? I do not know your name, so also your family and your virtue. How can I, being in a chariot, conquer you who go on foot (i.e. are a foot-soldier), by following the prescribed course of conduct?" Then, he got very angry, and again said these words: "O warrior, what is the use of (your knowing) my family, my virtue, or my name? I am Lava and will in a moment vanquish all the soldiers of my enemy. Now I shall even make a warrior like you (seated in a chariot) go on foot (i.e. a foot-soldier)."

25b-33. Speaking like this, that mighty Lava made ready his bow; he made the twang-sound (of the bow) and scared the soldiers at heart. Having recollected Vālmīki first and (then) his mother Jānakī, Lava discharged sharp arrows which instantly took away the life (of his enemies). Kālajit who was angry, made his bow ready and he who was quick and proficient in fighting, struck Lava. The younger brother of Kuśa (i.e. Lava) in a moment quickly cut off his arrows into hundred (pieces) and deprived the general of his chariot by means of bright, excellent arrows. He who was deprived of his chariot, mounted upon an intoxicated, very speedy elephant which (i.e. whose ichor) was flowing in seven ways (i.e. streams) and which was brought by his soldiers. The victor (i.e. Lava), seeing him mounted upon an elephant, laughed, and pierced all the hosts of the enemies with ten arrows fixed on his bow. Kālajit, seeing his valour, and with his mind amazed, threw (at him) a big mace made of great (i.e. strong) iron. (Lava), the younger brother of Kuśa, seeing the mace, made with (i.e. weighing) a myriad of bhāras coming to him speedily, cut it off quickly into three pieces with arrows having sharp, horse-shoe-shaped heads.

34-40. He then discharged (at Lava) a sharp, fierce iron club, out to take away his life. Lava, full of speed, cut it off. Having cut off the fierce iron club, he, with his eyes red due to anger, observing him to have mounted upon the haunch of an elephant, became angry. At that moment (only) he cut off with his sword the trunk of that elephant. Supporting his feet with (i.e. standing on) the tusks of the elephant, he mounted on his head. Having cut off the general's crown into a hundred pieces, and his armour into a hundred pieces, and having dragged the general with (i.e. by seizing) his hair he knocked him down on the ground. The general knocked down from the haunch of the elephant, again got angry. He struck him on his chest with his thunderbolt-like fist; he, struck with fists, having bent his bow, quickly discharged arrows with sharp horse-shoe-shaped arrows at his chest. He who had bent his bow and who had put on a helmet and an armour unbreakable even by crores of arrows, shone on the battlefield. He pierced by sharp arrows, took a sword to kill him.

41-48a. Lava, gnawing his teeth through anger, and repeatedly heaving and breathing, cut off the centre of the arm of the general who was coming with a sword in his hand. He, with the sword in his hand fell down. The general, seeing that his (right) hand holding the sword was cut off, angrily went to strike him with a mace (held) with the left (hand). That arm of him along with the armlets was also cut off with sharp arrows. Then the hero, getting extremely angry struck Lava with his feet. Lava, (though) struck by his feet, did not move on the battlefield. He bore up the cutting off of the feet like an elephant struck with a garland. Even then he started striking him with his head. Then Lava, looking upon the general as having superior valour, took a sword resembling the destructive fire at the end of the world in his hand, and cut off his head adorned with a large crown. When the general was struck down, there was a great wailing. The angry soldiers came (forward) to kill Lava.

48b-57a. By striking them with his arrows, Lava made them intent on fleeing. Some were broken; some were pierced; some went (away) from the battlefield. Having warded off all soldiers, he gladly penetrated the army, as the hog, having heaved, plunges into the great ocean at the time of the deluge. The elephants were pierced and cut into two, and the earth was filled with pearls, and became inaccessible for the great warriors (when) it is covered with mountains. Horses, shining with power, having golden saddles, charming, and decorated with gems, fell into the pool wet (i.e. full) with blood. The warriors fighting from chariots, who looked lovely on account of the bows in their hands, fell into the interior of the chariots like gods going to heaven. Warriors skilled in fighting, who bit their lips, marked with charm revolving round their faces, were seen to have fallen there. A river of blood, with the tortoises in the form of horses' heads and charming due to its great stream and causing fear to the enemies, flew (there). The arms of some were cut off; the feet of some were chopped off. The ears and noses and armours and earrings of some were cut off. When the general fell in the battle, such (was the) destruction (that) took place. All heroes fell down. None survived then.

57b-67. Lava, having got victory in the battle and having vanquished the host of his enemies, thinking that someone else might come, looked (everywhere). Some who were spared from the battle, did not die on the battlefield. They went near Śatrughna to tell him (about) the wonderful account. Having gone (to him), they told him (the account) as it took place on the battlefield—the death of Kālajit from (i.e. at the hands of) the boy, and his wonderful effort in the battle. Hearing that, Śatrughna who was amazed, laughed, and remembering the seizure of the horse by the boy, gnawed his teeth in anger, and said to them: "O heroes, were you intoxicated, or were you cheating imps? How did incompetency overcome you? How did Kālajit die? How would a boy vanquish him who was fearful to the hosts of enemies in the battle, who was (always) victorious in a battle, and who was invincible even for Yama?" Hearing the words of Śatrughna, the warriors, wet with blood, said: "We were not under the influence of intoxication etc. There was no fraud, nor gambling. O king, know that Kālajit had his death from (i.e. at the hands of) Lava. The boy having matchless skill, shook the entire army. (Now you decide) what is to be done hereafter, or which excellent men should be sent (against Lava). Thinking him to be a child, you should not use your force rashly." Then Śatrughna, having heard these words of the warriors, spoke to Sumati, the best intellect, about the waging of the war.

CHAPTER SIXTYONE

Hanūmat Falls Unconscious

Śatrughna said:

1. O great minister, do you know who is the boy that took away the horse and who destroyed all my army like an ocean?

Sumati said:

3-5. O lord, this is the great hermitage of the best sage Vālmīki. O you who torment your enemies, kṣatriyas do not at all live here. It might be that Indra became (i.e. took the form of) the great sage and snatched the horse, or it might be Śiva. Otherwise, who else would take away your horse? O great king, who else but Puṣkala can go to (i.e. march against) him who killed the very fearful Kālajit? O you destroyer of your enemies, go there surrounded by all your brave warriors, kings, and your great army.

6-8. Having gone there, having bound the hero, I shall show it to Rāma, who has a curiosity. This is my careful (i.e. well-considered) view.

Hearing these words, he ordered all his warriors: "Go with a great army. I (shall) come after you." In a moment the soldiers went there where the mighty one (i.e. Lava), stretching his very strong bow furnished with a string, stood.

9-11. Having seen that very mighty army full of warriors, coming, the powerful Lava was not at all afraid in his mind. Lava, looking upon all the warriors as deer, angrily stretched his bow, and discharging arrows in thousands, stood up like a lion. They, being afflicted by the arrows, and full of great anger, looking upon the hero as a boy, then rushed to him.

12-14. Seeing thousands of warriors arrayed in a circular arrangement of the troops, Lava, full of anger, quickly fixed arrows (on his bow). The first circular arrangement had a thousand (soldiers). The second had ten thousand as the number (of soldiers). The third had twenty thousand; the fourth had fifty thousand; the fifth had a lakh of soldiers; the sixth had ten thousand more; and the seventh had a couple of lakhs. He was surrounded by seven (such) circular arrangements of the troops.

15-16. In the midst was Lava, surrounded by the circular arrangements of the troops; and moving like fire he burnt (i.e. destroyed) all the soldiers forming the circular arrangements. The noble one destroyed all the arrangement(s)—some with swords, some with arrows, some with barbed missiles, some with lances, (some) with spears having sharp edges, and some with clubs tipped with iron.

17-21. The younger brother of Kuśa, freed from the seven circular arrangements of the troops, shone like the moon freed from the group of clouds at the advent of the autumn. He with his disc cut off many trunks of elephants and mighty heads of warriors, and completely struck (down) the warriors. Afflicted by Lava's arrows many fell and fainted on the battlefield; others, very timid, fled away. Seeing the army afflicted by Lava's arrows, intent on fleeing, the hero named Puṣkala went to the battlefield to fight. The mighty one, seated in his chariot, charming due to good horse, saying, 'Wait, wait' and with his eyes full of anger, went to (i.e. marched against) Lava.

22-23a. That Puṣkala knowing the (use of) great missiles, said to Lava: "Stand in the chariot adorned with good horses in the battle. How shall I fight with you—a foot-soldier—in the battle? Therefore, stand in the chariot, and then I shall fight with you."

23b-26. Hearing these words, Lava said to Puṣkala: "If I standing in your chariot, fight in the battle, then my victory would be doubtful. O hero, we are not brāhmaṇas given to receiving (gifts), but we are kṣatriyas, always engaged in acts of charity. Now, through anger I shall break your chariot. Then you will (also) be fighting on foot. Then you will fight (with me)."

27-29. Puṣkala having heard these words full of righteousness and courage, was amazed in heart for a long time and made ready his bow. Lava seeing him having taken a bow, got angry and cut off the bow in his hand, and took an aim with his arrow. The powerful one, laughed and being excited broke his chariot in the battlefield, while he was stringing his bow.

30-35. Seeing his chariot broken and his bow cut off by the noble one, he regarded him as a great hero, and the fighter on foot ran away in the battlefield. Both heroes were heroes; both had raised their arrows; both were wet with blood; both had their armours cut off. Both were seen to have their bodies shattered with the strokes of arrows of each other; both desired victory; both desired to kill each other like Jayanta and Kārtikeya or Śiva and Indra. In this way they fought with each other on the battlefield. Puṣkala said to the boy: "O crest-jewel of the brave, I have not seen a crest-jewel (i.e. best) of the brave like you. Today I shall knock down your head with arrows having sharp, fine joints. Do not run from the battlefield. Being restrained, protect your life."

36-39. Saying so he put brave Lava in the cage of (i.e. formed by) arrows. Puṣkala's arrows settled on the ground after having pervaded the sky. Lava, being in the cage of (i.e. formed by) arrows, said to Puṣkala: "O hero, you have done a great feat that you harassed me with arrows". Saying so, the hero skilled in taking aim with an arrow and cutting off the volley of arrows, said to Puṣkala: "Take care of yourself (while) standing in the battle. Afflicted by the strokes of my arrows, you will fall covered with blood, on the earth."

40-45. Having heard these words, Puṣkala, full of anger, fought with the very strong hero in the battle. Lava, getting angry in a moment angrily took out a sharp arrow (capable of) killing the enemy and resembling a serpent from the quiver. That blazing arrow discharged from Lava's bow and ready to pierce his chest was quickly cut off by Bharata's son (Puṣkala). When Bharata's son cut off with his fatal arrow (the arrow of Lava), he got very angry and took another fierce arrow. The sharp arrow discharged from the bow drawn up to the ear, pierced the chest of that Puṣkala in the great battle. The crest-jewel of the very brave, pierced in the chest by that fast going arrow, fell on the ground.

46-54. Seeing Puṣkala fallen, the son of Wind (i.e. Hanūmat) took him who was unconscious and handed him over to (Śatrughna) brother of Rāghava. Seeing him unconscious, he, with his mind overcome with grief and full of anger, ordered Hanūmat to kill Lava. Hanūmat, burning with rage, uprooted a śālmali tree and quickly went (i.e. rushed) to vanquish in the battle the very powerful Lava. The mighty Hanūmat struck on Lava's head with the tree. Lava, seeing it falling upon (him), quickly cut it off into hundred (pieces). When the tree was cut off, the very mighty one again angrily uprooted trees from the root and struck them on his chest and head. The mighty one speedily cut off with his arrows of sharp joints those trees which Wind's son (i.e. Hanūmat) took, and with which he struck him. Then the monkey, Wind's son, having uprooted rocks like high rocks thrown down by an earthquake, speedily threw them on the head (of Lava). Struck by those multitudes of rocks in the battle, he raised his bow and powdered them with his arrows as particles with turners' wheels.

55-62. Then, in the battle the angry blessed Hanūmat encircled the mighty Lava with his tail. Seeing himself tied up with his tail, he the powerful one, remembering his mother in his heart, struck with his fist Hanūmat's tail. Distressed by the strokes of the fist, Hanūmat freed him. He the powerful one, freed from the tail, discharged arrows in the battle. The monkey with his body afflicted by the unavoidable strokes of arrows, looking upon the shower of arrows as very unbearable thought: 'What should we do here? If I run away then it is shameful for my lord; (If I stay here), the boy would strike me. Due to the boon given to me by Brahmadatta, I had neither a swoon, nor did I die. The affliction caused by the arrows is unbearable. Let Śatrughna go to (i.e. march against) Lava in the battle and get victory over the boy. I desiring victory, shall lie in false swoon!' Thinking like this in his mind, he fell on the battlefield, fraudulently unconscious when all the heroes were seeing (i.e. in the presence of all the heroes). He, skilled in discharging arrows, knowing that the very mighty Hanūmat was unconscious, struck all the kings (with arrows).

CHAPTER SIXTYTWO

Lava Becomes Unconscious

Śeṣa said:

1-14. Hearing that Hanūmat was unconscious, Śatrughna was distressed: 'What should I do in the battle? This boy is very powerful.' Himself seated in a golden chariot along with excellent heroes he went where Lava, skilled in fighting in a wonderful way, stood. He saw Lava, as if Rāma reduced to childhood had come on the earth, having a bow and arrows in his hand and discharging (arrows) in the battle. At that time he thought: 'Who is this having Rāma's form and having a charming body dark like the petals of a blue lotus? This must be the son of (Sītā) the daughter of (the king of) Videha; not otherwise (i.e. none else), (who) having vanquished us in the battle, will go like the lord of beasts. There is no possibility of the victory of us who are void of power. What shall we, (though) proficient in fighting, (yet) being weak, do?' He, having thought like this, said (these) words to the boy who fought with vehemence, knocking down crores of heroes: "O boy, who are you that are knocking down our heroes on the ground? You do not know the power of Rāma who killed the demons. Who is your mother? Who is your father? Being very lucky, you got victory. O you very mighty one, what is your name well-known in the world? Release (the horse); how (i.e. why) have you caught the horse? (Since it is) due to your being a child, I forgive you. Come, see Rāma, he will give you large (wealth)." The boy who was addressed like this, said (these) words to Śatrughna: "What have you to do with my name, or my father, or my family, or my age? O hero, if you are endowed with power, then fight (with me) in the battle; otherwise, salute the hero Kuśa (by falling) at his feet; otherwise you cannot go. You are the brave brother of Rāma; (but) for us you are not the best among the mighty. If you have power, then forcibly release the horse." Saying so, the mighty warrior, taking aim with his arrow, struck him on his chest, head and arms on the battlefield.

15-27. Then the king (Śatrughna) got angry, and making a grave sound like that of the clouds, and as it were scaring the boy (i.e. in order to scare the boy) made his bow ready. The best among the mighty discharged innumerable arrows. The boy powerfully cut off all those volleys of arrows. The surface of the earth was pervaded by the arrows discharged by Lava in many ways. They became inexhaustible (i.e. did not fail) like gifts given on a day of a great portentous calamity. Those arrows fixed (on his bow) by Lava pervaded the entire sky. Having reached the sun's orb, they proceeded uninterruptedly everywhere. Even the wind did (i.e. could) not enter the cage of his arrows. Then what can be said about human beings said to live for a moment? Seeing these arrows spreading on, Śatrughna was amazed. Skilled in discharging arrows he cut off a hundred thousand (arrows). Seeing all his arrows cut off, the younger brother of Kuśa (i.e. Lava) quickly cut off the bow of king Śatrughna. When, having taken another bow, he discharged his arrows, he shattered the chariot with arrows having sharp joints. He cut off, the very strong bow in his hand, that had a string. The heroes remaining on the battlefield, appreciated that feat. He, with his bow cut off, deprived of his chariot, with his horses killed, with his charioteer killed, resorted to another chariot, went to fight forcibly with Lava. Pierced with many arrows, with blood flowing from his body, he shone in the battle like a kiṁśuka tree with flowers. Struck by the arrows of Śatrughna, he, skilled in aiming with an arrow, and having bent his bow became very angry. He made Śatrughna's body such that its armour was shattered, that the head was bereft of the crown and wet with the flowing blood.

28-38. Then Rāma's younger brother (Śatrughna) got angry; and he who was extremely angry discharged ten fatal arrows having sharp tips. Having reduced them to very small pieces like the sesamum seeds with his arrows having sharp joints, he struck on Śatrughna's chest with eight arrows. Very much afflicted with (the strokes of) the arrows and thinking of the mighty Lava and regarding him to be invincible, he discharged arrows at that time. Then Lava pierced him in his large chest with an arrow resembling the crescent moon and looking charming in the joints. Pierced in the chest, he received a terrible affliction. He, having a bow in his hands and well-adorned, fell into the interior of the chariot. Seeing Śatrughna unconscious, Suratha and other kings, eager to get victory in the battle ran to Lava. Suratha, the brave Vimala, so also king Vīramaṇi, Sumada, Riputāpa and others surrounded him in the battle. Certain kings struck him all round with arrows having sharp horse-shoe-shaped heads, pestles; some with very fierce arrows; some with darts and hatchets. The crest-jewel among the fighting heroes, seeing them eager to fight unjustly, struck them (each) with ten arrows in the battle. They, struck with showers of arrows in the battle, were very angry. Some fled away and some fainted on the battlefield. Just then, king Śatrughna, full of might, gave up his unconsciousness (i.e. regained consciousness) and went to fight with the great warrior Lava.

39-47. Having come (to him), he said to that Lava: "You who are like a boy, are lucky. You are not a boy; you are a god; you have come to outwit (us). I was never vanquished by any hero in battle. You have made me unconscious, when I am seeing (i.e. under my very nose). Now see my valour. I shall knock you down in the battle; put up with (at least) one arrow; O boy, do not run away." Saying so, he who had destroyed Lavaṇa, fierce like Yama's face, took an arrow in the battle. (Then) he fixed a blazing arrow and decided to strike on the chest of Lava who was like fire burning everything, all the heroes. Seeing that blazing arrow illumining the ten quarters, he remembered Kuśa who knocked down his enemies. 'If at this time my strong, brave brother were here, I would not have been humbled by Śatrughna, and there would not have been excessive fear.' When the noble Lava was thinking like this, a mighty, fierce arrow resembling the destructive fire at the end of the world, stuck to (i.e. struck) his chest. At that time the hero, struck by the king's arrow became unconscious in the battle adorned with the heads of all heroes.

CHAPTER SIXTYTHREE

Kuśa's Victory

Śeṣa said:

1-3. Seeing Lava, the destroyer of his enemies, unconscious, Śatrughna, the very mighty one, obtained victory in the battle. Putting Lava, the boy adorned with a helmet etc. and the likeness of Rāma in form, in the chariot he desired to go from there. Seeing that their friend was arrested by the enemy, the boys who were full of grief, quickly reported it to his mother, Sītā.

The boys said:

4-9. O mother Jānakī, your son forcibly snatched the horse of some proud king endowed with power. Then, O Jānakī, the great brave boy vanquished all the army. Later also he got victory. Having made that king unconscious, he obtained victory in the battle. Then the very fearful king, having given up the swoon (i.e. having regained consciousness), got angry and knocked down your son on the battlefield. We had in the beginning warded him off (saying): "Do not seize this excellent horse." Despising all of us, the brāhmaṇas who have mastered the Vedas, (he seized him)."

Hearing these very terrible words of the boys, she fell on the ground and full of grief she wept.

Sītā said:

10-20. How is the cruel king fighting with the boy? He who

has vanquished my son, has a wicked mind as a result of impious deeds. O hero Lava, where are you, full of great power? How (is it that) you seized the excellent horse of the unkind king? You are a boy, they are invincible and proficient in (the use of) all weapons. They were in their chariots, (while) you were without a chariot? How can the fight (be said to) be (between two) equal (parties)? With you (i.e. in your company) I gave up (i.e. did not mind) the unhappiness due to Rāma's having abandoned me. Now without you, how shall I live in the forest? Come to me; release the sarcificial horse; let this king go. You who wash away (i.e. remove) my sorrow, do not realise my sorrow. Had Kuśa, the crest-jewel of the brave, been here today, he would have (by) now freed you from the vicinity of the king. Due to my (bad) luck he too is not nearby. Now what shall I do? It is just my fate that is the cause for the rise of (this) sorrow.

The glorious one scratching the earth with the toe of her foot and with tears in both her eyes, wept much like this. She said to the boys: "This one (i.e. Lava) is a child, and he (i.e. Śatrughna) is a king. How and where will he go on having vanquished my son in the battle?" When this Jānakī who looked upon her husband as her god was speaking like this, Kuśa along with great sages came (back) from Ujjayinī. After having worshipped Mahākāla on the fourteenth day of the dark half of Māgha and after having secured many boons from him, he came in the vicinity of (i.e. to) his mother.

21-28a. Seeing Jānakī afflicted and overcome with fear and with tears produced in her eyes, and helpless due to being overcome with grief, he, being anxious, said. At that time, his (right) arm, throbbing and indicating fight, said (to him). In the heart of the mighty warrior there was great enthusiasm to fight. He spoke to his mother, speaking piteously in a faltering voice: "When I, your son, have stood by you, your affliction has gone. When I am alive, tears should not fall from (your) eyes." He, of a courageous mind, said to his mother who was sad with tears, who was speaking in a piteous and faltering voice, who was instantly unhappy due to Lava's being bounded by grief. "Where is my brother, the destroyer of his enemies, who having come to have known that I have arrived, would always come near me?

How (is it that) the hero is not seen? Where has the hero gone to play? Or with whom has he, due to his being a child, gone to see (i.e. look for) me? O my mother, why do you weep? Where is that Lava (now)? Tell me all that is the cause of your grief."

28b-32. Hearing those words of her son, she who was afflicted, said to Kuśa: "Some king, protecting a horse, has seized Lava. My boy bound here the horse fit for the sacrificial rite. The mighty one, all alone vanquished many guards (of the horse). The king, having made him unconscious, bound him in the battle. The boys who had gone with him, told me like this. Then having heard that Lava was arrested, I became distressed. (Now) you who have come in time (should) forcibly release him from the excellent king." Having heard his mother's words, Kuśa, full of anger, biting his lips and gnawing his teeth, said to her:

Kuśa said:

33-38. O mother, know that Lava is (surely) freed from the binding by the noose. With my arrows I (shall) now kill him with his entire army and horses (and elephants). Even if a god or a deity comes, or even Śiva comes, I shall free him with arrows having sharp joints. O mother, do not weep; vigourous fight here (i.e. in this world) leads to fame; (but) running away leads to infamy. O mother, give me a divine armour, and a bow with a string, so also a helmet and a sharp sword. Now I shall go to the battlefield; I shall vanquish the mighty army; I shall free my brother fainted on the battlefield. If, O mother, I do not to-day release your son from the great battle, then let your feet be angry with me on the earth.

Śeṣa said:

39-44a. With these words Jānakī, of auspicious characteristics, endowed him with blessings and gave him all the multitude of missiles: "O (my) son, go to fight, and free the unconscious Lava": Thus ordered, Kuśa who had put on an armour, who was decorated with ear-rings, who was powerful, who had worn a crown, who had a sword, who had a shield, who held a bow after putting the inexhaustible quiver on his shoulders powerful like those of the lion, and who was the best among the warriors, saluted his mother's feet, and quickly went (to fight). When he speedily and quickly went to fight, he saw his (brother) Lava, the destroyer of hosts of enemies. The very great warriors saw Kuśa coming like Yama approaching to destrory the entire universe.

44b-51. Lava, seeing his very mighty brother Kuśa resembling wind, coming, shone very much like fire. Having freed himself from the chariot, he went out to fight. Kuśa threw all the heroes on the battlefield into the eastern direction. Lava, through anger, urged on (i.e. made flee) all of them into the western direction. O sage, the men in the army, pervaded by affliction caused by Kuśa's arrows and troubled by Lava's arrows resembled the eddies in the ocean with the waves rising. The entire army, troubled by the volleys of the arrows of Kuśa and Lava, did not get happiness. The frightened army repeatedly scattered here and there. No one endowed with might remained anywhere on the battlefield and desired to fight. At this time Śatrughna who tormented his enemies went to fight with the hero Kuśa resembling Lava. The killer of the heroes of his enemy seated in a golden chariot, seeing Kuśa full of power and resembling Rāma's form, said:

Śatrughna said:

52-56. Who are you, very mighty one, and resembling your brother Lava? O great hero, what is your name? Who is your father? Who is your mother? O best of men, how (is it that) you are staying in the forest resorted to by brāhmaṇas? O very powerful one, tell me everything so that I shall fight with you.

Hearing these words, Kuśa, filling with noise the battlefield with his voice grave like that of the clouds, spoke to the king: "(I know) only (that) Sītā, devoted to her husband, gave me birth. Devoted to worshipping the feet of Vālmīki, we two live in the forest. O sinless king, we are engaged in serving our mother, are proficient in all lores (sciences and arts); we are known as Kuśa and Lava.

57-65. Who are you, the hero, desiring to fight? Why is the excellent horse let loose? Today in the fight, you, possessing power, are the victor. O king, if you are a warrior, fight with me. Now I shall knock you down in the battle." Śatrughna, knowing him to be the son of Sītā from Rāma, was amazed in his heart and angrily took his bow. Seeing him having taken a bow, Kuśa, full of anger, stretched his own very strong and excellent bow. Śatrughna who knew (the use of) all weapons discharged sharp arrows. Kuśa, laughing, easily cut them off in the battle. O sage, hundreds and thousands of arrows of (i.e. discharged by) Kuśa and the king (i.e. Śatrughna) pervaded the entire world. It was a wonder. The mighty Kuśa quickly burnt all of them with the missile presided ovey by the Fire. The brave king quelled it with the missile presided over by Rain. The king who was very brave, put it down with the missile presided over by Vāyu. Then everywhere on the battlefield strong wind blew. He covered the wind that disturbed (everything) with the missile presided over by Mountain. The king cut off the mountain-stones with a thunderbolt-like missile. Then that very great warrior Kuśa discharged the missile presided over by Nārāyaṇa (i.e. Viṣṇu). That missile presided over by Nārāyaṇa, was not able to hurt the king.

66-79. Then Kuśa got very angry. He, given to anger, spoke to Śatrughna having great might and valour: "I think you are a great hero, getting victory in the battle, as my fearful missile presided over by Nārāyaṇa, did not hurt you. O king, today with three arrows I shall knock you down on the ground. If I do not do this, hear my solemn declaration. I shall have in this world the sin of the man who, having obtained human body (i.e. birth) due to crores of religious deeds, does not honour it through delusion. On this battlefield you should be attentive. I shall instantly knock you down on the ground." Saying so, he fixed on his bow a fierce arrow resembling the destructive fire at the end of the world after aiming it at the great expansive, hard chest of the enemy. Seeing that arrow fixed, Śatrughna, full of anger, discharged sharp arrows piercing the skin of Kuśa. The arrow of a terrible form, resembling fire, and hissing like a serpent, went forth to pierce his chest. The best king, remembering Rāma, quickly noticed the arrow. He cut off that arrow having sharp joints and discharged by Kuśa. Then, Kuśa who was very angry due to his arrow being cut off, fixed on his bow another arrow with sharp joints. While he, full of power decided to pierce his chest (with an arrow), he cut off his arrow resembling the destructive fire at the end of the world. Then Kuśa, full of anger, remembered his mother's feet, and fixed on his arrow a third wonderful arrow. Śatrughna too, quickly took an arrow to cut it off. Just then, he, pierced by the arrow fell on the ground. When Śatrughna fell, there was a great wailing. Kuśa proud of his might, obtained victory then.

CHAPTER SIXTYFOUR

Rāma's Army Revives

Śeṣa said:

1-5. Seeing Śatrughna fallen, the excellent king Suratha getting into his very wonderful chariot fashioned with jewels went (to fight). Realising that Puṣkala was formerly defeated in battle, he went to fight with Lava, the crest-jewel (i.e. the best) of the great heroes. Suratha, the crest-jewel (i.e. the best) of the great heroes, having reached Kuśa and discharging arrows in various ways, troubled him. With ten arrows with rising flames he deprived Suratha of his chariot. He speedily cut off his bow, strong and strung. The battle between the two heroes (fought with) destruction of missiles and counter-missiles and throwing and counter-throwing of missiles was fierce and thrilling.

6-11. When the invincible king Suratha was very much exerting in the battle, Kuśa thought: 'What should I do (now) in the battle?' He, possessing great power, having thought, took a sharp, fierce arrow to kill the king. Seeing the arrow resembling the destructive fire at the end of the world, coming (towards him), he decided to cut it off. Just then the great arrow struck him. Then the very brave hero fainted in the battle, and fell in the interior of his chariot. The charioteer took him (away). Seeing on the fall of Suratha Kuśa getting victory and scaring the hosts of heroes, (Hanūmat), the son of Wind, went (to fight with him).

Seeing the powerful monkey, the son of Wind, coming (to fight), he grinned, as it were provoking him to become wrathful.

12-17a. He said to Hanūmat: "Come face to face with me. I shall pierce (you) with a thousand arrows. You will go to (i.e. fall on) the ground dead." Hanūmat, who was addressed like this, realising that Rāma's son was very powerful and that the duty for the master should be done, ran (to him). The very powerful one, having quickly uprooted a lofty śāla-tree having a hundred branches and aiming at Kuśa's chest, went to fight with him. The mighty one, seeing Hanūmat with a śāla-tree in his hand coming (to him), pierced him on his chest with three arrows having sharp horse-shoe-shaped heads and resembling the (crescent) moon. The son of Wind (i.e. Hanūmat), being quickly pierced by the powerful Kuśa, gnawing his teeth struck him on his chest with the śāla-tree. The bov (though) struck with the śāla did not shake a bit.

17b-22. Then the heroes through amazement (i.e. being amazed) praised him on account of his being a child. That hero Kuśa, knowing (the use of) great missiles (and) being struck with the śāla-tree, took through anger a destructive missile to kill his enemy. Seeing the invincible destructive missile discharged by Kuśa, (Hanūmat) mentally meditated upon Rāma, the destroyer of the difficulties of his devotees. Then that missile causing great pain, which was discharged by Kuśa, stuck to (i.e. struck) the chest of Māruti and he again swooned. Seeing the monkey (fallen) unconscious, the powerful one (i.e. Kuśa) pierced with sharp arrows that entire huge army. That entire army consisting of four divisions, shattered with myriads of arrows of (i.e. discharged by) him on the battlefield took to fleeing.

23-28. Then Sugrīva, the lord of monkeys and a great protector uprooted many trees and ran to the great warrior Kuśa. Kuśa, laughing, easily cut off all (those) trees. The mighty one again speedily cut off the trees that came to him. Afflicted by many arrows on the battlefield, Sugrīva took a fearful mountain (to hit it) on the head of Kuśa. Seeing the mountain coming (to him) Kuśa pounded it with arrows (discharged) in many ways and quickly rendered it fit for Mahārudra's body (i.e. converted it into ashes). Seeing that great feat performed by the boy, Sugrīva was averse to the hope of (i.e. was disappointed towards) victory on the battlefield. Seeing in the battle invincible Kuśa striking (Hanūmat's tail) and becoming very impatient and overpowered with anger, he took a mountain to strike him (with).

29-36. Seeing Sugrīva eager to strike him, he carefully struck him with many arrows with sharp joints. He, struck with arrows of different kinds, and being afflicted, was exasperated to kill Kuśa, (and) went, (and) took a śāla-tree. Then also that hero Kuśa took a missile presided over by Varuṇa and he, the elder brother of Lava, bound him with that strong noose. He being (thus) bound with soft nooses by the powerful Kuśa, fell on the battlefield adorned by great heroes. Seeing Sugrīva fallen, the warriors fled everywhere. Lava's brother, the crest-jewel (i.e. the best) of great heroes, got victory. Just then, Lava, having vanquished warriors, also Puṣkala, Aṅgada, Pratāpāgrya, Vīramaṇi, and also other kings, got victory in the battle, and came to his brother who got victory in the battle and who destroyed crores of enemies. O sage, pleased with each other, they embraced each other. They obtained victory. Then, being elated they talked (to each other).

Lava said:

37-42. O brother, because of your grace, the ocean of the battle has been crossed (by me). Now we shall cleanse the well-adorned battlefield.

Saying so the heroes, Kuśa and Lava, went (to the battlefield). (Lava) took the beautiful crest-jewel of the king which was decked with gold; so also the hero Lava took the auspicious crown of Puṣkala. He also took the very costly armlets of Śatrughna, and of someone else. Seizing the heap of weapons and also Hanūmat, the lord of monkeys, they went near Sugrīva and tied both (Hanūmat and Sugrīva). The younger brother of Kuśa held the tail of the son of Wind and said to his brother: "I shall take (him) to my (i.e. our) abode holding him by his tail, to please our mother, for the sages' sons to play (with) and for (satisfying) my curiosity."

43-49. Hearing these words, Kuśa then spoke to Lava: "I shall seize this strong, powerful monkey." Speaking like this, the two, best among the mighty, having bound the two at their tails and holding the two powerful ones, went to their hermitage. The two best monkeys (i.e. Hanūmat and Sugrīva) seeing them going to their hermitage, trembled and said to each other in frightened words (i.e. words full of fear). Hanūmat, with his mind soft through fear, said to the lord of monkeys: "These two sons of Rāma will take us to their hermitage. Formerly I who had gone to Jānakī, had done a (good) act for Jānakī. At that time the lovely queen Jānakī was (well) disposed to me. That Vaidehī will see me bound with a noose by my enemy. The excellent one will then laugh (and) I shall be ashamed. What should I do now? My life will end. A great misery has befallen. What will that Rāma do."

50-52. Hearing his words (Sugrīva said): "O great monkey, my (condition) is the same. If he will take me like this, I shall die." When the two who were very much frightened, were telling like this to each other, Kuśa and Lava energetically reached the house of their mother. Seeing them to have come, their mother was delighted. With great affection she embraced her two sons, one by one.

53-57. Jānakī, having seen the two monkeys, Hanūmat and Sugrīva, the best among the heroes and the lord of monkeys, held by the two (i.e. by Kuśa and Lava) by their tails, laughed. The excellent lady, seeing them tied with nooses, speaking for their release, said these excellent words: "O my (two) sons, free these very brave and very powerful monkeys. If the two big ones see me, they will cast their life. This is the hero Hanūmat, who burnt the city of (the son of) Danu (i.e. the demon Rāvaṇa). This also is the lord of bears, the king of all monkeys. Why have you, and where have you arrested them? What have you done (to them) through disrespect? That (you) two young ones have seized them by their tails makes me wonder."

58-66a. Hearing these soft words of the mother, the two sons, best in politeness and possessing great power, then said: "Mother, there is a strong king (named) Rāma, the son of Daśaratha. He has released a horse, well-adorned and having a golden note on his forehead. O mother, this is what is written there: 'My mother has given birth to one brave (son only).

Those who are (i.e. call themselves) kṣatriyas, may seize (the horse); otherwise, they should worship the soles of (my) feet.' Then, O you chaste lady, I thought in my heart: 'Are you not a kṣatriya lady? Would you not be the mother of heroes? (i.e. Have you not given birth to heroes?) Seeing the arrogance of the king, I have forcibly seized the horse. (Our) hero Kuśa has conquered and destroyed his army in the battle. O you who look upon your husband as a deity, know this to be the crown of the king. This also is the crown of another hero, the noble Puṣkala. Know this to be another crown, adorned with gems and pearls. O excellent one, know this to be the king's attractive horse, going at will, which is for my strong brother to ride upon. I have brought these two monkeys, the best among the strong, to play (with). They, who fight, are (brought here) for (i.e. to satisfy) your curiosity?"

66b-67a. Hearing these words, Jānakī, who looked upon her husband as a deity, repeatedly said to her brave sons: "Release them".

Sītā said:

67b-69a. You have done injustice. You have snatched Rāma's great horse. You have knocked down many soldiers. You have bound these lords of monkeys. The brave horse of your father is let loose by him for a sacrifice. You have snatched his horse too (which is to be used) in the best sacrifice.

69b-75a. Release these two monkeys; release this best among horses. Apologise to the very angry Śatrughna, the brother of the king.

Hearing these words of their mother, the best among the mighty, said: "We have conquered that king possessing might in the manner of kṣatriyas. Unfairness is not possible in the case of us who fight in the manner of kṣatriyas. Formerly Vālmīki said to us who were learning (under him): 'In the hermitage a horse fit for a sacrificial rite was seized. Therefore, a son would (i.e. could) fight with his father, or a younger brother with his (elder) brother; or a disciple with his teacher. By that no sin accrues.' By your order now we shall give (back) the excellent horse. We shall release these two monkeys. We shall do (i.e. carry out) your words (i.e. your order)."

75b-80. Saying so, the two went to the battlefield, released the lords of monkeys, so also the horse fit for the horse-sacrifice. Queen Sītā, having heard from her sons about the destruction of the army, reflecting in her mind upon Śrī Rāma, looked at the sun, the witness. "If by mind, words or deeds I worship Raghunātha and none else, then let this king revive. O you lord of the worlds, due to my truth (fulness) let the entire big army, forcibly destroyed by my sons, revive." While Jānakī who looked upon her husband as her deity, was talking like this, the entire army revived on the battlefield.

CHAPTER SIXTYFIVE

Sumati Describes the Adventurous Events to Rāma

Śeṣa said:

1-4. In a moment Śatrughna, the hero, gave up his swoon on the battlefield. Other mighty warriors also, who had fainted, revived. Śatrughna saw the best among the horses, standing before him, and saw (i.e. found) himself to be without the helmet and the army revived. Seeing this he wondered in his mind and spoke to Sumati, the best among ministers, who had then revived: "Having shown pity, the boy has returned the horse for the completion of the sacrifice. We (shall) quickly go to Rāma desiring (i.e. waiting for) the horse's arrival."

5-11. Saying so, he, having got into the chariot and without (the sounds of) kettle-drums and conches, quickly went to Rāma far away from the hermitage. After him moved the great army full of four divisions and making the lord of serpents broken down due to (i.e. under) its load. Having quickly crossed Gaṅgā, full of water having waves, he went to his own country adorned with his own men. The king was accompanied by Puṣkala and Suratha; he, holding a bow, was seated in a jewelled chariot; he had put the horse in front; the horse was adorned with jewelled necklaces; and on his head only shone the white umbrella. Surrounded by thousands of chariots and mighty kings who were adorned with heroic cries, he in due course reached the city, adorned by the solar dynasty, decorated with many excellent flags, and shining with citadels.

12-18. Rāma, having heard that the army along with this Śatrughna and with the brave Puṣkala had reached the city, was delighted in many ways. Showing Lakṣmaṇa the great army with four constituents, he sent him, his brother, best among the mighty (to receive it). Lakṣmaṇa having along with the army gone to his army, and being beside himself due to joy, embraced him whose body was adorned with wounds. Being asked about the safety everywhere, he told him the news. Śatrughna became very joyful and met with happiness. The brave and noble-minded son of Sumitrā, being seated along with his brother (Śatrughna) in his own chariot, went along with the great army to the city. Sarayū had sacred water, had purified the three worlds, was purified by the dust of Rāma's feet, was bright like the autumnal moon, was crowded with swans and ducks, was adorned with the ruddy geese, and was very much resounding with birds, having very strange colours.

19-33. Rāmacandra had abundantly got constructed there pavilions resounding with the separate recitals of brāhmaṇas knowing the Vedas. There were many kṣatriyas with their hands well-adorned with bows, and filling the earth with the noise of the various twangs of their bow-strings. There brāhmaṇas enjoyed (i.e. ate) charming and various kinds of food. Praising one another, they talked about (i.e. discussed) interesting news (topics). There were foods like rice boiled with milk, which were white and resembled the moon. They were full of (i.e. mixed) with profuse milk and ghee and were mixed with sugar. There were many small round cakes resembling the orb of the moon in beauty. They were very lovely and were made fragrant with perfumes of camphor etc. There were soft components of macaroni having hundred holes or no holes. With sweet food there were baked thin cakes that were dressed. There was boiled rice which resembled lotuses, which was mixed with kidney-bean-seeds, which was having a perfume, and which gave delight. The boiled rice was (mixed) with curd, and accompanied by (i.e. mixed with) camphor. It was prepared by cooks cooking tasty food, and served by waiters. There, certain brāhmaṇas on seeing the rice boiled with milk put (i.e. served) in their dishes, said to one another: "What is this wonder that is seen (here)? Is it the orb of the moon fallen from the sky through the fear of darkness? Here there is the wonderful nectar which puts an end to death." Hearing that, another excellent brāhmaṇa, with his eyes red through anger, said. "The orb of the moon is not at all wet with nectar. The form of the moon is one (only). Then how can it be seen to be similar in every individual dish of a thousand of brāhmaṇas? Therefore, know that it may be a lotus or camphor. Do not regard it to be the moon's orb endowed with white lustre." Just then another (brāhmaṇa) overcome with anger, shaking his head (said): "These foolish brāhmaṇas, not proficient in the knowledge of tastes, do not know: This is cooked with the bulb of campaka. They are sweet lotuses."

34-40a. O sages, brāhmaṇas who (generally) ate bulbs and roots, were pleased and were very eager to know the tastes and thus conjectured among themselves. Just then another brāhmaṇa said: "The existence of the kṣatriyas is excellent. They will enjoy food like that served on account of their great religious merit." To him a brāhmaṇa said at that time: "Such is the fruit of charity. Those who give to brāhmaṇas, obtain what is desired. Such food will never be seen by them who have never repeatedly worshipped Viṣṇu with various offerings of eatables. Those men who feed brāhmaṇas with (foods of) various tastes, enjoy (food of) sweet taste abandoned by (i.e. kept away from) the sight of the sinners. Those best brāhmaṇas, proficient in the Vedas, thus fed with (foods of) desired tastes, recited (the Vedic texts) in the pavilion. Being delighted, some danced, some laughed and some cried. A great festivity took place there.

40b-52. Then Śatrughna came there. Rāma, seeing Śatrughna coming along with Puṣkala, could not contain the joy rising (in his heart). Then Rāma got up (to greet his) brother stuck to (i.e. fallen at) his feet. Seeing his brother fallen at his feet, Rāma firmly embraced him who was full of politeness, and whose body was adorned with wounds. Shedding tears in various ways (i.e. profusely) on his head, Rāghava got great delight which is far away from (i.e. which cannot be expressed in) words. He, overcome with (Puṣkala's) modesty, took polite Puṣkala who had bent at his feet, between his arms, and embraced him much (i.e. closely). Raghunātha himself closely embraced others also like Hanūmat, the hero Sugrīva, so also Aṅgada, Lakṣmīnidhi, the son of Janaka, Pratāpāgrya, conquering his enemies, Subāhu, Sumada, the hero Vimala, the gem(-like) Nīla, Satyavat, Vīramaṇi, and Suratha, the servant of Rāma—who were affectionate and had bowed at his feet. Sumati, the lofty one, being pleased and standing in front of Rāma, closely embraced Śrī Raghupati favouring his devotees. Then Rāma, the best among the eloquent, seeing his minister come near him, spoke with great delight to him: "O Sumati, O best among speakers, O best among ministers, tell me who are these kings. How (i.e. for what reason) have all of them come here? Where (i.e. to which places) did the horse go? By whom was he arrested? How was he released by my brother having great might?"

Śeṣa said:

53. Thus addressed that very intelligent Sumati, the best among ministers, laughed and spoke in a voice grave like the (sound of the thundering) clouds.

Sumati said:

54-59a. How should I speak before you, the omniscient one? You are asking in the manner of the world. You who are everything, know all. Yet, O crest-jewel (i.e. the best) of all kings, always holding your order on my head (i.e. obeying your order), I shall speak; today (i.e. now) listen to it. O lord, by your grace, your horse, adorned with a note on his forehead, wandered on the surface of the earth. No one, proud (through the pride) of his name and power, seized him. (On the contrary) having given their kingdom (to you), they saluted your lotus-like feet. Who, desiring victory (and) free from old age and death, seized (i.e. would seize) the best horse of the killer of Rāvaṇa, the lord of demons? Your lovely horse had just gone to Ahicchatra (city).

59b-62. The king of that city, Sumada, heard that your horse had come; and the very powerful one, with his sons, and surrounded by his entire mighty army, offered his entire kingdom in which the elements causing nuisance were destroyed, O lord, That king Sumada who having propitiated the mother, the leader of the worlds, Jagadambikā, obtained a long life and a kingdom free from bad elements, salutes you, served by lords. Accept, with a favourable eye, him who desires to see you for a long time.

63-71. Then in king Subāhu's city, full of army, his son Damana seized the best horse. With that Damana a great battle took place. Having caused (Damana,) the son of Subāhu, to faint, Puṣkala obtained victory. Then Subāhu, getting angry, fought, in the battle with (Hanūmat,) the son of Wind, the servant of your lotus-like feet, and best among the mighty. Being struck by his foot, he obtained the knowledge covered due to the curse. Having dedicated everything to you, he has become the protector of the horse. This king Subāhu, of a lofty body, salutes you. Sprinkle with a favourable glance king Subāhu, proficient in political wisdom. Then the horse that was let loose, plunged into the puddle in Revā. There the mighty Śatrughna obtained the deluding missile. Then the horse went to Śivapura, adorned with the residence of Śiva. You know what happened there, as you yourself had come there. The demon Vidyunmālin was killed; Satyavat then joined (us); O you highly intelligent one, you know about our battle with Suratha. Then the horse, released from Kuṇḍalaka, roamed everywhere. Nobody proud of his might, seized him.

72-80. Then the horse reached Vālmīki's hermitage. O best among men, listen to what curious thing took place there. Then a strongest boy, sixteen years old and having resemblance with you, seeing the horse marked with a note, seized him. Then O best of men, a great battle with Kālajit took place. He was struck by the hero with a sharp missile. Many very mighty ones like Puṣkala were killed in the battle. The crest-jewel of the heroes made even Śatrughna unconscious. Then the brave king, the best among the mighty, feeling great pain in his heart, angrily made him unconscious. When he was made unconscious by the king, another (warrior) came (there). He and this one, having revived, destroyed your army. Having seized the weapons and ornaments of all that were unconscious, and taking (with) them the two monkeys that were bound, the two (i.e. Kuśa and Lava) went to their own hermitage. Having favoured (us) he gave (back) the great sacrificial horse. The entire army that was dead was brought back to life. Having taken the horse, we have come to your vicinity. I have told you these words (since) I knew this only.

CHAPTER SIXTYSIX

Singing of Rāmāyaṇa by Kuśa and Lava

Śeṣa said:

1. Having come to know that the two boys in Vālmīki's hermitage were his sons, he (i.e. Rāma) went to Vālmīki.

Śrī Rāma said:

2-5. Who are the two boys having my resemblance and the best among the mighty? Why do the two, skilled in archery, live there? Having heard what the minister told about them who easily bound Śatrughna and Hanūmat, I am amazed. Therefore, O sage, tell me all the deeds of the two boys, since a great, desirable delight thus comes to me.

Hearing those words of the intelligent king of kings, he (i.e. Vālmīki) spoke important words, with clear syllables.

Vālmīki said:

6-11a. How is it that you who live in the heart of men, would not have the knowledge (of the deeds)? Yet, to delight you I am telling it now. O king, these two boys, the best among the mighty, who resemble your form, and have charming bodies like yours, (live) in my hermitage. When you abandoned in the fierce forest the pregnant, innocent Jānakī, afflicted with grief and repeatedly crying like an osprey, I saw the daughter of Janaka and brought your righteous wife to (my) hermitage. The sages' sons constructed a lovely hut of leaves for her. In it she gave birth to the two sons illumining the ten quarters. It is clear that I named them Kuśa and Lava.

11b-15. As the moon waxes in the bright half of the month, they grew there continuously. In due course I performed all (sacraments) like the thread-ceremony. O king, I made them grasp (i.e. taught them) all the Vedas with their limbs. From my mouth they learnt all the Upaniṣads, so also Āyurveda, archery, science of (the use of) weapons, so also the lore of magic; I made them skilled in music. The two, unsteady and fickle of heart, skilled in all lores, sang on the bank of Gaṅgā and in the bowers of creepers and in groves. Then, O best of Raghus, I got the highest delight.

16-21a. Having given them all the missiles, I put my hand on their heads (i.e. I blessed them). Seeing them extremely skilled in singing and proficient in knowing the difference among the notes like the first, the fifth and the third (notes of the gamut), people were wonder-struck. Seeing them like that I made them sing charmingly. Due to my knowledge of the future, I composed the holy Rāmāyaṇa. The two, skilled in (playing upon) the tabor, musical instruments, lutes, sang in every forest and infatuated the beasts and the birds. O Rāma, the sweetness of the singing of your sons is wonderful. One night Varuṇa took the two boys to hear them. By the order of the god the two boys who have a charming age and form, who have crossed the ocean of the science of music, sang sweely there.

21b-28a. Varuṇa along with the members of his family and singers, heard your highly sweet, charming pure deeds. Having heard with Mitra your deeds sweeter than even nectar, O Rāma, Varuṇa was pleased. With the functions of his life and senses taken away by the joy of music, he did not direct (i.e. allow) your sons to come back (to the earth). The two boys, though enticed by charming, great pleasures, did not swerve, as a result of (their) remembering the feet of their teacher and their mother. I too then went to the excellent abode of Varuṇa. O lord, Varuṇa, having affection (for me), worshipped me. To Varuṇa who, though he knew everything about the birth and deeds of the two boys, too asked me (about them), I told everything about the birth of the boys and their acquisition of knowledge.

Hearing that they are Sītā's sons, he (presented them) with garments and ornaments. To honour my words 'the (articles) should be accepted, as they are given by a god,' the two princes accepted whatever was given by Varuṇa who was pleased with their musical instruments, singing, knowledge, age and virtues.

28b-36. Then the fortunate Varuṇa asked me with reference to (i.e. about) Sītā: (He said:) "Sītā is at the head of chaste ladies; she is endowed with beauty and good character; she has brave sons; she is noble; she does not deserve to be abandoned. O descendant of Raghu, there is a great loss (to Rāma) in (i.e. due to) abandoning her. She is the greatest well-being of all well-beings, which never perishes. O Rāma, the hearing about and narration of the account of whom is holy, what loss is thereby if the stupid sinful persons do not realise her greatness? Her purifying behaviour is always before us. Those who reflect upon Sītā's feet, instantly attain perfection; by the mere thought about her, these divine functions of the worlds like origin, maintenance and destruction, take place. Sitā is death; is nectar; (it is) she (who) gives heat; she sends down rain. Your Jānakī is heaven, salvation, penance, deep abstract meditation and charity. None else but your dear Sītā alone creates Brahmā, Śiva and other gods like me. You are the father of all the worlds, and Sītā is the mother. Therefore, your erroneous view about her is not at all proper for (i.e. will not at all lead to) happiness.

37-43. You, the omniscient one, the lord, yourself know that Sītā, the daughter of the Earth, who is dearer to you than your own life, is ever pure. Therefore, you should respect Jānakī who is pure and dear to you. (If you do this,) there will be no mortification of the curse for Sītā or for you. O Vālmīki, O best sage, you should actually tell these words of (i.e. uttered by) me to Rāma, the lord of the worlds." O lord, thus was I told by Varuṇa about your receiving Sītā. I was also told in the same way by all other gods. The gods, demons, all the gandharvas also, with minds full of curiosity, have heard the recital of Rāmāyaṇa done by your two sons. All of them were pleased, and they praised your two sons. By means of their form, singing, age and virtues, they have enticed the three worlds. Whatever was given by the gods to your two sons, has been accepted. Sages (gave) them blessings; and from others they (received) fame.

44-51. Formerly the sages saw the world to be full of one Rāma (only). Now the entire world has become full of three Rāmas on account of your two sons. Formerly in the world only one form of Cupid was seen; but now with four Cupids (i.e. Cupid, Rāma, Kuśa and Lava), he will be born (i.e. will have four forms). O lord of kings, everywhere else Kuśa and Lava are declared to be Rāma's sons. Then why do you, a learned man, shrink (from accepting it)? O you crest-jewel among those having an auspicious fame, except in the case of your having abandoned Sītā, praise about all your deeds is heard. O Rāma, you who are the lord of the three worlds and are following a householder's life, should accept these two sons who are endowed with knowledge, good character and virtues. They will not leave their mother and stay with you. Therefore, you should invite your sons with their mother. Now by reviving the army, she has given a pious, convincing proof to all the people—even the sinking ones (i.e. sinners) (of her purity). O you who cut off the pride (of your enemies), it is, therefore, not unknown to us or to gods. In her purity (being established), what was (supposed to be) lost for the people, is indeed (proved to be) eternal.

Śeṣa said:

52-54. Thus Vālmīki enlightened Rāma, though he was omniscient. Praising and saluting Vālmīki, he spoke to Lakṣmaṇa: "O deer one, go, resorting to a chariot with Sumantra to bring Sītā, (my) virtuous wife, along with (our) sons. Telling her these my words and also the words of the sage and having (thus) enlightened her, quickly bring her back."

Lakṣmaṇa said:

55-59. O supreme one, O lord of all of us, by your order I shall go. If the queen will come, then my journey will be fruitful. If the chaste one, being displeased with me for my former fault (of having abandoned her in the forest), does not come, then I, coming (back alone) should be forgiven.

Speaking thus to Rāma, Lakṣmaṇa getting with Sumitra and a disciple of the sage into the chariot by the king's order, went to Sītā's hermitage. 'How should I propitiate Sītā who would know (i.e. remember) the former fault of me who always depend upon Rāma?' Thinking like this and (oscillating) between joy and fear, Lakṣmaṇa reached Sītā's hermitage, destroying fatigue.

60-69. Having got down from the chariot, he with his eyes (i.e. sight) checked by tears, repeatedly addressing her 'O noble one, O revered one, O respected one, O auspicious one', and with his entire body trembling, fell at her feet. She who was beside herself by love, caused him to rise (and said): "O dear one, why have you come to the forest dear to the sages. Is the king, the pearl from the pearl-oyster (in the form) of Kauśalyā, all right? Carried away merely by his fame, is he without anger towards me? By all he is called the ocean of auspicious virtues. Entering into the fear of infamy, he appointed you to abandon me. If after that his fame has become spotless, then the fame of me who, even by dying, spread his good fame, will be very firm. O brother-in-law, let me quickly have the proximity of my husband. Though he has abandoned me, I have not, in the least, forsaken him. The fruit (effect) depends upon the means (cause); but the cause is not dependent upon the fruit. Is Kauśalyā whose son is the protector of the three worlds, who is free from heart-rending grief, and who has always been full of compassion for me, all right? Are all kinsmen like Bharata all right? Is the noble Sumitrā, to whom I am dearer than her own life, all right? Have you also been abandoned like me (by the king) for his fame? What is difficult for the king, to whom his own self is not dear, to abandon (anything)?"

70-86. In this way she asked Rāma's younger brother in many ways. He said to her: "The king is all right. He is asking about your well-being. O queen, Kauśalyā, Sumitrā and other royal ladies that there are, have with love and with blessing asked about your well-being. O you auspicious one, I report to you the salutation, preceded by a question about your well-being, offered to you by Śatrughna and Bharata. O Jānakī, the preceptors, and all their wives, have given you blessings and O auspicious one, have enquired about your well-being. The self-possessed one, not finding delight in anything else but you, is, truthfully inviting you, O beautiful lady. O daughter of Janaka, the lord, finding all the quarters vacant without you, weeps and makes others (us) also weep. O you born in the Videha country, he always remembers the place where you have stayed and looks upon it as occupied (by you), and says: "This hermitage of Vālmīki where Jānakī spends her time in (talking about) tidings about me, has become blessed." Our lord, while weeping, said something more to you. Listen to it: "There is no doubt that whatever is in the heart of the speaker does find an expression. People call me alone the lord of their lord; but I say that for them the unseen (destiny) is the independent cause. Even the lord of everything follows destiny in all his acts. Then, would not those that are ruled (by him), follow it in (times of) happiness or of misery? That inevitable cause which bore fruit at the time of bending the bow (of Śiva), the frenzy of Kaikeyī, the death of my father, going into the forest, your being kidnapped there, crossing of the ocean, killing of the lord of demons, at the time of receiving you (back), the truthfulness of my pledge, at the time of the murmur about (you, my) chaste wife, at the time of my again being connected with my relatives, my acquiring the kingdom, O beautiful lady, again at the time of separation from you, is again succeeding at the time of our re-union. Due to that (destiny) which falsified the Veda, due to which I followed (the ordinary) people (in abandoning you), I have become the first cause. The wise people follow destiny. Destiny wears out by fruition (enjoyment and suffering). That you (have exhausted) in the forest.

87-92. O Sītā, O you not seen by people (or by light), my causeless love for you, which is growing, having abandoned you (now) invites you respectfully. The merging of the purity of love takes place (i.e. the purity of love disappears), even if a fault is suspected (to be present in an individual). The wise ones should always enjoy that (pure) love. O good one, I have purified my love for you. It is not otherwise. It should be thought (i.e. borne in mind) that by me, following eminent persons, has been protected even this world in all conditions for the sake of purity, (even) through our censure, O queen;

for due to the acts of the great this confused world would perish. The fame of both of us is bright; the love of us is splendid; the families of us are bright; the acts of us are splendid. On the earth there would be bright singers of the fame of us. Those who are the devotees of us go to the end of (i.e. cross) the ocean of the worldly existence."

93-100. Being pleased with your virtues you were thus addressed by him. Make your mind compassionate to see the lotus-like feet of your husband. For you are prepared lovely garments, great ornaments, fragrant unguents, charming scents. For your delight Rāma has sent chariots and female servants; so also an umbrella, white chowries, elephants and horses, O beautiful one. Followed by me and praised by best brāhmaṇas and by bards and panegyrists, saluted by the ladies in the city, served by warriors, covered with flowers by celestial ladies, giving wealth to brāhmaṇas as desired by them, having put in front the two sons mounted on elephants, you the queen, the ruler of men, (should) go to Ayodhyā, your city. When you have gone there and are united with your husband, today there will be songs (sung) for all royal ladies and all the wives of sages that have come from all (places), so also for those (that have come) from Kosala.

Śeṣa said:

101-104. Hearing this request that respectable Sītā said to him: "I have not been the cause of the king's fame; on the contrary I myself am infamy. Void of good *dharma, kāma* and *artha,* what can I accomplish for him? Under the circumstances who would have faith in your autocratic king? By one like me born in an auspicious family the faults of my husband that are in my mind should never be told directly or indirectly. He does not move away from my heart in that form in which he settled in my heart at the time of (our) marriage.

105-109. O Lakṣmaṇa, these two sons of me are born from the portion of his lustre. They are the sprouts of his family; they are very brave; they are skilled in archery. Take them to their father and carefully fondle them. Staying here at will I shall propitiate Rāma by means of penance. O noble one, you should tell (i.e. convey) my salutation to the feet of the revered ones;

so also (you should tell) all after going from here about my well-being." Sītā directed her sons (as): "Go to your father. You have to serve him only, who would give you his position." The two boys, Kuśa and Lava, though thus ordered, were, unwilling (to go), (but) went there with Lakṣmaṇa due to the words of (i.e. due to being ordered by) Vālmīki.

110-111. The two sons went near the lotus-like feet of Vālmīki. Lakṣmaṇa also, going along with the two boys, saluted him. These i.e. Vālmīki, Lakṣmaṇa, and the two boys—gathered, and knowing Rāma to be in the assembly, they, being eager (to see him), went (there).

112-120. The very intelligent Lakṣmaṇa, full of joy and sorrow, having saluted (Rāma), reported to Rāma all the words of (i.e. uttered by) Sītā. By the words of Sītā's message Rāma fell into a swoon (i.e. he became unconscious). Having regained consciousness he said to Lakṣmaṇa who knew the way of life: "O friend, go there again and having told her my words bring her quickly by making great effort; well-being to you. (You should say to her:) 'Have you, practising penance in the forest, thought of, heard of, or seen any other course than (coming to) me, that, O Jānakī, you are not coming (to me)? By your own desire you went from here to the forest, dear to sages. You honoured those wives of the sages and saw the groups of sages. O beautiful lady, your desire is fulfilled. Then why no you not today come (back)? Taking note of (i.e. considering) your own desire you would not find fault with me. O you lady of beautiful thighs, to a lady, whether she goes or does not go (away from her husband), her husband alone, whether he is without virtues or is an ocean of virtues, is the recourse. Then what about him who is desired by her mind? Whatever act is done by a noble woman, is (done) for pleasing her husband. I was pleased with you formerly; now I am extremely pleased (with you). Sacrifice, muttering prayers, penance, charity, vows, (visits to) sacred places, (showing) pity etc., all become fruitful and deities are pleased, when I am pleased. There is no doubt about it.' "

Śeṣa said:

121-122. Taking this message to (i.e. for) Sītā from the lord of the world (i.e. Rāma) Lakṣmaṇa bowed down through attachment for Rāma and said to the lord of souls: "I shall tell those words full of politeness, which this one has uttered for bringing back Sītā."

123-125. Saying so and saluting the feet of Raghunātha, Lakṣmaṇa getting into a speedy chariot quickly went to Sītā. Having looked at the fortunate and very energetic sons of Rāma, making his face lovely by having a smile on Vālmīki said: "O sons, playing on the lute, sing (songs describing) the wonderful good deeds of Rāma, adorning them with your sweet voice."

126-133. Thus addressed, the two noble sons (of Rāma) sang Rāma's good deeds which give great religious merit, which were beautified with good sentences and words, in which the way of righteousness was actually present, in which chastity was present, so also were present brotherly affection and devotion to the teacher, where appeared in a bodily form the behaviour of the master and the servant, where punishment to one behaving unrighteously was actually (found to be inflicted) from (i.e. by) the descendant of Raghu. The singing pervaded the world; even in heaven gods remained (motionless); hearing which singing even kinnaras fainted in a moment. The entire assembly there on hearing the sound of the lute adorned with beating of time and measure, became (motionless) like a doll painted (in a picture). Rāma and other kings shed tears of joy; they being enticed by the singing of the fifth note, remained like (being) painted (i.e. motionless). Then seeing (Rāma) intent on (giving) a gift they laughed and with their eyebrows knit a little spoke to the best sage Vālmīki:

134-136. "O sage, a great injustice is being done by this king, since he (trying) to allure us desires to give us gold coins. Accepting gifts is recommended for brāhmaṇas and not for others. A king (i.e. a kṣatriya) intent upon receiving a gift is fit for hell only. (This) king is enjoying the kingdom, let free by us through compassion. How does he, adorned with good fortune, desire to give (us) gold coins?"

137-140. Vālmīki, full of compassion, looked at them who spoke like this and told them: "O you who are most prudent, know (this to be) your father." Hearing these words of the sage the two boys, full of modesty, and extremely pure due to their devotion to their mother, stuck to (i.e. fell at) the feet of the king. Full of joy, Rāma firmly clasped the two boys to his body. He thought that the actual likenesses of his wife had stood by him. O best sage, the assembly too, seeing the charming faces of Rāma's sons, regarded Jānakī's devotion to her husband to be true.

141. Having heard this spoken from the mouth of Śeṣa, Vātsyāyana said: "I have a mind (i.e. I desire) to hear Rāmāyaṇa, full of all morality."

Vātsyāyana said:

142. At what time was this great Rāmāyaṇa composed? Why did he (i.e. Vālmīki) compose it? What is described in it? Tell me that.

Śeṣa said:

143-146a. Once the brāhmaṇa Vālmīki went to a great forest where there were tāla (trees), tamāla (trees) and blossomed kiṁśuka (trees); where ketakī (tree) made the forest fragrant with its pollen and was seen like the great lustre of the moon by having white heads; where there were many blossomed trees like campaka, bakula, and kovidāra and kuraṇṭaka. The forest sounded with the notes of cuckoos and the hummings of bees; it was charming everywhere and full of lovely birds.

146b-149a. There a pair of curlews, which was lovely, which was afflicted with Cupid's arrows, which was delighted with each other, which was (having) affection for each other, enjoyed. Then, a certain cruel hunter, greedy for eating flesh, came there, and killed one lovely (bird) of the two. Then the female curlew seeing her husband (i.e. her mate) killed by the hunter, became afflicted, and giving out loud cries through grief, lamented.

149b-151a. Then the sage (Vālmīki) who was angry, touching the holy water of the river, cursed the hunter who killed the (male) curlew: "O hunter, since you killed one of the two curlews infatuated by love, you will not attain glory for eternal years."

151b-153a. Then the brāhmaṇas—his followers, thinking that the composition of a verse had taken place, were delighted, and praising the sage with the words 'Well (done), well (done)', they said: Lord, in the words that rose from the curse Sarasvatī has produced a verse. O best sage, this verse has been an extremely attractive one. O best brāhmaṇa, then the mind of the sage was extremely delighted.

153b-157. At that time, Brahmā having arrived with his sons said (these) words to Vālmīki: "O best sage, you are fortunate, (since) Sarasvatī, residing in your mouth, has become a verse. Therefore, compose the lovely Rāmāyaṇa of sweet words, by which your fame will last till the end of the world. Blessed is the speech in (your) mouth which is accompanied by the name of Rāma. Other stories about sensual love of men generate sin only. Therefore, compose the biography of Rāma, well-known in the world, by which the sins of the sinners will perish at (i.e. by means of) every word."

158-162. Saying so the Creator along with other gods disappeared. Then he thought; 'How would Rāmāyaṇa be (composed)?' Then on the charming bank of the river he became engrossed in meditation. Then in his heart appeared the lovely Rāma. Seeing Rāma who was dark like the petals of a blue lotus and whose eyes were like lotuses, and observing his past, future and present deeds, he met with great joy, and composed Rāmāyaṇa full of charming words and many kinds of metres, in which Rāmāyaṇa there are, O sinless one, six very charming divisions. (They are): Bāla, Āraṇyaka, Kiṣkindhā, and Sundara; so also Yuddha and Uttara.

163. O highly intelligent one, a man who listens to these six is freed from (i.e. absolved of) all sins.

164-167. In it, in the Bālakāṇḍa (is the description how) king Daśaratha who was pleased, obtained by performing the sacrifice to obtain a male issue, four sons, actually Viṣṇu, the eternal Brahman. Then (he, i.e. Rāma) goes to Viśvāmitra's sacrifice, marries Sītā, (meets) Paraśurāma, comes (back) to the city (of Ayodhyā), is allotted the position of heir-apparent; (then) at the words of his mother, he, with his wife and Lakṣmaṇa went to the forest after having crossed Gaṅgā, (then) to Citrakūṭa mountain. Having heard that he (lived) in the forest, Bharata, the wise one, went to his brother. Not securing him (i.e. unable to get him back), he himself lived in Nandigrāma. (This is what) you listen to in the Bāla (kāṇḍa).

168-170. The description in the next takes place in Araṇya (i.e. forest). It describes his residence in the hermitages of the sages. At places there is a minute description. (Then there is the description of) the cutting of Śūrpaṇakhā's nose; (so also is the description of) the destruction of Khara and Dūṣaṇa; (then of) the killing of the illusory (deer) Mārīca; (the description of) the kidnapping of his beautiful wife by the demon (Rāvaṇa); the wandering of him separated (from Sītā) in the forest; (thus) he was endowed with human deeds. (Then follows the description of) his seeing Kabandha there, and his arrival at Pampā; (then is the description of) his meeting with Hanūmat.

171-174. This (kāṇḍa or division where these events are described) is called Vana (or Araṇya kāṇḍa). O sage, listen to (the description occurring in) the next division. I shall abridge it and tell you (i.e. I shall tell it to yon in brief). The breaking of the seven tāla (trees); the wonderful killing of Vālin; giving the kingdom to Sugrīva, and the description of the trees; then the message (i.e. advice) of Lakṣmaṇa about his act (i.e. duty); expulsion of Sugrīva; so also the full description of the army, and search for Sītā; then meeting Sampāti, crossing the ocean, meeting with the monkeys on the other shore. (This is the description that occurs in) the wonderful Kiṣkindhā (kāṇḍa or division).

175-182. Listen to (the description occurring) in the Sundarakāṇḍa where (you find) the wonderful story of Rāma. The error of the monkey of seeing the picture in every house; then (Hanūmat's) seeing Sītā there, and (his) talk with Sītā; breaking of the forest (by Hanūmat); the monkey (i.e. Hanūmat) being bound by the angry (demons); then (the description of) the burning of Laṅkā; then joining the monkeys; then the giving of the token of recognition (given by) Rāma; then the march of the army; then (the description of) constructing a bridge over the ocean; meeting with Śuka and Sāraṇa. (The kāṇḍa which contains) this (description) is called Sundara. In the Yuddha (kāṇḍa, is given the description of) union with Sītā. In the Uttara (kāṇḍa) (is given the description of) the conversation with sages and the commencement of the (horse-) sacrifice. There are many tales about Rāma, which destroy the sins of the listeners. Thus these are said to be the six Kāṇḍas (i.e. divisions, listening to which) removes the sin of a brāhmaṇa's murder. I have told you in brief (this) very charming (account). That is Rāmāyaṇa destroying great sins, having twentyfour thousand (verses), and marked with (i.e. having) six Kāṇḍas. Having heard it, Rāma was pleased, and putting (i.e. seating) his sons on the seat, and embracing them closely, he remembered (his) dear Sītā.

CHAPTER SIXTYSEVEN

The Commencement of the Sacrifice

Śeṣa said :

1-5. Then Lakṣmaṇa, having come (there) repeatedly saluted her, and with (his voice) faltering through love, he told her the words uttered by Rāma. Having seen Lakṣmaṇa full of modesty to have come (there) and having heard Rāma's message through his mouth, Sītā being abashed, said: "O Lakṣmaṇa, how (i.e. why) have you come? I forsaken by Rāma in the great forest and remembering Rāma, am staying in Vālmīki's hermitage." Having heard the words that came out from her mouth Lakṣmaṇa said: "O mother, O you chaste lady, Rāma is inviting you again and again. A chaste wife does not bring to her mind the fault committed by her husband; therefore, seated in an excellent charriot, come with me."

6-10. Hearing these words Jānakī who looked upon her husband as god, gave up the anger in her heart and sat in the chariot with Lakṣmaṇa. Having saluted all the female ascetics and the sages bright with (the knowledge of) the Vedas, and mentally remembering Rāma, she sat in the chariot and went to the city (of Ayodhyā). She having costly ornaments, reached the city in due course. She reached the river Sarayū where Rāma was waiting. Having got down from the chariot with Lakṣmaṇa, the charming one, devoted to her husband, stuck to (i.e. fell at) the feet of Rāma. Rāma, having seen that Jānakī, beside herself due to love, (said): "O good lady, I shall complete the sacrifice with you."

11-16. Having saluted Vālmīki and other best brāhmaṇas, she, eager to salute the feet of his mothers, went (to them). Having showered blessings on that dear Jānakī, the mother of the heroes, Kauśalyā became glad in many ways. Kaikeyī, seeing the daughter of the Videha-king bowing at her feet, gave her the blessing: "With your husband and sons live long". Sumitrā, seeing the daughter of the Videha-king bowing at her feet, gave her blessing giving sons and grandsons. O brāhmaṇa, the chaste Sītā, dear to Rāmacandra, having fully saluted them indeed obtained great joy. Seeing the religiously wedded wife of Rāmacandra come there, the Pitcher-born (i.e. Agasti), disregarding the golden (image of Rāma's) wife, placed (in its place) (his) chaste wife.

17-19. In the sacrifice Rāma at that time shone with Sītā, like the Moon having rising lustre in the autumn along with the star (Rohiṇī). With his chaste wife Vaidehī, he performed the sacrifice removing all sins when the lovely time had come. (People) seeing Rāma engaged with Sītā in the sacrifice, were, being full of eagerness, very much delighted.

20-34. At that time of the best sacrifice Rāma said to the intelligent Vasiṣṭha: "O lord, what needful things should be done hereafter?" Hearing Rāma's words the very intelligent preceptor said: "Worship of brāhmaṇas, giving delight to them, should be done. Formerly (king) Marutta[1] made the sacrifice ready with preparations. Then brāhmaṇas were gratified with (gifts of) money etc. The brāhmaṇas were unable to carry large loads of the gifts. The brāhmaṇas unable to carry the loads of gifts threw them in the region of Himavat. Therefore, O foremost king having wealth, O best king, you too give gifts etc. to brāhmaṇas, so that there will be excellent (i.e. great) satisfaction." Hearing this the foremost king, looking upon Agasti as venerable, first worshipped Brahmā's son, the treasure of penance. He worshipped delightful Agastya with his wife by means of many loads of gems and various loads of gold surrounded by (i.e. together with)

1. Marutta—A king of the solar race, who is said to have performed a sacrifice in which the gods took part as waiters.

countries and people giving great delight. In the same way he honoured Satyavatī's son Vyāsa with gems, gold coins, and various countries. He worshipped Cyavana with his wife with good gems. He also honoured all other sages, priests, the treasures of penance, in many ways with heaps of gems and loads of gold. At that time, in the sacrifice Rāma gave large presents to brāhmaṇas. He gave a lakh of gold coins to each brāhmaṇa. He gave various gifts to the helpless, blind and poor with lovely gems given according to their satisfaction. There he gave, as laid down in the sacred texts, variegated garments, soft food, giving joy to all. The city crowded with well-fed and delighted people, grown (more populous) with all beings, surrounded (i.e. crowded) by women became very much delighted. The brāhmaṇa, the pitcher-born sage (i.e. Agasti), seeing him (i.e. Rāma) giving gifts to all, was very much delighted.

35-41. Then he called sixty-four kings with their wives, to bring nectar-like water to bathe (the horse). Rāma with Sītā, adorned with all (kinds of) ornaments went to bring water in a pitcher of a golden colour. Saumitra (i.e. Lakṣmaṇa) also (went) with Urmilā, king Bharata with Māṇḍavī, Śatrughna with Śrutakīrti, and Puṣkala with Kāntimatī. Subāhu (went) with Satyavatī, Satyavat with Vīrabhūṣā, Sumada with Satkīrti, and king Vimala with his queen. King Vīramaṇi went with lovely Śrutavatī, Lakṣmīnidhi with Komalā, Riputāpa with Aṅgasenā, Bibhīṣaṇa with Mahāmūrti, and Pratāpāgrya with Pratītā. Ugrāśva (went) with Kāmagamā, Nīlaratna with Adhiramyā. Suratha (went) with Sumanohārī and the monkey with Mohanā. The sage Vasiṣṭha sent these (and other) kings.

42-44. Vasiṣṭha who knew the sacred hymns, having gone to Sarayū flooded with holy and auspicious water, consecrated the water: "O water, purify this horse with this charming water for the sacrifice of Rāmacandra, the protector of the entire world." All kings like Rāma brought that water touched by the sage to the pavilion praised by best brāhmaṇas.

45-50. The pitcher-born sage (i.e. Agasti) having bathed the horse, white like milk, consecrated him with a hymn through the hands of Rāma: "O great horse, purify me in this crowd of the brāhmaṇas. May all the delighted gods be pleased by your sacrifice." Saying so, king Rāma with Sītā touched him. Then all the kings through curiosity looked upon it as a wonder. They said to one another: "What does that Rāma by remembering whom men are freed from great sins, say?" When king Rāma spoke like this, the pitcher-born sage (i.e. Agasti), consecrated a sword and gave it into Rāma's hand. When Rāma held and touched the sword, the horse gave up the beast's form and assumed a divine form at the sacrifice.

51-53. Surrounded by celestial nymphs, fanned by chowries, and decorated with a necklace, he got into an excellent divine car. Then all the people seeing him to have given up the horse's form and to have assumed an excellent divine form, were wonder-struck at that sacrifice. Then that very righteous Rāma, knowing it himself, and making the people all around to know it, asked him of a divine form:

54. "Who are you who have obtained a divine form; for what reason are you turned into a horse? How are you accompanied by a divine woman? What do you desire to do? Tell it (to us)." Having heard the words of Rāma, the god said to the king (i.e. Rāma):

55-56. He laughed, and spoke very charming words with a voice resembling that of clouds: "To you who move without and within, there is nothing anywhere that is not known. Yet, I shall tell you who ask me, everything properly.

57-67. O Rāma, O tormentor of enemies, in the former existence I, an exteremely righteous brāhmaṇa, behaved in a manner opposed to the Vedas. Formerly, sometime I went to the bank of Hutapāpā which was charming with trees and lovely everywhere. O you of mighty arms, having bathed there and gratified the dead ancestors, having duly given gifts, I took to meditation upon you (in a manner) acceptable to the Vedas. O King, at that time many kings had come there. To deceive them, I practised this religious hypocrisy. An excellent enclosed place was fixed with the preparations for many sacrifices. That charming and big place was covered with garments and had wooden rings on the tops of sacrificial posts. The smoke rising from the sacrificial fire and having a wonderful form, made the wide firmament charming and matchless. I whose body was beautified with many beautiful marks, whose penance was great, who was adorned with darbhas, who had the sacred fuel in his hands, was indeed religious hypocrisy in an embodied form. (At that time) Durvāsas, of a great lustre, roaming at will over the world, came there on the bank of the river Dhūtapāpā. Before him he saw me practising religious hypocrisy, observing silence, not offering him materials of worship, arrogant, and not uttering words of welcome. Seeing (me), the very intelligent sage, over-powered with anger like the ocean on a parvan-day, cursed me, a religious hypocrite: 'O you of a wicked mind, O you mean ascetic, since you are practising religious hypocrisy on the bank of the river, obtain beasthood (i.e. be born as a beast) which is fully censurable'

68-74. Having heard that curse given (by him), I became extremely distressed at that time; and I indeed seized the feet of that sage Durvāsas. Then, O Rāma, the brāhmaṇa showed me an excellent favour. (He said:) 'O ascetic, be a horse at the sacrifice of the king of kings. Then, due to contact with his (i.e. Rāma's) hand, go, after taking up a divine, charming form, free from religious hypocrisy, to that highest position.' Even that curse given by him became favourable to me, since I obtained the lovely touch of your hand. O Rāma, I have obtained the touch of your hand, difficult to be obtained, which was difficult to be had by gods etc. even after many births. O great king, give me an order. Through your favour I shall reach that great, eternal place of you, which is free from misery etc. O king, O lord of men, through your favour I shall go to that place where there is no grief, no old age, no death, no confusion about time."

75-83. Saying so to him and turning round, he got into that excellent divine, car decked with jewels, and very much honoured by all gods. By the grace of Rāma's feet he went to an eternal place, free from re-birth, and bereft of grief and delusion. Having heard what he had told, the other people knew Rāma (properly), and mad with joy they were amazed. O brāhmaṇa, O you very intelligent one, even if Viṣṇu is remembered with religious hypocrisy it gives salvation. Then what (will happen) by avoiding religious hypocrisy! Somehow or other Rāma should be much remembered, by which a man obtains the highest position, difficult to be obtained (even) by gods etc. The sages having seen that wonder regarded themselves blessed. When the god who formerly had a horse's form, went to heaven, Rāma said to the treasures of penance and the best among those who know the Vedas: "O brāhmaṇa(s), what should I do? The horse is lost; he has obtained happiness. How will the sacrifice, gratifying all deities, will (now) proceed? May the sages do that by which the gods would be gratified, my sacrifice will be excellent, and I would have what is told by the sacred rules."

84-87. Hearing these words, the best sage Vasiṣṭha, skilled in knowing the hearts of all sages, said: "Quickly bring camphor, due to which gods having first received oblation, will now accept it, after being impelled by my words." Hearing these words Rāma quickly brought very shining camphor for pleasing the gods very much. Then the sage, with his heart very much delighted, invoked the wonderful gods. All of them surrounded by their attendants, came that moment only.